The Hero and the Historians

Alan Gordon

The Hero and the Historians
Historiography and the Uses
of Jacques Cartier

UBCPress · Vancouver · Toronto

20 19 18 17 16 15 14 13 12 11 10   5 4 3 2 1

Printed in Canada with vegetable-based inks on FSC-certified ancient-forest-free paper (100% post-consumer recycled) that is processed chlorine- and acid-free.

Library and Archives Canada Cataloguing in Publication

Gordon, Alan, 1968-
   The hero and the historians : historiography and the uses of Jacques Cartier / Alan Gordon.

Includes bibliographical references and index.
ISBN 978-0-7748-1741-7

   1. Cartier, Jacques, 1491-1557. 2. National characteristics, Canadian – Historiography. 3. Canada – History – To 1763 (New France) – Historiography. 4. Canada – Discovery and exploration – French – Historiography. 5. Canada – Historiography. I. Title.

FC301.C37G67 2010   971.01'13092   C2009-907134-7

Canadä

UBC Press gratefully acknowledges the financial support for our publishing program of the Government of Canada (through the Canada Book Fund), the Canada Council for the Arts, and the British Columbia Arts Council.

This book has been published with the help of a grant from the Canadian Federation for the Humanities and Social Sciences, through the Aid to Scholarly Publications Programme, using funds provided by the Social Sciences and Humanities Research Council of Canada.

UBC Press
The University of British Columbia
2029 West Mall
Vancouver, BC V6T 1Z2
www.ubcpress.ca

Contents

Illustrations

Acknowledgments

This study began life as an unanswered question posed during the defence of my doctoral dissertation. Asking historians questions they can't answer is a cruel thing to do, and in this case, it led to more than ten years of on-again, off-again work. So, for that initial question, I thank Jim Pritchard. I hope an answer lies somewhere in this book, although in the process of researching and writing, I ended up asking myself a different set of questions. Earlier ideas appeared in the *Journal of the Canadian Historical Association* for 1999, and the anonymous reviewers of that journal made some excellent suggestions. I also learned a great deal from Viv Nelles and Ron Rudin, who shared a panel with me on hero making at the Canadian Historical Association (CHA) meeting that year. Although he probably doesn't remember the encounter, André Pratte of *La Presse* made some astute observations that helped me rethink how I imagined the interests of my Cartier enthusiasts. More recently, friends and colleagues have offered helpful suggestions, listened to my rants, and encouraged me to finish by setting their own fine examples. I owe particular thanks to Russ Johnston, who offered encouragement during a trip to Quebec City, and to Stuart McCook and Peter Goddard, who shared with me their own insights and made casual comments that had serious effects. Suzanne Zeller read a terrible early version of a chapter – and gently told me where I was going wrong – and Karen Racine lugged a full draft of the manuscript to Tahiti, where she read it, made countless suggestions, and shipped it back to me. At UBC Press, I am grateful to have worked with Melissa Pitts, whose guidance and encouragement, as well as deft skill, steered me through the publication process. And I owe a debt to the anonymous readers for their professional and thoughtful commentary on earlier drafts. But, of course, none of this would have been possible without the love of Adrienne Warren. During the long years of underemployment that followed my PhD, she encouraged me to keep going and gave me the support – especially emotionally – to persevere. In this, as in all things in my life, my greatest debt is to her.

A Note on Translations

This work relies heavily on citations from French-language sources. For the comfort of English-language readers, I have translated the passages I quote into English. I have not always translated word for word, but rather I have provided the sense of the original quotation and adjusted the syntax to flow more freely in English prose. I know there is some debate over these practices among translators, and I hope my approach has not altered any of the meaning in the passages. Readers interested in assessing the original French quotations can find them reproduced in the endnotes. There are a few exceptions to this general rule. In one instance, where the French syntax is important to the discussion, I reversed my practice and placed the English translation in the notes. I have not translated brief passages or institutional names where the meaning should be self-evident. Where possible, I have used existing English translations. For the accounts of Cartier's voyages, I use H.P. Biggar's work. I recognize that there are some problems with Biggar's translations, but I know of no significant disputes around the passages I quote. Finally, I have not attempted to translate poetry and song. I leave that task to scholars of literature and professional translators, whose skills far outweigh my own meagre abilities.

The Hero and the Historians

Introduction

In June 1542, Jacques Cartier set sail for France from Newfoundland's eastern coast. He never again saw the country he had explored at his king's behest, or the great river to Canada that he had followed for nearly a thousand miles into the North American interior. Perhaps, as he left harbour, he cast a glance over the stern of his ship and spent a silent moment reflecting on the failure of his little colony at Charlesbourg-Royal. His departure might well have been bittersweet. Although his hold was packed with "diamonds" and "gold," which eventually proved worthless, his effort at colonization had failed. He had abandoned his tiny fort, nestled beneath the cliffs overlooking today's Cap-Rouge River, a minor tributary of the St. Lawrence, some ten kilometres from today's National Assembly and the modern walls of Old Quebec.[1] The account of his voyage neither mentions nor explains his decision to desert the colony, but the winter had been bitter. This first effort to plant a permanent French presence in North America ended in dismal failure. And Cartier departed for France in defiance of a command to return to Charlesbourg-Royal given by his master on this expedition, the sieur de Roberval.

Jacques Cartier, a sea captain from the Breton town of Saint-Malo, never knew the fame or the success his little ventures later brought his name. He could never have realized that future generations would credit him with the discovery – or even the founding – of a new nation. How could he have guessed? He had no references in his own time. The "founding fathers" of the North American settler societies did not yet exist in the first half of the sixteenth century. Christopher Columbus – recognized, to be sure – was not revered in Spanish Cuba or in Spain as the discoverer of the New World. Nor did the European nations, such as they were understood in the sixteenth century, attribute their origins to great men. Certainly, France could look back upon the great Charlemagne, who had unified the Franks and carved an empire out of western continental Europe, or to Charles Martel and Clothar I before him. But even had France not been a fractured kingdom in the days of François I, the late-Renaissance French did not think of such things.

Three and a half centuries after Cartier last saw the North American shore, he had reached the height of popularity. The citizens of Saint-Henri, an industrial suburb of Montreal, gathered in a local park to unveil a monument honouring the great explorer as an expression of their gratitude for his heroic deeds. "Cartiermania" swept the St. Lawrence valley during the second half of the nineteenth century, and the residents of Saint-Henri embraced it enthusiastically. On the evening of 14 June 1893, much of the town turned out to witness a lavish ceremony inaugurating a fountain topped with a statue of Cartier. Two stages stood near the fountain: one held the fanfare and the other was jammed with orators and distinguished guests. This was a fairly typical late-Victorian inauguration of a monument, the likes of which were seen across North America around the turn of the century. Many similarly honoured long-dead explorers and military commanders. The only oddity at Saint-Henri was that the ceremony was held at night. The evening setting permitted the event to be celebrated with fireworks, which lit up the sky and cast their flickering glow on the statue of the intrepid sailor.[2]

Local sculptor Joseph-Arthur Vincent had been commissioned to create this tribute to the man who, probably, had only glimpsed the future site of Saint-Henri from atop Mount Royal three and a half centuries earlier. Vincent was in his early forties in 1893 and had just begun to make his mark on Canada's artistic scene. Having worked many years in an iron foundry, he was uniquely qualified to cast statues resistant to the harsh Canadian weather. Indeed, for an earlier statue at the Collège des Oblats in Ottawa, he had specially adapted a new technique for outdoor decorations. By the 1890s, he was well established teaching sculpture and casting techniques at the École des arts et métiers de Montréal.[3] In the centre of a town with little connection to Jacques Cartier, Vincent created the first public monument to display his sculpted likeness. Set at the top of an overwrought iron fountain, Vincent's statue captured the dignity characteristic of the mature imagination of Cartier. Dressed in Renaissance clothing, he was depicted as a middle-aged man, a hardy sailor with a distinctive profile and a determined, jutting chin.

Beneath Cartier, fixed to the fountain, a plaque explained the veneration of the Saint-Henri citizens: "To Jacques Cartier, born at Saint-Malo on 31 December 1491, sent by François I to the discovery of Canada on 20 April 1534. Dropping anchor 16 July of the same year by the entrance to the St. Lawrence, he took possession of the whole country in the name of the king his master and called it New France. 1893."[4] In their minds, Cartier had claimed Canada for France and thus initiated the history of the French presence in America. He represented the founding of New France and the eventual development of French Canada. Thus, displaying his image in Saint-Henri was entirely appropriate. Although Saint-Henri briefly boasted the only public sculpture of the explorer, it was just one of many towns to be caught up in Cartiermania. Across Quebec, squares, schools, streets, and even a bank took the name "Jacques Cartier" to symbolize their connection to a certain view of French Canadian history and their place in the French Canadian nation.

There is no obvious explanation for why the residents of this little industrial suburb, or of many other communities, felt driven to honour this long-dead sailor from another country. Cartier was not a Canadian and would never have imagined himself as such. Nor could anyone seriously claim that Cartier, whose three voyages ended abortively, was responsible for the development of modern Canada. He had no children of his own, and his explorations were surpassed by those of Champlain and his successors in the seventeenth century. Any realistic claim of the founding of a French colony in North America would date only from Champlain's efforts. And yet, people across Quebec created a national fiction that Jacques Cartier was the father of New France and the first hero of their own history. Such national fictions are not merely reflections of ideology, but are components in it. National historical heroes do not, as many students argue, simply mirror the nationalist ideal: they play a fundamental role in defining it. Thus, in inventing Cartier as a national historical hero, nineteenth-century French Canadians were also inventing an identity for themselves. Although the creators of this Cartier cult, and its most prominent guardians, sprang from the ranks of Quebec's middle-class nationalist intellectuals, Cartiermania's broad embrace suggests that it resonated with ordinary people. By the 1930s, government agencies, both federal and provincial, were also drawn to adopt Cartier as a symbol of (often competing) national identities.

A great deal has been written about nationalism and national identity in recent years. With some exceptions, most current scholars of nationalism would accept that modern nations are social, political, and cultural constructs. Scholars such as Benedict Anderson, Ernest Gellner, Eric Hobsbawm, and Elie Kedourie have connected the rise of nationalism and of the nation-state to modernity. Secularization, capitalism, and increasing technological and institutional sophistication in the eighteenth and nineteenth centuries reshaped the social relations of "modernizing" societies, particularly in Europe and America. Modernity reordered and expanded social relations in ways that broke down older communal face-to-face associations. In their place, people "imagined" a broader sense of community, with individuals living in a given territory, speaking a similar language, and sharing a common sense of history. In other words, living in the condition of modernity encouraged people to imagine themselves living in a national community.

Heroes fit into the story of modernity and national identity in a number of ways. They aid in forming the bond that citizens need to imagine so as to identify themselves with the broader national community. Historical heroes served a function similar to that of national ideal types, such as Jean-Baptiste in French Canada, John Bull in England, or Brother Jonathan and Uncle Sam in the United States. These figures were allegorical personifications of the nation, but historical heroes pushed the idea further because they were real people. The celebration of national heroes, then, was a crucial dimension in the construction of national consciousness. It is no coincidence that the nineteenth century saw both the entrenchment of nationalism and the rise of the hero cult across Europe and the Americas. However, hero veneration is also connected to modernity in other ways. Modernity, and its constituent intellectual and cultural trends, played a role in shaping the form of hero celebration. A convergence of intellectual trends helped produce specific ways of thinking about the past in which "great men" were particularly feted. Modernity helped shape social relations in ways that produced audiences for those "histories." And the lived environment of modernity created anxieties that hero veneration helped to assuage.

French Canada was not alone in generating historical heroes during the nineteenth century. This was the century in which most recognized historical heroes were fashioned for the needs of a society to which they themselves never belonged. Christopher Columbus is perhaps the most famous New World example. In his own time, and immediately following his death, he was a laughingstock, disgraced by his administrative failures, imprisonment, and almost continuous legal difficulties. However, his reputation was rehabilitated by the end of the sixteenth century and he was especially revered by Anglo-American colonists. Still, it was not until the eighteenth century, especially during and after the American Revolution, that the association of Columbus and America took root in the popular imagination. During celebrations to ratify the new American constitution in the 1780s, Columbus began to figure as the founder of a historical process culminating in the achievement of freedom in the New World. By 1792, the Columbus myth had spawned commemorative ceremonies led by New York's Columbian Society, an organization better known as the corrupt Tammany Society, which ran New York City politics. In the next century, Columbus was elevated as *the* founder of America, an American Moses.[5]

John Cabot, often seen in modern English-speaking Canada as the man who discovered Canada, was another such figure. Although his exact landfall during his 1497 voyage to North America remains disputed, it is generally accepted that he landed somewhere on the eastern coast of what is now Canada. However, Cabot himself was only recently rediscovered. For centuries, his name was obscure, known only to a handful of historians. Even then, he was frequently confused with his son, Sebastian. The fact that a Cabot left Bristol on a transatlantic voyage in 1496, 1497, 1498, or 1503 was not forgotten, but credit for initiating the English presence in North America usually went to Sebastian. Although the Elizabethan chronicler Richard Hakluyt kept alive some memory of John's achievement, these accomplishments became widely known only in the nineteenth century. Cabot's resurrection accompanied a growing Victorian imperialism and an effort to justify the British possession of North America. Indeed, upon investigating these "myths of discovery" and "inventions of tradition," a recent author has concluded that the Cabot legend is in many ways a fabrication. Numerous competing traditions overlap through the narrative of Cabot's landfall, rendering a definitive claim impossible, despite the 1997 Canadian government-sponsored celebrations of the five hundredth anniversary of the arrival of his ship *Matthew* at Bonavista, Newfoundland.[6]

Taken together, historical explorer-heroes such as Christopher Columbus, John Cabot, and Jacques Cartier are suggestive of how national communities make use of history. First, and perhaps most importantly, they symbolize the arrival of Europeans in the New World and, despite the specious logic inherent in such claims, legitimize the possession of North America by Christian Europeans. For the former European colonies of the New World, these first explorers represent founding fathers. Thus, their history provides a binding social myth. Such a collective emotive experience – an entire society idolizing the same figure or founding event – strengthens the bond of brotherhood that nationals are supposed to feel for one another, so that individual historical figures become surrogates for the collective bond of nationalism. Although such veneration need not function in service of nationalism, it has tended to do so in the modern world. Whether nationalist or not, celebrated individuals lend a sense of purpose and accomplishment to abstract, collective ambitions. For national communities, the first objective is to create a sense of unity. It hardly matters that the hero could never have represented these ambitions in his own day, for they are projected back into the past. Nowhere is this more clearly seen than in historical heroes. Scotland, for instance, was long a country divided by clans, geography, language, and ethnicity. However, well before the Mel Gibson film *Braveheart* attempted Scottish myth making, Scottish nationalists read into Scotland's past a national unity and purpose that pitted the common Scot against English overlordship. Scotland's "War of Independence" began in the late thirteenth century as a struggle on the part of some clans to overthrow English occupation. Partly because the Scottish nobility had been discredited, the early resistance was fought by commoners under the leadership of a lesser nobleman, William Wallace. Their effort failed (although Robert the Bruce later succeeded) and Wallace was brutally executed in London. However, as Graeme Morton has demonstrated, Scots saw Wallace's failures as noble resistance that helped define Scotland in opposition to England and, through that, helped graft a national unity onto a fragmented pattern of identities.[7] Indeed, failed heroes are often more resonant than successful ones. In noble failure, positive values are more easily constructed: failures become sacrifice. A hero sacrifices himself defending principles that subsequent generations come to value. Thus, in failure, the lesson of right conduct is more readily learned. William Wallace never united Scotland against the English, and he died horribly in defeat, but he became a symbol of Scottish bravery, ingenuity, and independence of spirit. Adapted for American movie audiences in *Braveheart,* he also came to stand for "freedom," a rallying cry that would have meant little to Wallace himself but that resonated deeply with modern viewers.

Historical heroes also perform another crucial social function for the nation. Although they may be seen to embody *timeless* national characteristics, they give the nation a sense of time. Nations are relatively recent historical constructs. However, nationalists frequently cite an ancient national past in which historical heroes figure prominently. Again, praise of historical heroes is not a nationalist's innovation: the ancient Greeks canonized such heroes in the works of Homer. But the cult of great men surged in Europe during the late eighteenth and early nineteenth centuries. Like the stories of the *Iliad* and the *Odyssey,* these Romantic-era cults focused on men of the distant past and made little distinction between myth and historical fact. Walter Scott, to continue with Caledonian examples, wrote a series of historical novels that reflected his own imagination and a past as he thought his readers wanted it to be. As Anthony D. Smith notes, heroes, such as Scott's Rob Roy MacGregor, were portrayed as vessels of a national essence, embodying virtues such as martial valour, generosity, temperance, self-sacrifice, endurance, loyalty, and patriotism.[8] Thus, nationalists make use of a selective reading of history to construct heroes as the embodiment of national virtue.

A reading of Benedict Anderson suggests another important connection to the past that historical heroes provide in modern nations. Anderson notes that humans construct their own identity through private memories and personal narratives. Yet, such individual accounts are insufficient; too much of our personal past relies on outside supporting evidence. Each personal narrative, a story that tells of our continuous development from child to adult, requires the manufacture of "historical" narratives through documents such as photographs and birth certificates. These documents, coupled with the oral traditions passed down to us from older relatives, help complete the task.[9] The cult of heroes provides a similar record for the nation. Through their martyrdom or success, heroes build a narrative, or a genealogy, of the nation that connects past and present. Like photographs of ourselves as children, heroic stories provide the framework of a narrative that connects or identifies previous people with ourselves. The key is that nations imagine these heroes as part of their community, as part of their families, or as part of themselves. As modernity progressed, this sense of time became more important. In Canadian historiography, modernity is usually described as some variant of the lived experience of the self and others under the capitalist revolution that transformed North America in the nineteenth and twentieth centuries. It is a lived experience of the unremitting process of rapid social change and its consequences. In brief, modernity is a social environment that anticipates, even orchestrates, change. Under such conditions, reference to a heroic figure who, although existing in the past, can be presented also as a timeless individual, can be a powerful tool of social cohesion.

In this display of shared national characteristics, figures from the past are reinterpreted so that their own actions become those of a people. Historical heroes are conscripted to the service of nationalist historiography. Anderson argues that nationalism requires an empty, homogeneous, simultaneous time and that national sentiment is formed in the "meanwhile" of historical narrative. A nation's members live, not only at the same time, but *in* the same time. Yet, they also live in communion with the past. However, a nation's past is one that escapes the constraints of conventional time: heroes and events are extracted from the past and projected as living memory in the present. No one believes that long-dead figures, such as Jacques Cartier, remain alive in any biological or metaphysical sense. However, because memories of their exploits inform the identities of living people, in a sense some element of the hero continues to exist in collective imaginations. This process involves reinvigorating and repackaging real historical people in order to fit them for the needs of the present in a continuous negotiation between history and politics. The heroes, origins, myths, and struggles of the national past thus live in the present of the imagined community. Nations picture their history as part of their community and imagine their identity with it. The strengths of the past are shared and timeless national characteristics. Their very timelessness is confirmed by the actions of heroes from the distant past. Jacques Cartier could never have become such a figure in his own day – he could never have been interpreted to represent the values of a yet unborn Canadian nation. Even if Cartier was an important man in Saint-Malo during his lifetime, he became more crucial in the imaginations and inventions of nineteenth-century Canadians.

This study uses the example of a single national hero – Jacques Cartier – to examine how certain notions about the past are created and passed on from generation to generation. It investigates the diverse historical meanings that Canadians, both anglophone and francophone, have invented for Jacques Cartier since the nineteenth century and used to embody particular ideas about the world. In many ways, then, Cartier constitutes a point of contact between English and French Canadian nationalisms. However, as this investigation reveals, the nature of the contact between the two was profoundly limited. Each expression of nationalism, although none were static, relied on its own reading of history. Given this, *The Hero and the Historians* is largely historiographical in its approach to the evidence. It argues that the particular forms of celebration of Jacques Cartier were related to the way in which historical studies developed during the nineteenth century but were also connected to the cultural and political currents of nineteenth-century nationalism. The image of Cartier changed only gradually as long-term ideological changes altered the nature of historical understanding and national identity, and eventually the heroic image fell from favour among Canada's "professionalizing" historians of the mid-twentieth century. Ultimately, a convergence of historical method, culture, and politics, similar to that which created Cartiermania in the nineteenth century, led to its demise in the twentieth.

Historians have long been involved in the manufacture of national identity, as well as in its study. The expression of nationalist sentiment relies on historical narratives and historical memory, and therefore historians figure prominently among the creators and devotees of nationalism. Jules Michelet, the French Romantic historian of the nineteenth century, turned his great studies of the French Revolution into poetic praise for the French nation. Writing from a similar republican tradition, the American John Bancroft derived a providential history of the United States in which the American republic expressed a fulfillment of God's plan. Washington Irving, whose *Life and Voyages of Christopher Columbus* set in place a series of "Columbus myths," presented Columbus as the first "American," a free-thinking individual who overcame the backward superstitions of Europe.[10] Canada has been no exception to this rule. Through the nineteenth and twentieth centuries, Canadian historians, both English speaking and French speaking, have been instrumental in furthering diverse ideas of Canadian national identity. Donald Creighton crafted a national narrative centred on the commercial potential of the Great Lakes and the St. Lawrence River that gave a justification to Canada's east-west orientation and its resistance to the continent's north-south pull. W.L. Morton imagined a Canada united by history; the Canadian Centenary Series of monographs was a partial expression of his devotion. Although David Cannadine once dismissed Canada as lacking "national monuments, national myths, national heroes and national traditions," heroes have figured prominently in these nationalist narratives.[11] Among francophones, Lionel Groulx was the most famous nationalist historian. A great deal has been written about Groulx, both as a nationalist and a historian, and more darkly as a racist and an anti-Semite. Like many historical figures, Groulx was a complex person whose good and bad should be carefully assessed.[12] If, for the moment, we set aside judgment of the man, Groulx demonstrates the dual role of historians as nationalists. He was foundational in developing a cult around the exploits of the seventeenth-century soldier Adam Dollard des Ormeaux among French Canadian youth early in the twentieth century. He also played a prominent role in the story of Cartiermania. Historians, then, help to establish a popular memory about the national past.

But historians, both amateur and professional, produce history in more than textbooks and learned articles. History is found in public plaques, in monuments, and in festivals and pageants. History is told in song and in verse. And it appears in the association of places with specific events and heroes. Taken together, these recollections combine with the more formally written history to create a popular historiography, or perhaps even a popular memory, of the past that defies traditional critiques because it is not overtly expressed. What develops out of this memory is a set of assumptions or premises that form the starting place for popular thinking about the past. In the case of Jacques Cartier, the memory begins with his voyage of "discovery" to Canada.

1
The Sixteenth-Century World and Jacques Cartier

Although the heroic figure of Jacques Cartier, as we recognize him today, was forged by relatively recent imagination, the historical Cartier was a product of his own times. His lifespan (1491-1557) was virtually coterminous with the transition from the Renaissance to the early modern period of Western civilization. He lived on the fringes of northwestern Europe during the first half of the sixteenth century, as religious discord, commercial revolution, imperial rivalry, war, and the gradual consolidation of royal power altered the contexts of European life. A cultured European of his century would have read the works of Thomas More, Erasmus, and Rabelais, and known of the art of Michelangelo and Raphael. The exploration of the New World came as Martin Luther and John Calvin proselytized a new Christian faith, and the Catholic Church, no longer unifying western Europe, struck back with the Counter-Reformation. In Italy, such politicians as Machiavelli began to grasp the importance of the new alignment of power. Cartier himself played a small role in the geopolitical struggles of a developing states system, especially the rivalry between the Habsburg emperor Charles V and his own king, François I. And, of course, he fit into a line of great navigators, beginning with the disciples of Henry the Navigator and extending through Vasco da Gama, Columbus, Cabot, Ferdinand Magellan, and into the seventeenth and eighteenth centuries. Yet, the so-called Age of Discovery was more importantly a period of imperial rivalry, beginning as a Christian struggle against the maritime commercial hegemony of the Muslims and their control of the Holy Land.

In the decades before Cartier was born, Christians pushed Muslims out of the Iberian peninsula, and Muslims finally conquered the vestiges of the Eastern Roman Empire. The impact of the fall of Constantinople, today's Turkish Istanbul, on the history of the northern Atlantic is not well known. The capture of the old imperial capital by the Ottoman Turks on 29 May 1453 signalled more than the final collapse of the Eastern Roman Empire. Nor was its influence on the Christian West confined to the migration of classical scholars and the establishment of a permanent European enemy for the Catholic Church. The taking of Constantinople effectively shut off the land route to India and Asia opened by Marco Polo only a few years earlier and forced the West to seek new routes to the riches of the East. True, goods continued to flow into Europe via Arab and Venetian merchants. But, as the Turks advanced into the Levant, Turkish customs duties had made the Arab trade more costly. According to myth, the Portuguese prince Henry the Navigator therefore opened Europe's first school of navigation in the hopes of some day circumventing the Arab stranglehold on trade in Oriental spices and finery. Throughout the fifteenth century, Portuguese sailors established commercial and slave trade relationships with western African tribes. By 1487, they had rounded the Cape of Good Hope at the southern tip of Africa and glimpsed the hope of a sea route to the Orient.

With the Portuguese controlling the African route, other navigators considered their alternatives. One option was to reach the east by sailing west. In the 1490s, the Genoese mariner Christopher Columbus convinced the Spanish court of Ferdinand and Isabella to fund his expedition across the western sea. On 12 October 1492, Columbus landed at the island he named San Salvador, which he thought to be on the fringes of Asia, and thus demonstrated to everyone's satisfaction that one actually could sail around the world. Of course, no educated European thought that the world was flat. Nicolaus Copernicus invented this "belief" in the sixteenth century to satirize his opponents. Even the simplest sailor could not long have subscribed to it against the experience of life at sea. Some uneducated Europeans may have believed in a flat earth before 1300, but the true shape of the earth was well known as far back as the time of St. Augustine of Hippo, who learned of it from the Greeks. After all, Aristotelian-Ptolemaic cosmology, effectively church dogma after 1250, was built on a system of concentric *spheres* with the earth at the centre. In actuality, Columbus' campaign to disprove the flat earth theory was invented by Washington Irving. What Columbus actually had to overcome was the widespread belief that the globe was much too large to circumnavigate. In a series of possibly deliberate miscalculations, he devised an estimate of its circumference that was a scant 20 percent of its actual size, and he put together an impressive lobby at the Spanish court to convince Ferdinand and Isabella of its accuracy.[1]

Columbus' "discovery" (he insisted he had reached the edge of Asia itself) initiated a frenzy of seafaring activity. Serving first the court of Spain, and then that of Portugal, the Florentine navigator Amerigo Vespucci sailed the coast of South America in 1499 and 1501. Columbus himself returned to the Indies three more times, and his adopted countrymen carried the flag of the Spanish Habsburgs deeper into the New World. In 1513, Vasco Núñez Balboa reached the Pacific Ocean by crossing the Isthmus of Panama; in 1519, Hernando Cortés advanced on the Aztec Empire in central Mexico, crushing it in three years of bloody war. His countryman Francisco Pizarro repeated the feat among the Incas of Peru between 1531 and 1534. Meanwhile, Spain's European rivals joined the excitement. Although Portuguese attention had been directed to the African route to the Orient, around the Cape of Good Hope, Portugal maintained an interest in the New World and a foothold in Brazil. The 1493 papal bull *Inter Caetera* divided the world into Spanish and Portuguese halves, and these two countries confirmed their self-appointed hegemony the following year with the Treaty of Tordesillas. However, England did not long respect the papal position. In 1497, a Genoese captain, John Cabot, reached North America, probably at Newfoundland, searching for an "all-English" route. Some Victorian-era English Canadians suggested that Cabot's landfall might have been in Nova Scotia and that Cabot therefore took precedence over Cartier by being first. Interest in this claim was short-lived. Nevertheless, claims that English-backed voyages to the territory that eventually became Canada predated Cartier's voyages by decades demonstrate the relative lateness of France in venturing into the unknown waters of the Atlantic, or at least in recording it.

In 1503, Binot Poulmier de Gonneville, a trader from Honfleur, sailed his 120-ton vessel *L'Espoir* into the Atlantic in the hopes of rounding the Cape of Good Hope and following the Portuguese route to the Spice Islands. However, de Gonneville floundered in the ocean for over three months before sighting land at about 26° south. He had been blown off course to South America but so liked what he found that he stayed a year in Brazil, from January 1504 until about the following Christmas. The return trip was nearly as arduous as the outward voyage. After five weeks at sea, de Gonneville finally sighted the North Star, the key to sixteenth-century navigation, coming over the northern horizon. Along the way, *L'Espoir* lost its cargo of dyewood and over half of its crew, but news of the voyage and the riches of Brazil spread quickly, aided by the spectacle of de Gonneville's prize trophy, the Brazilian Indian Essoméricq. Yet, although de Gonneville was credited with being the first French sailor to land in Brazil, Malouins and Dieppois may have been loading up on Brazilian redwoods for some time.[2] At the very least, French mariners readily braved the waters of the Atlantic for commerce: Breton fishermen had been at Newfoundland by at least 1504. Hardy Breton sailors were so famous that, although the Portuguese brothers Gaspar and Miguel Corte Real may have landed at Newfoundland in as many as four separate voyages between 1500 and 1502, the court of Aragon hired Breton pilots to guide its expedition to the Grand Banks fisheries in 1511.[3]

The most spectacular of the early French voyages was led by the Florentine Giovanni da Verrazano. In 1524 (some suggest accompanied by a young Jacques Cartier), Verrazano cruised along the coast of North America, looking for a passage through the continental barrier to the riches of the Orient.[4]

At one point, off the present-day Carolina coast, he spotted a stretch of open water behind a narrow swath of mainland. Imagining that he had found the western ocean, he searched in vain for a passage through.[5] Undaunted by his failure, he continued north as far as New England, or perhaps Newfoundland, before returning to France. But, although Verrazano brought news that the breakthrough to the Pacific Ocean was imminent, France did not capitalize on his voyage. Events on the European continent stifled overseas exploration. The Valois king François I fought his cousin, the emperor Charles V of Spain, for domination in Europe. Verrazano had sailed during a war between the two that ended poorly for France. Captured at the 1526 Battle of Pavia and imprisoned in Madrid, François I was in no position to follow up Verrazano and challenge Spanish hegemony in the New World. And, reliant on income from the church, he could not risk angering the pope by defying *Inter Caetera*. Further French exploration awaited favourable turns of fortune in European diplomacy.

This was the political context of Jacques Cartier's world, and his discoveries seem tame compared to the Spanish and Portuguese advances to the south. Yet, Cartier also helped open a new continent for Europeans. Born in Saint-Malo, probably in 1491, to a wealthy bourgeois family of stature, Cartier took up seafaring as a natural and honourable profession. Saint-Malo, clinging to the rugged Channel coast of Brittany, had long thrived on its fishermen; and generations of French kings looked to the Malouin fishery as the "nursery of the French Navy." Malouin men had been going to sea for generations, helping supply the fish that fed Europe's faithful on the numerous fast days of the Catholic calendar. Little is known of Cartier's early life. Indeed, little is known about him at all. Fragments of his life can be pulled together from court and other legal records; however, the only sustained documentary evidence of the man comes from the various accounts of his voyages, often grouped together and styled his *Relations* as a kind of shorthand. There is little doubt that he first went to sea in his youth. By 1520, he was considered a master mariner; that year, he married Catherine des Granches, the daughter of a local notable. That such a family would accept Cartier suggests he had established considerable stature for himself in Saint-Malo. Henry Percival Biggar, a scholar of Cartier's life, concurred, tracing his prestige through baptismal records in which Cartier was frequently asked to stand as godfather.[6]

The First Voyage, 1534

In 1532, Jean Le Veneur, abbé of Mont St. Michel and bishop of Lisieux, presented Jacques Cartier to the king, who was then on a pilgrimage to Mont St. Michel. Le Veneur offered to pay half the costs of an expedition to the New World should the king consent to it. To add to Cartier's credibility, Le Veneur informed the king that Cartier had already been to Brazil and Newfoundland, something that seems quite plausible given his knowledge of the Portuguese language and the Malouin trade in redwoods.[7] The following year, Le Veneur negotiated a favourable papal interpretation of *Inter Caetera* that effectively freed France to explore and claim any "undiscovered" lands. The diplomatic turn of fortune had come in the form of the engagement of the pope's niece, Catherine de Medici, to the dauphin, the future Henri II. The opportunity to challenge Iberian hegemony had arrived. Le Veneur, patron of Jacques Cartier, advanced his own client and made sure that he received the commission to undertake the first expedition.

Preparations for Cartier's voyage would not have been easy. Jealous local fishermen, fearing a scarcity of able hands for their vessels, had convinced enough of Saint-Malo's sailors not to sign on for the mission. Despite a royal commission, the master pilot had to petition local authorities to slap an embargo on the fishing fleet until he had recruited enough hands to man his two ships. At last, on 20 April 1534, Cartier set sail from Saint-Malo with a total complement of 122 men. A scant twenty days later, he made land at Cape Bonavista, Newfoundland. Arriving this early in the northwestern Atlantic carried certain risks. Ice forced the two ships into a small harbour where they laid at rest for another ten days, making repairs and awaiting more favourable sailing conditions. On 21 May (30 May by the present calendar), Cartier put out to sea again, heading north to l'Isle des Ouaiseaulx (Funk Island) where he doubtless knew he could replenish his stores from the flocks of birds that nested there.[8]

At this point, Cartier and his crew were still in known waters, as is made abundantly clear in accounts of the voyage. Even after entering the Strait of Belle Isle, which divides Newfoundland from Labrador, Cartier cannot be accurately described as the first European to visit the region. In his day, the strait was already well sailed; French fishermen had named it the Baie des Chasteaulx for the castle-shaped island that guards today's Chateau Bay on the Labrador coast. The southern coast of Labrador is studded with rocky islets and reefs hidden beneath dark waters, but Cartier sailed confidently as if he knew his route, naming geographical features and stopping here and there to take on water and wood. Passing the harbour of Blanc Sablon, Cartier entered the Gulf of St. Lawrence. Even now, he was still sailing in known waters: not only was Blanc Sablon already named, but on 12 June, more than a hundred miles from the Atlantic, his little convoy encountered a fishing vessel from La Rochelle. Its crew, Cartier insisted, had become lost. He escorted the errant fishermen into a nearby harbour, which he named Havre de Jacques-Cartier after himself, and observed that it was among the best in the world. Cartier was not generous with this sort of praise. He was not at all complimentary about the land he saw, famously concluding that it must be "the land God gave to Cain."[9] Perhaps this impression influenced his decision to reverse course, returning to a well-used harbour near the western entrance to the strait. At this point, on 14 June, Cartier made a right turn and sailed due south to explore the west side of Newfoundland. Only at this point did he pass from the known world into the unknown.

No one is sure why Cartier took this departure, but it diverted him from proceeding directly up the north shore of the St. Lawrence River. Instead, he established two facts hitherto unknown about Newfoundland: it was an island and it hid a great inland sea. After sailing through thick Newfoundland fog, Cartier made land at Point Rich on the western coast of the island. From 14 to 24 June, he explored the coast, finding little to spark his interest other than abundant fish. (In an hour, the crew of one of his vessels pulled up more than a hundred cod.) Turning west from today's Cape Anguille, the southwestern point of Newfoundland, the company headed into the Gulf of St. Lawrence. After passing small islets and naming today's Brion Island, Cartier deduced the true nature of this inland sea: "I am rather inclined to think, from what I have seen, that there is a passage between Newfoundland and the Breton's land [Cape Breton Island]; if it were so, it would prove a great saving in both time and distance, should any success be met on this voyage."[10] He was correct, of course, but he did not opt to investigate the possibility at the time.

However, his decision to continue west was fortuitous. After passing the Magdalen Islands and exploring the coast of Prince Edward Island (which Cartier believed was a peninsula), the ships reached the mainland near Miramichi Bay. Weather forced them back out to sea, but the company returned to the coast on 3 July, rounded Cape Esperance, and entered Baie des Chaleurs. Certainly, after the ice and fog of the Gulf of St. Lawrence, the sunny climate of early July in New Brunswick and the Gaspé Peninsula, not to mention the comparatively warm water of the bay, was a relief to the crew. It must also have raised the crew's spirits, for the descriptions in the *Relations* are much more optimistic here than before. Cartier commemorated the warmth of the season in the name he chose for the bay. And, on 6 July, the French had their first significant encounter with the inhabitants of North America. While the captain and his men explored Baie des Chaleurs in a small boat, two fleets of canoes set upon them, waving furs in an effort to open trade. The French panicked. As the *Relations* describe the encounter, "We did not care to trust to their signs and waved them to go back."[11] However, the Natives ignored the signs and quickly surrounded the French so that, to frighten them off, Cartier fired two cannon shots over their heads. Obviously not greatly intimidated, the Natives quickly returned, and the French repeated the threat, this time with greater success. The next day, however, affairs got off more amicably. Nine canoes met the French rowboat, and the two sides conducted a brisk impromptu trade of furs for trinkets. These Natives were most probably the Mi'kmaq, with whom French explorers and settlers enjoyed good relations for the following centuries.

Subsequent interactions with the Mi'kmaq were equally profitable, but Cartier's most famous encounter with the locals came near the end of July. After exploring the southern and eastern coasts of the Gaspé Peninsula, the French met another group of Natives on a fishing expedition. Some two hundred people in forty canoes approached the French ships at anchor in Gaspé Bay. They seemed as friendly as the Mi'kmaq, so Cartier allowed them close enough to make the usual trade of pelts for trinkets. These Natives, however, differed from the Mi'kmaq, as Cartier quickly noted. He described them as the poorest people imaginable, for they carried virtually no possessions and went about nearly naked. Their heads were neatly shaved, except for a single lock near the crown, which was allowed to grow long and bound tightly with leather strips. The significance of this "scalp lock" was, as yet, beyond French comprehension. Whether these people had already encountered Europeans is unclear, but they seemed at least to have heard of them. Like the Mi'kmaq, they knew how to trade profitably with the sailors, immediately offering their only valuable possessions. They are commonly assumed to have been a branch of the Iroquoian peoples who occupied the temperate zones of northeastern North America. At Cartier's arrival, according to the archaeologist Claude Chapdelaine, the St. Lawrence Iroquois were divided into three main groups. The Hochelagans, who were the most populous of the three, lived farthest west, with their principal village on today's Island of Montreal. The central group lived near Lac Saint-Pierre. Farther east, the Stadaconans congregated around present-day Quebec City. Although they were divided among approximately eleven villages, their major settlement was Stadacona.[12] It was this final group, under the leadership of Donnacona, that met Cartier in Gaspé Bay during the summer of 1534. These peoples had been living in the St. Lawrence valley for centuries, cultivating crops (mostly corn, squash, and beans) and supplementing their diets with game and fish. They typically lived in small, generally unfortified villages of about four hundred inhabitants. In Cartier's time, they seem to have been at war on a number of fronts: versus the "Agouyada" to the west and the Mi'kmaq and the Maliseet to the south and east. Some time between Cartier's explorations and Champlain's arrival, Native peoples abandoned the St. Lawrence valley, leaving it a virtual corridor of no-man's land in the midst of northeastern North America.

On 24 July, as he prepared to leave Gaspé, Cartier had his men erect a wooden cross carved with the words "Vive le Roy de France" and the three fleurs-de-lys of François I's arms. This was not the first cross Cartier had raised during his explorations, but it has certainly become the most famous and the subject of the most significant Cartier commemoration. Fraught with controversy during the twentieth century, the cross was no less controversial in the sixteenth. Donnacona immediately raised an objection: he came to Cartier's ship and conveyed, by signs, that this country was his and that Cartier might not raise such a totem without his consent. But Cartier managed to quiet him with gifts and the unlikely reassurance that the cross was a simple beacon to help the French find their way back. Emboldened, Cartier decided to snatch two young men and take them back to France with him. As the canoes of the Stadaconans came alongside the French vessels, Domagaya and Taignoagny, possibly Donnacona's own sons, were pulled on board and spirited away below decks.[13] Of course, Cartier promised to return the youths on his next voyage, but Donnacona was understandably upset that the French violated Iroquoian custom by failing to exchange some of their own party for Domagaya and Taignoagny. Nonetheless, he acquiesced to the situation, probably for political reasons. He needed a powerful ally against his enemies and no doubt thought that Cartier fit the bill. In any case, the French were determined to have their way and set sail with the two Stadaconans on deck.

From Gaspé, the fleet headed north, exploring much of the coast of Anticosti Island, and thus Cartier again missed his chance to find the St. Lawrence River by himself. From there, the passage home to Saint-Malo was almost direct. One can only speculate regarding what Domagaya and Taignoagny thought when they first saw Europe. No doubt they were startled to discover the many technological wonders of European civilization. But did they, like Essoméricq before them, hide their surprise as a matter of pride? Certainly, coming from an egalitarian and permissive society, they would have found little in European social relations or child rearing to impress them. However, their thoughts can be inferred only from their actions during Cartier's second voyage. As for Cartier himself, the first trip greatly enhanced his status, and the stories that he, his men, and his captives told enabled him to quickly raise support for a second one.

The Second Voyage, 1535-36

Although the names of the ships and crewmembers from Cartier's first voyage are unknown, we know more regarding the preparations for his second trip because we have a more detailed record. Cartier set sail with three vessels (the *Grande Hermine*, the *Petite Hermine*, and the little *Émerillon*) and, according to one roll, 112 officers and men. A few months passed between the date of this roll and the mission's departure. No doubt some sailors signed on but found other pursuits in the meantime. Two names in particular have sparked controversy among historians: Dom Anthoine and Dom Guillaume Le Breton may or may not have been priests, and they may or may not have accompanied Cartier later that spring. At least this time, Cartier's objectives were stated more clearly: he was to explore beyond Newfoundland and discover "certain" countries. Apparently, Domagaya and Taignoagny had described their homeland to the French. But, as Samuel E. Morison points out, the absence of instructions to bring back gold or gems suggests that, perhaps deliberately, the two boys had not mentioned the fabled Kingdom of the Saguenay, rich in mineral wealth and thought to lie north of the St. Lawrence. Nor, for that matter, did Cartier's commission contain any suggestion of missionary activity.[14] Despite the assumptions of some later historians, neither Cartier nor his king considered conversion and proselytization to be of much value.

The fleet left Saint-Malo on 19 May 1535, but this time the Atlantic crossing was difficult. Foul weather tossed the ships for a full month and separated them from each other. It is a testament to the skill of the Breton mariners that, after more than two months at sea, all three ships survived to reunite at Blanc Sablon on 26 July. Only then, in the late summer of 1535, did Cartier again don the cap of the explorer. The westward voyage was relatively uneventful; however, on 10 August, Cartier entered a small bay on the coast opposite Anticosti Island, which he named for St. Lawrence, whose feast day it was. This was the first appearance of the name St. Lawrence in Cartier's toponymy. A few days later, after realizing that Anticosti was an island after all, Cartier consulted Taignoagny and Domagaya, who assured him that the great river (at the western end of Anticosti, the St. Lawrence is hardly recognizable as such) was the river of Hochelaga and the way to Canada. Within about a week, a third historic name entered the European vocabulary: Domagaya and Taignoagny began to tell Cartier of the great Kingdom of the Saguenay lying somewhere to the north and west of them.

As they directed the French up the river, the two guides explained the riches to be had in the Saguenay, a populated place with an abundance of metal wealth. Either by deliberate misinformation or through a misunderstanding, Cartier became convinced of the mineral riches of the country. His excitement is reflected in the account of the second voyage. By the end of August, the fleet had reached the mouth of the Saguenay River, which ran "between lofty mountains of naked rock."[15] However, the Saguenay flows from the north, and Cartier knew that it was not the route to the interior (or possibly to Asia) for which he sought. He continued up the great river and encountered some of Domagaya and Taignoagny's countrymen within a week. Soon Donnacona himself came aboard the *Grande Hermine* and greeted his two sons and the captain. Taking to the ships' boats, Cartier followed the Stadaconans upstream past the magnificent views of Montmorency Falls and the approach to what would one day be Quebec City, with Cap Diamant standing majestically over the river. He made no comment regarding either. His concern was to get his ships into a good harbour: this he promptly did in a crook of the St. Croix (today's St. Charles) River, which flows into the St. Lawrence below Quebec City. The French had arrived at Stadacona, and Domagaya and Taignoagny had come home.

However, Cartier was hardly content with his accomplishment. His guides had promised to lead him as far upriver as Hochelaga, but their father proved reluctant to let him go. Donnacona probably hoped to use his geographical proximity to the French to control their interaction with other Aboriginal peoples and to exert a hegemony over his rivals at Hochelaga. He tried repeatedly to dissuade the French, even resorting to a "warning" from the god Cudouagny. Great dangers lay ahead, Donnacona's Cudouagny cautioned: the French faced ruin if they proceeded inland. Cartier, good Christian that he was, laughed off such an effort and, claiming to have reassurances from his own priests, decided to press on without local pilots. On 19 September, he set sail in the little *Émerillon* with a company of gentlemen volunteers, leaving behind the crews of the other two vessels. For nearly two weeks, the little company journeyed upriver, encountering more of the country's inhabitants along the way. At the western end of today's Lac Saint-Pierre, unsure regarding how to navigate the archipelago that hides the river's main channel, the company met a group of men, one of whom was so strong that he hoisted Cartier in his arms and carried him ashore with no appreciable effort. After sharing a meal with these Natives, who were kind enough to show the French the way through the islands, Cartier left behind the *Émerillon,* pressing on with his longboats and thirty-four hands. At last, on 2 October 1535, the boats arrived at Hochelaga.

Perhaps a thousand people rushed to the river's edge to greet the visitors as the longboats drew near the Island of Montreal. There is some dispute as to where Cartier landed and, more to the point, where Hochelaga stood. Perhaps historians have discussed the events of the Hochelaga visit more than any other incident in Cartier's itinerary. However, the conventional wisdom is that Cartier landed on the southern shore of the island and that Hochelaga stood somewhere on the southern slopes of Mount Royal. All night, these Natives stayed on the riverbanks, dancing and singing by the light of their bonfires. The following morning, dressed appropriately and accompanied by four gentlemen volunteers and twenty sailors, Cartier marched through the forest, past fields of maize, and up to the town itself. Hochelaga was probably a community of fifteen hundred people.[16] Cartier counted fifty longhouses surrounded by a palisade of sorts and further defended by two redoubts of roughly piled stones.

Cartier's descriptions of Hochelaga and its inhabitants are amply recorded elsewhere in the *Relations*. However, two incidents are of particular note. The first was Cartier's excursion to the summit of Mount Royal where he and his companions were rewarded with the magnificent view that still brings thousands of Montrealers to gaze over the modern city, the river, and the vast Montreal Plain. Cartier was able to take in the Laurentian mountains to the north, to glimpse the Adirondacks to the south, and to trace the silver strand of the St. Lawrence running west to the distant horizon. However, to his dismay, he saw a set of impenetrable rapids just upriver from where he had beached his longboats. Scholars differ regarding the identity of these rapids. Some claim that Cartier's route to the interior was blocked by the Lachine Rapids, named years later by René-Robert, Chévalier de La Salle. An alternative hypothesis suggests that Cartier could not have seen the Lachine Rapids from his vantage point on Mount Royal, and so the barrier must have been the Sault-au-Récollet on the Rivière des Prairies. Either way, Cartier could not advance further inland by the river. As he contemplated this new obstacle, a second frequently described incident occurred. Apparently without prompting from the French, the Hochelagans confirmed that a consolation prize of gold and silver was to be found in the Kingdom of the Saguenay. Touching Cartier's silver whistle and a sailor's gilt dagger hilt, they indicated, or more properly the French inferred, that such items were in abundance somewhere to the north and west.

After a whirlwind tour of Hochelaga that occupied only a single autumn day, the French returned to the *Émerillon*. Travelling with the current this time, they reached Stadacona on 11 October and settled in for a winter of suspicion and intrigue. Relations with the Stadaconans had deteriorated in Cartier's absence, and even his return could not maintain the peace. The bitter Laurentian cold shocked the French, whose winters were never so harsh. Their stores of beverages froze in their casks, and, one by one, they developed scurvy; by mid-February, nearly all of Cartier's men had the disease. Suspicious of the Natives, and fearing attack should he reveal his predicament, Cartier and a handful of healthy men made a great show behind their fort's walls, shouting and carrying on to suggest a large number of strong men enjoying themselves in the winter cold. At last their prayers for salvation were answered in the unlikely form of Domagaya. Cartier's erstwhile guide had suffered from scurvy, but suddenly he seemed cured. He had been healed by a tea made from a certain tree, and he gladly showed Cartier how to identify it. Everyone who was brave enough to try the remedy recovered. At spring thaw, the company stood at eighty-five men.

Meanwhile, Cartier and Donnacona continued to play a game of cat and mouse, testing and tricking each other as to their strength. At one point, Cartier became convinced that Donnacona had amassed a force of allies to crush the weakened French. He had indeed brought back reinforcements, but they were political reinforcements. Donnacona faced challenges to his leadership from his own people, and he suggested that Cartier intervene on his behalf. To prove his worth as an ally, Donnacona spun out further tales of the wealth of the Saguenay, even claiming to have been there himself. If these accounts were intended to win Cartier's support and secure his position in Canada, the plan backfired. Cartier decided instead to seize Donnacona and carry him back to France to tell his wondrous stories. That spring, following yet another cross-raising ceremony, Cartier abducted ten Stadaconans, including Donnacona, Taignoagny, and Domagaya, and whisked them to

Europe despite the wailing and crying of the victims and their families. Arriving at Saint-Malo in mid-July 1536, Cartier had lost twenty-five Frenchmen but gained ten Native curiosities to entertain France's social circles. Taignoagny and Domagaya quickly turned to mischief, as Cartier had no doubt expected of them. Donnacona visited the court of François I where he converted to Christianity, received an annual pension, and spent four glorious years spreading the lore of the Kingdom of the Saguenay. One hopes that Cartier thanked him, for Donnacona's tales of gold and diamonds must have helped to deflect the failure of his mission. He had returned from Canada with nothing but the word of his former host to buttress his claims that the Canadian adventure would produce anything of value.

The Third Voyage, 1541-42

By the time Cartier began preparations for another voyage across the Atlantic, all but one of the Stadaconans in France had died. What happened to the last survivor, a young girl, no one knows. Donnacona, at least, was given a Christian burial, but Cartier never fulfilled his promise to return the Stadaconans home "within ten or twelve moons" of their capture.[17] Indeed, as he embarked upon his return trip, Cartier was not in much of a position to promise anything. François I had determined to send a third expedition; Donnacona's well-spun tales had seen to that. But a fresh war with Spain intervened, ending with the Treaty of Nice in 1538. In the meantime, Cartier did very well for himself, living in his Saint-Malo house or at his country cottage in Limoilou. He may also have engaged in some privateering or have played a minor role in an Irish rebellion.[18] Eventually, in October 1540, he secured another commission to return to "Canada and Hochelaga."[19] However, the king intended to exploit the Saguenay from a permanent colony on the banks of the St. Lawrence, an effort that required more than a simple sea captain. Admittedly, Cartier was appointed captain-general of the expedition in the fall of 1540, but shortly thereafter, he was subjected to the command of another – Jean-François de La Rocque, sieur de Roberval, appointed by commission in January 1541 as "lieutenant-general, chief, commander, captain of the said enterprise."[20] Approximately ten years younger than Cartier, Roberval was a soldier and a courtier. Although he was a Protestant, the king gave him complete authority over the new lands and every Frenchman, Catholic or Protestant, who went there.

Jacques Cartier does not seem to have suffered this humiliation well, but he soldiered on under his king's orders. The king emptied his prisons of both men and women to stock the colony, and Roberval and Cartier recruited a few nobleman volunteers. (No doubt this eased Spanish and Portuguese concerns. A Spanish spy in Saint-Malo took a very dim view of the potential success of the venture.)[21] On 23 May 1541, the fleet of five vessels, led by

Cartier as Roberval was not yet ready to depart, set sail for Canada. Again they had a rough crossing, which, in hindsight, was not a good omen. The first ship reached Newfoundland after a month at sea; the others, which had become separated, trickled in one by one. Not until 23 August, three months after setting sail from Saint-Malo, did the fleet reach Stadacona. The inhabitants greeted the French with the usual joy and did not seem too put off by Cartier's explanation for the continued absence of the ten abductees. They were all living as lords in France, the captain-general lied, and did not wish to return home. Perhaps not trusting his hosts to believe him, Cartier continued upriver a few more miles to plant his settlement at the site of the modern suburb of Cap-Rouge. There he put his cast of colonists to work building a fortified settlement called Charlesbourg-Royal and a second small fort on the heights above it for extra protection.

With the work under way, Cartier left Charlesbourg-Royal on a second visit to Hochelaga. There, he explored the Lachine Rapids and learned that the route to Saguenay was blocked by yet another set of rapids much further upstream. His objective of learning the route accomplished, Cartier returned to Charlesbourg-Royal no nearer to the Saguenay riches than he had been seven years earlier. To make matters worse, he discovered that relations with Stadacona had taken a foul turn. The Natives no longer made friendly visits to the French settlement, and the colonists expected a sinister plot. The surviving narrative of the voyage ends at this point, but some of that harsh winter's tale can be pieced together from fragments of gossip told in the ports of France. The Stadaconans attacked the French, probably during the traditional Iroquoian war season of November, killing as many as thirty-five colonists.[22] Scurvy broke out, as expected, but was quickly cured. It was a miserable season. Roberval never appeared and Cartier, convinced that he lacked the manpower to remain, broke camp in June 1542 and set sail for France. He carried off all he could (including eleven barrels of "gold," seven barrels of "silver," and a basket of "precious stones"), leaving behind the empty hulk of Charlesbourg-Royal.

However, for Cartier and the colonists, the ordeal had not ended. Reaching St. John's Harbour, Newfoundland, at the end of June, they discovered that Roberval had not been lost at sea. He met them there with three ships full of reinforcements, nearly four hundred men in all. He had taken the better part of a year to set off after Cartier left, biding his time with a bit of piracy and profiteering in the English Channel. He had left France only in April 1542, piloted by Jean Alfonse. He had reached Newfoundland just as Cartier and his advance party were breaking camp and was in no mood to turn back, as Cartier advised. As Cartier's legal commander, he ordered a return to Canada, but that night, Cartier and his vessels disobeyed the order, stealing away under cover of darkness. No doubt the urging of the remaining colonists weighed on this decision; it is unlikely that any relished the thought of another winter in Canada, especially after a return to France had been promised. Roberval linked Cartier's decision with a desire to cash in on his New World diamonds. In any event, Cartier's reputation at home remained unsullied. François I agreed to pay any outstanding debts and consulted Cartier on naval matters. He was never elevated to the nobility, but the king did make a present of the *Grande Hermine* and the *Émerillon* for his pilot. The silver, gold, and diamonds turned out to be worthless. Despite this failure, and his insubordination, Cartier returned to find respect and some wealth. He appears to have spent the rest of his days at Limoilou, his estate. He continued to appear at baptisms and as a court witness in Saint-Malo until his death in 1557.

Cartier never returned to Canada, but Roberval carried on. His story, although peripheral to that of the development of Jacques Cartier as a national hero, completes the tale. Alfonse piloted the fleet up the St. Lawrence toward Stadacona. However, along the way, one of the saddest love stories never to become a major motion picture unfolded. A cousin of Roberval's, a young woman named Marguerite de La Rocque de Roberval, had taken a lover from among the colonists. Roberval's Calvinist morals were outraged, and he marooned the poor woman, along with her maid, on an island in the Gulf of St. Lawrence with a few provisions and two arquebuses. As the ships sailed away, Marguerite's young lover leaped overboard and swam for the island to join his beloved. At first, the little group managed well enough. The young man built a cabin and the three survived on fish and fowl. But that winter, things took a turn for the worse. The man died and, unable to dig a grave in the frozen earth, Marguerite guarded his body from the wild animals until spring. No sooner had she laid him to rest than her child was born. It, too, died. The following winter, the maid died and poor Marguerite was left alone. Amazingly, she survived. Defending herself against bears and impending insanity, she persevered until the spring of 1544 when a passing fishing vessel discovered her and brought her home to France. André Thevet recorded the story in his *Cosmographie universelle* of 1575, but it was also cleaned up and transformed into a respectable fable about fidelity and devotion to God by Marguerite de Navarre, sister of François I, in *nouvelle* 67 of *The Heptameron.*[23]

Roberval, meanwhile, had continued to Cartier's camp and rebuilt a settlement on the heights of Cap-Rouge, which he called France-Roy.[24] Winter set in, cruel and cold as always. About fifty settlers died of scurvy; the food stores were stretched thin. Roberval maintained strict discipline, clapping people in irons and flogging for transgressions. But at least the Stadaconans did not attack. France-Roy was far better fortified than Charlesbourg-Royal. In the spring, the company made a renewed effort to reach the riches of the Saguenay through the two known routes. Roberval travelled up the St. Lawrence and dispatched Jean Alfonse to the Saguenay River. Neither attempt proved fruitful, and, some time in the summer, Roberval decided to return to France. With that, the excursions of the Valois French into Canada came to an end. The dream of New World riches to rival Spanish wealth also died.

Discovery, Invention, Common Sense

Cartier helped initiate the "Age of Discovery" that propelled European interlopers around the globe in search of riches, profit, and commercial and religious expansion. Few European explorers "discovered" much of anything, if we take that word as referring to the first human to set foot on a given territory. It is estimated that, at the time of European contact, some 90 million people lived in North and South America combined. About 10 million lived in what is today the continental United States and Canada. Evidence suggests that these peoples first began migrating into the western hemisphere between 50,000 and 30,000 BC, or possibly earlier. Archaeological evidence also indicates that the first migrants reached the St. Lawrence valley by about 9,000 BC.[25] Nonetheless, from the European perspective, such lands and peoples were unknown. The admittedly Eurocentric title of "discoverer" is thus a relative description of the human encounters that constituted the first contacts between European and American peoples.

Of course, discovery is as much a political act as a geographical one. Originally, the word had a legal sense of "making known" certain facts, a sense that is still used in criminal law. In this sense, it implies not the first to know but the act of making knowledge public.[26] In the nineteenth century, the term began to be applied to geographical discoveries in a manner that suggested finding lands hitherto uninhabited. In this modern guise, the notion of discovery is more difficult to reconcile with Cartier's accomplishments. He was not the first European, or even the first Frenchman, to visit the shores of northern North America. Nor was he likely to have been the first into the Gulf of St. Lawrence. Perhaps, then, his claim to the discovery of Canada rests on his reconnoitring of the coasts of Prince Edward Island and Canada's founding provinces New Brunswick and Quebec. And yet, some scholars express nagging doubts about even this "discovery." Had Cartier been first, one would then need to explain why the Mi'kmaq and Stadaconans already seemed to know how to deal with Europeans, holding up furs to show they had things of value for trade. Perhaps, then, Cartier was the discoverer of Canada not in 1534 but in 1535 when he sailed up the St. Lawrence to the land originally known as "Canada." Yet doubts arise here as well. Some scholars, such as the nineteenth-century American Francis Parkman, have made claims for a French discovery of the St. Lawrence by 1506.[27] And there is some evidence to suggest Portuguese penetration of the Gulf of St. Lawrence before 1534 by João Alvarez Fagundes, Miguel and Gaspar Corte Real, or even their father twenty years before Columbus sailed. Portuguese tradition holds that the Corte Real brothers reached the "River of Canada" some thirty years before Cartier. Certainly, Gaspar Corte Real reached Newfoundland in 1500; his brother, Miguel, followed suit in 1501. The following year, Miguel disappeared while searching for his missing brother, and, though the hypothesis is unlikely, both may have been wrecked in the St. Lawrence River. At the very least, Henry Percival Biggar established that Portugal attempted to set up a small colony in Newfoundland around 1520.[28] Indeed, historians still know surprisingly little about the navigations of sixteenth-century Europeans. Some historians of Portuguese exploration have even suggested that their sailors, not the Genoese Columbus and his crew of Spaniards, discovered the Americas in a series of secret voyages. The Portuguese clearly reached the New World early, but any documentation of the secret voyages, if ever kept, was apparently lost in the catastrophic Lisbon earthquake of 1755. Although it is unlikely, Basque whalers and fishers may have been in the St. Lawrence before the arrival of Columbus, but any such voyages were not recorded in Europe's courts.[29] Given current historical sources, it is not possible to establish conclusively who first landed in Canada or the New World. The question descends from evidential shortcomings to epistemological labyrinths and semantic squabbles. In light of the political baggage hung on the debate, it is best simply to acknowledge what is problematic about the word "discoverer."

Nevertheless, Cartier has long been credited with the discovery of Canada. Today, this claim is difficult to reconcile with John Cabot's probable Newfoundland landfall at about the time Cartier was born. Yet, even if we assume that Cabot did disembark in Newfoundland (a point that has been hotly contested by partisans of a Cape Breton Island landing), he did not actually "discover Canada" until 1949. Newfoundland's history, though closely tied to that of mainland Canada, is nonetheless that of an independent dominion in the British Empire. Newfoundland joined the Canadian Confederation in 1949 (by the slimmest of margins in a referendum), so Cabot became the discoverer of Canada some 450 years after his death. This perhaps more semantic aspect of the question began to arise only in the 1890s and is treated in greater detail in Chapter 5. Nevertheless, semantics and antiquarian trivia have the potential to divert attention from the greater question: what did Cartier discover?

Doubtless, in 1534, Jacques Cartier was not the first European to reach the coast of what would become Canada. It has even been suggested that Cartier himself first saw Canadian shores ten years earlier. The twentieth-century historian Gustave Lanctôt argued that Cartier learned of North America by accompanying Verrazano in the *Dauphin* in 1524 and again in 1528.[30] According to Lanctôt, Cartier had probably been to Brazil. Verrazano's second voyage reached Brazil in 1528 and returned to France in March 1529, although Verrazano himself did not survive it, having been eaten by cannibals, probably at Guadeloupe.[31] But Cartier compared North American maize to Brazilian millet corn and likely spoke Portuguese. Although the proper place to discuss Lanctôt's assertions is in Chapter 7, the basis of his claim should be clarified. Lanctôt's hypothesis rests on Cartier's absence from Malouin birth registers and marriage certificates during the very dates that Verrazano was at sea, as well as his reading of the letters of the seventeenth-century Jesuit Père Pierre Biard, who wrote in 1614 that "Canada ... was discovered principally by Jacques Cartier in 1524, and then in a second voyage ten years afterwards in 1534."[32] However, Biard wrote his account from memory, which explains why he dated Verrazano's voyage to 1523 and gave 1524 for Cartier's first voyage on only two of five occasions.[33] Moreover, Cartier was frequently absent from the Malouin registers during the seafaring months, a fact which reflected the nature of his profession. He may have been to Brazil, and he appeared to know Newfoundland well, but Lanctôt's evidence is insufficient to provide anything more than conjecture.[34]

None of this should diminish Cartier's rightful place in Canadian history. Whether or not he was the first European to visit Canadian lands, he was the first to capitalize on the potential for further exploration offered by the Gulf of St. Lawrence. And he was certainly the first to exploit the potential of the great axis of penetration into the continental interior that the St. Lawrence River affords. Moreover, his exploration upriver as far as the Island of Montreal added significantly to European geographical knowledge. Cartier blazed a trail followed by European explorers and settlers for centuries, and his river dominated Canadian commercial history from his day to the twentieth century. Despite its failure, Cartier's little colony at Charlesbourg-Royal was the first substantially documented European attempt to settle in northern North America. He initiated French contact with and claims on this part of the New World. And although Cartier's gold and diamonds proved worthless, subsequent explorers, such as Champlain, who followed in his footsteps found other wealth in the land. In this sense, Jacques Cartier discovered Canada. Canada, as we know it today, might not have existed without the leadership of an intrepid Breton mariner in the service of the king of France.

Jacques Cartier, then, is clearly a recovered historical hero. Forgotten to all but a few erudite scholars for over two hundred years, he was resurrected and reinvented during the nineteenth century. The traditions that surround Cartier, in this light, must be seen as "invented." The English historian Eric Hobsbawm has developed the notion of "invented tradition" as a means to understand the sudden appearance of appeals to the past in justification of nationalism and national policies. Following the 1983 publication of his path-breaking collection of essays under the title *The Invention of Tradition*, historians latched onto the concept as a key explanatory theme. Invented traditions have since been flushed out of their hiding places in popular culture and exposed as bourgeois constructions. For Hobsbawm, as for his legion of followers, such traditions are novel responses to novel situations, which take the form of reference to the past. An invented tradition is one whose origins can be dated in a relatively short period of time and whose inventors can be identified by historians.[35] However, as many recent critics have pointed out, the category of *invented* traditions implicitly sets up a paradigm of invented versus authentic traditions. Hobsbawm never investigated the opposite pole; nor did he seem to have contemplated that some national traditions may well have spontaneously sprung from the authentic sentiments of a people. All traditions are invented at some point, and invented traditions evolve to suit the needs of those who keep them. To offer an invented tradition, or an invented historical hero, as a static reflection of a narrow class interest, as a reading of Hobsbawm suggests, is to deny both a historicity of past cultures and an agency for present people. This is not to imply that Hobsbawm's model is useless or that such distinctions are unimportant. However, the exaltation of a hero such as Jacques Cartier, although he was invented, opens one route to an understanding of changing national sentiments. And it presents a case for the authenticity and persistency of many brands of nationalism, even in Canada's brief history.

Perhaps a more constructive approach to the perseverance of such inventions would examine not simply their moment of creation and dispersal but the roots of their reception by ordinary people. Ideas and beliefs may have been invented, but dating their genesis offers little insight into their influence in a culture. People experience invented traditions as authentic; this simple fact is more important in understanding human history than is knowing that the traditions are invented. What is crucial in explaining the actions of individuals and groups is understanding what they believed to be true. Many people argue that Columbus was motivated by a desire to disprove a common myth that the world was flat. For Jeffrey Russell, this claim reveals much more about nineteenth-century Americans than it does about fifteenth-century Europeans, who did not insist on a flat earth.[36] Nineteenth-century Americans genuinely believed that earlier peoples clung superstitiously to the idea of a flat earth. Indeed, this tradition became a matter of common sense despite being incorrect. In part, this common sense belief underlined a religious prejudice in which Protestantism – the faith of American patricians – was superior to the Catholicism of much of Europe (and many recent immigrants to America). Nevertheless, common sense traditions are experienced as, and believed to be, authentic or real; as such, they help guide people's perceptions of the world around them. This study aims to uncover how certain "facts" about the past are discovered and presented to the public, and how they enter into common sense knowledge.

Common sense is unlike other forms of human knowledge. Following Antonio Gramsci, some scholars represent it as the ability of the dominant class to project its own way of seeing the world so that those who are subordinated by it accept it as natural. To the extent that this prevailing consciousness is internalized by the population, it becomes part of what is generally called "common sense" so that the philosophy, culture, and morality of a particular elite come to appear as the natural order of things. Such scholars, following Gramsci, stress that this process involves the active consent of the subordinate.[37] Common sense is the way through which a subordinate class lives its subordination. But, for the common sense of national identity, it is still more subtle. Here, common sense is akin to what Michael Billig has termed "banal nationalism." Billig argues that "our" nationalism is forgotten as a sort of common sense world view, whereas that of others – in the Balkans, for instance – is portrayed as dangerously irrational.[38] Yet nationalism, even when explicitly and openly conceived as such, involves a necessary consensus on the meaning of key symbols and an unspoken agreement about natural laws of human societies. Common sense, then, is an unsystematized set of values that affects all classes, although it may advantage some. Yet, it is not rigid and immobile. It is continually transforming itself. The creation of new aspects of common sense knowledge, such as the "facts" of Cartier's "discovery of Canada" requires a system of ideas to permeate throughout society. An entire system of values, attitudes, beliefs, and morality that has the effect of supporting specific relationships of power and identity is wrapped up in the elevation, celebration, and veneration of historical heroes. The story of Jacques Cartier's rise to the status of historical hero, of the transformation of the political meaning of his image across time, and of the audiences to which his life was presented is one that illustrates how diverse elements of societies compete to enshrine common sense, a specific way of looking at the world that is accepted as the natural order.

2
Forgetting and Remembering

Canadians rediscovered and rehabilitated Jacques Cartier in the nineteenth century. At the start of the century, research into Canada's past had not progressed beyond the mid-eighteenth-century writings of Père François-Xavier de Charlevoix. This Jesuit's published volumes remained the essential source for historical writing through the early decades of the century. In 1804, George Heriot published his *History of Canada* in which he translated substantial portions of Charlevoix's sixty-year-old manuscript for a British audience. Although he made some of his own judgments (for instance, he attributed the weakness of settlement in New France to a French desire for quick profits and gold), Heriot remained faithful to Charlevoix's original. Following directly from Charlevoix, Heriot also ended his account at 1731. Some ten years later, another Englishman, William Smith, brought the narrative forward from that date. The son of a former chief justice of Lower Canada, Smith was himself connected to a circle of influential would-be aristocrats and office seekers, often termed the "Chateau Clique," gathered around the governor general in Quebec City. His connections secured him a position as clerk of the Lower Canadian Legislative Assembly and, later, as an executive councillor. But, unlike many of his associates, Smith avoided controversial statements. Like Heriot, he relied heavily on Charlevoix, supplemented with a reading of Louis-Léonard Aumasson de Courville's then unpublished manuscript.[1] In the process, he shouldered judgment out of the narrative, treading so delicate a path that his plodding prose trampled the life out of the past. Cartier barely figured; only Champlain survived as a heroic figure.

From this inauspicious beginning, accounts of Cartier's voyages were widely circulated less than a century later, and students of history, from the early primary grades to university, learned about him. In the span of a few generations, Cartier emerged from the mists of history and moved to the forefront of Canadian heroism. This change was a product of the genesis of a national historical consciousness, especially among French Canadians, that can be linked to two interrelated developments of the century. First was an emerging – and in Canada only gradually emerging – social and cultural modernity. Over the course of the nineteenth century, and particularly from the 1840s, the social and institutional environment of Canada became increasingly complex and sophisticated. Brian Young has commented on the post-rebellion use of "positive law" to reshape Lower Canada's antiquated institutions and legal codes.[2] Rising modernity reshaped Canadian society. But it also influenced historical consciousness and set standards for historical knowledge. The nineteenth century, a time of rapid social, political, and economic change in Canada, was paradoxically also the first "historical" century. Out of the tumultuous years between the reign of George III and the end of Victoria's long life, Canadians developed a particular interest in, and appreciation of, their history. Associated with an increasingly abstract and rule-bound social environment (as opposed to a pre-modern world of face-to-face personal interaction), historical understanding also gradually came to adopt certain standards. Probably the most important of these involved the use of documentary evidence as the arbiter of historical fact.

Yet modernity, which eventually produced twentieth-century "mass societies," is also linked to an understanding of the world that emphasized the accomplishments of elites or particular "great men." Perhaps the most notorious outcome of this connection was the emergence of the cult of the leader exemplified by the totalitarian states of the mid-twentieth century. But such a hypothesis is beyond the scope of this investigation. As for historical studies, modernity helped connect historical development to individual heroes. Certainly, Christianity, liberalism, and Romanticism were individualistic ideologies that directed attention to the individual. But they may not have coalesced as they did to produce a cult of heroes without other developments linked to modernity. This chapter will outline the social and cultural forces that reshaped historical understanding in the nineteenth century. The next chapter will examine how the memory of Jacques Cartier became its chief Canadian beneficiary.

A Hero Forgotten

When Cartier returned home to a comfortable retirement in the summer of 1542, he could never have imagined what people would make of his image centuries later. In his own day, "history" was less important than "description," as European nations sought out new riches and wonders in the Age of Discovery. Explorers did not venture into the unknown with an eye to their historical legacy but for personal profit. And Cartier, though a successful explorer with, according to all available records, an impressive social status at home, had many successors. As he neared the end of his life, he no doubt heard tales of many new discoveries and watched his own accomplishments slide from memory.

One means of assessing Cartier's contemporary reputation is to analyze the popularity and diffusion of the relations of his voyages. An account of the second voyage was edited by Ponce Roffet and printed in Paris in 1545 as *Brief recit, et succincte narration, de la nauigation faicte es ysles de Canada, Hochelage et Saguenay et autres, auec particulieres meurs, langaige, et cerimonies des habitans d'icelles: fort delectable à veoir*, but usually shortened to *Brief recit*.[3] The awkward title, a characteristic of late-Renaissance publishing, indicates more than just the substance of the work. Unlike modern published reprints, the original did not identify who made "the navigation," suggesting that Cartier himself was less important than the voyage. Although some manuscript accounts also appear to have been in circulation during the previous decade, this *Brief recit* was probably the chief source on Cartier's voyages during his lifetime. Yet, this little tract must have had a very short print run. Very few examples remain. Copies exist in the Bibliothèque Mazarine in Paris and the Bibliothèque municipale de Rouen, but for years the only known surviving copy was held by the British Museum in London. Giovanni Ramusio translated the *Brief recit* into Italian in 1556, and this version was itself translated into English by John Florio as *A Shorte and Briefe Narration* in 1580. Richard Hakluyt used the Florio translation for his *Principal Navigations*, which was published in the final years of the sixteenth century.

Many experts, including Henry Percival Biggar and Charles-André Julien, agreed that the *Brief recit* probably derived from a manuscript copy of Cartier's original sea journal (now obviously lost) in the hand of Jean Poullet, who sailed with the captain. Others have presented more imaginative suggestions of authorship, including François Rabelais. Marcel Trudel provides a good summary of these debates in Volume 1 of his *Histoire de la Nouvelle-France*.[4] However, the best account is found in Michel Bideaux's introduction to Cartier's *Relations*, published in 1986 as part of the Bibliothèque du Nouveau Monde series. In this essay, Bideaux makes a convincing case for Cartier's authorship of the *Brief recit*. Bideaux argues that, though the accounts are all narrated in the third person, this was a common rhetorical technique of the sixteenth century. The accounts also provide examples of the first person as, for instance, when the narrator names newly discovered places. Such naming is, of course, the prerogative of a captain. Moreover, Cartier's nephew Jacques Noël referred to "the booke of Iacques Cartier" in a 1587 letter to John Growte, suggesting that Cartier himself was indeed the author. Bideaux concurs.[5]

Ramusio's *Navigationi et viaggi* of 1556 revealed to Europe that the discoveries of the New World were not the unique contributions of the Portuguese and Spanish. The third volume included a version of Cartier's first two voyages, as well as an account of Verrazano's letter to François I outlining his own American itinerary. Enjoying numerous reprintings, Ramusio's version was probably the most successful account of Cartier's voyages; through it, educated Europeans first learned of the exploits of Jacques Cartier. Even André Thevet, the French geographer and self-proclaimed close friend of Cartier, relied on Ramusio for his descriptions of North America. Florio's and Hakluyt's English versions, as noted, also relied on "this famous learned man Gio. Bpte. Ramutius."[6] Through Hakluyt's work, people learned of Cartier's third voyage as well as the travels of Roberval. No published French-language account of the third voyage existed prior to the nineteenth century, and what has survived is but a partial record, ending some time in the middle of Roberval's sojourn in Canada. Indeed, Christian Morissonneau has commented that Europeans knew only of Cartier's second voyage and that the rest of his exploits passed unnoticed.[7]

Certainly, the geographical knowledge that Cartier brought back with him wound its way into European consciousness. The Harleian map carefully reproduced the discoveries from his second voyage, including the St. Lawrence as far as Hochelaga and what some have taken to be a portrait of Cartier himself. Curiously though, the map appears to place Canada east of the Saguenay River. Some have speculated that it was drawn by the famous cartographer Pierre Desceliers of Dieppe in 1542. At the very least, a known Desceliers map, that of 1546, follows the lead of the Harleian map, although it differs in many details. Other maps drawn by cartographers such as John Rotz, Nicolas Des Liens, and Nicholas Vallard appeared through the 1540s to confirm Cartier's discoveries and help entrench his nomenclature, but not, despite the scattering of small unnamed figures on the maps that may or may not represent Cartier, his name and face.[8]

It thus seems probable that Cartier was not widely celebrated during his own day. Some have even suggested that Roberval's pilot, Jean Alfonse, played a greater role in spreading European awareness of North America.[9] Certainly, the king rewarded Cartier with a modest estate near Saint-Malo, but official French attention turned away from the Atlantic to the French hexagon itself. The bloody wars of religion erupted to overshadow any exploits in the northern Atlantic shortly after Cartier's final voyage. Cartier is mentioned in Jehan Mallard's *Description de tous les portz de mer* (1545) and in Guillaume Postel's *De orbis terræ concordia* of the previous year.[10] Following Cartier's death, the Huguenot colonists Jean Ribault and René Laudonnière cited him. Ribault in particular praised him for his skill as a navigator but compressed his voyages to two and gave the Protestant Roberval credit for the second one. Laudonnière condensed all the voyages into one in 1535.[11]

By the 1580s, important tracts rarely mentioned Jacques Cartier at all.[12] One notable exception is the work of the cosmographer André Thevet. An imaginative author given to exaggeration and poetic licence, Thevet saw Cartier as a grand enough authority to rest his own geographical credit on Cartier's name. In his *Cosmographie universelle* (1575), Thevet claimed to have lived with Cartier in Saint-Malo for five months.[13] From this cohabitation, and their blossoming friendship, Thevet derived his particular knowledge of the western Atlantic. Although the modern scholar Frank Lestringant calls this "fiction" a means by which Thevet lowered Cartier's status to elevate his own, it might be seen another way.[14] By elevating Cartier's status and associating himself with a great mariner, Thevet hoisted his own authority to the level of a traveller's first-hand knowledge. Thevet, most generously described by Samuel Morison as "a teller of tall tales," often invented his trips to faraway countries and conjured up a personal travel history that would be the envy of the modern jet set.[15] As if validation through Cartier were insufficient for Thevet's ego, he also concocted a mariner's summit held in Saint-Malo between himself, Cartier, and Sebastian Cabot. Attributing John Cabot's discoveries to Sebastian, Thevet thus placed himself in the company of the two great North Atlantic explorers. His participation at the summit made Thevet an equal of Cartier and Cabot. Unfortunately, no such conference ever occurred. It is possible that, during the brief reign of Edward VI, France and England did hold a naval summit aimed at ending Spain's maritime hegemony, but nothing confirms that either Cartier or Cabot attended. As Lestringant rightly points out, there are simply too many contradictions and inconsistencies in the stories to support the claim.[16]

Among the participants in this alleged summit, Thevet included another great sixteenth-century figure: the raunchy French satirist François Rabelais. According to Thevet, Rabelais visited Cartier, looking for material for the fourth book in the chronicles of Pantagruel, a comic adaptation of the *Odyssey* in which Rabelais satirized politics, religion, and common superstitions. Although few modern scholars have made much of the naval summit itself, many have taken Thevet at his word that Cartier inspired Rabelais. Pierre Margry, the nineteenth-century head of the French Archives de la Marine, believed Cartier to have been the inspiration for Pantagruel's fictional voyages. In 1934, a Canadian folklorist, Marius Barbeau, penned an article for the *Canadian Geographical Journal* outlining the sections of the fourth and fifth books of *Pantagruel* that corresponded to Cartier's various *Relations*. Barbeau made no mention of Thevet or Margry but took it for granted that Cartier and Rabelais were acquainted and that the latter was familiar with the *Brief recit*.[17] His evidence is seductive: Rabelais' story of the quest for the Temple of the Bottle, in which Pantagruel voyages through frigid northwestern seas, begins in Saint-Malo. But Barbeau's strongest piece of evidence is the appearance of Cartier himself, along with Roberval (as Robert Valbringue), in the posthumously published fifth book of *Pantagruel*. According to Rabelaisian scholars, Cartier is represented in *Pantagruel* by the character Jamet Brayer. "Jamet," Barbeau informs us, was the name of Jacques Cartier's father. It was also the sixteenth century's familiar version of Jacques.[18] Nevertheless, though the accounts of Cartier and Rabelais do contain similarities, and it is not impossible that the one inspired the other, this is not a necessary conclusion. The landlubber Rabelais did not need Cartier to learn nautical terms, and many Rabelaisian students have questioned the authenticity of the fifth book. Naval historians such as Samuel Morison have argued that the nautical expressions shouted in Rabelais' tales are better suited to Mediterranean than to Atlantic seafaring; some are nearly complete gibberish.[19] Of course, accuracy was hardly Rabelais' goal. Still, though Barbeau's account is unconvincing, corroborating evidence does exist. A seventeenth-century Malouin historian, Jacques Doremet, published a small tract in 1628 confirming that Rabelais visited Cartier. Doremet drew this suggestion from the oral tradition of the city, but he reported it as a simple fact.[20]

True or not, the suggestion that Cartier inspired Rabelais is intriguing. It implies that Cartier's explorations were better known than the evidence of cosmographers and geographers indicates. And, in connecting Cartier with Rabelais, Barbeau followed Thevet's lead in the practice of greatness by association. Rabelais, then, became a tool to elevate the value of Cartier (and, by extension, of Canada) in the minds of sixteenth-century French thinkers. If the popular satirist had found value in stories of Canada, surely the place was not without worth among his contemporaries as a locus of wonder. Indeed, as Barbeau specified in his article, this Rabelaisian assessment serves as a counterpoint to Voltaire's later dismissal of Canada as "a few acres of snow." Voltaire was probably referring to Acadia, but the Canadian imagination reassigned his epigram to an insult encompassing Canada as a whole, despite the fact that it was uttered by a fictional character in a satirical novel.[21] Still, for Cartier and Rabelais, according to Barbeau's reading, Canada was not a pathetic waste of resources as imagined by Voltaire but the symbol of a hope for Oriental splendour. This, he suggested, was the true image of the country among Voltaire's contemporaries. He added that Bougainville, who circumnavigated the globe after the fall of Quebec, "became the flagbearer of the very utopia which Cartier and Rabelais once had grafted upon the soul of ancient France." The inference here is spectacular. From Cartier, Barbeau drew a line through Rabelais to Bougainville and from Bougainville to the Rousseauian celebration of the primitive life of the South Seas: "It revived the vision of the Millenium [sic], which Cartier and Rabelais once had conjured. Jean-Jacques Rousseau penned eloquent diatribes against civilization and urged upon all the 'état de nature' – which was the true incentive for an upheaval among a tax and war-ridden people ... Out of this chimera the reformers drew the humanitarian motto which inspired the French Revolution: LIBERTÉ, EGALITÉ, FRATERNITÉ."[22] Although the line between Cartier and the French Revolution is hardly a direct one, Barbeau inserted him at the head of a hitherto unimagined interpretation of French intellectual history. Alas, what Barbeau's vision actually boils down to is hardly unique: Cartier was among the first French sailors to imagine a route to the riches of Asia through or around North America. Of course, Barbeau's claims were made during the 1930s at the end of a long period of glorifying Cartier, and they mirrored an anglophone pattern linking explorers in a chain of successors. European fascination with exploits such as Cartier's was much more restrained in the sixteenth century. Only after 1560 did the existence of the New World begin to attract attention outside a small circle of enthusiasts and scholars, and even then there was little interest in France.[23] There is scant evidence to suggest that either Rabelais' fictional Jamet Brayer or any allusions to historical events kept the name of Jacques Cartier in the forefront of the European consciousness. The only certain and overt sixteenth-century effort to cultivate his memory was spearheaded by his nephew, Jacques Noël, and supported by the Breton merchant community. During the 1560s, Malouin merchants began to trade in furs with the inhabitants of North America at Tadoussac, at the mouth of the Saguenay River.[24] In the 1550s, Noël, who had sailed with his uncle, returned to Canada to investigate the interior, and his sons likewise may have led transatlantic expeditions. Indeed, if they themselves did not see Lake Ontario, they at least uncovered tales of it. In 1584, a certain M. De Leau informed Richard Hakluyt that a Malouin had discovered "the sea on the backside of Hochelaga."[25] These sixteenth-century Malouin traders had a vested interest in perpetuating the memory of Jacques Cartier: their claim to trading rights rested on the discoveries of their townsman. Noël did his best to keep the Cartier name fresh by corresponding with geographers and cartographers to correct their estimates of terrain and their toponymy. Along with his partner, Etienne Chatan de la Jannaye, Noël secured a commission from Henri II granting a twelve-year trading monopoly in Canada. The commission expressly stated that the two men deserved this honour because of their inheritance from Jacques Cartier. The merchants of Saint-Malo rejoiced. But their celebration was short-lived, for, six months later, the king revoked the commission. Unfortunately for those who sought to capitalize on Cartier's discoveries, such an interdiction violated the traditional trading liberties of the towns of Brittany.[26]

By the beginning of the seventeenth century, Cartier's legacy was greatly diminished. Champlain, who knew of him, at first insisted that Cartier had not penetrated as far as Montreal. Although he later revised his opinion, Champlain persisted in playing down his predecessor's accomplishments in favour of his own. His colleague Marc Lescarbot attempted to correct this misdirection, repeatedly reminding his readers that Champlain was following Cartier's lead. For instance, in his *Histoire de la Nouvelle France*, Lescarbot prefaced his account of Champlain's expedition by observing that "Monsieur Champlain [has] of late made the same voyage which the Captain James Cartier had made."[27] Moreover, repeatedly citing Cartier's accounts as his source, and making comparisons between Cartier's *Relations* and his own observations, Lescarbot set up Cartier as an authority. But seventeenth-century scholarship continued to reduce the significance of Cartier's legacy. The description made by the Baron de Lahontan ten decades later is typical. After travelling in North America between 1683 and 1692, Lahontan published his journals in about 1704. Like Champlain at the opposite end of the century, he downplayed Jacques Cartier and attributed the discovery of Canada to Verrazano. He summed up Cartier's three voyages with the following statement: "Jacques Cartier went there next, but after travelling above Quebec with his vessels, he returned to France thoroughly disgusted with the country there."[28]

By the eighteenth century, the name and accomplishments of Jacques Cartier, when remembered, were deemed inconsequential. Among Frenchmen interested in North America at that time, the geographers Claude and Guillaume Delisle performed the most intensive research. With voracious appetites, they pored over documents in the various archives, reading all they could about the voyages of La Salle, Iberville, Louis Hennepin, Jacques Marquette, Champlain, and Cartier. Guillaume Delisle incorporated this information into his secret brief to the Conseil de la Marine and the regent in 1717.[29] Thus, when the council and the regent sent Père François-Xavier de Charlevoix to North America in search of the western sea – the very question "les Delisle" had been investigating – they probably armed him with a knowledge of Cartier's expeditions. Such a supposition is borne out by Charlevoix's *Histoire de la Nouvelle France*, published in 1744. Although Charlevoix persisted in crediting the discovery of Canada to Verrazano, his history partially rehabilitated Cartier's name. Admittedly, Charlevoix devoted three times the space to Verrazano that he allotted to Cartier, but he also asserted that, after the miserable winter of 1541-42, Roberval convinced Cartier to return to his abandoned fort, that he rebuilt it, and that he stayed another winter.[30]

In part, Cartier's slide into obscurity was due to the culture of the times. Having neither established a Christian colony nor paid much attention to the proselytization of the Natives, Cartier was of little use to Jesuits and explorers, such as Charlevoix. Control of the French trade with Canada likewise slipped from Breton hands. The rapid expansion of Malouin capitalism in the eighteenth century, although initially built on the Newfoundland and Quebec trade, shifted to a focus on privateering, the cod fisheries, and illegal trade with the Spanish West Indies. By the eighteenth century, shipping between Saint-Malo and Canada was irregular at best, and even merchants at Rouen and Dieppe routinely sent their ships via the better-established ports of La Rochelle and Bordeaux.[31] Assertions of a Malouin pedigree in the trade were no longer necessary or politically astute. The educated interests of the seventeenth and eighteenth centuries were only beginning to encourage historical scholarship. The French in North America had an empire to build and conquests to protect. The relentless push west, even when officially curtailed by the great minister Colbert, gave little pause to reflect on the echoes of the past. The use of the past was simple and practical. Explorers and missionaries turned to prior accounts for what they could learn about the terrain, climate, and inhabitants of the American interior. Cartier's misfortune (and more so that of the Hochelagans and Stadaconans) was that the original inhabitants of the St. Lawrence valley had long since abandoned their homes by the time Champlain planted the first permanent colony at the foot of Cap Diamant in 1608. Having penetrated no further than Montreal, Cartier offered little of practical value in the pressing search for the western sea.

The Invention of History

History was of greater interest during the nineteenth century than in the eighteenth. Although historical studies were not invented during that century, and many innovations in history can be traced to eighteenth-century developments, the particular responses to emerging modernity of the nineteenth century sharply altered historical research and historical thinking. Authors such as Hugh Trevor-Roper and Stephen Bann have argued that the intellectual roots of modern historiography are to be found in the broad movement known as Romanticism.[32] Although Romanticism cannot be reduced to a simple set of principles, it can be characterized by certain recurrent themes. European Romantic movements shared a philosophical revolt against excessive rationalism. The basic aims of Romanticism were a veneration of nature, an exaltation of the senses and emotions over reason and intellect, and a rediscovery of the artist as a supremely individual creator. Romanticism obviously derived from many sources. It is often said to have begun in France with Jean-Jacques Rousseau but is more clearly linked to Immanuel Kant, the upheaval of the French Revolution, and German idealism. Indeed, Romanticism arrived most clearly in Germany about 1781 in the writings of Friedrich Schiller and Johann Wolfgang von Goethe. A useful simplification to help identify the movement claims that these writers rejected the dry rationalism of Voltaire's Enlightenment and embraced the primitive, the grotesque, and the mysterious. They discarded the stylistic conventions of drama and poetry; they encouraged a more personal and intimate tone; and they invoked the feeling of the sublime, a sense of inexpressible, inarticulate emotional awe instilled in individual consciousness by the natural world. The basic factor in this revolutionary dismissal of the Enlightenment was subjectivism: for Kant, the mind was not simply the Enlightenment's passive observer of the universe but an agent active in shaping reality. Romanticism shifted the emphasis from the observable passive object to the subject. Under this regime, the mind became not a blank slate or a human tool to uncover reality but a creative force imagining and shaping the world it perceived.[33]

Romantic literature focused on often dark secrets, which, if uncovered, could hint at a new understanding of human creative powers. Many Romanticist writers employed the play of memory across time in order to narrate a voyage of the self from childhood into maturity. Although Romanticism must be construed as politically ambiguous, much Romantic literature, in part because of its focus on the environment and its revitalization of language, reinforced emerging images of nationalism. Romantic writers, such as Henry Wadsworth Longfellow, William Wordsworth, Victor Hugo, Robert Burns, Alexander Pushkin, and Johann Wolfgang von Goethe, connected nature, the folk, and the passage of time in a way that infused nations with a past and a sense of purpose and belonging. The wealthy built themselves replica ruins and follies in an effort to capture a fantasy past or to invoke the sublime passage of time. In many ways, Romanticism entailed a conservative vision and a retreat to a safe past; several of these early writers became conservatives later in life. But it also indicated a new, and in some ways revolutionary, historical consciousness. It reoriented the study of the past toward folk histories, the more recent human past, and especially national histories. It also relied heavily on a belief that history's meaning could be felt and sensed in a nation's age, its folklore, its landscape, and its character. George Heriot's *Travels through the Canadas,* published only two years after his *History of Canada,* featured descriptive sections entitled "romantic appearance" and noted Quebec City's "romantic situation." Showing Heriot's concern with the sublime – that catch word of early nineteenth-century Romantics – the *Travels* included a discourse on the "influence produced on the mind by positions of extraordinary elevation."[34]

There has been some debate concerning the advent of Romanticism in Canada. Conventional wisdom suggests that it arrived, at least in French Canada, with *La Capricieuse* in 1855. This French warship, so the story goes, not only came to Canada with a hold crammed with the great French literature of the first half of the nineteenth century but re-established political and cultural contact between France and French Canada.[35] Mason Wade, an American student of Canadian history, disagrees. Wade insists that Romanticism was fashionable in Canada during the early 1800s and that, though they were not as popular as classical authors such as Voltaire, France's leading Romantics regularly appeared in the Canadian press, borrowed by editors to fill out their fledgling newspapers.[36] However, according to Maurice Lemire, Romanticism came late to French Canada. French Canadian authors eschewed the style until at least the 1860s, not because they were unaware of it but because it held little resonance for them.[37]

Nevertheless, the Romanticist ideas of the century certainly penetrated Canadian culture. Heriot was not alone in his appreciation of the sublime.

If French Canadian authors, with exceptions, avoided the Romantic style, the reading public appeared more interested.[38] Benefiting from the lifting of the Continental Blockade, Canadian booksellers conducted a brisk trade in European books after 1815. Announcements of books for sale multiplied in the local papers. From 1816 to 1822, a Montreal merchant named Hector Bossange placed sixty advertisements in five newspapers. As early as 1816, the catalogues of Quebec City booksellers listed the titles of leading Romantic writers. In that year, G. and B. Horan in Quebec City and Bossange in Montreal advertised the sale of works by Germaine de Staël, François-René Chateaubriand, and Alphonse Lamartine, among others.[39]

Chateaubriand makes an interesting case. Although the implicit leader (along with Benjamin de Constant and Germaine de Staël) of early French Romanticism, Chateaubriand planted himself on somewhat unique ideological ground. Appalled by the godlessness of the French Revolution, he wrote an apology for Catholicism, *La génie du Christianisme,* which celebrated the emotional and spiritual uplift that candlelit church interiors evoked in the senses. He marvelled at the sight of sunlight playing through stained-glass scenes and dancing through the vastness of a Gothic cathedral. His defence of the sublime beauty of medieval architecture and the emotive power of devotional music helped bring ancient Catholicism into line with the new ideals of Romanticism. Later in life, he broke with Napoleon and became a staunch supporter of the Bourbon restoration, serving as Louis XVIII's ambassador to England and, following the July Revolution of 1830, supporting the claims of Charles X and his grandson.[40] Thus, although subsequent leaders of the Romantic movement, such as Victor Hugo, would threaten the Canadian Catholic clergy, Chateaubriand offered a possible concord between Romanticism and Catholicism.

Some have attempted to establish connections between Romanticism, historical consciousness in Lower Canada, and the works of the German nationalist Johann Herder.[41] However, a link between nineteenth-century French Canada and Herder seems anachronistic. Herder's works were scarcely known in Canada, whereas those of Chateaubriand were in demand: his novels *René* and *Atala,* set in the forests of North America, offered a particular appeal to New World audiences. In 1822, the library of the Legislative Assembly of Lower Canada acquired a number of his books, and during the 1830s, *Le Canadien* published extracts from Chateaubriand's works, as well as those of Lamartine.[42] And, of course, Chateaubriand had a keen admirer in the person of the abbé C.-F. Painchaud, the curé of Sainte-Anne-de-la-Pocatière and founder of the college there. Painchaud was so moved after reading *La génie du Christianisme* in 1826 that he wrote Chateaubriand to congratulate him: "I devour your works, their melancholy is killing me, all the while they delight me; it is ecstasy." Some authors have tried to establish an even closer association between these two men, alleging that they spent a week together at Niagara Falls. This seems unlikely. However, Painchaud was also in contact with the leaders of the Patriote movement in the 1820s and 1830s, even professing to its leader, Louis-Joseph Papineau, to be a supporter.[43] His choice of reading materials certainly suggests that he shared similar tastes with the voracious readers of the Legislative Assembly.

Historical scholarship in the nineteenth century was also influenced by a broad understanding of material reality, one form of which was eventually systematized as "positivism" by Auguste Comte. Although much of Thomas Malthus' writings anticipated Comtean positivism, these methods were not popularized in the English-speaking world before 1843 and the publication of John Stuart Mill's *System of Positive Logic*. From the mid-nineteenth century, the Comtean method dominated the study of society and had a not insignificant influence on historical studies. Comte himself sketched a theory of history, but the real credit for developing the methods of modern "scientific" historiography belongs to Leopold von Ranke. Lord Acton once credited Ranke with perfecting objectivity in historical writing and congratulated him for creating a neutral style of prose.

It is too simplistic to see the genesis of "scientific history" as a mere transcription of a monolithic nineteenth-century positivism. Positivism's influence on historical writing, like that of Romanticism, was not so straightforward. Certainly, some positivist historians, such as Ranke himself, accused Walter Scott of distorting the past by writing more from imagination than anything else. But this should not imply that Ranke rejected the use of imagination in historical inquiry. Even fellow Romanticists accused Scott of inventing a "false genre" of historical writing.[44] Ranke's effort to see history "as it actually was" has often been mischaracterized as uncomplicated positivism. Yet, his thought retained many vestiges of German idealism, and he expected historians to interpret their documents through an almost mystical process.[45] And, despite Lord Acton's opinion, his prose cannot be described as neutral. His methodology relied on Romantic inspiration and insight as well as on a dogged materialistic interpretation of the sources. Nonetheless, the English-speaking world *did* misinterpret Ranke as the harbinger of a noble dream of objectivity. In Canada, this approach appears in Robert Christie's six-volume *History of the Late Province of Lower Canada,* which covers 1791 to 1841; its prose is more neutral than that of George Heriot, whose works exemplify Canadian Romantic history. Christie adopted a rigorously documentary approach to his study, in mimicry of Acton's dictums.[46]

These trends coalesced in ways emerging from the mania for collecting that captivated the middle classes of Europe and its colonies during the eighteenth and early nineteenth centuries. This was a peculiar interest that became even more pronounced in the Victorian age and may itself be one of the first manifestations of modernity. Collecting, much like capitalism, satisfied a drive to acquire wealth. And, as collections grew, they required their owners to categorize, structure, and organize their holdings according to "rational" schemes they dreamed up. This was a modern way of systematizing, and therefore of controlling, knowledge. Such "scientific" forms of knowledge appeared during the eighteenth century but reached a point of maturity in the nineteenth. For the material world, this fascination helped nurture the developing natural sciences of geology, botany, biology, and zoology, as collectors amassed sample after sample of known and newly discovered curiosities. One offshoot of this cultural phenomenon was the creation of cabinets of curiosities. Initially the private displays of an individual collector's holdings, some of these cabinets were eventually opened to a wider public, becoming the forerunners of museums familiar to a later age. This sort of open display of curiosities was part of the Enlightenment enthusiasm for equality in opportunity for learning. Museum historians have suggested it is no coincidence that the British Museum opened in the mid-eighteenth century, at roughly the time when Ephraim Chambers' *Cyclopaedia* was published. They discern the same pattern in France, for the Encyclopédistes published at about the time when parts of the royal collections were opened to public display at the Luxembourg Palace.[47] This spirit crossed the Atlantic: in Charleston and Philadelphia, museums opened before the dawning of the nineteenth century, but not until the 1820s in Canada.

During the instigation of these public displays, private collectors continued their own idiosyncratic pursuits. Indeed, throughout the nineteenth century, the personal collection remained the most widespread expression of the collector's impulse, and private enthusiasts became recognized as experts among their social peers. Although historians of science have described a "professionalization" of the natural sciences through the nineteenth century, distinguishing the professional from the amateur remained difficult before the century's end. The problem is even more acute in historical collecting, and especially antiquarianism. The latter, a curious private and personalized blend of interest in old books, documents, and artifacts, was the first serious development in "modernizing" historical studies. The recognized modern methods of history and archaeology eventually grew out of antiquarian pursuits. Yet, despite this gradual development, which could be termed "professionalization," the antiquarian mindset persisted for some time. Indeed, though the slow nineteenth-century emergence of the disciplines of archaeology and history from antiquarianism resembles that of the natural sciences, the distinctions remain more difficult to delineate. Philippa Levine has demonstrated how the more "scientific" disciplines began to diverge from antiquarianism in England at midcentury, particularly as archaeology increasingly drew on the physical sciences and history developed more rigorous rules for reading and interpreting documents. By the end of the century, the words "historian" and "antiquarian" meant very different things in England, with historians institutionalized in universities, leaving the antiquarians to their amateur hobbies.[48] Yet, though historians displayed a growing scorn for the local and county histories developed by antiquarians, they continued to rely on the sources compiled and methods pioneered by their amateur predecessors. In Canada, with its less-developed institutions of higher learning, the amateur tradition persisted into the twentieth century. Even past the First World War, librarians, retired military men, and well-read jurists were sometimes considered the peers of professional historians holding positions in the country's universities.

Antiquarianism also emerged as part of the collector's impulse. Antiquarians first delighted in ruins and relics, demonstrating as well a kindred spirit with the inclinations of Romanticism. Possessing the past in the form of artifacts and ruins represented a means to hold physical remains linked to famous stories and myths. Indeed, the desirability of an individual artifact lay in its connection with a known or acceptable story; otherwise, owning this skeleton as opposed to that skeleton made no sense. The artifact had to tell a tale, and the story had to connect to widely known tropes, myths, legends, and memories.[49] Yet, at the same time, early antiquarians saw no point in amassing complete collections. They remained concerned only with fragments of personal interest and steered away from linking elements to form coherent narratives accessible to wider audiences.

To modern historians, antiquarianism is a quaint anachronism. Relying on a Nietzschean distinction, Stephen Bann suggests that the "antiquarian historian" has been equated with an inability to rise to the standards of the true history practised by professionals, a characterization he describes as "not entirely false."[50] Historian Arnoldo Momigliano similarly saw antiquarianism as "so near to my profession," and yet so mysterious. He recognized the sincere enthusiasm and commitment to the vocation but had difficulty reconciling this interest in historical artifacts with the lack of interest in history itself.[51] However, not all antiquarians can be so categorized. Sir Walter Scott ridiculed earlier antiquarians as behind the times of historical understanding: they had failed to progress from the idiosyncratic collection to recognizing the place of artifacts in recounting national histories.[52] By Scott's time, antiquarianism itself had moved into new areas of compiling and publishing collections of documents. By the end of the 1830s, printing clubs had formed, first in Scotland and then across England. Following the foundation of the Camden Society in 1838, private printing clubs became the accepted means for distributing the kind of historical sources required to produce a "Rankean" study. A widespread availability of documents thus affected the ways in which people understood and wrote about the past.[53] Similar, if less widespread, developments reached Canada. Jacques Viger, the Montreal political organizer and office holder, was an avid collector. As a young man, he began amassing a series of documents and notes that eventually became the forty-three-volume collection "Ma Saberdache." Although somewhat unique in Canada, his attention to the documented record influenced an emerging Canadian historiography, both francophone and anglophone, through the nineteenth century.

Despite this invigoration of historical methodology in the early nineteenth century, historical studies in Canada rarely surpassed the work of Charlevoix, who became the chief source for anyone with a passing interest in the Old Regime. Certainly the Parti patriote was interested in improving the level of historical knowledge. Jacques Labrie, a medical doctor and supporter of Papineau, produced a history of Canada for publication by the spring of 1831. However, Labrie died before his manuscript could be typeset and published by the Legislative Assembly. After his death, the appointed Legislative Council amended the relevant bill in order to fund the purchase of his manuscript and notes by Quebec City's Literary and Historical Society. By 1838, the manuscript had still not been published, and it was unfortunately lost in a fire shortly thereafter.[54] But in truth, few people much cared about the French regime, or any Canadian history, in those days. When an old French well was discovered in Montreal in 1834, it was seen as an intriguing curiosity but nothing to spark an interest in the city's past. A bust of King George III, long thought to have been destroyed by American troops in 1775, was found near that well, but again it was not seen as important.[55] Nevertheless, this general lack of interest in the Canadian past was on the verge of changing. A fascination with history had been sparked by the flint and steel of Romanticism and the new, more rigorous methodology. In a country as young as Canada, documentary evidence was most certainly preserved and available; much was immediately accessible. Romanticism's absorption with the mysterious and sublime past cast some Canadian eyes to their own heroic past.

Liberalism, Individualism, and Great Men

Even if interest in history was growing, it would not necessarily lead to public commemorations of long-dead men. British and European monuments of the eighteenth and early nineteenth centuries tended to commemorate reigning sovereigns or the recently deceased. In France, heroes were more deeply politicized after the revolution, which made a point of developing cults around public figures. Of course, no French hero could rival Napoleon Bonaparte, who maintained followers even in exile and after death. Indeed, Napoleon cast a long shadow over French hero worship through the nineteenth century and significantly affected French political symbolism.[56] In England, early nineteenth-century Whigs invented a cult around Charles James Fox, the rotund statesman. Their efforts were clearly aimed not so much at the memory of Fox as at continuing to fight for their cause.[57] Living heroes, such as the Duke of Wellington, served to legitimize middle-class pretensions, not to mention the hero's own status and ambitions.[58]

This practice quite naturally crossed the Atlantic with the settlers who came to colonize American soil. The memorial for Sir Isaac Brock, Upper Canada's first national hero, was begun shortly after the general drew his last breath.[59] Montreal's Horatio Nelson monument, erected in 1809, is another case in point. More than anything else, it performed a memorial function marking the mourning for the loss of a contemporary military leader. (The more famous Nelson's Column at Trafalgar Square in London bucks the trend. Erected in the 1840s, it suggests a more historical, commemorative function. However, Nelson memorials were also built in Glasgow and Dublin, as in Montreal, only a few years after the hero's death.[60]) The Wolfe and Montcalm obelisk in Quebec City, on the other hand, was aimed less at commemoration than at political concern, such as the soothing of ethnic tensions in the new provincial capital. It was proposed by Lord Dalhousie, the governor general, and inaugurated on 8 September 1828 to help rebuild amity between French and English in the city.[61] Herein lies a partial explanation for the interest in historical heroes: it was motivated by political concerns. In the same vein, Brock's monument at Queenston Heights, constructed during the 1820s, became even more of a symbol after it was blown up, presumably by a Fenian sympathizer, in 1840. Reconstructed as a taller and more elaborate column between 1853 and 1856, the new monument commemorated the hero under different political circumstances. No longer a simple column marking the general's grave, it was reminiscent of the Trafalgar Square Nelson's Column, surrounded by allegorical representatives of Britain and topped with a statue of the hero. By midcentury, Brock had become a symbol of loyalism more than a man.

It would be tempting to attribute the sudden nineteenth-century interest in historical heroes to political liberalism. On the ascendant in the Western world during the nineteenth century, liberalism is committed to individualism and takes the rights of individuals to be basic or fundamental. Individuals constitute the primary building blocks of society; thus, few restrictions on their freedoms or liberties can be justified. Liberal language is evident in the demands for greater democracy made by Canadian political leaders such as Pierre Bédard. Liberalism was the key ideology of many historians who were attempting to justify the constitutions of England and America, and especially the emerging capitalist economic system. Certainly, liberal historians celebrated historical heroes under the guise of what has become known as the "great man" theory of history. Thomas Carlyle's 1840 lectures on the hero in history explained how a succession of great men had redefined their world in their own image. In this guise, history was narrated as a series of actions of great men: kings, prime ministers, generals, and explorers.[62] Many liberal historians of the nineteenth century went out of their way to elevate certain individual heroes, those who fit characterizations of the liberal "self-made man," in their works. Thus, the progress of history became inextricably tied to individual initiative. American historians, for instance, attempted to portray Christopher Columbus as just such a new man, a bourgeois of talent, whose achievements were based on merit rather than position or class. Columbus' success, then, represented confidence in the capitalist individualism of the nineteenth century.[63] Yet, though there has been a tendency to associate great men with the emergent liberal individualism of the nineteenth century, even doctrines of individualism do not necessarily connote liberalism. Individualism is evident in the Cartesian system of philosophy, which grounds the foundations of certainty in individual reason and evidence *(cogito ergo sum)*. And elements of Cartesian philosophy were accepted by some Catholic teachers, such as abbé Jacques Odelin. The German philosopher G.W.F. Hegel also posited history as a series of acts by great men, but his great men were simply the vehicles through which History itself unfolded according to the logic of the dialectic. In Hegel's formulation, individualism began with Christianity.

Certainly, early Christianity was an individualist faith. Its concentration on the salvation of the soul and affirmation of the imminent end of all things intensified the spirit of individuality developing in the Roman Empire. Such a spirit was bequeathed, in often vastly different ways, to the medieval Christian church and to the Protestant faiths of the Reformation. But, despite the writings of some propagandists, Christian individualism is apolitical in nature. The doctrine of the original equality of all souls is compatible with a broad variety of political arrangements. Nevertheless, medieval Christianity did construct heroes out of historical figures, heaping all manner of differing values onto them. Charles W. Jones provides but one example of this type of cult, in his investigation of St. Nicholas. Nicholas himself may have been a living historical person in the fourth century AD, but Jones' use of the designation "N" rather than "Nicholas" reinforces his point that the saint venerated by later followers was purely imaginary.[64] For many other saints, groups of followers banded together into cults to celebrate and teach the meaning of "N" as they understood it and according to their own circumstances. The pattern was constantly repeated throughout the long centuries of Christian Europe, often with encouragement and sponsorship from civil or ecclesiastical authorities, as the various saints provided a symbolic focus for abstract concepts and principles guiding good conduct and belief. Long before political liberalism elevated the great man as the hero of history, Christianity had elevated a series of inspirational men and women.

Many authors have sought less confessional origins for individualism. Romanticism was likewise individualist from its earliest conception. It was at root a celebration of the creative self and an effort to reconcile the unique individual with the collective, at least in fiction. Moreover, at least one scholar has pointed out that this individualism was not the negative, defensive variant of liberal political theory. According to Gerald Izenberg, such a conception was at odds with Romanticism's project of a creative, unique individual because liberalism imagined individuals as atomized and yet narrowly homogeneous.[65] Although Izenberg may be overstating the case on both sides, his claim further cautions against presuming the celebration of individuals to be uniquely liberal.

However, following Stephen Lukes, Alan Macfarlane points out that "individualism" within liberalism describes a multitude of possible meanings. Lukes uncovered no fewer than eleven distinct, although related, meanings. All seem to lead to an understanding that society is based on autonomous units – individuals – which are ultimately more important than any larger group. This belief is especially reflected in liberalism's sacralization of private property, religious toleration, and legal and political liberties. It lies at the very heart of liberalism. This ideology is traditionally dated from the mid-seventeenth century, in the writings of James Harrington and Thomas Hobbes, and is associated with a shift in socio-economic systems from limited communal ownership to absolute private ownership. Occasionally it is traced to the Protestant Reformation's reorientation of Christianity inward to the primacy of the individual soul. Macfarlane pushes the origins of individualism, in England at least, much further back, arguing that it cannot be explained by such conventional devices as Protestantism or the market economy.[66]

Perhaps aspects of the increasingly hegemonic ideology of liberalism, such as individualism, became "common sense" attributes of all nineteenth-century ideologies. By the end of the eighteenth century, even English conservatives relied on at least the language of liberalism to defend conservative principles. Edmund Burke, to cite the most famous example, attacked the French Revolution on the basis that it violated the natural order of things, but he phrased his opposition in the language of individual rights. According to Burke's 1790 *Reflections on the Revolution in France,* these rights existed, at least for Englishmen, because they had been inherited from the past.[67] This infusion of the elements of liberalism into opposing or contradictory ideologies was certainly present in Lower Canada. Ultramontane Catholics made use of scientific methods normally associated with liberalism, and, in the middle decades of the century, they were able to denounce secular liberalism while selectively employing some of its rhetoric.[68] However, the Catholic leaders of French Canada rejected liberal individualism, and especially the idea that society was a simple collection of atomized individuals, at the same time that they celebrated historical heroes.

The influence of the French priest Felicité de La Mennais, more commonly known as Lamennais, reveals the difficulty of tying specific ideas too closely to broader intellectual or social movements. At the very least, Lamennais shows how modernity is not necessarily connected to a liberal or secular mindset, and therefore the easy association of liberalism with the celebration of historical heroes is not always accurate. Indeed, to trace the development of Lamennais' thinking is to uncover the diverse influences that early nineteenth-century modernity could produce, even in one mind. Moreover, the varied acceptance of his ideas in Canada sets the association of liberalism with hero celebration on its head.

Born in Saint-Malo in 1782, Lamennais followed his brother's path into the religious life in the first decade of the nineteenth century, although he was not ordained until 1817. He began his intellectual career by writing defences for a Catholicism labouring under partial suppression in Napoleonic France. His most notable early piece was his "Essay on Indifference in Religion," written in 1817, the year he became a priest. The second edition of the essay, published in 1820, argued for a new theory of certitude, which would overcome the indifference to religion pressed by individualist thinking. Lamennais claimed that certitude could not be supplied by individual reason; it belonged only to the general reason, to the universal consent of mankind, the *common* sense. Certitude derived from the unanimous testimony of the human race and from authority; it was not found through objective evidence but was a matter of faith.

At first, Lamennais was respected by Canadian ultramontanes. The future bishop of Montreal, Jean-Jacques Lartigue, came across Lamennais during his sojourn in France in 1819 and 1820, and praised his attacks against impiety, describing him as a great force for Catholicism. Lartigue helped ensure that Mennasian ideas reached across the Atlantic. Ten years later, Bishop Lartigue was happy that Lamennais had become well known among the Canadian clergy, for those who read his works "will quickly become ultramontanes."[69] It was Lamennais' attacks on Gallicanism, a doctrine that placed the administration of the French church beyond papal authority, that inspired Lartigue and his followers. But Lartigue must also have accepted the theory of certitude, which was central to Lamennais' attack on Gallicanism.

Of course, episcopal approval did not mean that all Canadian Catholics accepted these teachings. The Sulpicians, for one, denounced this system of philosophy, and these philosophical disputes sometimes spilled out of the seminaries and into public discourse. In 1833, a Cartesian priest berated students at the Collège de Saint-Hyacinthe for adhering to Mennasian ideals.[70] As Lamennais drifted leftward in politics, his earlier supporters became nervous. After the July Revolution of 1830, Lamennais began to defend the church against a new French government that resented the influence it had enjoyed under the Bourbon monarchy. Yet, even as he worked to ward off fresh dangers menacing the church, Lamennais hoped to unite it with the cause of liberalism, setting up his defence of Catholicism on the basis of equal rights. This effort jeopardized his reputation among Canada's ultramontanes. Lamennais founded the journal *L'Avenir* in the fall of 1830 and in its pages began to formulate a Catholic brand of liberalism and democracy. He was denounced, at least indirectly, by the papal encyclical *Mirari vos* of August 1832. Quieted, but not silenced, Lamennais was denounced again in the encyclical *Singulari nos* of 1834 and forced to break with the Catholic Church.

Initially a reactionary and a follower of the French royalist Louis de Bonald, but later a proto-socialist, Lamennais consistently rejected doctrines of individualism. Indeed, it was only after 1830, when he began to approach liberalism (although through its democratic alliance with the sovereignty of the people), that he was attacked by the ecclesiastical authorities. In Canada, he came to be associated with democracy and the struggle for liberty, and thus against his earliest partisans in the church. At the very least, his stated faith in the separation of church and state forced ultramontanes to reconsider their earlier approval. In June 1836, Lamennais' anti-Vatican polemic *Paroles d'un croyant* was printed and distributed in the Lower Canadian countryside by the Parti patriote, the political faction on the verge of leading the rebellions against constituted authority in the province.[71] Yet the Patriotes resisted celebrating historical individuals in their propaganda. Certainly, they elevated specific political leaders, such as Papineau, or honoured political martyrs, but with the possible exception of Dr. Labrie, they eschewed appeals to the past. Their project was to overthrow the past. By contrast, opponents of rebellion drew heavily on the past to buttress their resistance to the radical change they feared liberalism might bring.

The memory of Jacques Cartier was first conscripted to local history and quickly became a servant of conservative purposes. Liberals involved in the first Jacques Cartier monument project in 1835, such as Hector-Simon Huot, were moderates who split with the Parti patriote over the issue of armed rebellion. Perhaps, then, a more complete answer to the question of why historical heroes emerged when they did involves the social and intellectual developments of the century, of which liberalism was only a part. Liberalism helped people establish a meaning and a use for some historical heroes, such as Columbus, but it was not the cause of their veneration. It was simply one means to interpret the significance of those heroes whom people honoured.

Many scholars have presumed that the celebration of heroes developed as a means to motivate those who followed them. Most nineteenth-century hero-worshippers, to borrow Carlyle's formulation of the practice, pointed to the hero's ability to inspire subsequent generations, much as their Christian predecessors looked to the saints to encourage devotion. Cartier's French Canadian proponents frequently made such pronouncements in their appeals for Cartier monuments. His conduct was an example of virtuous behaviour. The hero's brilliant achievements are inspiration for the great life but remain beyond the reach of ordinary people. Perhaps, though, his role was more one of providing comfort than of offering inspiration. The nineteenth century was a transitional period in many Western countries. Its middle decades were rife with social, economic, and political upheaval and uncertainty, and the exploits of heroic figures pointed to a simpler time when clear-cut virtues led to glory. Historical heroes were both a product of, and a reaction to, emerging modernity. They provided comfort that the values of the past were indeed the right ones, and in the face of political, and especially spiritual, upheaval, they offered the moral anchor for a society seemingly adrift. Supporters of historical heroes borrowed from the intellectual currents of liberalism and Romanticism, and later sought material evidence of their truth through historical documents, in order to adapt their values to the progress of modernity. In this sense, historical heroes represented not only the confidence of the Victorian age but its anxieties as well.

3
The Invention of a Hero

Cartier Discovered

In September 1835, a group of citizens of Quebec City met at the Hôpital de la Marine in the Lower Town to commemorate the tercentenary of Cartier's arrival at Stadacona. The centre point of the brief ceremony was the raising of a wooden cross in mimicry of the one that Cartier left behind at his fort during the winter of 1535-36.[1] For many people, this simple ceremony and its ephemeral marker were insufficient: they decided to meet again to discuss raising funds to erect a more permanent indicator of the great explorer's presence. Near the end of the month, a public meeting resolved to construct such a monument, paid for by public subscription, within a year. This memorial was to mark the exact spot where Cartier had discovered "Quebec," a word that, in the 1830s, designated Quebec City rather than the province of Lower Canada. At this moment of his heroic resurrection, Cartier represented the origins of Canada only by extension – his greatest connection was with the local history of Quebec City. The monument was to be, in the words of one local newspaper, "something elegant, but modest at the same time," and placed at the Hôpital de la Marine, one of the commonly accepted sites of Cartier's fort.[2] This hospital had been constructed on the Pointe-aux-Lièvres, formed by an oxbow bend in the St. Charles River in the Lower Town immediately to the east of Quebec City proper. Its location, far from even the emerging working-class suburb of Saint-Roch, revealed its purpose of keeping at bay the series of immigrant-borne epidemics affecting the city. Fifteen leading citizens signed the petition calling for public subscriptions to the monument fund, including Dr. Joseph Morrin, a founding physician of the new hospital; a moderate liberal politician named Hector-Simon Huot; the adamant conservative Michel Clouet, who happened to have been the business partner of Huot's late father; Colonel Joseph Bouchette; Jonathon Sewell; William Burns Lindsay; the mayor; J.C. Fisher; and Georges-Barthélemi Faribault.[3] An executive committee was struck to supervise the project, and Jacques Cartier's next voyage began: his rise to historical heroism.

The leadership for this push came from J.C. Fisher and Georges-Barthélemi Faribault. John Charlton Fisher was a printer, journalist, and publisher who, in 1823, accepted an offer to come to Quebec City to take over publishing the *Québec Gazette*. Lord Dalhousie had lost faith in the *Gazette* as published by John Neilson and looked to Fisher's impeccable conservative credentials to re-establish an official newspaper favourable to his administration. Dalhousie was not alone in benefiting from Fisher's arrival in Quebec City: Fisher was a leading figure in the city's English-speaking cultural milieu during the second quarter of the nineteenth century. This former member of the New York Literary and Historical Society helped establish a similar organization in his new home. Fisher served as treasurer and corresponding secretary of the Literary and Historical Society of Quebec in its first year. He also helped develop the city's libraries and gave popular lectures on British history and antiquity. His notoriety was such that, when Charles Dickens visited Quebec in 1842, Fisher was selected as his host.[4] But, in the matter of raising the Cartier monument, this Anglican erudite took second place to Georges-Barthélemi Faribault, a clerk in the Legislative Assembly.

Faribault was born in Quebec City in 1789, the son of a merchant and grandson of one of Fraser's Highlanders from the Siege of Quebec. He became a lawyer in 1810 and within eighteen months had secured a civil servant's position in the Lower Canadian assembly. By 1815, he was effectively the parliamentary archivist, without ever holding that title, a role he continued to play until his retirement in 1855.[5] In 1830, Faribault initiated a project to gather and catalogue all documents relating to the history of Canada. With government support, his copyists scoured the collections of Europe and America, looking for documents to transcribe and ship back to Quebec City. And Faribault maintained a correspondence with many of the leading antiquarians, historians, and collectors of the day, including Jacques Viger, Pierre Margry, the philanthropist Nicolas-Marie-Alexandre Vattemarre, and the American historian George Bancroft.

In the fall of 1836, Faribault received a number of plans for the monument project, and though none were implemented, they are nevertheless instructive. Tellingly, few included a likeness of the explorer himself. Most took the form of obelisks or columns, common architectural devices for early nineteenth-century monuments.[6] Numerous obelisks adorned the capitals of Europe following Napoleon's theft of an Egyptian trophy in 1802. Indeed, the neoclassicism of the proposals suggests the continuing influence of conservative artistic forms in the New World. Quebec City's Wolfe and Montcalm memorial, raised in 1828, was a simple obelisk inscribed with the names of the two generals, who were mortally wounded during the Battle of the Plains of Abraham. One of the Cartier proposals, attributed to "Philomène Demosthene," took classical tradition to extremes. Demosthene envisioned a ten-foot-high circular pedestal upon which would rest six Corinthian columns supporting an elaborate crown and topped with a globe. This may not have been a serious suggestion, but the globe motif proved popular. At least five of the seventeen proposals featured one. John Ostell, later a celebrated architect, designed a naval column topped with a globe divided into halves representing nature and civilization.

A few brave proposals did venture a depiction of the explorer. Charles Dugal, a rural notary from the south shore of the St. Lawrence, submitted ten plans, each of which was topped by a tiny nondescript figure. Presumably, these represented Cartier. But only a design by George Browne focused on Cartier himself. Browne envisioned a simple square pedestal upon which would sit a statue of a man holding a map, compass, and telescope. His left foot would rest on a globe. With the telescope, the accompanying explanation indicates, the figure would point to the site of Cartier's landing. However, not knowing much about the historical Jacques Cartier, Browne portrayed a man wearing a Roman-style tunic with a robe draped around his shoulders. Early nineteenth-century artists often depicted near contemporary figures anachronistically clad in classical attire. Among the most famous examples was an image of Napoleon as Caesar, which briefly topped the Vendôme Column in Paris. Obviously, the idea was to associate current political leadership with the glory of ancient Rome, and perhaps Browne was making a similar statement about Cartier. However, Faribault responded cynically, commenting that no one knew anything about the sixteenth century.[7] A modern art historian has pushed this criticism further. Browne's Cartier, Jacques Robert notes, has a disproportionately small head, which hides a crucial detail: it has no mark of individuality.[8] No one knew what Cartier looked like! This is not to say that the nineteenth century had no models for his depiction. As early as 1556, Ramusio's edition of Cartier's *Relations* included an illustration of old Hochelaga adorned with a tiny picture of Cartier greeting its inhabitants. Some scholars believe that Cartier is also figured on the Harleian map published by Pierre Desceliers in 1542. However, these rough sketches did not circulate in North America. Few of the contributors to Faribault's contest would have had the opportunity to travel to Europe and examine those illustrations.

Family, Nature, and National Development

Although Faribault's Cartier movement began before Carlyle delivered his famous lectures on heroism, he was clearly awash in the general current of contemporary ideas. And he had models to direct his interests. American republicans had previously seized on the image of Christopher Columbus to symbolize their break with the Old World and to assert the novelty of the

New World. Columbus was portrayed as a new Moses, leading the virtuous away from the corruption and moral decadence of old Europe. In his own day, Columbus was hardly this scourge of the corrupt. He was so inept a governor as to be shipped back to Spain in chains, but Americans tied his memory to the wider struggle of the New World colonists against imperial domination. After the American Revolution, Columbus came to symbolize the superiority of the New World. Indeed, Thomas Schlereth has commented that, as an American symbol, Columbus was as malleable as he was durable. In a sense, Columbus was even able to change gender. To early republicans, he became the mock-classical deity Columbia, an allegorical figure symbolizing liberty and progress, before gradually transforming back to the male hero Columbus as the nineteenth century marched forward and the quartercentenary of his first voyage of discovery approached.[9]

Although no one ever imagined a feminine "Cartia" to symbolize French Canada, there are considerable similarities between the cases of Cartier and Columbus. Across Latin America, Columbus symbolized the distinction between the Old and New Worlds marked by independence. In the United States, supporters of the revolution used Columbus to legitimize their national project and to differentiate the new nation from its motherland. For instance, King's College in New York, founded in 1754 by royal charter, changed its name to Columbia College in 1784 to demonstrate its rejection of England and its monarch. Two years later, South Carolina established Columbia as its capital city, the new capital of the new state symbolizing the glory of America. The Columbus myth thus helped create a long pedigree of American liberty culminating in the revolution and the constitution. It also helped check the kind of popular agitation feared by leaders of the revolution. Terrified of the social disorder that accompanied European political upheavals, men such as Thomas Jefferson and George Washington saw in great men a source of stability and leadership they hoped would reflect on themselves.[10]

Interest in Cartier also accompanied social and political turmoil. The charged political atmosphere of the 1830s herded people into rival camps. Reformers became more extreme under the influence of Papineau as the Parti canadien became the Parti patriote. Although they did not rely on historical heroes, the Patriotes did create politically charged symbols. For instance, Ludger Duvernay founded the Association Saint-Jean-Baptiste, using John the Baptist as a national symbol and linking him directly to the resistance against the colonial administration.[11] However, though Cartier's revival began in this atmosphere, it was not tied directly to the struggles between the majority in the elected assembly and the colonial administration. Students of Lower Canada argue that political opinion swung markedly to the right following the failure of the 1837-38 rebellions. This shift can be seen in many ways. Duvernay's association became part of a church-led temperance movement during the 1840s. Indeed, in 1849, at the height of his influence, the temperance crusader abbé Charles Chiniquy delivered the annual Saint-Jean-Baptiste Day sermon in Montreal. A rightward move can also be seen in parliamentary politics. Differences between the clergy and liberals became open when Papineau returned to political life and events drove the supporters of Louis-Hippolyte LaFontaine into an alliance with the clergy.[12] Two conservatives led the push to honour Cartier, and it was no coincidence that this effort began to succeed after 1840.

Massive social change accompanied the failure of the Patriote vision. In the first decades of the century, Lower Canada slowly turned its economic orientation away from the western interior. The west began to slip from popular imagination as the fur trade declined in economic importance. The Montreal-based fur trade, in trouble following the American Revolution, managed to stave off collapse only due to the 1805 merger of the XY Company and the North West Company. But even this new company struggled and eventually submitted to its chief rival, the Hudson's Bay Company, in 1821. The interior, which had held a fascination and a promise for generations of voyageurs, shifted its orientation. It was transformed from a wilderness to a frontier of settlement by English-speaking immigrants. Between 1815 and 1845, some 400,000 people arrived at Quebec from the British Isles. Meanwhile, declining wealth in the Lower Canadian countryside, as documented by such researchers as Allan Greer and Christian Dessureault, indicated a general decline of the Lower Canadian rural economy. Greer points out that the individual independence represented by farm ownership, once a near universal rural experience, was nearly at an end.[13] French Canadians suffered through a sort of proto-urbanization and proto-industrialization. The number of "urban villages" in Lower Canada (villages populated by the families of artisans and landless labourers) expanded from about twenty-four at the Conquest to over two hundred by 1831.[14] They were hardly towns, but their growth underscores Greer's assertion of a dramatic transformation in the social organization of the countryside. Even large towns were changing. French Canadians rapidly became a minority in the major centres as British and Irish immigration flooded them. The urban hierarchy was also shifting: Montreal's population outnumbered that of Quebec City by 1831 and it became the economic and cultural centre of the province. Lower Canada – indeed, all of British North America – was changing swiftly. With this alteration, old ways of life disappeared.

People reacted to social changes in a number of ways: armed rebellion had failed; an alternative response was to reorganize society. A number of scholars have looked at how Canada, and Canada East in particular, restructured itself in the 1840s. The Special Council, which governed when armed insurrection suspended the constitution, carried out much of this restructuring at breakneck speed. As one scholar has claimed, "the Special Council's work subjected a whole envelope of social relations – the family, childhood, marriage, community, work, and region – to a regime of positive law and an expanding role for the state."[15] However, the council's work is better understood as an acceleration of a modernization process that began during the 1820s and continued in subsequent decades. For instance, the council planned the gradual extinction of seigneurial land tenure in 1840, but the process was continued by the reform democracy that officially abolished it on behalf of railway interests in 1854.

Amid this uncertainty and change, the study of history occupied a more important place. The failure of the rebellions and the insecurity of the 1840s drove many younger people into both a nostalgia for a more distant past and a hope that history would teach them the way to a better future. The political contexts of the post-rebellion era made it possible to imagine New France as a conservative alternative to the model regimes imagined by the secular leadership of the rebellions. Thus, from the 1840s to the end of the 1860s, a growing body of literature chose the "national past" as its privileged theme. This was also a time when French Canadians found themselves outnumbered by anglophones in Montreal and Quebec City. The "national past" pointed to the agricultural settlement of New France as the rural foundation of French Canada. This theme was evident in more than the histories of François-Xavier Garneau and abbé Etienne-Michel Faillon. Authors such as Joseph Doutre, Georges Boucher de Boucherville, and Philippe Aubert de Gaspé made French Canadian history important aspects of their works. The Canadian visits of the performer and philanthropist Nicolas-Marie-Alexandre Vattemarre in the 1840s helped popularize the notion of a national institute. Vattemarre urged Montrealers to merge their literary and educational associations into one institution that would provide a lending library, a museum, and opportunities for intellectual discussions under one roof. He urged the citizens of Quebec City to take the same step. The liberal – or eventually Parti rouge – youth formed the Institut-Canadien in 1844 as a debating society and lending library to encourage discussion of social and political issues, modelled on Vattemarre's suggestion.[16] Many of the institute's members focused their energies on historical pursuits, which they made public in 1854, with the opening of a museum in Montreal. As one student of the Institut-Canadien has observed, the museum chose to emphasize nationalist themes in its exhibits.[17] But Vattemarre's dream of a unified association never came to pass. The Institut-Canadien, like many other organizations, simply built on precedents extending back to the 1820s. Three years after the 1824 foundation of the Literary and Historical Society of Quebec, Montreal established a natural history society, which opened its own museum in 1828. That same year, following a trend in Britain and Europe, Montrealers founded a mechanics' institute. It was intended "to instruct the members in the principles of the arts and in the various branches of science and useful knowledge."[18] In other words, its aim was to help tradesmen be more economically useful. Although ostensibly non-sectarian, the institute's membership was, not surprisingly, drawn from the city's anglophone Protestant community. Mechanics' institutes originated in Britain and were carried to North America by British immigrants. Montreal's was organized by the Reverend Henry Esson, minister of St. Gabriel's Presbyterian Church. No doubt this inspiration kept the city's Catholics away. However, Catholics also created civic associations such as the St. Patrick's Society and the Société Saint-Jean-Baptiste. Many of these lapsed due to political uncertainty in the tail half of the 1830s, but the habit of establishing them accelerated once political stability returned in the 1840s. Although no single institution could speak for all, they proliferated, particularly among French Canadians. The Société des Amis and the Oeuvre des bons livres de Montréal both organized themselves in 1844. Each aimed at promoting a literary culture.

The acceleration in this associative movement was also driven by a demographic shift in the province. During the period of British rule, the population of Lower Canada doubled roughly every twenty-five years. Thus, although the province's birth rate slowly declined from a peak in the 1760s and 1770s, the continuous population growth of the nineteenth century meant that, in absolute terms, increasing numbers of babies were born every year.[19] The 1851 census reveals that the number of men aged twenty to thirty had jumped from about forty-five thousand to nearly seventy thousand in a decade, accentuating a long-felt need for educational improvements. Even the educated youth demanded supplements to the college and apprenticeship system that had served them since the Conquest. Population growth in previous decades forced dramatic expansion in the number of schools, a figure that nearly tripled during the 1840s. The numbers of children enrolled in school also soared from less than five thousand at the start of the decade to seventy-five thousand by the end. Institutions of higher learning kept pace. New colleges opened across the province after 1840: eighteen existed in 1875 where there had been only eight at the time of the rebellions. Educational concerns had been caught up in the political struggles of the 1830s and continued to be embroiled in ideological conflict for decades to come. However, the failure of the rebellions and the political demise of Papineau greatly weakened any calls for secular state-run schools. A real breakthrough in higher education occurred in 1852, with the founding of Laval University under the control of the Catholic Church. From that date, all classical colleges were required to affiliate with Laval. Five years later, the first three teacher-training colleges in Canada East, the Laval and McGill Normal Schools, and the École normale Jacques-Cartier, opened their doors. The first two were ostensibly named for their affiliated universities (themselves named after the seventeenth-century Bishop François de Laval and James McGill, the Scottish immigrant whose bequest helped found McGill). Montrealers, lacking a francophone university of their own, and with the local clergy divided between the bishop and the Sulpician order, chose the national figure of Cartier for the Catholic normal school in their city. Although only a minority of teachers took professional training at such institutions, their presence helped raise the standards of education in French Canada.[20]

Enhancements in the educational infrastructure both improved the quality of graduates and widened their number. A middle-class reading public emerged, joined the associative movement, and became immersed in the culture of print-capitalism. Literacy rates in Lower Canada were persistently low for much of the nineteenth century, especially among francophones. One scholar has estimated that, at the time of the rebellions, only 26 percent of Lower Canada's population could read and write. This figure masked more striking inequities. Rural and French-speaking people demonstrated the lowest levels of literacy. Whereas the urban literacy rate neared 60 percent, the countryside reached only 22 percent. Within this large rural cohort, anglophone literacy matched the high standard of the towns, but a mere 12 percent of rural francophones could read and write. Lord Durham was particularly concerned about the lack of education in rural Lower Canada, especially as the more rebellious Montreal region was chronically less literate than the more peaceable eastern portions of the province.[21] Nonetheless, literacy improved over time. The two decades between the rebellions and the 1861 census saw a remarkable rise in Quebec literacy rates. By 1861, urban literacy was at 82 percent, but the improvement among rural Quebecers was even more pronounced. The 1861 census claimed that 62 percent of them were literate. Admittedly, these figures are difficult to compare. The measure of literacy was not always consistent, and occasionally those who could read but not write were considered literate. Other measures might include those who could write but not read, whereas sometimes "literacy" required the ability to do both. Moreover, literacy itself is a much more complex phenomenon than such simple measures can capture.[22] Nevertheless, the sharp rise in rural literacy rates where francophones were in a clear majority suggests a significant improvement in francophone literacy between 1840 and 1860. Thus, the combined efforts of educators and bourgeois debating-society members conspired to create a reading public in French Canada for the second half of the nineteenth century.

Benedict Anderson has emphasized the importance of the printed word in the building of national sentiment, an insight Walter Bagehot had earlier attributed to Charles Dickens.[23] According to Anderson, reading is central in forging a national consciousness. The written word has the power to reach a far greater number of people, presuming a general degree of literacy, than does the spoken word. Spoken words hang in the ether between speaker and listener; they are ephemeral. Written words, however, pass from writer to reader, to reader, and to reader. Simply put, in an era that predates audio recording, written words lasted longer than their spoken equivalent. They also diffused more widely. Thus, the nineteenth-century written word was both spatially and temporally more significant than its spoken counterpart. The dissemination of the written word had a twofold effect on the development of nationalism. On the one hand, it contributed to the standardization of vernacular languages and thus helped break down local distinctions in vocabulary, grammar, and dialect. In Quebec, this was not crucial as even eighteenth-century travellers frequently commented on the consistency of the French language throughout the St. Lawrence valley. Perhaps more importantly, the written word made it possible for one person to be aware of events happening far away and to communicate with, for instance, other French speakers around the nation. The printed word helped to forge a sense of community. At the most basic level, people read in their own language and thus associate primarily with those who do likewise. At a deeper level, the sudden surge in print-capitalism helped create the intellectual environment in which it was possible to read "in one's own language." For French Canadians, this process accompanied the associative movement. In 1844, for example, seventeen new newspapers began publishing in the province. Many of these were short-lived, and few had circulations of more than a thousand copies. Nonetheless, the middle decades of the century witnessed significant advances in domestic print-capitalism. Important newspapers, such as *L'Aurore des Canadas* (Montreal, 1839), *Le Journal de Québec* (Quebec City, 1842), *L'Avenir* (Montreal, 1847), *Le Pays* (Montreal, 1852), and *Le Courrier de Saint-Hyacinthe* (1853), saw the light of day in these years. Among the most successful, the weekly illustrated paper *L'Opinion publique* (Montreal) launched in 1870 with a circulation of over five thousand. By the mid-1870s, it was selling twelve thousand copies a week.[24] Quite clearly, a reading public had emerged in francophone Canada by the 1870s. This public spearheaded interest in historical heroes.

Similar patterns were unfolding among English-speaking Canadians. Literacy rates were on the rise throughout the nineteenth century, although not as spectacularly as among francophones. And anglophones were also forming debating associations, opening libraries and museums, and printing newspapers. However, the intellectual climate of English-speaking Canada did not lend itself to the support of French regime national heroes. Anglophone interest in Canadian historical heroes really only developed during the last decades of the nineteenth century.[25] This may have been due to some smouldering anti-French sentiment but more probably to the general weakness of anglophone literature and science in the first half of the nineteenth century. In this climate, English-language intellectual activity focused on concerns other than Canadian history. Among the most prevalent concerns was natural history, a peculiar Victorian intellectual discipline mixing science and faddishness. It is best understood as both a popular diversion and a branch of scientific inquiry joining geology, botany, and zoology. Although it became fashionable in Great Britain during the 1820s and grew in popularity with each subsequent decade, its roots go back to the seventeenth century. Some of the nineteenth century's greatest minds, including Charles Darwin and Thomas Huxley, pursued natural history, but it was primarily the pastime of leisured amateurs. Armies of Victorians roamed the British seaside, stooping here and there to inspect and gather diverse specimens, which they added to their personal collections or sent to similarly occupied friends. Indeed, by midcentury, the sight of men and women ankle deep on the tidal flats, bent at the waist and rummaging through the muck, was common enough to be lampooned in such satirical publications as *Punch*. One historian has commented that the popularity of natural history was directly related to the boredom of Britain's new leisure classes. As British national wealth grew by leaps and bounds in the nineteenth century, increasing numbers of people suddenly found themselves with too much time on their hands. Admittedly, only a few Victorians shared the enjoyment of this new wealth, and although natural history was, by Victorian standards, remarkably democratic in its appeal, by modern standards, it was disproportionately the preserve of the landed gentry.[26]

However, interest in natural history was not solely the product of leisured boredom. It was also connected to the culture of acquisitiveness – the collector's impulse – and associated with the rise of industrial capitalism. Capitalism made a virtue of amassing wealth; it is no surprise that Victorians turned to amassing collections in their leisure time as well. Collecting was a peculiar Victorian passion indulged in by more than naturalists alone. People collected coins, stones, butterflies, and eventually even postage stamps. Victorian fairs and expositions were exhaustive displays of collections of natural specimens and man-made artifacts, suggesting an underlying belief that, if an example of every specimen could be possessed and displayed, the Victorian mind could grasp the entirety of the universe. No naturalist would have cited anything so mundane as boredom, or anything so crass as acquisitiveness, as the source of his fervour. In *The Naturalist in Britain*, his classic study of natural history, David Allen rejects the argument that the interest in natural history was driven by economic motivations. Instead, Allen posits that it was more a product of the Enlightenment, especially its emphasis on pursuits of practical importance. Writing explicitly about geology, Allen suggests that collecting was also a means of establishing a gendered class status for wealthy practitioners. It made a man appear rational, learned, progressive, and almost noble.[27]

Frequently, naturalists found further justification for their activities in William Paley's *Natural Theology*, published in 1802. Following a scientific tradition from the seventeenth century, Paley argued that nature revealed the majesty of the work of God. Under Paley's logic, to examine a plant or animal is to discover that it possesses exactly those structures and abilities that allow it to survive and reproduce. Moreover, these qualities are so elaborate, and so clearly "designed" for the survival of the species, that they point to a conscious design. Thus, the study of nature confirmed the existence of God and suggested that God the Creator had structured the universe in just such a way as to make it function properly. Natural theology became a useful defence for the study of natural history, and naturalists took it up with vigour.

Natural history accompanied its practitioners as they moved from Britain to Canada in the nineteenth century. Canadian contributions to natural history include, most prominently, Catherine Parr Trail's *The Backwoods of Canada* and P.H. Gosse's *The Canadian Naturalist*.[28] Canada, a country of vast wilderness, offered boundless opportunities for the study of nature. Not all Victorian English-speaking Canadians were naturalists or devotees of natural theology, but these notions remained just below the surface of Canadian intellectual life. Expansionist interest in the northwest, for instance, drew on evidence offered by natural history that the prairie west was not uninhabitable as had long been imagined. "Scientific" rhetoric found its way into everyday public discourse. Even the Confederation debates echoed with the language of lay science.[29] However, this anglophone attention to the findings of natural history directed English-speaking Canadians to an understanding of their country that emphasized its close connection to the world's "natural state." In other words, their vision of Canada did not turn to human history: Canada was too young for a human past. It was too closely linked to nature's expanse to be seen as a place with a human history.[30] This attitude changed only at the dawn of the twentieth century. Toward the end of the 1870s, some Canadians associated natural history and human history, but the study of history did not become a field for English-speaking Canadians until the 1890s.[31]

While anglophones in Canada focused on the natural world, their French-speaking compatriots developed an interest in national, rather than natural, history. Some French Canadians also practised natural history. The abbés Léon Provancher and Louis-Ovide Brunet published their own scientific findings and encouraged the study of entomology, botany, and horticulture. Yet, natural theology, with its notion of direct individual communion with God through nature, more closely reflected Protestant sensibilities than Catholic ones, and Canada's natural history societies were primarily English-speaking groups. On the other hand, French occupation of the St. Lawrence valley dated from 1608, when Champlain established his habitation beneath Cap Diamant. As Colin Coates informs us, by the mid-nineteenth century as many as seven generations of St. Lawrence valley inhabitants had transformed its natural landscape into one reminiscent of the Old World. In the

1860s, the American author Henry David Thoreau, greatly taken by the settled area between Montreal and Quebec City, remarked that it reminded him of medieval France and that it "appeared as old as Normandy itself."[32] Of course, Coates also cautions us that Thoreau was wrong: the St. Lawrence was not an ancient landscape. However, it was cast as such in the Romantic imaginings of post-Conquest English colonists who sought to establish themselves as a semi-feudal seigneurial gentry. The apparent antiquity of the region inspired such late Romanticists as Thoreau to imagine a long history untouched by nineteenth-century progress and modernization. For Victorians interested in progress, most famously Lord Durham, this situation was deplorable. For those interested in the romance of the past, it became a rallying point. Durham's infamous slight, that French Canadians were a people without history, motivated François-Xavier Garneau to complete his monumental *Histoire du Canada*. Following Garneau, the intellectual current of French Canada focused on the debate regarding the human past. Francophone intellectuals turned more directly to the humanities and the arts, producing a national literature rather than a national science.

Much of this interest was directed toward the study of ancestors, a form of antiquarian inquiry not unique to nineteenth-century French Canadians but of particular interest to them. Genealogy, the study of one's ancestors, helped put a human face on history. Some genealogical passages appear in the historical writings of Garneau, Faillon, and J.-B.-A. Ferland, but the earliest published works devoted to family biographies date from the 1860s. The first significant study appeared in 1867: François Daniel's *Histoire des grandes familles françaises du Canada, ou aperçu sur le Chevalier Benoist et quelques familles contemporaines*. The abbé Daniel, an avid promoter of genealogy, was a French-born Sulpician priest but seems also to have taken an interest in printing. He had been a business partner of Chrysologue Sénécal, the brother of Eusèbe Sénécal, who published the *Histoire des grandes familles*. After the Daniel-Sénécal partnership collapsed in 1859, Daniel relied more on writing about the past and the nation to pay his bills. During the 1860s, his historical writings appeared in a number of publications, such as the *Revue canadienne*. He seems to have translated Julia Smalley's 1861 *The Young Converts*, which focused on three sisters who converted from Protestantism in midcentury. His *Histoire des grandes familles*, described by some as a parlour book, or "luxury volume," of interest only to those wealthy bourgeois whose ancestors might appear in its pages, makes a clear link between family history and national history.[33] Part historical sketch and part genealogical survey of some eighteen Canadian families, it opens with a brief history of Canada, which is divided into nine "epochs" from Cartier's first arrival to Confederation. The division is reminiscent of the marquis de Condorcet's ten epochs of the development of the human mind. Daniel's ninth and last epoch corresponds with Condorcet's ninth, the present. Daniel's unnamed but implied tenth epoch is like Condorcet's tenth – it represents the hopeful future, foreshadowed by Confederation via which "Canada escaped assimilation."[34]

After this brief overview of national history, Daniel delved into the family history of the Chevalier Benoist, a French military officer who served in North America from 1735 to 1759. Dotted through the text are illustrations of celebrated figures from Canada's past, such as Cartier, Champlain, Laval, Montcalm, Duvernay, and Papineau, interspersed with portraits of the lesser-known ancestors of the "grandes familles" covered in the book. To add further authenticity to his subjects, Daniel included the signatures of some forty great men of the past. These additions attest to the original research of the author, a point Daniel himself made explicit in his defence of archival research.[35] But the signatures also add to the emotive feeling promoted by the book. They serve as traces of the passing in this world of these illustrious people. Although only facsimiles, they offer souvenirs of the lives of great men. But perhaps more importantly, to a literate world the signature is a mark of authenticity. Similarly, Daniel's tracing of the generations of the Benoist family, or of the de Montigny family, into the then present forges a link between the distant past and the here and now.

Of course, one should not overestimate the influence of abbé Daniel on the intellectual development of nineteenth-century French Canada. Daniel was a minor figure.[36] But his association with Sénécal helped to popularize genealogy. Eusèbe Sénécal's publishing house dominated the early production of genealogical studies in Quebec, though this zeal may have contributed to the eventual collapse of the firm. One scholar has speculated that Sénécal was nearly ruined by the enormous costs of publishing Cyprien Tanguay's seven-volume *Dictionnaire généalogique des familles canadiennes depuis la fondation de la colonie jusqu'à nos jours*.[37] Still, with the publication of abbé Tanguay's first volume in 1871, genealogical studies in Quebec had arrived. Born in 1819, Tanguay had been ordained a priest in 1843, just as his compatriots began to pay some attention to Canada's history. He had been interested in genealogy since his childhood, and the project of a complete genealogy of the French Canadian people was closely related to the work of his friend Joseph-Charles Taché. Formerly the editor of the clerical newspaper *Le Courrier du Canada*, Taché had become deputy minister of agriculture in 1864 and had embarked upon a project to restructure the government census along "scientific" lines. Tanguay's own brand of statistics figured in the project. For Taché, making a genealogy was as central to forging a nationality as was his own census, and he defended dispensing government funds to his friend.[38]

Genealogy was part of a search to define the nation, a search given urgency in the mid-nineteenth century. In the thinking of nineteenth-century Catholic nationalists, the family, not the individual, was the foundation of the nation, and, rhetorically, the nation was an extension of the family. This, the first social unit, found its place at the centre of national life fortified by the rhetoric of nationalism. In uncertain times, such as the latter nineteenth century with its social transformations, people often look for symbols of continuity and stability. A genealogy that demonstrated the prestige of a family lineage might help assuage fears about the decline of the family fortune. It might also ease the anxieties of a bourgeoisie facing a structural crisis in the transition to monopoly capitalism. It helped to establish descent from "original" settlers and to cement a family's social status. But, most crucially for nationalists, a genealogy that demonstrated an unbroken chain of national survival, especially after the Conquest, helped relieve concerns over waves of French-Canadian emigration to the United States. It could serve as a call to arms to defend what the forefathers had built. Tanguay at least knew how to judge his contribution to cultural life in French Canada. He argued in his introduction to Volume 1 that his work might seem a little strange but that his purpose was national. On the one hand, as a curé charged with enforcing the laws of the church, he was astonished by the way in which the poor understanding of family ties complicated potential marriage unions. Some of the young betrothed had no knowledge of the closeness of their family ties until actually standing at the altar. Genealogy could help prevent potentially embarrassing situations. On the other hand, Tanguay noted an enormous growth in tastes for literature and history in Quebec. In this, he considered his own work to be "eminently national." It was national precisely because it fit together generations of ancestors with the history of the nation. Tanguay remarked that "the dates, the names, the genealogies are the elements of history."[39]

Cartier Emerges

These ideas had also gained the support of earlier bourgeois gentlemen such as Faribault (see Figure 1). Following the unveiling of that first temporary Jacques Cartier monument in 1835, he continued to investigate Canada's history. In 1837, he published a bibliography of Canadian historical writings. And in 1843, supported by the Literary and Historical Society of Quebec, he released the first new edition of Jacques Cartier's *Relations* since 1598. From Pierre Margry, we know that Faribault himself translated the account from the 250-year-old *Principal Navigations* of Richard Hakluyt.[40] As clerk of the Legislative Assembly, and prompted by a legislative committee chaired by Robert Christie, he also directed the collection of documents for the archives of the United Province of Canada through the 1840s and 1850s. After the destruction of the parliamentary library in the Rebellion Losses riot of 25 April 1849, Faribault travelled to Europe to reassemble a collection based on French and British originals. Accompanied by his wife, he sailed for New York in October 1851, reached London later that month, and was in Paris

Figure 1   Portrait of Georges-Barthélemi Faribault, by his son-in-law Théophile Hamel. *Library and Archives Canada, R11549-0-5-E, copy negative C-151490*

by November. The trip cost him his wife, who succumbed to a long illness in March 1852. Faribault's own health similarly deteriorated, but he recovered sufficiently to complete his mission.[41] Through the intermediary of Margry, he assured the completion of a three-year project to transcribe French records related to the history of New France. His works were continued by the likes of historians Félix Martin, Maximillien Bibaud, Hospice Verreau, and Charles-Honoré Laverdière.

Upon his return to Canada, Canadian political leaders conferred upon Faribault a £250 pension in gratitude for a mission so fruitful for the country but painful for its leader. Perhaps, however, the more fitting tribute came from the poet L.J.C. Fiset, who delicately addressed Faribault's personal suffering in a poem comparing him to his hero Jacques Cartier:

Lorsqu'à travers la plaine humide
Cartier, l'intrépide marin,
N'ayant que son grand coeur pour guide,
Vers nos bords s'ouvrit un chemin;
Songeait-il, au fond de son âme,
Aux faveurs exemptes de blâme
Qui se lieraient à ses traveaux;
Ou bien, pesait-il seul dans l'ombre
L'or et les richesses sans nombre
Dont il chargerait ses vaisseaux?

Oh! non, la gloire plus réelle
Enflamme l'esprit du héros:
Fils de la France, c'est pour elle
Qu'il brave les vents et les flots;
Non, le seul rêve de sa vie
Se résume en ce mot, patrie!

Whereas Cartier had braved the winds and seas for his *patrie*, Faribault had braved the death of his wife for his own patrie:

Fidèle à sa tâche sublime,
Nouveau Cartier, bravant la mort,
Il part décoré de l'estime
Qui couronne son noble effort.

Ce n'est pas que de nouveaux mondes
Découverts au loin sur les ondes,
Il veuille sonder les secrets;
Mais il apportera de France,
Pour nous tous, les arts, la science,
Pour lui, hélas! Deuil et regrets.[42]

Although he retired from the civil service in 1855, Faribault continued to promote the veneration of the great figures from Canada's French past. He was a principal advocate of a monument to Montcalm, unveiled at Quebec City on the centennial of the Battle of the Plains of Abraham. However, Faribault's greatest contribution to the celebration of his first hero, Jacques Cartier, was a supporting role in a pair of earlier discoveries.

Although Faribault led the drive to learn more about Cartier, his personal passion alone could never have sparked the Cartiermania that developed in mid-nineteenth-century Quebec. His efforts were decisive, but interest in the great explorer was widening. Even before Faribault and Fisher had organized the first commemoration of Cartier's presence – their cross of 1835 – the curator Pierre Chasseur advertised that his collection contained a bronze cannon formerly belonging to the famous Malouin explorer.[43] Chasseur's museum, among the first in Canada, was devoted predominantly to natural history. It opened in 1824 alongside the first stirring of scientific inquiry and the associative movement that characterized the emerging bourgeoisie of that decade. Although in financial straits by 1832, Chasseur made important contributions during the 1820s to the development of Canadian science.[44] The bronze cannon had been discovered in a sandbank in the Trois-Rivières area; Chasseur advertised it as having been uncovered at the mouth of the Jacques Cartier River. According to Charlevoix, Cartier had indeed lost a cannon at that spot during his 1535 voyage. However, Charlevoix's account displays considerable confusion as to exactly what happened when and where. Charlevoix believed that Cartier's Ste-Croix, where he spent the winter of 1535-36, was not the currently accepted St. Charles River at Quebec City. Instead, he placed Ste-Croix further up the St. Lawrence, at a spot some forty-five kilometres west of Quebec City, at the mouth of the Jacques Cartier River. He went so far as to chastise Champlain for misreading Cartier's *Relations*.[45] Rising north of Quebec City, the Jacques Cartier River flows southwest to drain into the St. Lawrence at the present-day town of Donnacona (coincidently across the St. Lawrence from a town called Ste-Croix) about midway between Quebec City and Trois-Rivières. Thus, in the 1830s, there were two competing traditions regarding the location of Cartier's 1535-36 fort, reflecting the limitations of historical scholarship during the period. However, as further documentary evidence concerning Cartier's time in Canada became available in subsequent decades, a more standardized common sense "truth" about the events of his life and exploits became established.

Although the discovery of Chasseur's cannon predates Faribault's interest in Jacques Cartier, efforts to locate Cartier's fort represent the first sign of the expansion of that interest. In 1842, Michel Boivin, a local hunter, found the remnants of an old ship along the north bank of the St. Charles River, a small tributary of the St. Lawrence beneath the heights of Cap Diamant. Not knowing what vessel this might be, Boivin asked the Quebec City engineer if he knew of any recently sunken ships at the mouth of the St. Michel Stream, which emptied into the St. Charles near where he spotted the wreck. The engineer, Joseph Hamel, admitted that he knew of no record of a sunken ship in that river, unless it were Cartier's *Petite Hermine*. Hamel verified his theory by referring to Faribault's recently published account of Cartier's voyage, which confirmed that Cartier had indeed left one of his ships behind in 1536. In May 1843, when Faribault sent a copy of his translation to Saint-Malo as a gift to its mayor, Louis-François Hovius, he mentioned that he would have liked to send some artifacts from the *Petite Hermine*, recently discovered, for authentification.[46]

However, in the summer of 1843, Hamel and Boivin found it difficult to relocate the remains of the presumed *Petite Hermine*. Some time had elapsed since Boivin last visited the spot, and he was unable to find the ship again. Hamel asked other local hunters for help. One, a printer named Décarreaux, offered his assistance, but finding a convenient time proved difficult, and it was not until 10 August 1843 that Décarreaux, Hamel, Faribault, and the historian François-Xavier Garneau set out in search of their quarry. A week later, another hunter, a merchant from the Faubourg Saint-Jean, directed Hamel to the remains of an old submerged vessel in the mouth of the tiny St. Michel stream at about the point of the first Dorchester Bridge. William Shephard, the president of the local Literary and Historical Society, and Faribault returned on 19 August to confirm the discovery.[47] Almost immediately, the name *Petite Hermine* was on everyone's lips. The vessel was a relic, a sacred relic, of the founding moment of Quebec's history.[48]

Faribault and Joseph Hamel arranged for M. Lamare-Picquot, a friend of the Saint-Malo mayor, to transport some sections of wood, nails, and other iron pieces retrieved from the wreck to Brittany for verification. These relics, carrying a powerful allusion to the cross of Christ, were nevertheless treated "scientifically" as antiquarian artifacts. Once they arrived, a committee was struck to determine their provenance. By 13 December 1843, after its only meeting, this committee concluded that the objects were indeed surviving portions of Cartier's *Petite Hermine*. Although little evidence connected the wreck to any specific ship, the committee was certain that "these fragments ... will become precious documents for the history of our town [Saint-Malo]; in effect, sirs, they recall the greatest phases in the life of our dear compatriot, phases which glorify his hometown, Saint-Malo."[49] Indeed, the Saint-Malo government built a monument out of the scraps of wood and iron for display in a museum at the city hall.

As spring came to the St. Lawrence valley, the mails carried a return letter from Mayor Hovius to Faribault, thanking him for his manuscript and the relics of the *Petite Hermine*. More importantly, Hovius mentioned that a portrait of the explorer hung in a gallery at the Saint-Malo City Hall.[50] This was astonishing news! No one yet knew what Cartier looked like, as the various abortive proposals for Faribault's monument had demonstrated. But suddenly, across the Atlantic, there was an authentic portrait of the great man. Actually, it was only a four-year-old painting by an artist named François Riis. He claimed to have produced it from memory, based on an original sketch at the Bibliothèque impériale in Paris. However, no one has ever found the sketch; as early as 1857, a scant eighteen years after Riis made his "copy," researchers at the Bibliothèque impériale were unable to locate it. Francis Parkman also looked for it. Edouard Charton, though he published a sketch of the Riis painting in his *Voyageurs anciens et modernes,* likewise searched for the original but eventually came to doubt its existence.[51] That something could disappear so completely in so brief a time casts considerable doubt on the authenticity of the Riis copy and thus, by extension, on the accepted likeness of Jacques Cartier. Still, the portrait was presumed to be a true likeness by those, such as Faribault, who hungered to put a face on their hero.

The problem was getting that face to Canada. This was accomplished when a copy of the Riis copy was offered to the Literary and Historical Society of Quebec. The popularity of the painting prompted the Legislative Assembly to commission more copies, a task assigned to a promising young artist named Théophile Hamel, a cousin of Joseph Hamel and soon to be Faribault's son-in-law. Born in 1817 in Sainte-Foy, Hamel studied painting under Antoine Plamondon before opening his own studio in 1840 on rue Buade in Quebec City. One of Canada's first great artists and a gifted portraitist, he served as a quasi-official portraitist for the Canadian government during much of his career. In 1853, the Legislative Assembly commissioned him to paint the portraits of every Speaker of the House of both Upper and Lower Canada since 1792. But in the spring of 1843, he found himself in Europe, studying his craft in Italy. He travelled Italy and France, and may have seen Riis' *Cartier* in 1846, while working as a copyist at the Louvre.[52] Mayor Hovius of Saint-Malo had sent the Riis *Cartier* to Paris where it was copied by Louis-Félix Amiel. Amiel's copy was lent to Quebec City in March 1847, arriving in April of that year, where Hamel's work was commissioned.[53] Thus, by a rather convoluted route, Faribault had managed to secure a copy of a copy of a copy of an allegedly authentic portrait of Jacques Cartier.

Establishing a true portrait was crucial to the development of the cult of the hero. Few fully developed historical heroes do not have a widely accepted physical image, often captured in an official portrait. The face, the dress, and the body language in such images helps to solidify the acceptance of the hero and people's ability to read into him (or her) certain attributes and values they wish to venerate. Whether the portrait is an exact reproduction of the physical traits of the hero is less important than its ability to inspire an emotional connection between the subject and its audience. Adapting Benedict Anderson's phrase, we can call this connection an "imagined community." The difficulty for the historian is to interpret this emotional evidence, which cannot be viewed directly. A similar problem hangs over the question of the past's authenticity, which cannot be verified as easily as that of a work of art. The latter task, though not always easy to accomplish, is simply to discern the work of the correct hand. The former case is more troublesome. Few historians ever consider what it means to be historically authentic. It is far easier to "debunk" national myths than to point to a single incidence of authenticity. Historians are vulnerable to such accusations precisely because of the nature of historical research. Many modern professional historians doubt the existence of a single version of historical truth, preferring instead to sift through multiple possibilities to derive the best approximation of what actually happened. But such an understanding of the past is of no use to those who would look to their history to establish the grounding of their own national values. This is the purpose of the veneration of historical heroes like Jacques Cartier. For historians who would study such subjects, the struggle is to gauge the experienced connection between the hero and the audience. Obviously, we cannot know the thoughts of people twenty, fifty, or a hundred years ago. Nor can we know how the individual members of a past society understood the history of their country, or even how they appreciated particular historical heroes. Historians must instead look at the indirect evidence of their thoughts. A few people did record these in detail, and their writings offer a glance at the collective imagination of their society. But more crucially, indirect evidence can be found in the repetitions of key symbols and phrases, or in the attendance figures at public ceremonies. We find this snapshot not in the details of erudite discussion but in the general lines of agreement on broadly defined topics. By looking for the general, though shifting, consensus on such questions as why Cartier was important, we can glimpse popular reception of ideas about him. Paying attention to the widely repeated elements of the Cartier story, and to the broadly accepted meaning of his accomplishments, we capture an element of unspoken popular perceptions.

Hamel made two oil-on-canvas copies of the Cartier painting and a number of line drawings, which were sent to New York to be lithographed.[54] The next year, his lithographs were ready for wide distribution. Suddenly, Faribault's personal obsession became widespread. *La Minerve* urged everyone to buy a copy of the portrait, both to support the talented young artist and because owning such an image was patriotic.[55] Cartiermania was born. Jacques Cartier became ubiquitous. In 1847, the City of Montreal voted to rename its old market square (then known as the New Market) as Place Jacques-Cartier, and Quebec City opened its own Marché Jacques-Cartier the following year. Within a decade, Hamel's and Faribault's Cartier, a figure primarily of local history, became French Canada's Cartier, a national hero.

It is difficult to overestimate the importance of the Hamel portrait in popularizing Jacques Cartier (see Figure 2). Volumes of sales of the lithographs alone did not spread interest in the hero. The artist's skill made Cartier's face aesthetically pleasing. Hamel faithfully reproduced the Riis Cartier, paying particular attention to the details of dress and facial features. But his great talent was his ability to render his subjects with both technical accuracy and emotional depth. His Cartier is an inspired man, one of cunning intelligence,

Figure 2   Portrait of Jacques Cartier, by Théophile Hamel, 1844. *Library and Archives Canada, acc. no. 1997-218-1*

a perfect leader whom sailors *would* willingly have followed into the unknown. Hamel's heroic portrait solidified popular appreciation of Jacques Cartier. As the sensationalist newspapers of the end of the century were to discover, pictures work far better than text at arousing popular enthusiasms. Certainly, other traditions exist for Cartier's likeness, but Hamel's appeared at the right moment, had the greatest common sense claims to authenticity, and was the most widely known.[56] His affordable lithographs and artistic skill must therefore be placed in the first order of importance in popularizing Faribault's particular fascination with Jacques Cartier. Indeed, as other copies quickly followed Hamel's success, the endurance of the model created in 1839 persisted. The Riis portrait was destroyed by Allied bombing during 1944, and the copy sent to Quebec City burned with the Parliament buildings in 1854, a fire that also destroyed the remains of the *Petite Hermine* and some seven thousand of the twenty thousand volumes Faribault had collected in Europe. Thus, the question of the authenticity of Hamel's work will probably remain unresolved.

4
Cartiermania

By the eve of Confederation, Jacques Cartier appeared nearly everywhere in the province of Quebec. The efforts of Faribault and Hamel had popularized the Malouin explorer's reputation as the discoverer of Canada. Less than a decade after Confederation, much of Cartier's image had become a sort of common sense knowledge to French Canadians: they knew what Cartier represented, what he had accomplished, and they placed him at the head of a list of national historical heroes. In other words, Cartiermania, a sudden and massive outpouring of representations of Jacques Cartier, carried with it certain ideological assumptions hidden in the historical "facts" surrounding the great figure. Extracted from history by men who had come of age before the rebellions, Cartier was transformed into a national hero by subsequent generations.

Transatlantic Appeal

Among the first indicators of Cartier's rising star was a small bust made by Théophile Hamel's student Napoléon Bourassa. Another in a direct line of gifted French Canadian artists, he was born at L'Acadie in 1827. Although originally planning to study law after his education at the St.-Sulpice seminary in Montreal, he turned to painting instead, apprenticing under Hamel for two years in Montreal and Toronto. In 1852, he travelled to Europe to pursue his studies and was in Italy while Faribault was busy collecting documents and caring for his dying wife in Paris. Returning to Canada in 1855, he opened a studio on rue Bonsecours in Montreal, married one of Louis-Joseph Papineau's daughters, and took up sculpture. Bourassa was little known in Montreal as a sculptor until he produced his first notable work – a bust of that "great and noble figure," Jacques Cartier, which he exhibited at the Provincial Exposition in October 1858. Standing modestly amid the displays of industrial equipment and agricultural implements, Bourassa's Cartier was based on Hamel's portrait, itself "known to everyone."[1] Much like his master, Bourassa had executed a fitting portrait of a national hero:

In the Jacques Cartier of Mr. Bourassa, there is the mark of real inspiration; this face so forcefully chiselled, these features are no doubt those of the hardy pilot from Saint-Malo, and in his piercing eye there is certainly the stare of a discoverer. We are, as a French Canadian, greatly satisfied with this work; it is no longer a generic figure, more or less cut from the raw material. It is an artist's creation, an idea and not merely an object.[2]

One might wonder if this veneration of Cartier was confined to a relatively small circle. Although Bourassa's work was exhibited in Montreal, he had a personal connection to the first generation of Quebec City's Cartier enthusiasts. Another sculptor, François-Xavier Berlinguet, had also produced a Cartier sculpture for Quebec City's Marché Jacques-Cartier. However, his wooden effort was rejected by the city council, probably because it was seen as self-serving.[3] Thus, Berlinguet used it as a sort of advertisement for his own studio, erecting it above his door on rue de la Fabrique in Quebec City's Old Town. For many years, Berlinguet's wooden work sat above his studio door, although he himself gave up sculpting.[4] But more evidence suggests that interest in Cartier had spread beyond Quebec City and Faribault's circle of friends. In 1857, the Government of the United Province of Canada issued a postage stamp bearing the image of Hamel's Cartier, and the 1850s saw the coupling of Cartier with the idea of a French Canadian nation.

In Montreal, Cartier made his first significant appearance at the annual Saint-Jean-Baptiste Day parade. The idea of a parade to celebrate the accepted patron saint of French Canadians originated in the temperance movement, reviving what had previously been a Patriote holiday, as French Canadians sought to restabilize their society following the rebellions. The post-rebellion church, especially in Montreal, launched a campaign to make religion more public and relevant to everyday life. Creating a national holiday was a central component of that campaign. Although the feast of St. John was celebrated in Canada during the seventeenth century, its modern incarnation was invented by Papineau's supporters in the 1830s. In the lead-up to the rebellions, Saint-Jean-Baptiste Day had become very popular in the villages around Montreal. After the restoration of civil order, the Catholic Church renewed the holiday as a means to direct the rising national sentiments of the people of the St. Lawrence valley. By the end of the 1840s, the holiday came to represent a particular brand of Catholic nationalism. Developed by Montreal's Catholic temperance society, the parade itself first marched between the city's cathedral and its parish church (Notre-Dame Basilica) in 1847; its participants wore temperance uniforms and ribbons, and brandished anti-alcohol banners. By the end of the decade, the parade had become a fixture of the holiday in the city, routinely winding through the francophone neighbourhoods as a special reminder of the slogan "l'union fait la force."[5] Over the years, the symbols of Saint-Jean-Baptiste Day multiplied, as triumphal arches and images of the saint joined the omnipresent maple leaf. By the end of the 1840s, the French Canadian people were represented by images of their patron saint and stereotypical depictions of themselves. Banners compared the French Canadian habitant and Saint-Jean-Baptiste as "allegorical representatives of the French-Canadian nation."[6] Before long, pictures were not enough. A young boy dressed as Saint-Jean-Baptiste marched in the procession in 1851. No longer satisfied with a two-dimensional representation, nationalists created a living, breathing, walking allegory for their nation. This idea to incorporate young boys as living allegories was the brainchild of a Montreal tailor named Alfred Chalifoux, who designed and manufactured the costumes. In 1854, Chalifoux added two other children, one boy dressed as an Indian, representing nature, and another dressed as Jacques Cartier. Thus, by the mid-1850s, a coherent image of the nation marched at the end of the national parade on the national holiday. George-Etienne Cartier, speaking to an assembled crowd after the parade, praised the rising national sentiment of the French Canadian people and drew heavily on the rhetoric of nineteenth-century nationalism as he compared French Canada to a great extended family. He also made sure to insert his namesake at the head of that extended family, alongside the patron saint of the French Canadian people. In his words, Jacques Cartier and Saint-Jean-Baptiste were "travelling companions."[7]

The next year, Chalifoux's little Cartier figured on the margins of an event of international importance: the arrival of *La Capricieuse*. This French corvette was sent on a goodwill mission to Canada in the summer of 1855. Its arrival was an offshoot of improving Anglo-French relations, themselves issuing from the joint effort of France and Britain to wrest control of the Crimean peninsula from Imperial Russia, thereby opening shipping on the Black Sea. That year, Canadians raised a fund to aid widows and orphans of French soldiers, for which (through the appropriate intermediary of the governor general) Napoleon III personally thanked the people of Canada. The year was flush with grand gestures of entente between the British and French Empires. In April, just prior to the opening of the Paris fair, Napoleon III paid a cross-Channel visit to London to meet with Queen Victoria, where he stayed at the Crystal Palace, the site of the 1851 London Universal Exposition. That August, Britain reciprocated, as Victoria and Albert crossed the Channel themselves to visit the Parisian answer to the London Exposition, the Exposition universelle.

Canada also participated in the Paris universal exposition; a young Joseph-Charles Taché, MP, along with William Logan, supervised the Canadian exhibits. Logan and Taché divided their efforts, with the latter taking responsibility for attracting the attention of the press. To this end, he had printed five thousand copies of his pamphlet *Esquisse sur le Canada*, publicizing himself and his country at the same time. The results were well received by his masters across the Atlantic. Numerous newspapers praised the work of the Canadian commissioners and gushed over the Canadian pavilion, especially its central display, the Trophy of Canada. Taché was personally rewarded by Emperor Napoleon III, who made him the first Canadian to receive the Chevalier de l'Ordre de l'Empire.[8] Seizing on this warming of relations and his new-found interest in Canadiana, Napoleon III decided to send, via a warship from his Newfoundland division, a goodwill and commercial mission to Quebec.[9] Paul-Henri de Belvèze, a career sailor with an aptitude for diplomacy, captained *La Capricieuse* up the St. Lawrence, and, on 13 July 1855, it became the first French warship to land at Quebec City since the Conquest.

The arrival of Belvèze and *La Capricieuse* was *the* cultural event of 1855, and for many French Canadians of the day, the event of the century. It symbolized the reunion of the original mother country with its orphaned colony. Antoine Plamondon celebrated the event in his painting *Le flûtiste*. Octave Crémazie wrote poems in honour of the event. His "Chant du vieux soldat canadien" captured the joy of seeing the French flag on the St. Lawrence once again:

Voyez sur les remparts cette forme indécise,
Agitée et tremblante au souffle de la brise:
C'est le vieux Canadien à son poste rendu!
Le canon de France a réveillé cette ombre,
Qui vient, sortant soudain de sa demeure sombre,
Saluer le drapeau si longtemps attendu.

Et le vieux soldat croit, illusion touchante!
Que la France, longtemps de nos rives absente,
Y ramène aujourd'hui ses guerriers triomphants,
Et que sur notre fleuve elle est encore maîtresse:
Son cadavre poudreux tressaille d'allégresse,
Et lève vers le ciel ses bras reconnaissants.[10]

His "Drapeau de Carrillon," published a few years later, was equally moving. No one seriously suggested reforging the lost colonial link to France; most commentators simply agreed that French Canadians, although now loyal to Britain, remained French in their hearts and that the renewed acquaintance with the original source of Canadian culture and life was invigorating. Although he was later reprimanded following British complaints about his mission, Belvèze was feted in Quebec City, Montreal, and even in Toronto.[11] He attended a ceremony honouring the recently discovered remains of soldiers killed at the Battle of Sainte-Foy, the last French victory in North America.[12] And Chalifoux, the Montreal tailor, presented him with

Figure 3 "Au Commandant de Belvèze." Alfred Chalifoux with children dressed in Saint-Jean-Baptiste Day costume. From left to right, Chalifoux, Saint-Jean-Baptiste, an "Indian," Jacques Cartier, and a French officer. Daguerreotype by Thomas Coffin Doane. *Collection André L'Homme, Library and Archives Canada, PA-139248*

a daguerreotype portrait of himself and four costumed boys representing "all the religious and patriotic memories of the French Canadians" (see Figure 3).[13] The image itself is of technical interest as it was taken by Thomas Coffin Doane, one of Canada's most skilled daguerreotypists, but is of particular importance for what it says about memories of Jacques Cartier.[14] The text accompanying the picture, signed by Chalifoux, explains the symbolism of the costumes worn by the children. Beside Chalifoux, who stands at the extreme left, is John the Baptist, the patron saint of Canada, dressed in skins and holding a cross. Next in line is "the Indian chief who welcomed the French to Hochelaga"; beside·him is Jacques Cartier, "who in the sixteenth century brought the gospel to this country." (The original text reverses the positions of Cartier and the "Indian chief.") The Cartier costume, worn by young Théophile Deschambault, achieved "historical accuracy" and was closely modelled on the Théophile Hamel portrait of less than a decade earlier. Finally, in honour of the visit of the *Capricieuse* and the Crimean alliance, Chalifoux had dressed a fourth boy as a "young Canadian wearing

the colours of France." Newspaper discussions of this child called him vari-
ously a "French officer" and a "French general."[15]

Chalifoux placed his daguerreotype in a velvet case and presented it to
Belvèze. It was a private gift intended for the Empress Eugénie in order to
assert that French Canadians remembered and honoured their patriotic and
religious connection to French civilization. It thus helped frame a transatlantic expression of patriotism and amity in which the memory of Jacques
Cartier figured prominently. But as a private gift, it had a very limited influence upon public memories of Cartier. Indeed, the empress probably never
received it, as it was later donated to the National Archives of Canada by a
descendent of Paul-Henri de Belvèze.[16] Although Joan Schwartz correctly
argues that the daguerreotype had too limited a circulation to help shape
French Canadian national identity on its own, it reveals something more
when combined with the national parade. It suggests the degree to which,
only two decades after his rediscovery, Cartier symbolized French Canada's
French origins. French Canadian nationalists felt a constant threat of assimilation, which had been the stated goal of Lord Durham's report and the Act
of Union that implemented parts of Durham's plan. Led by Louis-Hippolyte
LaFontaine and the church, French Canadians fought through the early
years of the union to establish language and cultural rights. The fight continued into the 1850s, but a new threat of assimilation by emigration had
developed. As thousands of French Canadians left for work in the United
States, the demographic survival of French Canada was again at risk. In this
environment, the use of Cartier to emphasize the French origins of the nation was both celebratory and cautionary. In Montreal, these four boys
participated in the annual Saint-Jean-Baptiste parade for the next several
years. In this way, Chalifoux's gesture influenced public memory.

Cartiermania did jump the Atlantic, even if it failed to inspire the hearts
of most citizens of the Second Empire or the Third Republic. In 1857, Edouard
Charton wrote a biographical sketch of Cartier for a French audience entitled
Jacques Cartier, navigateur français. Charton, a Saint-Simonian French politician, included Cartier in his longer series on the history of exploration since
the time of Christ, which he produced through the press of his journal
Magasin pittoresque. Although Canadians saw Cartier in conservative terms,
his ideological use in France was more ambiguous. Three years later, Henri-
Émile Chevalier published a fictional account of Cartier's second voyage.
Little is known about Chevalier's early life, except that he left the French
army to take up republican political journalism in about 1850. After Napoleon III's 1851 coup, Chevalier was arrested and exiled, arriving in America
in 1852. After working as a journalist and author in New York, he moved to
Montreal and joined the liberal Institut-Canadien (serving as its librarian),
where he arranged for French republicans to give a series of talks as they
passed through the city. Chevalier himself delivered a number of lectures

on French and Canadian history, and he continued to write novels and contribute to a variety of newspapers, including his own *La Ruche*. However, his opposition to Bonapartism was not strong enough for him to ignore Napoleon III's amnesty for political exiles in 1859, and he returned to France, profiting from his North American experiences by writing historical adventure novels set in the Canadian wilderness.[17]

Visiting Saint-Malo, Chevalier lamented that few of his countrymen remembered the Malouin explorer who opened half of North America for the French. No monument recalling his exploits graced any French city squares. But in Saint-Malo, he saw "a sign that recalled our Jacques Cartier, he who is known by, is venerated by, even the most ignorant among French Canadians, to whom all have made an altar in their heart; he whose portrait, whose name [Chevalier] had seen in public buildings, in public places, in the roads, on the ships, whether in Montreal or in Quebec."[18] Clearly, at least in Chevalier's interpretation, even the most "ignorant" French Canadian celebrated Cartier's memory, though he was remembered only locally in France. Chevalier's pronouncements concerning Cartier reflected his career ambitions more than anything else. His commercial success depended on portraying himself as an expert with a deep understanding of Canada, a country he probably knew only superficially. But for a liberal to promote what was, in Canada, a conservative national hero demonstrates the broad acceptance of the myth of Jacques Cartier. And, like the flow of republicans in exile whom Chevalier sponsored, or the visit of *La Capricieuse*, which he would have witnessed, his return to France is evidence of continuing cultural contact between French Canada and France. But a more substantial transatlantic connection was made from the movement of Canadian intellectuals to Europe.

The combined forces of romance and scientific history continued to shape Cartiermania in the 1860s, much as they had during the 1840s. Canadians were never as deeply enamoured of the German historical methods as were some of their American counterparts. Thousands of young nineteenth-century American scholars flocked to the universities in Göttingen, Berlin, Leipzig, or Heidelberg for professional academic training. There, they quickly fell under the spell of "objective" historical research, which they hoped to replicate in the new institutions of the New World.[19] No parallel existed among anglophone Canadians. In English-speaking parts of the country, young scholars who were interested in history had few options for professional development. Ontario universities, founded by competing religious denominations, reflected the acrimony that existed between them. Those universities that began to offer history as a subject in the 1860s did so with an eye to establishing a community of moral values, not to uncovering history "as it actually was." In English Canada, history was seen as a branch of literature, an approach in contradistinction to the developing American and

German conception of historical sciences. Although, in 1877, University of Toronto physicist James Loudon's presidential address to the Canadian Institute might mark the arrival of the German research ideal at Canadian universities, scholars in the arts were slower to embrace the "objectivity" of knowledge.[20] Until the latter years of the nineteenth century, Ontario's students, for instance, were subjected to a liberal arts education learned in an atmosphere of evangelical Christianity, which attempted to prevent the dominance of impartial intellect in educational life.[21] For francophones, higher education was less well developed, and French Canadian historians wrote to advance particular and often partisan causes. A historian's authority rested on his skills as a moral teacher, a man of letters using historical subjects to teach virtuous behaviour, depending more on insight and identification than on scholarly rigour. Until the end of the century, Laval University enjoyed a monopoly on higher education, and even the numerous classical colleges that sprang up in the educational awakening of the 1850s and 1860s were required to affiliate with it.

Still, young francophone scholars seeking to further their education often took advantage of sojourns in Europe. But their interests drew them to differing European capitals. For would-be men of letters, study in Paris was a necessity. For good Catholics, a visit to Rome was a spiritual antidote to the liberalizing tendencies of the City of Lights. Most famously, François-Xavier Garneau began his literary career with a trip to England and France between 1831 and 1833, preceded by trips to the Maritimes and the United States. These travels opened his horizons, as well as his eyes. While in London, he became secretary to Denis-Benjamin Viger, a member of the Lower Canadian assembly delegated to work in London as the assembly's unofficial liaison with the Colonial Office. He also boarded with another member of the assembly, Joseph-Isidore Bédard, son of the Parti canadien leader Pierre Bédard. This circle of associates allowed him to meet such notable figures as William Lyon Mackenzie, Daniel O'Connell, and the French scholar Isidore-Frédéric-Thomas Lebrun. In France, he made the acquaintance of Amable Berthelot, a lawyer from Quebec who eventually became his benefactor. And he came under the spell of Felicité Lamennais, Alphonse Lamartine, and Henri-Dominique Lacordaire. Although he did not show an interest in history before 1837, he ventured into Old World archives at Denis-Benjamin Viger's request in advance of Faribault. Historians Félix Martin, Maximillien Bibaud, Hospice Verreau, and Charles-Honoré Laverdière all followed a similar pattern. These Canadian historians borrowed from the intellectual currents of Europe, Canadianized their content, and developed a national historiography with one foot in the Old World and the other in the new.[22]

Despite their outward rejection of Rankean methodology, or at least of anglophone interpretations of it, French Canadian historians did develop a parallel archives fetish. Over the last third of the nineteenth century, French historians established themselves in the universities of France. They hoped to develop a professional methodology hinged on archival evidence, outwardly resembling the Rankean ideal. Perhaps the most direct statement of this noble goal was Gabriel Monod's 1876 insistence that the *Revue historique* publish only those works in which "each statement was supported by evidence, with notes referring to the sources," and that rhetorical flourishes be given no place in scientific history.[23] Thus Quebec historians had English, French, and American models of "scientific" methodologies to follow. But these examples never led to an all-out rejection of politically motivated writing. Canadian intellectuals of the second half of the nineteenth century were too directly plugged in to the ideological struggles that are generally characterized as between liberals and ultramontanes. These conflicts influenced the telling of history. Garneau's famous *Histoire du Canada* was just as famously reworked so that its "evidence" changed from the support of liberalism to the defence of conservative ideals. Thus, archival records came to be seen as the "proof" of history. But, though newly discovered documents might disprove long-held assumptions, they did not alter the substance of historical argument.

One might be tempted to perceive this adherence to the "truth of history" as a mark of the amateur, but such a dismissal draws on an artificial boundary between professional and amateur historians that is not helpful in this context. Through the twentieth century, Canadian historians, first in English Canada and then in Quebec, attempted to draw such a distinction and usually postulated professional history as an improvement over its amateur cousin. Donald Wright has recently suggested that this view, though common, is inaccurate and instead suggests that the difference is better understood as a distinction between two ways of doing the same thing.[24] They might also be seen as two ways of reaching different audiences. Yet, such thinking still makes the division appear clear. Wright proposes a "flat line" metaphor to explain how a clear distinction between the extremes can become blurred as they converge in the middle. There, distinctions are often based as much on structures of power as on rational criteria. For instance, Wright explicitly challenges the gender bias inherent in the concept of professionalization. As the historical profession developed, it classified the scientific methods in masculine terms and pushed other ideas about historical studies, typically the practices of women, to the amateur margins. This unveiling of the gender aspects of professionalization is instructive: it reveals the power implications behind the concept of professionalization and suggests that historians have engaged in an exercise of power entrenchment much like that which some scholars have analyzed in other professions.[25] However, despite efforts to distinguish amateur from professional, the hallmarks of professional history (such as specialization, objectivity, and argument supported by empirical evidence) can readily be found in amateur history. Indeed, those who initiated this professionalization were the very amateurs, such as Faribault, who were later marginalized by the professionals. Perhaps, instead of seeing nineteenth-century historical development as a philosophical shift toward an increased reliance on written primary source evidence and a resulting professionalization, one might better characterize it as a budding empiricism that university historians later associated with professional history. The evolving practice of history was affected by the continuing push of modernity. The modern economy and modernizing social relations became increasingly governed by practices of gathering and categorizing information and the efforts to systematize human knowledge. However much this trend focused on slotting things into groupings, so too did it demand that knowledge be retrievable. Historians' interest in documentary evidence was a reflection of the broader cultural forces of modernity. However, this was only one step toward professionalization, as history is currently practised.

In France, followers of Faribault's trail began to uncover hitherto unknown documents attesting to the historical significance of Cartier's adventures. Some early results were published in the 1862 *Transactions of the Literary and Historical Society of Quebec*. The same year, C. Desmazières de Séchelles released his *Notes sur la vie et les trois voyages de Jacques Cartier*. The following year, a Parisian bookseller named Edwin Tross discovered a copy of the *Brief recit* in the British Museum. After having it transcribed, Tross published it with an introduction by the French scholar Marie Armand Pascal d'Avézac (also known as Armand d'Avézac-Macaya) and an appendix noting three additional manuscripts at the Bibliothèque nationale in Paris. D'Avézac believed the oldest of these was the French manuscript 5653, which he designated "A." He founded this opinion on its apparent age, which he argued was confirmed by the fact that it was bound in restored sheepskin leather and stamped in gold with the arms of King Charles IX of France, whose reign (1560-74) followed shortly after Cartier's death. D'Avézac's conclusion was not without its critics. In 1865, shortly after reprinting the 1598 Rouen manuscript, a French translation of Ramusio's Italian account of the first voyage, Henri-Victor Michelant and Alfred Ramé discovered another manuscript at the Bibliothèque impériale. Michelant, an archivist at the imperial library, was working with the papers of an eighteenth-century Provençal lawyer named Moreau, in which he found a collection of narrations of sixteenth- and seventeenth-century voyages. Toward the end of the eighteenth century, Moreau had acquired some files of Philibert de la Mare, a seventeenth-century Parlement de Dijon councillor. Michelant and Ramé immediately rushed the Moreau manuscript into print through Tross.[26]

Archival work reflected modernity's influence and suggests the first steps of a professionalization of history writing in Canada, one that predated the twentieth-century revolution outlined by Donald Wright and Ronald Rudin.

Rudin argues against other distinguished commentators, such as Carl Berger and Peter Novik, that historians have been united in their quest for "the truth." He asserts that clerical leaders, who controlled the institutions of higher learning in Quebec, resisted efforts to turn Laval and later Montreal universities into institutions in search of material and secular truths: institutions filled with intellectuals more dedicated to scientific inquiry than to propping up a particular social order. Borrowing from Marcel Fournier, Rudin suggests that the economic marginalization of francophones opened a degree of space between themselves and the pressing needs of nineteenth-century modernity for practical scientific knowledge. As the century progressed, and even into the twentieth century, Catholic Quebec was insulated from modernity to a degree. Threatened by the industrializing, urbanizing, modernizing society, traditional francophone leadership reacted against modernity's intellectual currents, turning instead to a politicized Catholicism aimed at the preservation of social and moral values.[27] Hence (although Rudin does not make this point exactly), Quebec's Catholic leadership was compelled to respond to modernity and its social problems with traditional solutions such as colonization and cooperative movements. However, these solutions, be they the caisses populaires, Catholic trade unions, or the universities, had little choice but to respond to the modernizing forces pressuring Quebec society in the twentieth century. Out of this, Rudin argues, historical writing professionalized under the initial tutelage of Lionel Groulx.

Rudin's work has been particularly controversial. A generation of francophone historians has taken issue with his characterization of it as "revisionist" and with his connection of the professional discipline in Quebec to abbé Groulx, a historian noted as much for his religiosity, his distortion of history, and his racism and anti-Semitism as he was for being the first chair of Canadian history at a Quebec university.[28] However, viewed from another periodization, Rudin's hypothesis is much less controversial. Rudin suggests that, though Groulx gradually developed a "modern" or "professional" methodology, his sharp break from his amateur past did not occur until about 1945. An even longer-term view shows a developing professionalization of methodologies connected to the emerging archives fixation of the nineteenth century. Biographers, genealogists, and historians relied heavily on documents, either in archival collections or bound and published by historical societies. Indeed, the interest in new archival discoveries in Europe was widespread among Canadians, and Faribault's efforts of the 1850s were widely applauded. Presentations at historical and literary societies, and even the French section of the Royal Society of Canada, began to dwell on the significance of newly uncovered documents on prior interpretations of history. Indeed, one of the characteristics of amateur history is an excessive attention to empirical evidence, especially documentary evidence. The result, professional historians lament, is often a loss of perspective and a fetishization of documents. Yet, until the postmodern turn of the late twentieth century, this same insistence on documentary evidence was also a hallmark of professional history.

Although these mid-nineteenth-century efforts were indeed "amateur" interpretations that did not entail a sophisticated understanding of the nature of historical evidence and interpretation, they do reveal the fundamental attribute of the modern historian. Moreover, for historians unwilling to make an open declaration of their ideological sympathies, this archival fixation permitted them to avoid descending into partisan battles. The documents did not lie. This was hardly the Anglo-American interpretation of Leopold von Ranke, but it was a step in the direction of empiricism over passion, and it played a significant role in shaping the common sense knowledge about Jacques Cartier.

Abraham of America

Although the increasing interest in the heroes of the past was accompanied by a growing sophistication in historical research, there was still room for passion and emotion in the imagining of Jacques Cartier. For the bishop of Trois-Rivières, Monsignor L.F.R. Laflèche, Cartier took a special position in the line of heroes for the French Canadian nation: Laflèche suggested an astonishing link between the Hebrews of the Old Testament and the Canadians of the nineteenth century. In his *Quelques considérations sur les rapports de la société civile avec la religion et la famille* (1866), Laflèche argued that French Canadians constituted a true nation with a homeland in the St. Lawrence valley. Its mission, commanded by God, was to protect and promote the true faith on a continent of heathens, heretics, and Protestants. But, more importantly, he borrowed from the contemporary fashion for genealogical studies to argue that the French Canadian nation was bound not only by a common territory, a common history, and a common mission but also by family lineages. After describing the divinely ordained passage of Abraham and his children into the land of the Canaanites, Laflèche noted a similar pattern in Canadian history: "If the few families who left the France of yore to come and settle on the banks of the St. Lawrence some two hundred years ago have now become a million souls, this is not due to mere chance or to any blind force, but simply to the merciful designs of Providence."[29]

Once again, the image is one of a few families becoming a nation. National history, for the French of North America, is not solely political and economic history: it is also family history. The nation can be found in its genealogy. But Laflèche took the image further. Much as the biblical Hebrews were led into the promised land by Abraham, so too the Canadians were led by an inspired patriarch. For Laflèche, Abraham's arrival in Canaan resembled

Jacques Cartier's arrival in Canada. Both had been sent by providence; Abraham followed the word of God, and Cartier had his king's commission (according to some theories of the monarchy, the king was God's representative). Both were rejected by the heathens whom they encountered: Abraham in Canaan and Cartier at Stadacona and Hochelaga. And both were forced to leave their promised lands while God allowed the heathens time to amend their ways. Both sets of heathens were then vanquished by God. In Canada, this was accomplished by the mysterious, and still unexplained, disappearance of the Hochelagan and Stadaconan peoples from the St. Lawrence valley. Cartier, then, resembled Abraham, in whose seed all the nations of the earth were to be blessed. French Canadians were blessed, so the argument held, from the divine origins of their founding patriarch: Cartier. This argument was more emotional than factual. No one realistically claimed that Cartier's ephemeral colonies led directly to the French peopling of Canada. Another priest, Cyprien Tanguay, argued that the first Canadian families could be traced only from the time of Champlain: "It is not until the arrival of Champlain that we commence the long genealogical series of the Canadian people. Yes, it is to the immortal founder of the city of Quebec that goes the honour of establishing the first permanent families in Canada."[30]

But even here, there was room for dispute. Benjamin Sulte disagreed, saying that no one knew when the French peopling of Canada began. He noted that the French of Champlain's first colony were mostly itinerant, and he even raised the unlikely possibility that colonists from the Baron de Léry's Sable Island venture might have come to the mainland in 1518. He was fairly certain that none of Cartier's or Roberval's colonists had stayed behind.[31] Despite this, French Canada could envision itself as less imagined than other imagined communities. Even if it was not factually correct, common sense wisdom suggested that this nation was a truer extended family than others. A nation made by families, it traced its origins to its founding heroes.

Although many authors assert that French Canadian nationalism in the post-rebellion years rejected the liberal-national project generally attributed to the Parti patriote – there has been a tendency to conflate all French Canadian nationalist ideas into a single clerical vision – a liberal nationalist tradition did persist.[32] Despite the apparent triumph of conservatism, French Canadian liberalism survived. In the first nine provincial elections following Confederation, Liberals won an average of 45 percent of Quebec ballots, though this generally did not translate to an equivalent number of seats.[33] Moreover, liberal-minded people continued to support nationalist policies through the 1840s, 1850s, and 1860s. Rouge papers, such as *L'Avenir* and *Le Pays*, often made use of nationalist rhetoric to promote their visions. In arguing for repeal of the union in 1848, *L'Avenir* stood on the "natural" division of Canada into its French- and English-speaking halves (never mind the large anglophone population living in the "French" half). Nationality was its guiding political principle, and the union was "un acté contre nature" because, according to *L'Avenir*, different nations could not coexist in a unitary political formation.[34] Of course, *L'Avenir* was expressing a narrow ethnic vision of the nation, but one that was common in nineteenth-century thinking about nationalism. Louis-Antoine Dessaulles, the nephew of Louis-Joseph Papineau, likewise felt that the union was unnatural because it infringed on this principle of nationality.[35] And these liberals often pointed to historical heroes to personify their ideals, the most notable being Pierre Bédard, Vaudreuil, or the Patriote "martyrs" of the rebellions. But Jacques Cartier was not at first a major hero in the liberal pantheon. The earliest authors to discuss him were almost all conservatives. Faribault, for instance, began his career under the protection of the Dalhousie administration and remained connected to conservatives. And, before becoming the first bleu premier of Quebec, Pierre-J.-O. Chauveau wrote a poem called "Donnacona," in which the Canadian chief accepts the Catholic faith brought by Cartier and voluntarily exiles himself to France. Paul de Cazes, who presented papers on Cartier to the Royal Society during the 1880s, had been a friend of the Liberal leader Honoré Mercier in youth but remained a staunch enemy of the rouges. Indeed, of some fifteen essays, plays, and poems about Cartier written in French before 1890, at least twelve were by conservative partisans.

Cartier was, especially at first, a figure who justified the conservative vision of the French Canadian nation. It might seem obvious that an Old Regime figure would more easily validate an ideological position that, its opponents believed, wished to return French Canada to the eighteenth century. But not all Old Regime figures can be so easily characterized. Jean-Baptiste Colbert and Jean Talon found favour among liberals for their "modernizing" initiatives and status (however questionable) as "new men." François-Xavier Garneau wrote approvingly of Talon's struggles against the authority of the Jesuits and of "the greatest freedom that had been accorded to commerce" during his intendancy.[36] By contrast, ultramontanes saw Cartier as the founder of Catholicism in the New World. For instance, the abbé J.-B.-A. Ferland's *Cours d'histoire du Canada* insisted that Cartier was deeply religious and that he undertook his second voyage in order to convert the Natives.[37] Among the most explicit efforts was George-Etienne Cartier's comparison of the explorer to John the Baptist, claiming that both prophesied the coming of the true faith to North America. Of course, Monsignor Laflèche took the hyperbole even further in his comparison of the explorer to Abraham. To the conservative Catholic mind, Cartier represented the founding of French Canada's religious vocation, its divine mission to defend the Catholic faith in the New World. Thus, for conservative thinkers, Jacques Cartier embodied the link between their French ethnic roots and their religious origins. He stood for a particular view of the French Canadian nation that supported conservative politics. This connection between memories of Cartier and conservatism meant that his image commonly appeared at political celebrations. Nonetheless, the ubiquitousness of the image and memory of Jacques Cartier produced the first French Canadian "national" historical hero.

Behold the Hero

Until the 1870s, Jacques Cartier was the most prominent historical hero – the only truly national hero – for French Canadians. However, that decade saw the emergence of other heroes, all of whose exploits could be verified in historical documents. During the late spring of 1873, Quebec City celebrated the bicentennial of what they understood as the discovery of the Mississippi by Jacques Marquette and Louis Jolliet. Many American cities, anticipating the massive ceremonies for the centennial of the republic, used this bicentennial of discovery as a sort of warm-up. In Quebec City, on the other hand, important celebrations had recently honoured the old French regime bishop François de Laval, as well as the bicentennial of the founding of the Séminaire de Québec (which had been renamed Laval University in 1852). It was therefore fitting that the university lent its newly acquired expertise in centennial festivities to this project. On the night of 17 June, Quebec City's leading citizens assembled to feast and to hear speeches, poems, and the singing of two cantatas honouring these French regime figures. In his historical outline of the discovery of the Mississippi, the Sulpician historian Hospice Verreau noted that some would dispute the glory of Jolliet. "They say," he remarked, "the Spanish discovered the Mississippi, like the Scandinavians reached America before Columbus, like the Basques and Bretons discovered the Gulf of St. Lawrence before Jacques Cartier."[38] However, Verreau was unmoved by these arguments, for his passion could counter their cold chronological facts. In his mind, the hero was not an anonymous fisherman, blindly pursuing his quarry across the waves. A true explorer, a true hero, was one who set out to venture into the unknown and make his discoveries public. He was purposeful and conscious of the importance of his actions. In other words, he was a leader.

The following year, the number of historical heroes multiplied dramatically. Montreal's annual Saint-Jean-Baptiste parade had represented the saint and Jacques Cartier since the 1850s, but in 1874, during the fortieth anniversary of the Montreal *fête nationale,* the parade featured banners introducing a wealth of important historical heroes in French Canadian history. Students from the École normale Jacques-Cartier (Montreal's Catholic teacher-training college) carried banners naming twenty-five significant figures from French Canadian history. The banners honoured the patriarchs of such French Canadian families as Le Moyne d'Iberville, Vaudreuil, Boucher de Boucherville,

Saint-Ours, and de Salaberry. Each family also figured in François Daniel's expanded family tree. The banners also drew attention to French colonial heroes such as Jean Talon, Bishop Laval, Frontenac, Lévis, Champlain, and of course, Jacques Cartier. Almost all had been illustrated for abbé Daniel's *Histoire des grandes familles*, but this was the first appearance of any historical figures, other than Cartier, in the annual parade.

Picking up on this theme, the Reverend M. Deschamps delivered an 1874 Saint-Jean-Baptiste sermon on the need to erect monuments to these heroes from the French Canadian past.[39] Later that summer, Canada's two illustrated newspapers, *Canadian Illustrated News* and *L'Opinion publique*, published pictures of a Cartier sculpture proposed for Montreal.[40] At 1874's Saint-Jean-Baptiste banquet, Joseph-Adolphe Chapleau drew a stronger connection to the theme of family. After rather fancifully comparing the papal Zouaves to the Patriotes of 1837, Chapleau argued that French Canada was the oldest nation in North America. His analysis was strikingly narrow, having ignored indigenous peoples as well as the Spanish at St. Augustine. In the local context of francophone North America, the "other" was clearly confined to the English. And, although French Canadians might owe England their love, they could never forget their original "mother." Chapleau used the language of family to suggest something of the bond of nationhood.

A souvenir pamphlet of that fête nationale, this one published by Sénécal, commented that a goal of the Association Saint-Jean-Baptiste was to cement among all French Canadians the union that should reign within a single family.[41] The rhetoric drew on the metaphor of the nation as a family. Modern scholars may note that heroes help unite people in a political community, but a contemporary French Canadian observer argued that their existence demonstrated the accomplishments of the nation; the veneration of heroes confirmed its continuing patriotism. But more importantly, the recovery of lost heroes served a sacred purpose: "These studies, ladies and gentlemen, have as their goal not only to revive our past in its most striking features to be used to teach the people, but they contribute as well to pulling from the dust of ignorance heroes and unknown facts, to shed new light onto details otherwise obscured and to have us seek out in all things historical truth."[42]

It was once commonplace to date the start of Quebec's interest in historical figures as the June 1881 unveiling of Louis-Philippe Hébert's Michelle de Salaberry monument in Chambly.[43] But that moment was the result of a single man's efforts, and we should note that Hébert's teacher, Napoléon Bourassa, in addition to sculpting Cartier in 1858, began his *Apotheosis of Christopher Columbus*, a tableau gallery of great figures from history, in the 1860s. From the early 1870s, he also designed maquettes for monuments to French Canadian historical heroes, collaborating with one of Théophile

Hamel's students, Eugène-Étienne Taché, on a sort of pantheon of Canadian heroes. Taché, son of Legislative Councillor Étienne-Pascal Taché and cousin of Joseph-Charles Taché, was the principal architect of Quebec City's parliament buildings. He began his government career as a draftsman and surveyor for the Department of Lands and Forests in 1861. By the end of the decade, he was the deputy minister. In the 1870s, he began to turn his attention to architecture but had no real credibility. Although the more accomplished architects François-Xavier Berlinguet and Charles Baillargé had also submitted plans for the parliament buildings project, Taché's private connections ensured that he won the commission. His designs made explicit reference to the monumental architecture of France, especially the Napoleon III portions of the Louvre. In this sense, he was among the first Canadian architects to import the Second Empire style to North America, a style at once acclaimed as ideally suited to Canada's climate. Important Quebec City buildings, such as Baillargé's Laval University, had been given flat roofs, which tended to cause problems. As a result, sloped or even mansard roofs became preferable. For large public buildings, mansard roofs, a characteristic of the Second Empire style, were necessary: due to the depth of the building, a traditionally sloped roof would have been incredibly high.

When Taché began to consider the project of constructing an appropriate house for the provincial government in 1874, the idea of portraying history through statuary was hardly commonplace. In Europe, certainly, sculpture had long been used to teach public lessons in history, but the practice was novel in Canada. Baillargé's 1860 *Monument aux braves* was the first commemorative work in Quebec City to use free-standing statuary. Earlier efforts, such as the Wolfe and Montcalm obelisk, bore no statues, and Faribault's Cartier project was stillborn. Montreal was a little more advanced in this respect, with its Nelson monument at Place Jacques-Cartier being the oldest example in the city. In his designs of 1875, Taché proposed placing statues of historical heroes in niches along the exterior facade of the parliament buildings. This concept was not an innovation: Baillargé had earlier proposed such works. But Baillargé's idea followed the Italian precedent of placing the statues on pedestals atop portico colonnades such as at St. Peter's in Rome, whereas Taché employed a French style of recessed niches borrowed from the Louvre. Several of the figures from Bourassa's proposed *Apotheosis* formed part of the project for the building facade. Taché's initial version placed Jacques Cartier alone on the top floor of the central tower, with Champlain, Laval, de Salaberry, and Frontenac occupying places on the floor beneath, and Wolfe and Lord Elgin on the main floor.[44] Taché's statues would have replicated in three dimensions the hierarchy of heroes imagined by nationalists of his generation.

Taché's plan was never fully executed. He had called for thirteen statues, but historical zeal kept adding to the popularity and number of historical heroes. Projected changes seemed to concern figures from the recent past about whom very little real consensus could be established.[45] There was also a shift in thinking concerning more distant figures. Men of Taché's generation, such as Napoléon Bourassa, continued to hold Cartier in the highest esteem. For the interior of the assembly, Bourassa proposed a painting of Cartier arriving at Hochelaga, but this was met with muted enthusiasm. It would be too much to claim, as have architectural historians Luc Noppen and Gaston Deschenes, that "the image of Jacques Cartier had suffered a decline ... By the 1880s he was no longer in favour with historians."[46] Cartier remained popular; his decline was only relative. But he had been joined in the public imagination by a host of other idols. In October 1883, the government left the completion of Taché's project to future generations, and by 1894 the idea of Cartier alone on the central tower was dropped. Perhaps, as the Legislative Assembly was a public building housing the representatives of all Quebecers, not just francophones, such an ethnically associated figure was inappropriate. Cartier may have been widely acknowledged as the "discoverer of Canada," but, given his close association with French Canadian nationalism, placing him so conspicuously on the provincial legislature might have angered the powerful anglophone minority of Quebec. Certainly, English-speaking figures were part of this pantheon of historical heroes, but Taché's scheme clearly placed them below the first French Canadian hero. Nevertheless, subsequent generations took their time finishing the job and continued to commission sculptures of historical heroes for the walls of the parliament buildings into the 1960s.

Cartier-Brébeuf

Another possible explanation for removing Cartier from the central tower was the overt partisanship with which Cartiermania came to be associated. In the second half of the nineteenth century, Cartier was established as the leading figure in the national family of heroes. In part, this was because control of membership in the "official" family rested with conservative thinkers, especially the priests who ran the educational system and the lay leaders of French Canada's national societies, the Associations Saint-Jean-Baptiste. Cartier's name became increasingly prominent in toponymy. His image routinely figured on stamps, on medallions, and at public festivals. In Montreal's Saint-Jean-Baptiste parade, he annually appeared alongside the patron saint in the person of a costumed child.

Cartier, then, had taken on a universalizing function in harmony with the social order espoused by clerical and political leaders. And this harmony reached a crescendo at the Saint-Jean-Baptiste Day unveiling of a new Cartier monument in Quebec City's Lower Town. During the 1880s, the Cercle catholique de Québec, a sectarian literary and historical society, initiated a drive to replace the long-vanished cross at the site of Cartier's first winter in

Canada. The Cercle catholique was founded by nine Quebec City residents on 26 May 1876. Its goals were to encourage social peace by ensuring the triumph of certain doctrines and principles, such as obedience to the church and the pope, recognition of the rights of the church, submission to the bishops and priests, and, in those areas of free inquiry, assiduous research in order to uncover the truth. In this latter goal, the Cercle catholique encouraged the study of history, literature, arts, and sciences. Its program included helping to create parish libraries so as to spread the enjoyment of reading approved literary works and religious tracts. In other words, it was designed to serve ultramontanism. Highly conservative, Cercle membership included the lay leaders of the ultramontanes: Jules-Paul Tardivel and Senator F.-X. Trudel, as well as Narcisse-Eutrope Dionne, briefly the editor of *Le Courrier du Canada*.[47]

After 1882, lay ultramontanes in Quebec politics called themselves the Castors. They emerged, initially, as a segment of Quebec's Parti bleu that opposed its leader, Joseph-Adolphe Chapleau, and his questionable associations with the ex-Liberal politician and financier L.-A. Sénécal. When Chapleau quit provincial politics for Ottawa, the Castors (and especially the Cercle catholique) turned their attacks on his friend and successor J.-A. Mousseau. They never took control of their party, but the Castors influenced a number of ministers and policies. Still, many abandoned the bleus and rallied to Honoré Mercier's calls for a national front to defend French Catholic interests against Anglo-Protestant attacks following the Riel affair of 1885. Many ultramontanes initially opposed Mercier's use of the Riel affair to form a new political movement, his Parti national. After all, Mercier was a liberal. Bishop Laflèche insisted that Mercier's agitation was "evil," but differences between the ecclesiastical hierarchy and the lay Castors divided conservatives in Quebec. Certainly, Mercier further exploited this division as Castor support helped bring his Parti national to power.

In the midst of this manoeuvring, in September 1885, the Cercle catholique decided, through its literary and historical committee, to celebrate the 350th anniversary of Cartier's arrival at Quebec City. At 8:00 p.m. on 23 September 1885, members of the Cercle catholique opened their soirée with the singing of Ambroise Thomas' "Dieu protège la France."[48] They opted for 23 September out of respect for Hospice Verreau's demonstration of the changes in the Christian calendar that had occurred since Cartier's time.[49] In the nineteenth century, the Gregorian calendar typically had dates shifted by ten to twelve days from the old Julian calendar, so the ceremony was not held on the thirteenth, as it had been in 1835. At the conclusion of the song, Thomas delivered a lecture on the life of Jacques Cartier. The evening was a happy mix of patriotism, politics, and music. Frédéric-Ernest-Amédée Gagnon led the Union musicale in the singing of old Breton folk songs. By the 1880s, Gagnon was an accomplished musician and folklorist.

His song transcriptions, published during the 1860s as *Chansons populaires du Canada*, did more than put a previously oral tradition to paper: they were the first great contribution to a developing study of French Canada's folkloric heritage.[50] Moreover, Gagnon's participation at the soirée verified to other participants that they were not simply honouring the past but communing with it, making it part of their own lived experience. Similarly, Honoré Chassé's reading of Pierre-J.-O. Chauveau's poem "Donnacona" connected the present to the distant past by invoking the changes in the physical and human landscape over three centuries. This ceremony, much like Faribault's efforts half a century earlier, emphasized the connection between Cartier and Quebec City's local history. But, by the 1880s, Cartier's presence beneath Cap Diamant was no longer simply a matter of local history: he was clearly the first hero of French Canada, a figure of national importance.

When the Cercle catholique decided to pay double homage to Cartier and the Jesuit missionaries of New France, particularly Father Jean de Brébeuf, it was using Cartier's stature as political shorthand to further the cause of the Jesuit estates. A full understanding of this plan requires a brief voyage through the politics of religion and education in nineteenth-century Quebec, for, although the Jesuit Order was founded during Cartier's lifetime, there is very little historical connection between the two.

Established in 1542 as a missionary society by Ignatius Loyola, a former soldier, and organized along quasi-military lines, the Jesuits first came to Canada with Samuel de Champlain during the 1620s. They very quickly became the dominant missionary and educational order in New France, as they had in Europe. After the Conquest, Protestant Great Britain would probably have preferred to eliminate all vestiges of Catholicism in Canada, but its tenuous hold over the French population necessitated a moderate stance. Despite this, the detested Society of Jesus did not benefit from the full leniency of the Treaty of Paris. In and of itself, the Jesuit organizational system was not particularly offensive, but Jesuit efficiency and success had incurred considerable Protestant hatred. Moreover, the Jesuit emphasis on practicality exposed the order to accusations of Machiavellianism. To be fair, even Catholic countries had become apprehensive regarding Jesuit influence in their courts, and pressure from France's House of Bourbon convinced the pope to abolish the order in 1773. By church law, Jesuit property was to revert to the diocese. But complications occurred in Canada, with the result that the thirty-four Jesuits in the colony had been permitted to stay and retain their property, though no new Jesuits could replace them. Their numbers slowly dwindled until the last of them, Père Jean-Joseph Casot, died in 1800. In accordance with civil law, the order's property reverted to the Crown. Neither the Crown nor the Catholic Church would fully accept the legitimacy of the other's claims, and another claim by the estate of Jeffrey Amherst further complicated the situation.

Successive efforts to settle the issue failed, and by 1831 the Colonial Office had limited the use of the Jesuit estates to education. At Confederation, this restriction, coupled with the division of powers under the British North America Act, transferred control of the estates to the new Government of Quebec. However, the educational restriction meant that interest in the estates pitted the archbishop of Quebec, head of the Catholic Church in Canada, against a Society of Jesus reconvened by the pope in 1814. In 1849, the Jesuits founded the Collège Sainte-Marie in Montreal and set up a rivalry with the Séminaire de Québec (which was incorporated into Laval University in 1852). Competition between the archbishop and the Jesuits, who were backed by the ultramontane bishop of Montreal, was intense, particularly where the control of education was concerned. The bishop of Montreal desperately wanted a degree-granting university of his own, and the archbishop of Quebec desperately defended the monopoly of Laval University.

These issues wound their way into public policy during the late 1880s. When Mercier manoeuvred the Parti national into power in early 1887, the Jesuits, at least, had reason to cheer. The new premier, who had been a student at the Collège Sainte-Marie, had retained close ties with his former instructors. Mercier did not disappoint them. He granted the Society of Jesus provincial incorporation and thus the right to own property. This first step aroused little controversy, but when Mercier began negotiating with the Holy See regarding compensation for the Jesuits' estates, he stepped into a seething cauldron of sectarian and intra-faith distrust and hatred that became known as the Jesuits' Estates Act controversy.

Negotiating compensation for what was, in legal title, Crown land was bad enough, but Mercier's solution enraged many Protestants. Mercier set the value of the estates at $400,000, which he agreed to divide between the Jesuits and other teaching orders. However, to forestall accusations of funding Catholic education with state money, he granted an additional $60,000 to Protestant schools. The result was exactly the opposite of what he had intended: the Protestant gift provoked cries of "popery" and discrimination, for, compared to the $400,000, it seemed a pittance.[51]

At the height of this dispute, the Cercle catholique sent out a solicitation for donations to its monument fund. Twenty-three people promptly pledged a total of $1,030, which encouraged the committee to reissue its request an additional fourteen times. Over three years, and fifteen calls for subscriptions, some 528 people offered a total of just over $5,000 toward the construction of the Cartier monument, which would also carry an inscription honouring the Society of Jesus. A breakdown of these pledges indicates that the appeal of the plan was probably not tightly restricted to the upper classes. Pledges ranged from a high of two hundred dollars to a low of twenty-five cents. Although much of the money came from large donations of twenty, fifty, or a hundred dollars, many subscribers pledged modest sums of a few dollars. If we assume that the average income for a Quebec industrial worker (about $260 per year) applies to this cohort, the average donation, of $9.48, would have represented about two weeks' pay.[52] However, this figure is a little misleading because the average is skewed by the large contributions of such notables as Lord Lansdowne ($100), the mayor of Saint-Malo ($200), Sir Donald Smith ($50), and Lord Stanley of Preston ($100).[53] Almost half of the total, 223 donations, consisted of no more than $2. Even if they were not truly "popular" in composition, the lists of subscribers point to a broad support for the project from local small businesses, professionals, priests, and otherwise undistinguished people. A full analysis of who gave and why is impossible. For similar reasons, we cannot know how audiences at monument unveilings reacted to and used the speeches and spectacles they witnessed.[54] Audience agency – active participation in shaping the meaning of performances – leaves behind little historical documentation. It can be discerned, but with great difficulty. Nonetheless, despite the peril of taking official memory at face value, the planned ceremonies do offer a revealing glimpse into one political use of a national hero and the resonance it had for many.

The site selected for the monument was a natural. In 1835, Faribault's committee had chosen to commemorate Cartier's winter near the Hôpital de la Marine, situated on the south bank of the St. Charles River on a peninsula called the Pointe-aux-Lièvres, which was formed by the river's oxbow meander. At that early date, it was generally accepted (Pierre Chasseur and others aside) that the fort had actually stood at the mouth of the Lairet River, a small tributary of the St. Charles. Indeed, in his biography of the martyr Jean de Brébeuf, Félix Martin claimed that, by the end of the seventeenth century, the area around the residence was known to locals as "le fort Jacques-Cartier," but he was not specific about which bank.[55] Faribault had fixed the correct location to a series of mounds still visible on the left (looking downstream) bank of the Lairet.

Meanwhile, the Faubourg Saint-Roch, the neighbourhood hugging the "back" side of Quebec City's cliffs and near where the monument would stand, had grown immensely. Saint-Roch was one of the city's oldest suburbs. It began to develop at the end of the French regime as an overflow from the Upper Town, but in the nineteenth century, it became more associated with the industrializing Lower Town. By the time of the Great Fire of 1845, which wiped out most of the district, over ten thousand people called Saint-Roch home.[56] Largely a collection of the wooden homes of working-class people, it housed 85 percent of the city's labourers in 1842. Most of its residents were French speaking, but a mix of English and Irish comprised a sizeable minority of about 20 percent. Its wooden houses had spread in linear fashion toward the St. Charles River, where the Vacherie limited its growth. Across the river sat the Jesuit estates, the site of the order's first residence Notre-Dame-des-Anges, where such missionaries as Gabriel Sagard, Jean de Brébeuf, and Charles Lalemant spent their initial nights in Canada.[57] After the Great Fire, Saint-Roch was rebuilt and expanded further. By 1855, just in time for the abolition of the seigneurial system, the old seigneurial lands of the Hôpital Générale had been filled up. This popular area maintained its special connection to the memory of Jacques Cartier. Its main market was christened Marché Jacques-Cartier in 1848. The unincorporated district of Saint-Roch-Nord, which by Confederation housed twenty-five hundred people, took the name Limoilou in honour of the estate outside Saint-Malo where Cartier passed his final years. Another subdivision was given the name Jacques-Cartier in 1861. All told, the area remained Catholic and working class. Its population represented "the people." The 1891 census listed over thirty-six thousand inhabitants in Saint-Roch, Limoilou, and Jacques-Cartier.

The unveiling ceremonies were an interesting mix of civic and religious elements. (For an image of the monument, see Figure 4.) To a degree, this reflected, as Ronald Rudin has suggested, a "gentleman's agreement" to accord equal prominence to these aspects of French Canada's nationality.[58] On Sunday, 24 June 1889, Quebec City celebrated French Canada's fête nationale. The day's festivities opened with the Sixty-fifth Battalion of Montreal and the Ninth Voltigeurs based at Quebec City marching to the basilica for mass. Later, the same battalions lent a martial air to the monument unveiling, standing as honour guard and firing a thunderous cannon salute to greet the arrival of Lieutenant Governor Auguste-Réal Angers, whose presence that day was particularly symbolic. The Cercle catholique program noted that he was a French Canadian governor of Quebec, thus putting him in a line of succession that included such historical heroes as Frontenac, Vaudreuil, and La Galissonière. Despite the institutional rupture between colonial New France and Quebec as a province in the young dominion, Angers served as one other means to tie the glorious past to the present as a continuity of French ethnicity. But the sacred aspects of the ceremony predominated, for the balance between civic and religious elements was uneasy at best. One could interpret Cartier as a representative of the French state, but, given his presentation by ultramontanes over the years, he might also be used to tip the scales in favour of religion. Following Angers, the archbishop of Quebec and the president of the Société Saint-Jean-Baptiste de Québec took their places at the head of an assembly of perhaps 100,000 people gathered for mass.

The official speakers made a great deal of the importance of place in the past. The site, near the position of Cartier's 1535-36 fort and across the St. Charles from the spot of the short-lived 1835 cross, was also the location of the first Jesuit property in the New World. In 1625, Père Jean de Brébeuf

Figure 4 The Cartier-Brébeuf monument in what is now Cartier-Brébeuf National Historic Park on the north bank of the St. Charles River. *Jules-Ernest Livernois, Library and Archives Canada, PA-023570*

took possession of the land in the name of his order. An inscription on the Cartier-Brébeuf monument, which offers a dual celebration of both Cartier and the Jesuit missionaries, announced these facts. On one face, it read, "Jacques Cartier and his hardy companions, the sailors of the Grande Hermine, the Petite Hermine, and of the Émerillon, passed the winter of 1535-36 here." On another face, another inscription indicated that "On 3 May 1536 Jacques Cartier had planted, at the place where he had just spent the winter, a cross 35 feet high bearing a coat of arms with three fleurs-de-lys and the inscription 'franciscus primus dei gratia rex regnat.'"[59]

These two texts explained the nearby cross, erected as part of the same ceremony, but on another face, the inscription added a second interpretation: "On 23 September 1625, Fathers Jean de Brébeuf, Ennemond Massé, and Charles Lalemant solemnly took possession of the grounds known as the fort Jacques-Cartier, situated at the confluence of the St. Charles and Lairet Rivers, to establish the first residence of the Jesuit missionaries in Quebec."[60] Thus, the monument presented a vision of the past that connected the Jesuit claims of possession to Jacques Cartier's original assertion of possession in the name of the king of France. And, as many viewed Cartier as the first "French Canadian," this association helped legitimize Jesuit claims.

The tenuous link between Cartier and the Jesuits was not intended to be rational. Historical heroes do not assume their importance via the strength of rational discourse but are held in place by the power of emotion and symbolism. This case was deliberately emotional. Pierre-J.-O. Chauveau, former premier of Quebec, closed the ceremonies with a speech and a passionate reading of his celebrated romantic poem "Donnacona." The poem opens with the Stadaconan chief brooding in his forest kingdom:

Stadacona dormait sur son fier promontoire:
Ormes et pins, forêt silencieuse et noire.

The presence of Cartier, and the God he represents, troubles the old chief. He considers sending his warriors to kill the French interlopers, but "inutile espoir! Leur magie est plus forte." Eventually, he succumbs to the lure of the Christian God and consents to return with Cartier to France. Chauveau recounts the passing of time:

Douzes lunes et vingt, et bien plus se passèrent
Cinq hivers, cinq étés lentement s'écoulèrent
   Le chef ne revint pas.

Donnacona died during his long years in France, though Cartier did not admit it on his third voyage. But Chauveau's account draws upon a sublime connection between old vanished Stadacona and nineteenth-century Quebec City:

Vieille Stadacona! sur ton fier promontoire
Il n'est plus de forêt silencieuse et noire:
  Le fer a tout détruit.
Mais sur les hauts clochers, sur les blanches murailles,
Sur le roc escarpé, témoin de cents batailles
  Plane une ombre la nuit.[61]

And as the poem closed, Chauveau invoked the mysterious echo of the past, which haunts Quebec's mountains, forests, and plains. Then, suitably prepared to feel the sublime significance of this, each national or trade society filed past the Cartier-Brébeuf monument in turn. Each saluted the memory of Jacques Cartier, the silent hero of Chauveau's "Donnacona," before joining an immense triumphal procession through the Faubourg Saint-Roch to the Marché Jacques-Cartier. For more than three hours, the procession walked beneath flags and ornaments, as well as the watchful eyes of young women in the windows above the Saint-Roch streets. Much of the crowd remained: about half were still on hand that evening, when the last hours of the festival were signalled by the lighting of a bonfire at the Glacis cliff overlooking the monument.

Saint-Jean-Baptiste Day was itself an emotional holiday that united French Canadians through the dual pillars of nationality and faith. Passion was the link that unified the people and tied them to the historical interpretation offered by the monument. Of course, this understanding ignored the fact that the land had long been used by Aboriginal peoples, both before and after Cartier's pronouncement. It also ignored the industrial activity that began in 1688 (shipyards and pottery works). And curiously, it ignored the farm that, even in the 1880s, continued to occupy a portion of the surrounding area.[62] In other words, the past as presented by Saint-Jean-Baptiste Day was selectively chosen to affirm not only a particular national vision but a specific political policy as well. The Cartier-Brébeuf monument announced the dual identity of French Canadians, which in turn defended the Jesuits' Estates Act and Mercier's Parti national. That evening, Mercier delivered a famous speech in which he urged French Canadians to abandon their "fratricidal strife" and come together under his brand of unified nationalism:

When we disappear, we will say to the generation called to succeed us: we are Catholic and French, and when you, our successors, disappear in your turn, you must say to the generation that replaces you: we die Catholic and French! It will be our testament and theirs; the last wishes of a heroic people, transmitted from father to son, from generation to generation, until the end of the centuries.

To obtain this great result and to thus consolidate our destinies, we have but one imperial, urgent, solemn, duty to complete.

He concluded with this memorable cry: "Let us end our fratricidal strife; let us unite!"[63] It was perhaps Mercier's greatest speech.[64] For him, the message brought past, present, and future together; in honouring the historical hero, French Canadians honoured their unity.

Cartiermania was a political phenomenon, although it was not always so clearly partisan as in the case of the Cartier-Brébeuf unveiling. Nevertheless, Cartiermania represented a specific vision of the French Canadian nation, a particular ultramontane image. For supporters of Jacques Cartier, the hero directed attention to the French Canadian nation's assumed religious vocation. Indeed, Mercier further cemented the connection in 1891 when he dedicated a plaque in Saint-Malo commemorating the spot where Cartier received his benediction before sailing to "discover" Canada in 1535.[65] But in the ultramontane conception, French Canada was a nation born to secure the true faith, not through proselytization but via its own national survival. But that survival also meant the explicit rejection of alternative models of nationalism. In short, Jacques Cartier helped conservative and ultramontane leaders articulate French Canada's divine mission by providing a real-life symbol of it. Even if this view did not last, elements of it became common sense knowledge and thus guided the discourse concerning history and nationalism into the twentieth century.

5
Common Sense

The Cartier-Brébeuf unveiling of 1889 constituted the apogee of Cartier-mania. Political historians have agreed that it coincided with the peak of Honoré Mercier's career as well. Yet, whereas Mercier's star declined, Cartier remained at the top of the national family of heroes for many more years and continued to be evoked in story and carved in stone. The monstrous wrought-iron Victorian fountain in Saint-Henri was inaugurated only a few years later. And in 1905, Cartier's hometown erected its own monument to honour his birth on an occasion when Canadians, reversing the direction of Cartier's voyages, sailed for France to pay tribute to their country's "dis-coverer."[1] The 1905 monument, the project of Louis Tiercelin, a poet, playwright, and editor of the local Saint-Malo paper Le Salut, was designed in a spirit of Franco-Canadian cooperation during the years of the pre–First World War Anglo-French alliance. Yet, at the same time, Cartiermania was experiencing a relative decline. The set of forces that worked to propel Cartier's status to such heights also elevated other heroes of French Canadian history. Nevertheless, though Cartier himself no longer stood alone, he continued to represent a set of common sense ideas about the origins of the French Canadian "race" that many people had incorporated into their own memories.

Among the most imaginative late-nineteenth-century interpretations of Jacques Cartier's image was Ernest Myrand's Christmas story Une fête de Noël sous Jacques Cartier.[2] Myrand was born in Quebec City in 1854, in the same year that Chalifoux began dressing children for Montreal's Saint-Jean-Baptiste parade. He was one of the generation of young French Canadians to benefit from the post-rebellion stabilization of social order and attention to education. A writer and a scholar, Myrand began his career in 1872 as a journalist under Israël Tarte's supervision at Le Canadien, a Quebec City paper. He later worked at the Palais de justice de Québec in a position that allowed him to pursue his interests in historical investigations. By 1902, he had become the registrar of the provincial secretariat; ten years later, he assumed the post of Quebec Legislative Assembly librarian. These positions demonstrate the respect in which his contemporaries held him, as does his membership in the Royal Society of Canada from 1909.[3] This esteem stemmed primarily from Myrand's historically themed writings. His publications included an account of William Phips's confrontation with Frontenac at Quebec City (1893) and his later work *Frontenac et ses amis* (1902). But Myrand did more than simply write history: he was active in the research of new historical knowledge, and he also published, under the title *Noëls anciens de la Nouvelle-France* (1899), the first serious historical study of Canadian music and song.[4] This work continued his interest in French regime Christmas celebrations, which emerged in 1888's fantasy story *Une fête de Noël sous Jacques Cartier.*

Myrand's *Fête de Noël* focused on time-travel, ghosts, and Christmas. These themes were well established in nineteenth-century literature and most famously known to English-language readers in Charles Dickens' *A Christmas Carol* (1843). During the late nineteenth and early twentieth centuries, many authors experimented with science fiction and fantasy stories. Some of the most famous include Jules Verne and H.G. Wells, whose characters commonly faced the unknown in the distant future. In the United States, Edgar Allan Poe and H.P. Lovecraft cast their eyes back to an ancient mythical past of the mysterious, the magical, the grotesque, and the occult. Poe clearly influenced Jules Verne and other French authors, but this influence did not re-cross the Atlantic in French-language literature. Even Verne was little followed by French Canadian writers, who preferred the use of Gothic and *fantastique* to science fiction and borrowed from traditional oral *contes*. French Canadian fantastique, then, drew on the oral traditions that dated from New France and incorporated both the supernatural figures of Catholicism (including the devil, ghosts, and damned souls) and the mysticism associated with North American Aboriginal peoples.[5]

Myrand's tale, an example of the fantastique genre, opens with the narrator (presumably Myrand himself) walking the snowy Grande Allée in Quebec City on Christmas Eve of 1885. He encounters his old teacher, abbé Charles-Honoré Laverdière. A much admired instructor attached to the Séminaire de Québec, Laverdière taught a number of subjects there, but his true passions were history and archaeology. His interests led him to collect, edit, and publish historical documents related to the Old Regime of New France, including three volumes of the *Jesuit Relations* (1858) and the works of Champlain (1871). In 1866, his research convinced him that he had found Champlain's chapel beneath the rue du Fort in Quebec City.[6] And, of course, by 1885, when Myrand's tale is set, he had been dead for twelve years.[7]

After discussing Canada's heroic history with his former student, Laverdière escorts him on a journey back to the days of Jacques Cartier, to a Christmas Eve 350 years earlier. Winding their way through the streets of Quebec City, or more properly, passing the places where those streets would later be, the two companions arrive at the confluence of the Lairet and St. Charles Rivers where they find Cartier's snowbound fort of 1535.[8] Unseen by sixteenth-century eyes, they tour his ships. In the names of the company and crew, Myrand discerns an echo of the family names of his own day: Dubois, Legendre, Gilbert, Henault. And sadly, they visit the bodies of crewmen who have succumbed to the scurvy depicted in Cartier's *Brief recit*. Later, they watch the sixteenth-century Breton Christmas rites, and they witness Cartier's chaplain, Guillaume Le Breton, light a Christmas bonfire and celebrate mass. As Le Breton ends with the Latin invocation "Et claritas Dei circumfulsit eos," the pyre, as if on cue, collapses in a fury of light and heat that suggests divine attention to the mission.

Myrand intended his Christmas tale to provide more than mere entertainment. His was a religious view of Canadian history: He explained at length the importance of the number three in the success of French Canada, a message clearly aimed at the adoration of the Holy Trinity. And he demonstrated the close association of the Te Deum, an early Christian hymn, with the course of Canada's history. But, as he explained in his preface, the book was to offer a history lesson much as Jules Verne's fantasies taught geography. He backed his descriptions with footnoted evidence drawn from the best historical sources available to his day. And so, in fictional form, Myrand's tale explained the essential facts of the history contained in Cartier's *Brief recit*. But it did more than that. Through the writer's imagination, it also established the key themes of late-nineteenth-century historical wisdom regarding Cartier: that he was the discoverer of Canada, that he was the first French Canadian, and that he was deeply religious. Here was the common sense knowledge concerning Cartier, these most important aspects of Cartier's nineteenth-century heroism, which went largely unchallenged by any researcher, even when other facts came under dispute.

Cartier in Question?

The Cartier-Brébeuf unveiling continued to have a profound effect on knowledge about Cartier into the twentieth century. The Cercle catholique also sponsored an essay contest held in conjunction with the Cartier-Brébeuf celebrations, which produced the first book-length studies of Cartier. Prior to the 1880s, information regarding him was collected in scraps, bits, and pieces. The Cercle catholique's contest, endorsed by Lieutenant Governor Auguste-Réal Angers, awarded four medals: two went to Joseph Pope and Hiram Stephens for their English-language books, and two were awarded to Frédéric Joüon des Longrais and Narcisse-Eutrope Dionne for their works in French. Joüon des Longrais, later to become an eminent legal scholar of international renown, won his medal for his efforts in gathering in one volume all the documents relating to Cartier's life and voyages.[9]

Narcisse-Eutrope Dionne was among the best-known francophone intellectuals of the late nineteenth century. He was born in 1848 in Saint-Denis, the eldest in a poor family of twelve children. The local curé quickly identified Dionne's talent for storytelling and sponsored his studies at the Collège de Sainte-Anne-de-la-Pocatière. Originally, Dionne planned to enter the priesthood, but in 1869, he fell in love with his cousin, Laure Bouchard, and opted for medicine instead. He promised to marry her once he had completed his studies and fulfilled both his promise and his MD in 1873. Dionne's medical practice was not particularly successful, and after half a decade of struggling, he decided to pack it in. An old friend from Saint-Denis, Thomas Chapais, helped him land a job with the ultramontane newspaper *Le Courrier du Canada* in the fall of 1880. There, his real talents blossomed. Along with Chapais, he turned to historical research, a craft he had learned during his medical school days when he earned extra money as a temporary secretary to Francis Parkman. In 1880, Dionne published a prize-winning essay on Champlain's tomb, but his historical works were most productive at the end of the 1880s.[10]

Dionne's *Cercle catholique* essay on the life and exploits of the greatest French Canadian hero was the strongest piece of nineteenth-century Cartier scholarship. And it is no surprise that it quickly found its way to the printing presses of Léger Brousseau, a Quebec City publisher. His narrative followed the established "facts" of Cartier's life, from his birth, through his voyages to Canada, his retirement to his Limoilou estate, and his death. However, though the plan of the book was straightforward and chronological, Dionne openly weighed his evidence and spelled out the reasons for his conclusions. He questioned the received wisdom concerning Cartier's life and presented as many sides of an argument as possible before indicating his own sympathies. In this sense, his was not only a work of history, but one of historiography. Indeed, his final two chapters consisted of his critical examination of the assessments of Cartier throughout the centuries, from François I to Charlevoix, and from Faillon to Garneau. But, though Dionne's historiography was sketchy, his critical examination of the controversies surrounding Cartier's life and exploits was masterly. From the start, he was skeptical of accepted wisdom. Pointing out that a number of "Jacques Cartiers" lived in fifteenth- and sixteenth-century Saint-Malo, he sifted through the genealogical evidence presented by such authors as Pierre Margry, Frédéric Joüon des Longrais, Hippolyte Harvut, and Desmazières de Séchelles. Dionne pronounced himself suited to assess this contradictory evidence because French-Canadian surnames, much like those of sixteenth-century Saint-Malo, were often similar and French Canadians were therefore comfortable dealing with coincident names. In other words, his familiarity with genealogical confusion, as well as the improvement in available sources, permitted him to assess the known theories regarding Cartier's parentage, date of birth, and siblings. From the baptismal and parish registers, Dionne concluded that Cartier was born in 1491, not 1492 as was commonly believed, and had four, not two, siblings.[11]

Indeed, genealogy figured prominently in Dionne's study. He relied on genealogical methods to uncover the probable parents of Cartier and to trace the families of his brothers and sisters. He paid particular attention to Cartier's sister Jehanne, who married a man named Nouel or Noël, and whose son Jacques later revived Cartier's claim to possession of trading rights in New France. Dionne borrowed his genealogical approach from Cyprien Tanguay, whose method he described as "pitch[ing] his tent in each of the parishes and consult[ing] the archives, whether of the civil government, the notaries, or the court clerks, and tak[ing] all that a man of experience is capable of extracting. Without this work, we will never manage to do the true genealogy of a family as numerous as that of the Cartiers."[12] Tracing the children of Cartier's brothers and sisters (like every other researcher, Dionne unearthed no evidence that Cartier had children), he found that all branches of the Cartier family had become extinct during the eighteenth century. The sole exception, he discovered, was the last surviving descendant of Cartier's parents, who was living a quiet life in Sainte-Foy-la-Grande, near Bordeaux. Unfortunately, Dionne informed his readers, he was a Protestant.

Dionne continued to apply this critical approach through much of the Cartier story. He attempted to fix the dates of the main events in Cartier's life and offered subtle revisions for many. He revisited the old Quebec City debate concerning the location of Cartier's winter fort of 1535-36. He pored over the lists of seamen to reveal the identities of Cartier's companions. And he considered the popular belief that Cartier had undertaken a fourth voyage to North America. The theory of the fourth voyage originates with Marc Lescarbot: in his 1612 *Histoire de la Nouvelle France,* he reported having found a document, the *Règlement des comptes,* at the Parlement de Rouen. This was a settlement of the accounts between Roberval and Cartier, in which the latter demanded payment for a seventeen-month voyage and an eight-month voyage. The seventeen-month voyage was clearly Cartier's third voyage, but the eight-month voyage seemed to imply Cartier had also returned a fourth time, presumably to rescue Roberval. At least, this is how Lescarbot read the document. Charlevoix, likewise, noted that Cartier returned to Canada a fourth time, although he asserted that this crossing was with Roberval. Thus, the idea of a fourth expedition to Canada took on the mantle of truth. It was supported by what appeared to be Cartier's eight-month absence from Saint-Malo's parish registers. Cartier was a frequent witness or godfather at Malouin baptisms and other civil proceedings. In some of these instances, as it turned out, the witness was another man whose signature resembled Cartier's. Still, Jouön des Longrais compiled dozens of examples of Cartier's appearance in civil and religious proceedings between 1510 and 1557.

Although there are other periods of eight or more months during which Cartier's name does not appear on any notarized documents, abbé J.-B.-A. Ferland's *Cours d'histoire du Canada* of 1861-65, which popularized the fourth voyage theory, dated the trip to between the autumn of 1543 and April or May 1544.[13] Accepted by many leading historians, including Benjamin Sulte, the fourth voyage approached the status of historical "fact."

However, not all Ferland's conclusions survived Dionne's scrutiny. As early as 1884, Paul de Cazes argued that an eight-month voyage could not have permitted Cartier to spend another winter in Canada, though he accepted that Cartier's vessels the *Grande Hermine* and the *Émerillon* had been sent to rescue Roberval.[14] Ferland had speculated regarding the dates, but Dionne had at hand a copy of Joüon des Longrais' *Jacques Cartier: documents nouveaux* of 1888. Counting the months between Cartier's appearances in archival records, as cited by Joüon des Longrais, Dionne set the only possible dates for such a voyage as the seven-and-a-half-month period between 3 July 1543 and 17 February 1544.[15] This method also permitted him to conclude with certainty that Cartier never again had time to make a fifth return trip across the Atlantic.

As late as 1928, some experts still took the fourth voyage as factual, but most have disparaged its likelihood, and its existence is no longer accepted.[16] How was a historical "fact" revealed as an error of interpretation? Ironically, it appears to have been Dionne's analysis, coupled with more rigorous archival research, which triggered widespread skepticism about the probability of the fourth voyage. Dionne had established that Cartier could not have sailed on the dates suggested by Ferland. In 1906, his opinion became more of a certainty: during that year, J.P. Baxter, an American historian, published *A Memoir of Jacques Cartier;* widely read in Canada, it followed Dionne's reasoning regarding the fourth voyage. Baxter argued that the voyage "has been thought to be probable by a report of an Admiralty Commission [the *Règlement* cited by Lescarbot] ... to audit his accounts," but that further proof was needed.[17]

The confusion regarding the fourth voyage was exacerbated by the paucity of knowledge about Roberval, the commander of Cartier's third expedition. In 1857, T. Buckingham Smith had discovered a few documents in Madrid that suggested Spanish concerns, and espionage, surrounding Roberval's colonization attempt of 1542-44. And in 1872, Henry Harrisse had included a few documents about Roberval's commission in his *Notes pour servir à l'histoire, à la bibliographie et à la cartographie de la Nouvelle France.*[18] Dionne appears not to have known about this collection, and he was certainly unaware of the documents at the Chateau de Roberval, which were not discovered until 1891. Roberval's Canadian adventures ruined him financially, and in 1555, his chateau was threatened with seizure. When he was murdered in 1560, what remained of his assets passed into the hands of his creditors.

His nephew, Louis de Madaillan, purchased the chateau, but eventually it again passed out of the family. By 1817, greatly transformed, it had become the property of M. Davène de Fontaine as had the personal papers of Jean-François de La Rocque de Roberval.[19] By the time of J.P. Baxter's 1906 *Memoir*, however, scholars were in possession of a further document regarding Roberval: an order of 26 January 1543 from the French king in which Roberval's lieutenant, d'Aussillon de Sauveterre, was instructed to return to Canada to relieve his master. Baxter was not convinced that Cartier had accompanied this mission. Ferland had claimed Cartier set sail in the autumn of 1543, but Baxter doubted Cartier, with his knowledge of Canada's winter, would have risked an Atlantic crossing so late in the season. Ferland may have been wrong about the dates, and Baxter argued for the possibility of an eight-month voyage from March to October, but concluded only that the evidence just was not sufficient to claim Cartier had made the trip.[20]

Although Joüon des Longrais had won accolades for his efforts to uncover archival evidence of Cartier's exploits, his work was only a first brush. Following in the footsteps of Faribault and his research teams, Henry Percival Biggar scoured European collections. Educated at Upper Canada College, the University of Toronto, and eventually Oxford University, Biggar joined the staff of the Dominion Archives in 1905 as its principal agent in Europe and expanded the search for documents. In 1911, his collection of documents relating to the early exploration of Canada was published by the Archives Branch as *The Precursors of Jacques Cartier*. Biggar continued to produce important scholarly document collections. His *The Voyages of Jacques Cartier* appeared in 1924 and quickly became the standard English-language version, a status it retained for decades; Biggar's *A Collection of Documents Relating to Jacques Cartier and the Sieur de Roberval* was published in 1930. With the destruction of Saint-Malo during the Second World War, these collections have become even more important, as they are now the main sources for Cartier's life.[21]

From Biggar's research, historians became more certain that Roberval's lieutenant, d'Aussillon, was authorized on 26 January 1543 to provision the Canadian colony. The order makes no mention of either Cartier or of "rescuing" Roberval. At that point, France knew only that the colony would require fresh provisions by the spring of 1543. The supply ships duly left in May 1543, arriving in June at France-Roy, Roberval's settlement on the Cap-Rouge heights, where the decision was made to abandon the colonization effort. Biggar published the text of the Cartier-Roberval account settlement in his *Collection of Documents*, which permitted a wider range of scholars to scrutinize its language. The crucial passage interpreted by Lescarbot as referring to Cartier's rescue of Roberval is a settling of the accounts for "the third ship," which was probably the *Grande Hermine*. This ship spent seventeen months on Cartier's third voyage and eight months on an expedition to find Roberval:

"du tier navire mettrez pour dix-sept mois qu'il a esté audict voiaige dudict Cartier, et pour huict mois qu'il a esté à retourner querir ledict Robertval."[22] The key hinged on the French pronoun "il," which some read to refer to a man (Cartier) but more properly refers to a ship (navire). The eight-month voyage, then, is a reference to a ship's journey, not that of Cartier himself: he had become enmeshed in this mission via assumptions, the tendency to see evidence as pointing to famous events and people, and the original error of Lescarbot. Joüon des Longrais had revealed this mistake. Baxter had misapplied it, and Biggar's work solidified the demise of the fourth voyage. By 1914, Canadian authors such as Arthur Doughty and Stephen Leacock doubted the possibility that the fourth voyage had ever occurred.[23]

Although Dionne's work resembled that of an "objective" nineteenth-century historian grappling with the evidence to divine the past "as it actually happened," his was hardly a neutral effort. Dionne himself admitted that patriotism lay behind his interest in Cartier, whom he considered the foremost French Canadian national hero. His own Catholicism and his nationalism led him to draw certain conclusions from the evidence, and, in places, his critical eye failed him. Maurice Lemire has noted that Dionne's intent was to establish a portrait of Cartier as a citizen, sailor, and Christian who left Saint-Malo "to carry the light of civilization and faith to Natives, whom he always treated with humanity."[24] Viewing Cartier with these three qualities in mind, Dionne concluded that he was surpassed only by Christopher Columbus himself. He did not initiate the discovery of the New World or the conversion of its "miserable inhabitants" to the glory of the Christian faith. Nor had he, like Amerigo Vespucci, left his name on a continent. But Cartier was a great sailor, one recognized as such by no less an authority than his king. (If François I were qualified to rate a sailor's abilities, Dionne gives no explanation as to why.) As a citizen, he revealed a life devoted to public service, through his frequent participation at baptisms and as a witness in judicial proceedings. And his career as a Christian demonstrated that his principal motive was always to "procure the glorification of the Holy name of our Creator and Redeemer."[25]

Cartier's repeated practice of kidnapping Aboriginal people may be less than Christian, but it was not uncommon during his time. For Dionne, the abductions of Aboriginals were motivated by Cartier's zeal to ensure their conversion to Christianity and thus save their immortal souls. For late-Renaissance Christians, the existence of people in the New World, apparently untutored in the existence of God or of Christ, presented serious moral questions. As human beings, they were surely the children of the Lord. But because they knew nothing of the gospels and had had no opportunity to embrace the true faith, their souls were inevitably condemned to the agony of eternal damnation. At least, this was the motivation that Dionne, himself a devout Catholic, read into Cartier's actions. What else could explain his reactions to the sick and old at Hochelaga, those close to death, when he prayed for them and made the sign of the cross on their foreheads? In the kidnappings, his actions were not cruel but similarly motivated by a paternalistic desire to help these children of God. To modern eyes, Cartier's accounts of his kidnappings appear less benevolent. Admittedly, Aboriginal people of northeastern North America sometimes sent their children to live with other groups to cement alliances or as expressions of friendship. And Cartier certainly would have violated even this tradition by not reciprocating.[26] But for Dionne, following the traditions of Cartiermania established during his childhood, Cartier's faith and devotion were matters of common sense that justified his actions.

Two English-language entries in the Cercle catholique essay contest also won prizes. One of these was captured by Hiram Stephens, a Montreal journalist, and the other was taken by Joseph Pope, the personal secretary of Sir John A. Macdonald.[27] Anglophone Canadians were not, at first, interested in the French history of their country. Certainly, some prominent exceptions to this rule exist, especially in Montreal's intellectual community. Thomas D'Arcy McGee wrote two poems about Cartier shortly after arriving in Montreal in 1857.[28] The poet Mary Anne McIver recorded her thoughts on seeing Hamel's portrait of Cartier in 1869:

What quiet thoughtfulness rests on that brow,
What calm resolve on that unsmiling lip,
Alone he stands as lost in rev'ries now,
Upon the deck of his own gallant ship.
Was such his attitude, was such his mien,
When Canada's wild shores burst on his sight?
Or did he gaze thus moveless and serene
Upon its dim coasts by the parting light?
Ah, if indeed on these that far-off glance
In all its fixed intensity was cast,
Methinks 'twas thus he mused of his loved France,
And the vain visions of a youth long past,
Quitting a strange strand to return no more,
For the fair land which had been his before.[29]

McIver's verse demonstrates how images can be perceived differently, and this foreshadowed the eventual collapse of the common sense consensus. Rather than presenting Cartier as the father of his people, she imagined his nostalgia for his homeland and his vanished youth, ideas that softened and humanized him. Moreover, this nostalgic view seemed to suggest that his glory (and perhaps, by extension, that of French Canadians) lay in the past. By implication, the future of the new dominion belonged to English Canadians. Like McIver, the accomplished Montreal author Rosanna Leprohon made poetic use of Cartier. For her, Cartier helped explain, in verse, the name of Mount Royal.[30] He had certainly become known to English Canadians, but such attention was occasional and fleeting before the 1890s.

During the 1850s, the famous American historian Francis Parkman had praised some of Cartier's exploits. For the English-reading audience of North America, Parkman was probably the greatest factor sparking interest in the history of New France.[31] Indeed, anglophone Canadian attention to French colonial history began to percolate after the publication of Parkman's volumes. He improved the quality of prose, infusing it, to echo the sentiment of John Bourinot, with romance and adventure.[32] Certainly, Parkman's interpretations have been roundly criticized by twentieth-century scholars, and he continues to make good fodder for modern historians who wish to frame the intellectual climate of the nineteenth century as racist and Whiggish. Parkman did see the world according to nineteenth-century categories of progress and racial attributes. He imagined a hierarchy of peoples: English-speaking societies were superior to those who spoke French; European civilizations were superior to, not just "more advanced than," their Aboriginal counterparts. And within those categories, he further defined a hierarchy according to military prowess, so that the powerful Iroquois were the superior Indians.[33] Nevertheless, Parkman's skill with a pen brought life and adventure to an otherwise underappreciated aspect of the North American past. And, although his literary skill often overshadowed the works of other researchers, his popularity turned the attention of some to the French regime. His rediscovery of New France coincided with the revival of the Literary and Historical Society of Quebec: having lain dormant since Faribault's heyday, the society again began to publish its proceedings and transactions during the 1860s.

Although Henry James Morgan's 1862 *Sketches of Famous Canadians* proclaimed Jacques Cartier as the father of Canada, few midcentury anglophones paid much attention to him.[34] As early as 1885, an anonymous poet even tried to make a case for Cartier as a hero shared between English and French Canadians.[35] And by the time of the Cartier-Brébeuf unveiling in 1889, some English Canadians began to propose accepting Cartier as (almost) one of their own. The Toronto *Globe,* responding to complaints voiced by the Montreal anglophone community regarding the Cartier-Brébeuf monument, wondered "why should the French Canadians not show pride in their heroes?" But the *Globe* went further and suggested that Cartier might also be an appropriate subject of English Canadian celebration: "Why should we not rejoice with them? Jacques Cartier sailed up our great river and first found for Europe our land."[36] About the same time, in 1887, W.F. Ganong addressed the Royal Society of Canada on Jacques Cartier and his contribution to Canada's past.[37] The Cercle catholique contest came at this moment of dawning interest and helped propel Jacques Cartier's image into the collective memory of English Canadians as they began to awake to a curiosity concerning the Canadian past.[38]

Of the two English-language essays, that of Stephens is the less remarkable. His motive, as he himself stated it, was to provide "all the facts" known about Cartier, and to this end he simply synthesized or translated accounts from Ramusio, Hakluyt, the 1598 Rouen manuscript, Lescarbot, and the recently discovered manuscript of Michelant and Ramé. After a brief introduction to the early life of Cartier and a description of his Limoilou manor, Stephens ploughed through the accepted narrative of his first two voyages. For the third voyage, he relied most heavily on John Pinkerton, Hakluyt, and Faribault's 1843 work. These, of course, were all variations of Hakluyt's sixteenth-century version. However, for English-speaking Canadians, Cartier could not be used to legitimate a French and Catholic nationalism. He had to be remade to suit a different nationalism. Stephens, tellingly, compared Cartier to Columbus, setting up a discovery myth that was parallel to, but distinct from, the American version. Like Columbus, Cartier was the founding explorer who brought European civilization to a part of the New World. However, unlike Columbus, Cartier knew he was sailing to the New World. Also unlike Columbus, he did not immediately establish an imperial presence there.

For his part, Joseph Pope offered a more critical inquiry. Pope was an anglophone and a Catholic convert from Prince Edward Island who, as a young man, moved to Ottawa to join the federal civil service. In 1878, he signed on as personal secretary to John A. Macdonald and enjoyed a career in the federal bureaucracy under both Conservative and Liberal prime ministers. Although Conservative politically, he championed the notion of a neutral professional civil service. In 1896, when Wilfrid Laurier came to power, he expected to be fired from the civil service; instead, due to his personal friendship with Laurier and his connections, he was retained as undersecretary of state. In 1884, he had married Henriette Taschereau, daughter of Quebec's chief justice Sir Henri Taschereau, which brought him an alliance with the prominent Taschereau clan of Quebec Liberals. His memoirs, which reveal a fair-sized ego, pass over his Cartier biography with little comment other than noting that he had won a prize. Perhaps it was a lesser event in his life, for, while he was writing the biography, he was promoted to assistant clerk of the Privy Council.[39] However minor the book may have been in Pope's life, it played a greater role in the saga of Jacques Cartier, becoming a key reference for the anglophones who, at the turn of the century, were slowly discovering Canada's French regime past. Like Stephens and Dionne, Pope accepted the existence of Cartier's fourth voyage, allotting it a few sentences as an afterthought to the greater achievements of the first three. Like Dionne, Pope was willing to entertain various possibilities regarding the voyage before settling on April 1543 as its date.[40] For Pope, Cartier's main achievements were that, while at Gaspé, at the end of the first voyage, he "solemnly took possession of the country in the name of his royal master" and that he had discovered and explored the St. Lawrence as far as Montreal, the heart of the Canadian Confederation.[41] Pope, then, confirmed the Toronto *Globe's* understanding of Cartier's acts as the first link in a chain of secular events that eventually culminated in the Dominion of Canada.

By the end of the nineteenth century, authors could debate the specific facts of Cartier's career without undermining its common sense meaning. For example, many people believed that the French king had ennobled Cartier in recognition of his efforts. Few authors supported this claim, which, because so many of them explicitly denied it, was probably a widely held misconception. It stemmed mainly from a misreading of certain documents, the name of Cartier's wife, and the styling of Cartier as the sieur de Limoilou. Francis Parkman, considered by many English Canadians to be *the* authority on the French regime, certainly accepted Cartier's nobility and claimed that it was conferred by François I in appreciation of his discoveries.[42] Parkman seems to have based his understanding on Faillon and Desmazières de Séchelles. Similarly, Charles Cunat, often seen as the French authority on Saint-Malo history, argued for the nobility of Cartier.[43] Later authors were less certain. Dionne pointed out that Desmazières de Séchelles, using the same source evidence as Faillon, dated Cartier's patent of nobility to 1549 but was not in possession of the actual document. Indeed, no document conferring nobility on Cartier had been found by 1889, when Dionne was writing. Instead, Desmazières de Séchelles based his speculation on a passing reference to Cartier as "un noble homme" in a document and his unofficial title – the "sieur de Limoilou" – as owner of a small rural estate. Joseph Pope likewise doubted Cartier's nobility, noting that, though Faillon had found 1540 and 1550 references to "un noble homme," Cartier was also styled a "bourgeoys" in baptism records. To drive the point home, Dionne emphasized that these earlier claims were not based on the volume of evidence available for the Cercle catholique contest. Thanks to the work of Joüon des Longrais, more evidence was accessible; agreeing with that author, Dionne claimed that no Malouin was ennobled before the end of the sixteenth century.[44]

Although Dionne doubted Cartier's nobility, he did suggest that further research was necessary and important to settle the question. And the subject certainly left impressions in ideas about the explorer. A complicating aspect of this issue was Cartier's use of armour. On his arrival at Hochelaga, he apparently donned it in order to visit the town. This claim seems to have come from Biggar, who translated the French verb "accoutrer" as "having put on his armour," but later scholars have argued that this translation misrepresents the meaning in the *Brief recit*. Recently, Michel Bideaux has suggested that "accoutrer" should be translated as "having very gorgeously attired himself." Yet, Bideaux based his own improved translation on the fact that Cartier was not noble and therefore would not have possessed armour.[45] In 1919, Régis Roy took up the challenge at a meeting of the Royal Society of Canada and found Dionne's arguments to be wanting. Roy began by noting that nobility could be acquired in a number of ways: it could be inherited at birth, included in a grant of fief, or won via military or bureaucratic office. He rejected the idea that Cartier's Limoilou estate was a fief that established his nobility, even if it was associated with the arms of a nobleman. For Roy, Cartier's nobility came through his office, his commission as captain-general for the third voyage, which was registered at the Parlement de Rouen on 17 October 1540. Following this, Cartier began to be styled in baptismal records as either "noble capitaine" or "sieur de Limoilou." Thus, Roy concluded, arguments against Cartier's nobility lacked conviction. Much more would be required to convince him that Cartier, the founder of a noble people, did not deserve his title: "We await further evidence to convince us that our hero was not a man of quality."[46]

On the other hand, arguments against Cartier's nobility might also be questioned. Many writers have made a great deal of the commoner status of Christopher Columbus and have emphasized his role as an iconoclast, a development explained by some scholars as part of the nineteenth-century bourgeoisie's battle to secure the ascendancy of liberalism in the United States. Authors such as Washington Irving portrayed the Genoan explorer as a "new man" or a "man of talent," overturning Old World corruption and nepotism with his novel ways. Thus, invented stories, which ranged from the minor (that, for example, Columbus taught priests to stand an egg on its end) to the major (that he intended to prove the world was round), emerged to serve liberalism and American ideology. The reasoning of Samuel E. Dawson, who wrote about Cartier, might well fit with this approach: he insisted that Cartier was never a nobleman and also absolved him for abandoning Roberval on the third voyage, remarking that the incompetence of Roberval, the nobleman, provided a perfectly good reason for disobeying his orders.[47] The "new man" trumped the corruption of hereditary patronage.

Unlike these nineteenth-century liberal writers, Régis Roy saw nobility as a sign of quality. In 1918, along with E.-Z. Massicotte, he published a study of Canadian coats of arms called *Armorial du Canada français*. Sometimes his search for nobility in French Canada's past stretched credibility. Marcel Trudel accused him of fabricating the nobility of a seventeenth-century naval captain named Guillaume de Caën: "Régis Roy, convinced that de Caën was a noble, and having no proof whatsoever to offer, even supposes that the appellation 'de Caën' is a surname: there is nothing to substantiate this argument."[48] Better known for his comedies, Roy also wrote considerable history, which reveals him as a moderate defender of conservative ideals. Although he never claimed to be a historian, he was a regular contributor to such publications as the *Bulletin des recherches historiques;* at his death in 1944, one obituary proclaimed him an authority on history and Canadian heraldry.[49] But perhaps more importantly, he insisted that by the time of the third voyage under the command of Protestant nobleman Roberval, Cartier had been granted nobility. However, as long as Cartier was framed as deeply pious, conservatives did not need him to be noble in order to promote their world view, and Roy's opinions remained marginal.

One issue that might have struck at the heart of common sense knowledge was the question of whether Catholic priests accompanied Cartier to the New World. Myrand's *Fête de Noël* introduced readers to Dom Guillaume Le Breton, one of the priests who may have travelled on Cartier's second voyage. The inclusion of priests on Cartier's long expeditions might be taken as evidence of his religious sensibilities, a crucial aspect of his appeal to nineteenth-century ultramontane nationalists. Yet, the evidence on the matter is inconclusive at best, and the debate is largely confined to the second voyage of 1535-36. Most authors who claimed that priests participated in it, such as Faillon, Ferland, and Dionne, relied on the title "Dom," which applied to two of the company listed on a provisional roll for the voyage and the fact that the *Brief recit* mentioned the celebration of mass, for which a priest would have been required. But neither of these pieces of evidence are ironclad. Samuel E. Dawson, for one, noted that the *Brief recit* did not provide the names of any priests administering religious services, though it did mention three distinct services on the second voyage.[50] Paul de Cazes suggested that, because Cartier did not refer to the blessing of the crosses he planted during his travels, no priests were with him. Moreover, he disputed Dionne's claim that the names of the company furnished conclusive proof, suggesting instead that the roles of these individuals were not truly stipulated.[51]

However, Joseph Pope offered the strongest argument against the presence of priests on Cartier's voyages. In deliberating the issue, Pope attacked the three main reasons for accepting the premise – that Dom Guillaume Le Breton and Dom Anthoine were recorded on the roll of the second voyage, that the narratives speak of the celebration of mass, and that Cartier himself mentioned priests. In the fall of 1535, when Cartier planned to continue up the St. Lawrence to visit Hochelaga, Donnacona and the Stadaconans constructed a ritual in which the spirit Cudouagny warned against the danger of proceeding. Cartier, the *Brief recit* reveals, laughed off the warnings, telling Donnacona that his priests had spoken to Jesus and gained assurances not to worry. On the other hand, Cartier also claimed that he had no priests, which was why he had not baptized those Stadaconans who asked for the rite. The primary evidence contains no direct allusions to the services of priests; in the narratives, it is Cartier himself who explains Christianity to Aboriginal people and supervises the religious rituals. Here, Pope suggested that "mass" was not the formal celebration envisioned by Faillon but rather an informal ceremony. Had Cartier truly celebrated mass, would he not have made more of it in the *Relations*? It was Cartier who read from scripture at Hochelaga, led prayers, and laid hands on the sick. To corroborate, Pope added that Lescarbot claimed to have undertaken similar functions at Port Royal and that Champlain insisted the first mass held in Canada was that performed in 1615 by Récollet fathers at the Rivière des Prairies.[52]

Pope did not question Cartier's piety. Indeed, shortly after arguing against the presence of priests on the second voyage, he insisted on Cartier's devotion; later in the book, he spoke of Cartier's "deep piety."[53] This, however, raises questions regarding what it meant to be a devout Catholic in the early sixteenth century, before France's wars of religion or even the Council of Trent's response to the Protestant Reformation. Nineteenth-century ultramontanes infused piety with an increased reverence for the authority of the pope and the clergy. During that century, not all Catholics were ultramontanes, of course, and certainly the power of ultramontanism declined in Canada following the 1876 resignation of Ignace Bourget, the bishop of Montreal. However, ultramontane spirituality influenced the Canadian church so that its institutions were reshaped in ways that reflected the triumphal piety of the papacy. This emphasized a devotional life greatly dependent on the leadership of the clergy and regular, formal forms of worship.[54] Piety in Cartier's time might well have been understood in different terms. François Lebrun has claimed that most pre-Reformation Catholics attended church and took the sacraments primarily at great events. Such outward displays of devotion played little role in their daily lives. Piety may have been more flexible as ordinary people interpreted their own spirituality. A.N. Galpern has argued that emotion was the key to urban religion in sixteenth-century Champagne and that Christianity underwent a rapid vulgarization during that century. Popular devotions could often fall outside the direct supervision of priests and communal pietan activities, such as the joining of confraternities, which were routinely practiced without clerical oversight.[55] Taking priests on such long voyages of colonization may not have been necessary in Cartier's mind. On the other hand, the Huguenot Roberval, while in command of the third voyage (although never with Cartier), felt free to supervise the morality of his company and acted accordingly. Pope was the only author to suggest that Cartier may not have been pious, but he claimed simply to be repeating word of mouth complaints, which he dismissed as Protestant slurs much like those that criticized Catholics for mumbling their prayers.[56]

Not all authors perceived Cartier's piety as beneficial. William Kingsford, a Montreal Protestant, denounced the French "policy" of proselytization: "Even at that early date the mistaken policy of the French ministers in abandoning the functions of government to become the propagators of religious opinions is apparent. Cartier set forth that one of his objects was to be of humble service in the increase of the Holy Faith."[57] Most authors disagreed with Kingsford and saw such a service in a positive light. Many assumed that the goal of Cartier's voyages was the conversion of Aboriginal peoples to Catholicism. Indeed, this appears to be a common adjunct to Cartier's presumed piety, especially in the mid-nineteenth century. Allegations that Cartier's mission was the propagation of the faith can be traced to Ferland, who, in 1861, invented a story that Cartier told François I he would return to Canada to convert the Stadaconans.[58] Given this, it is curious that Cartier allowed Domagaya and Taignoagny, the two young men he kidnapped from Gaspé, to spend eight months in France and return home unbaptized. Nevertheless, the myth of proselytization persisted, in part because it fit with the common sense belief in Cartier's devotion. Parkman picked up on it and claimed that François I's interest in the New World was to counter the Lutheran heresy in Europe.[59] This suggestion dovetailed nicely with nineteenth-century French Canadian values and the imagination of the nation's divine vocation as a bastion of Catholicism on a Protestant continent. The founding French Canadian established the national vocation.

As with the dispute over the priests, the evidence seems to mitigate against this common sense belief. Cartier not only failed to baptize any converts on his missions, but he refused baptism when it was requested. Indeed, for the ten Stadaconans kidnapped in May 1536, who never again saw their homes, evidence exists of only three conversions (as confirmed by baptism) in France.[60] This need not necessarily speak against Cartier's piety, as he would not have been responsible for their religious education in France. And even the Récollet missionaries of the seventeenth century, who went to the New World specifically to convert the Natives, likewise withheld baptism until they were satisfied that the applicant had a sufficient understanding of the faith. Yet, missionary activity was one goal of the third voyage. The commissions supporting this expedition repeatedly proclaimed that its object was to spread the name of God through the New World. Both Roberval's commission and that of Cartier reiterated that its aim was to "induce the other peoples of these countries to believe in our holy faith" and to support "our mother the holy Catholic church."[61] Why did this sudden interest in proselytization strike the king of France? Marcel Trudel attributed it to political ambitions and François I's need to win support from the Holy See, whose bulls had previously divided the world between Spain and Portugal.[62] But again, placing a Huguenot in command of a mission allegedly intended to win Catholic converts suggests that Catholic piety in the sixteenth century was more complicated than nineteenth-century authors could admit.

Two related issues also spoke against the common sense understanding of Cartier. A hero, especially a pious explorer and founder of a nation, must be a person of the highest moral qualities. Cartier's character, by modern standards, is not so certain. On his third voyage, he abandoned Roberval, his commander, and he repeatedly kidnapped Native people during the other two. Although Frank Basil Tracy accused Cartier of making "the blunder of kidnapping two young Indians for use as an exhibit at home," most authors dismissed the abductions as at worst misguided but well meaning.[63] Ferland glossed them over and Arthur Doughty even suggested that Donnacona was a willing passenger on the trip back to France.[64] Admittedly, these issues reflect as much the smugness of Europeans and the persistent notion that Aboriginal peoples were untutored savages in need of civilizing as they do Cartier himself. Even fewer writers commented on the topic of Cartier's insubordination, in which, having encountered Roberval at St. John's Harbour during his retreat from Charlesbourg-Royal, he fled in the night rather than obey his commander's order to spend another winter in Canada. Parkman called Cartier's behaviour a betrayal, but few authors took up the challenge. It simply did not match the common sense notion of the heroic explorer.

Other issues could similarly pick at the margins of Cartier's story without shaking the faith in its essential meaning. Some authors suggested that Cartier had participated in earlier voyages of discovery and had perhaps been to Brazil. Some questioned the authenticity of the Cartier portrait in Saint-Malo, or of the wrecked ship discovered in the St. Charles River, or even suggested earlier Portuguese penetration into the Gulf of St. Lawrence. But none of these ideas – not even the suggestion that Cartier was not the first European to visit Canada – displaced from him the title of discoverer of Canada or altered the common sense knowledge. Nevertheless, anglophone secularization of the essential meaning of Cartier sowed the seeds of his fall.

Rivals: Cartier, Cabot, Columbus, and Champlain

One of Cartier's near contemporaries, John Cabot, also figures prominently in the discussion of common sense. The modern anthropologist Peter Pope alleges that anglophone Canadians promoted John Cabot as Canada's discoverer in order to diminish Cartier's claim.[65] Pope's assertions are somewhat overstated, but they are suggestive of the ways in which specific facts of history can be open to intellectual debate, whereas their underlying meaning may be more emotional. Pope bases his reasoning primarily on the writings of Samuel E. Dawson, a Montreal man of letters, and the rivalry between the Bonavista and Cape Breton claims for Cabot's landfall. His argument is

that Canadian nationalists rejected Newfoundland's claim on Cabot's landing and elevated Cabot, an Italian sailing under the English flag, to the status
of Canada's discoverer, deliberately displacing Cartier. In doing so, they
reinforced the legitimacy of English possession of northern North America.
Thus, by virtue of his English commission, Cabot gave Britain an unbroken
chain of claim on continental North America, which predated that of France
or even Portugal and Spain. As further support to such assertions, a letter
from Clement Markham of the Royal Geographical Society, read at the 1896
meeting of the Royal Society of Canada, proclaimed Cabot as the founder
of "British maritime enterprise."[66] Markham invoked the sea, a central feature
of British national pride and identity in the nineteenth century. Britain, the
nation that "ruled the waves," got its maritime start from Cabot. By extension, British greatness, connected to British sea power, found its roots in the
voyages of John Cabot; Canada (or the independent colony of Newfoundland) was cloaked in that same greatness and steeped in its heritage.

As the fourth centennial of Cabot's voyage approached, numerous British
North Americans advocated holding a historical celebration to commemorate it. No doubt, their eyes were firmly cast south to the United States, where
the fourth centennial of Christopher Columbus' first landing in the New
World had recently been feted. Americans had long folded this landing into
the larger discovery of the New World that set in motion the eventual rise
of the United States. By 1892, the Knights of Columbus, Italian American
organizations, the Grand Army of the Republic, and various other groups
had been lobbying Congress to declare a national holiday on the anniversary
of Columbus' first landfall. Across the nation, Americans turned out in
numbers for the patriotic festivals in honour of the great explorer. In New
York, a corner of Central Park was christened Columbus Circle, and a huge
Columbus monument was unveiled. The following year, the Chicago World's
Fair took the name World Columbian Exhibition.

English Canadians were keenly aware of these events, and many looked
to Cabot's arrival five years after Columbus as an opportunity to counter the
American founding myth with their own. In late 1894, Oliver Aiken Howland
read a paper at the Canadian Institute in which he proposed holding a
historical exhibition in Toronto to celebrate the quatercentenary of Cabot's
discovery.[67] Howland was no stranger to either historical writing or civic
boosterism. He had already published a treatise on imperial government, a
favourite topic of Canadian imperialists in the 1890s, which traced the
historical development of the British Empire.[68] He also came from an important Toronto family. His father, William Pearce Howland, was prominent in
the Reform Party during the middle decades of the century but was enticed
into John A. Macdonald's Liberal-Conservative Party after being expelled
from the Reform Convention for refusing to follow George Brown out of
the coalition that formed Confederation.[69] Oliver Howland continued in

the Conservative Party, winning election to the Ontario legislature in 1894, running unsuccessfully for federal election in Toronto-Centre in 1897, and eventually serving as mayor of Toronto in 1901-02. He died in 1905. The idea of an exhibition to commemorate Cabot received enthusiastic approval from Canada's intellectual circles. The Royal Society of Canada endorsed the proposal, citing Samuel E. Dawson's articles in its *Proceedings and Transactions* as proof that the English claim to the discovery of the Gulf of St. Lawrence took precedence over that of the French. Royal Society members were also dismayed by the possibility that Cabot's contribution might be forgotten, an apprehension worsened by the fact that a monument had been raised in Boston to honour Leif Eriksson's Vinland colony. The Royal Society concluded that this injustice could best be remedied by holding its 1897 annual meeting in Halifax, the closest comfortable city to the alleged Cape Breton landing site.[70] This was not at all what Howland had in mind, and the Toronto committee pushed on, holding an organizational meeting for its own Cabot exhibition at St. George's Hall in February 1896. What exactly Cabot had to do with Toronto was never satisfactorily explained.

When the Canadian Senate caught wind of this scheme, there was considerable resentment. The chamber of sober second thought spent a good portion of the afternoon of 18 March 1896 debating the merits of Toronto's planned exhibition and, more importantly, a bill to permit Parliament to contribute to the costs. In debate, Toronto's supporters were led by Donald MacInnes of Ontario, whereas Nova Scotian Lawrence Geoffrey Power led the opposition. Certainly the only francophone to participate in the discussion, Charles Eugène Boucher de Boucherville cited Dionne to insist that there was no proof for any claims about Cabot's discoveries. However, the debate did not devolve to focus on the merits of Cabot versus those of Cartier. Power's arguments against the bill boiled down to his opposition to Toronto as the site for a national commemoration of a Maritimes event. MacInnes defended this location on the grounds that the Ontario government had taken the initiative and offered space and funding. As a Nova Scotian, Power could hardly dispute the claims for a Cape Breton landing or, consequently, the implication that Cabot was the first European explorer to reach what eventually became Canada. But he did suggest that the site of Cabot's historic landing could not be fixed by parliamentary statute and that the subject ought to be left to the historians. Moreover, he felt that the organizing committee, comprising such Toronto notables as Howland, David Boyle, George Wrong, and James Mavor, could not pretend to represent all of Canada, even with the governor general's endorsement. Yet, in the end, he acquiesced as senator after senator stood to insist that invitations to the exhibition be extended to the scholars in their own communities.[71] In committee, the bill was greatly watered down so that Ottawa would contribute no money to the event. The issue fizzled out and with it the planned exhibition. Ultimately, Canada commemorated Cabot's quatercentenary with a plaque in Halifax, unveiled by the governor general.[72]

During these Senate debates, members on all sides of the discussion placed a great deal of weight on the authority of Samuel Edward Dawson. Dawson grew up surrounded by books, and it was only natural that he would develop a love of learning. His father, Benjamin Dawson, moved the family from Halifax to Montreal in 1847 where he operated a bookstore and circulating library on St. James Street. In 1860, his sons took over the business, and for nearly three decades, Samuel Dawson and his brother built it up, expanding its operations into publishing and printing. In the process, Dawson cultivated a reputation as an articulate, careful, and knowledgeable bookman who was also an expert on copyright law. After his partnership with his brother dissolved, Dawson was appointed queen's printer, with the prime minister's hope that he could clean up the corruption and inefficiency in the Department of Public Printing.

When the Senate debated the Cabot exhibition, senators had every reason to lean on Dawson's reputation and authority. He had recently been awarded an honorary DLitt by Laval University in recognition of his accomplishments, including his literary work. He frequently wrote articles for Montreal newspapers, and he published in magazines on philosophy, science, and history. He earned respect for thoughtfulness in the wake of the Jesuits' Estates Act controversy when his *Toronto Week* articles argued that the civil and religious rights of English Protestants were not in fact being impinged upon by the Catholic Church.[73]

Elected to the Royal Society of Canada in 1893, he presented his papers on the voyages of John and Sebastian Cabot at its 1894, 1896, and 1897 annual meetings. These maintained that Cabot had landed at Cape Breton, an assertion that never neared majority acceptance. Moreover, even Dawson hedged his argument, displaying the balance that characterized his scholarship, by admitting that Cartier opened Canada for exploration, whereas Cabot merely visited in 1497. In an appendix to his 1896 contribution to the *Proceedings and Transactions of the Royal Society of Canada,* Dawson responded directly to the suggestion that he was deliberately slighting Cartier. Insisting on a Cape Breton landing, he suggested, was in fact a defence of the claim that Cartier had discovered Canada. As part of Nova Scotia, Cape Breton did not become "Canada" until 1867. Therefore, Cartier was the first to reach "Canada" until Confederation altered the definition of the territory. It was the modern designation of territory that had changed, not the accomplishments of either explorer. Moreover, he continued, those who insisted on a Labrador landing were letting "national pride get into the historical argument" and undermining their own defence of Cartier.[74]

Southern Labrador was French and much of it in Quebec, which is in Canada. Therefore, if one applied the shifting territorial definition of Canada, this would mean that Cabot reached Canada before Cartier did. Later still, in his 1905 *Saint Lawrence Basin and Its Borderlands*, he continued to pay homage to Cartier, pointing out that though "the whole Atlantic seaboard of the Dominion of Canada had been explored" when Cartier arrived, it was he who had discovered the St. Lawrence, "the heart of Canada."[75] Peter Pope has suggested that Dawson was being disingenuous in these arguments, but such may not be the case.[76] To be sure, his reasoning hinged on games of semantics, but Dawson seems to have sincerely believed that his was an objective look at the evidence, and he does not appear to have intended to disparage the accomplishments of Cartier.

Certainly, Dawson, or more accurately his supporters, can be seen as countering Cartier's status. And certainly, Dionne and Joseph Pope attacked any notion of replacing Cartier with Cabot in most forceful tones.[77] But even Columbus had his doubters in the United States, and counter-Columbus activities flourished around the Columbus celebrations. Some New Englanders and some Americans of Scandinavian descent protested that the Norse had arrived five centuries before Columbus. However, much of this "counter-Columbianism" was directed against Italian Americans, and it was overwhelmed by the strength of support for Columbianism.[78] Similarly, in the Cartier case, Cabot simply did not have the widespread public support to become the discoverer of Canada. What was actually at stake here, for English-speaking Canadians, was a suitable rebuttal to American claims regarding Columbus. Cartier could not serve in this capacity, having taken possession of the land for France nearly three decades after the death of Columbus. Cabot, on the other hand, if he landed at Cape Breton, had made a claim of possession about a year before Columbus saw the North American mainland.[79] Hiram Stephens called Cartier the "Columbus of Canada," but for many anglophones, Cabot better fit the bill. However, over the long term, Cartier, not Cabot, retained the status of Canada's discoverer. One American even praised Cartier at the expense of Columbus. In dedicating a book to the president of the University of Michigan, Harvard University's Justin Winsor suggested that Cartier opened the continent for Americans: "No one knows better than yourself how the great valley which the American people shares with others in the north, and the greater valley of the interior which is all ours ... carry the streams of national life back and forth between the gulf which Cartier opened and that other gulf which Columbus failed to understand."[80] Cartier might have been greater even than Columbus.

These disputes reversed the pattern commonly seen in discussions of single explorers. Whereas the minor points of Cartier's life were debatable, no one seriously questioned the major ones. However, in disagreements regarding who discovered Canada, the facts of history, with the exception of the site of Cabot's landfall, were rarely much in dispute. At issue was the "meaning" of the facts: the notion of "discovery." Peter Pope suggests that discussions of the meaning of discovery tend to run to Edmundo O'Gorman's argument that nothing can be discovered until it is comprehended. But this presumes a modern understanding of the word. Instead, Pope suggests that, in the fifteenth and sixteenth centuries, discovery implied making something widely known.[81] This wise counsel echoes an argument made in 1889 by Dionne.[82] However, Pope's caution is also in accordance with a maxim of history that the past must be judged on its own terms rather than by the standards of the present. In these Victorian debates over who discovered what, "discovery" was inevitably tied up with founding: the act of discovery became a founding moment. When they looked at the actions of Cabot, English Canadians saw the commencement of the British Empire's rise to greatness. Others saw Cartier as opening up the heart of the continent to development and showing future Canadians the way forward. Aboriginal people rightly take exception to such haughty claims, and nothing in this book is intended as an endorsement of such Eurocentric views. However, those who accepted one claim of discovery in preference to another repeatedly cited the start of a chain of history.

The chain of events envisioned by French Canadians differed from that of English Canadians. In a review of Myrand's *Fête de Noël*, Pierre-J.-O. Chauveau, adopting a stance that looked to his own imagined community, attempted to forestall disputes regarding discovery before they arose. He poked fun at those intellectuals who would claim that Cartier did not discover Canada, joking that "these scholars, in my opinion, are ... too clever!" Moreover, he continued, one could say that Columbus did not actually discover America – might one then reasonably make a claim for the "Eskimos" as the discoverers of Canada? Certainly not: Cartier named Canada, he claimed it for France, and he set the stage for Champlain. Chauveau's point, clearly expressed before he embarked on his review, was that French Canada's history began with Cartier. He was and remained the first in a long line of heroes.[83] Interestingly, at the time of Cartier's quatercentenary in 1934, Clifford P. Wilson reversed Chauveau's argument. Speaking on the Montreal radio station CFCF, Wilson revisited the Cabot-Cartier dispute. Arguing that the Gulf of St. Lawrence had been explored by Cabot, Corte Real, Verrazano, Gomez, and John Rut, as well as innumerable Portuguese, Spanish, English, and French fishermen, prior to Cartier's arrival, Wilson suggested that it was improper to consider Cartier the "discoverer of Canada." However, he acknowledged that this appellation was widely in use. He felt that Canadians regarded Cartier as the discoverer because his narrative of the first voyage survived, whereas the others' did not. Also, his explorations were clearly linked with the westward push that uncovered the Canada of 1934. And finally, Cartier was French and thus "belonged to that race that began the settlement of New France, and was a fellow countryman of Champlain, La Salle and Montcalm, and all the ancestors of the French Canadians of today." Cartier, then, was more properly the discoverer of French Canada than of Canada.[84]

Almost as quickly as it had caught fire, this Cabot-Cartier dispute blew itself out. Certainly, a rivalry between supporters of Cabot and those of Cartier continued to smoulder through the years and occasionally flared up, but it never again reached the intense levels briefly seen in the late 1890s. For instance, a Cabot lobby, which promoted both the Italian's claim to the discovery of Canada and the erection of a Cabot monument in Montreal in 1933, provoked some controversy.[85] Indeed, Wilson's radio essay seems to have targeted the folly of this dispute, even laughing at the Montreal aldermen who entered learned debates about the distant past and tried to fix historical facts via municipal decree. However, Wilson also noted that Canadians, not solely French Canadians (and he clearly distinguished between the terms), held to Cartier as the discoverer of their country. His essential point was that such claims were foolish. *Toronto Mail and Empire* reporter Fred Williams also insisted in 1934 that Cabot had discovered Canada and that France had never understood its importance.[86] But by the 1930s, that opinion was decidedly in the minority. Even Williams grudgingly acknowledged that Cartier introduced Christianity to Quebec.

The Cabot-Cartier rivalry had largely been reduced to one between the Italian minority in Montreal and the francophone majority. In May of 1935, the year following the great Cartier quatercentennial, leaders of Montreal's Italian community, along with official representatives of the Mussolini government, finally donated a John Cabot monument to the city of Montreal. Accepted on behalf of the city by Mayor Camillien Houde, the monument occupied a prominent place in Western Square (now Place Cabot) at the corner of rue Sainte-Catherine and Atwater Avenue near the border of the town of Westmount. However, its inaugural ceremonies were overshadowed by that day's commemoration of Dollard des Ormeaux at his monument in Lafontaine Park, of the French Canadian veterans of the North West Rebellion, and of sailors lost at sea, held annually by the Last Post Fund. Speaking at the Cabot monument unveiling, Luigi Petrucci, Italy's consul general in Canada, used the opportunity to refer to the accomplishments of Italy in all branches of human affairs and commented that his homeland had "also left an undying legacy in the field of the discoveries."[87] Columbus, Vespucci, Verrazano, and Cabot were all Italians. Indeed, though Petrucci's speech remarked on the accomplishments of Cartier and Champlain, it made it clear that this celebration of Cabot was a celebration of Italy (and, by extension, of Italian greatness under Mussolini), not an Anglo-Canadian attempt to undermine the place of Cartier as Canada's discoverer.

Admittedly, one Montreal newspaper, *La Patrie,* did take the opportunity to publish a poem about Cartier's arrival at Hochelaga, no doubt in an effort to reinforce the primacy of the Malouin.[88] Nevertheless, this occasion actually constituted an effort by a minority community to stake a claim to legitimacy and to announce its presence in Canada's largest metropolis, as had been the case for the monument erected by Italian immigrants in honour of the Renaissance poet Dante Alighieri a decade earlier.[89] Organizers attempted to avoid specific rivalries with French Canadians, even opting to unveil the monument in May rather than on the 24 June anniversary of Cabot's landing, which was also the national holiday of French Canadians.

A greater threat to Cartier's status came from his compatriot Samuel de Champlain. Ronald Rudin has documented the rise of Champlain as a hero in Quebec City during the latter half of the nineteenth century. Charles-Honoré Laverdière takes some of the credit for elevating Champlain's stature in French Canada. He was reported to have discovered Champlain's tomb in 1866, although in actuality, he had only a theory regarding its location. More importantly, he also edited and published the collected writings of Champlain, as his *Oeuvres,* about the same time.[90] Interest in Champlain, which can be dated from this point, began to accelerate in subsequent decades. Like that of Cartier, Champlain's image offered possibilities for French Canadians to imagine their nationality deeply imbued with their faith.

Ironically, the first suggestion for a Champlain monument came from the largely English Literary and Historical Society of Quebec and included no reference to Champlain's religion, beyond his broad Christianity. Instead, Champlain was presented as the first European governor of Quebec.[91] However, French Canadians were also imagining Champlain in ways that connected his civil and religious roles. At about the time of the Cartier-Brébeuf unveiling, the Société Saint-Jean-Baptiste de Québec (SSJBQ) proposed placing a Champlain monument on the site of his Fort Saint-Louis, near the newly built Canadian Pacific Railway hotel, the Chateau Frontenac. Their Champlain was a founding father whose Catholicism was overt and who revealed the connection between civil and religious authority. This accord between the civil and the religious began to disintegrate as anglophone leaders noticed the importance of French regime heroes to national and imperial unity during the 1880s. Although Cartier-Brébeuf had inspired efforts to celebrate the early civil and religious leadership of Quebec City, as personified by Champlain and Laval, funding the erection of monuments to either man proved beyond the financial resources of French Canadians in Quebec City and its environs. This fiscal weakness is perhaps not surprising given the city's relative economic decline at the end of the nineteenth century. Similar difficulties had characterized monument projects throughout the century and would continue to prevent their realization through the twentieth. However, in the case of Champlain, an anglophone community with deeper pockets, or at least access to those with deeper pockets, emerged to fill the void. Anglophone interest split the traditional accord between the civil and religious elements of celebrating the past. Canada's largely Protestant anglophone communities saw no connection between their identities and the Catholicism celebrated in the commemoration of Laval. Although some, perhaps most notably Quebec City engineer Charles Baillargé, launched a campaign to preserve the traditional accord, anglophone money flocked to the secular notion of Champlain. In 1898, Champlain's monument on the Dufferin Terrace was unveiled, scandalizing those who resented his desacralized portrayal as the first of a series of civil governors, shorn of all religious connotation and mission.[92]

Rudin's lucid dissection of the motivations behind the monument shows that Champlain's image underwent many of the same manipulations as Cartier's. However, anglophones accepted Champlain as a hero more readily than they had Cartier. By the early twentieth century, Champlain monuments had been erected in Ottawa; Orillia, Ontario; Plattsburgh, New York; and Acadia National Park, Maine. Indeed, interest in Champlain spilled across the Canada-US border as easily as it crossed the Ottawa River. Perhaps the fact that Champlain's exploration encompassed a larger geographical area than that of Cartier might account for this wider interest. However, with Champlain, another curious development followed: the moment of discovery diverged from the founding moment, which opened cracks in Cartier's high position. One aspect of common sense knowledge began to be questioned. For English Canadians and Americans, Champlain was celebrated as a secular explorer, charting new discoveries and initiating a process of civic government. For French Canadians, he could not represent the same things. Certainly, he was an accomplished explorer, but by the end of the nineteenth century, it was all too apparent that his discoveries in Quebec had simply followed those of Cartier. Instead, Champlain's importance came in founding the first permanent French colony. He, not Cartier, came to embody the founding moment, even if he could not represent the first event in the nation's history. As Cyprien Tanguay had explained in his genealogy, the first families came only with Champlain.[93]

A similar pattern can be seen in the following decade, with the development of the tercentenary of Champlain's arrival at Quebec. In this proposed project, Lord Grey saw an opportunity to exhibit to anglophone Canadians the francophone contributions to Canadian history. He seized on the occasion as a means to cement racial harmony within the British Empire by demonstrating the greatness of French Canadian history within a larger narrative of the British imperial mission. Connected to Grey's idea was the notion of developing the Plains of Abraham as a sacred imperial site. Grey envisioned the battlefield as a stage in imperial progress during which both French and English lost a significant hero. Again, this idea had a long pedigree. The deaths of Wolfe and Montcalm allowed both sides in the battle on the heights above Quebec City to mourn a fallen hero. Although Britain eventually won the Seven Years War in Canada, the loss of Wolfe and Montcalm permitted advocates to portray the Battle of the Plains of Abraham as a decisive struggle. As early as 1828, the Wolfe and Montcalm obelisk had been erected in Quebec City. Wolfe, in particular, became a British military hero whose veneration is comparable to that later accorded Nelson and Wellington.[94]

But the tercentenary was planned to be more than a simple monument to Champlain or a static commemoration of these past heroes. H.V. Nelles has provided an account of the unfolding of this grandest of commemorative celebrations, held on the Plains of Abraham in July 1908. Nelles masterfully narrates the genesis, the planning, and the staging of the tercentenary events and suggests that, despite disputes and conflicts, the festival was a great success. In the tercentenary, Nelles catches glimpses of a distant future of bilingual harmony. Ronald Rudin has thrown cold water on Nelles' enthusiastic account of the ceremonies, noting that few francophones or working-class residents of the city attended. Indeed, even at a mass held at the pageant grounds, Rudin notes that the stands were only two-thirds full.[95] What does this suggest about the historical sense presented at this "national" celebration? By 1908, Quebec City was home to some seventy-five thousand people, and, given the international attention to the festivities and the numbers of tourists who flocked to the old capital (including the Prince of Wales) to take part, one might have expected the grandstands to burst under the weight. Rudin suggests that cost may have been a crucial issue, as workers' wages had not kept pace with the cost of living, and Quebec City was trapped in an economic recession. Moreover, the tercentenary was largely an anglophone affair. Lord Grey, the governor general, had ensured that it would reflect imperialist thinking regarding Canada's history and its people, and that it would promote the "fusion of the races." Ideas of racial fusion simply did not resonate with the majority of francophones who formed the bulk of Quebec City's population. Fusion was simply too close to the old threat of assimilation. Lord Grey's imperialistic celebration aroused no overt hostility, Rudin points out, but there was a sense of suspicion concerning its motivations.

Nevertheless, we should not discount the tercentenary so quickly. Its 1908 festivities at Quebec City emerged from a combination of the nationalist energies of the SSJBQ and the imperialist opportunism of the governor general. The original idea can be traced to H.J.J.B. Chouinard, the tireless secretary of the SSJBQ and clerk of city council. Late in 1904, he wrote an article in the *Quebec Daily Telegraph* proposing a tercentenary celebration of

Champlain's founding of Quebec City. His friends, among them a number of ambitious city councillors and Mayor George Garneau, established a committee to plan Chouinard's celebration and couple it with the coincidental bicentennial of the death of Monsignor Laval, widely seen as the founder of the Catholic Church in Quebec. Certainly, the event was taken over by federal and imperial authorities, but it retained much of its local inspiration. The historical pageant was staged by the international pageant master Frank Lascelles, but Québécois author Ernest Myrand wrote its scripts. Curiously, although Quebec City was the centre of the revival of Cartier's memory, and Myrand was a willing participant in Cartiermania, Cartier's position at the tercentenary was strikingly reduced.[96] Although Nelles has wondered why, in a commemoration of Quebec City's founding, Cartier was more prominent than might be expected, this glosses over his importance in the exploration history of the St. Lawrence valley.[97] Moreover, it misses the magnitude of Cartier in French Canadian nationalism. Yet, Nelles suggests an essential point: by 1908, Cartier's significance had declined. This process had been rapid. In 1888, Chauveau described Cartier as the first hero in a *city* of heroes.[98] He was the head of a Quebec City pantheon and, as the Cartier-Brébeuf celebrations confirmed, still a father figure for the nation. Twenty years later, he had become a mere prelude to Canadian history. No longer was he connected directly to the founding of the city. No longer was he the renowned father of New France. Instead, his position as founding father had been supplanted by Champlain and, to a lesser extent, Laval. This veneration of Champlain and Laval cannot be separated from a deeper confrontation between civil and religious memories that characterized much of the commemorative movement in the Western world. The lay and clerical leaders who planned the city's major commemorative events had always been careful not to separate the civic from the religious message. Following the example set in the veneration of Jacques Cartier, commemorations and the celebration of heroes always connected the Frenchness of the population with its Catholicism, an accord best reflected in the 1889 Cartier-Brébeuf festivities.

Myrand's scripts told the story of Canada's history, and Cartier's visits to Canada occupied the first four tableaux of Lascelles' historical pageant on the Plains of Abraham. Curiously, the pageant opened with Cartier's arrival at Hochelaga, an event from his second voyage. The first act of Canadian history, then, involved the presentation of the old and the sick for the explorer to cure, as well as Cartier's response with prayer. In the first lines of dialogue, Cartier asked God to enlighten the poor infirm Hochelagans who had mistaken him for a deity, and he appealed to the saints for intervention. The second tableau transported the audience to Stadacona on 3 May 1536, as Cartier and his crew made ready to leave for France. As part of these preparations, the pageant instructed the audience, Cartier planted a cross

Figure 5   An actor playing Jacques Cartier plants a cross during the second tableau of the tercentenary pageant on the Plains of Abraham. *John Woodruff, Library and Archives Canada, 1939-434 NPC, DAPDCAP271720*

to take formal possession of the country in the name of his king, François I (see Figure 5). Here, not at Gaspé a year earlier, the French came into possession of Canada. But other aspects of collective memory crept into the event as well, despite the growing historical literature questioning the smaller facts. Prayers at the cross raising were led by the two "priests" included on the provisional roll of 1535: Dom Guillaume Le Breton and Dom Anthoine. After this brief tableau, the pageant quickly depicted Donnacona's kidnapping. Cartier, addressing his newly raised cross, asked God to transform this barbarous frontier into a "sentinel" of Christianity and of France. This sentiment closely paralleled nationalist ideas about French Canada's divine role as the only French and Catholic society in the New World. But the implication was also that the kidnapping, never fully explained despite the fact that "kidnapping" was in the title of the third tableau, was part of this holy endeavour. Finally, in the lengthy fourth tableau, Cartier presented the New World chief to his Old World king. His efforts, in this case literally, served as intermediary between the Old and New Worlds.

Here, then, was 1908's common sense notion of Jacques Cartier. His voyages represented the founding acts of Canada's history, for he was the country's "discoverer" despite its earlier occupation by "savages." Cartier's second voyage, which constituted the formal and legitimate possession of Canada for Christianity, established France's dominion over these "terres inconnues." Moreover, Cartier's role was a divine one: he brought Christianity to the New World and brought the New World, in the person of Donnacona, to Christianity. Even though Canada was not the quick route to China, as François I had hoped, it presented marvels never before seen. Canada offered the French a cure for scurvy. It provided them with tobacco and a means to enjoy it.[99] But above all, Cartier's voyages to Canada initiated the French Canadian divine mission in the New World.

6
The Many Meanings of Jacques Cartier

In the years following the First World War, English-speaking Canadians became much more interested in the utility of knowledge and the professionalization of its creation. This was a broad-based trend among intellectuals who, like the president of Dalhousie University, saw the war as a clarion call for superior scientific education in order to make its sacrifices meaningful. The war had demonstrated the utility of science and encouraged scholars to see their social role in utilitarian terms. Canadian social sciences emerged, although underdeveloped by American or British standards, as a means to apply scientific knowledge to social and economic problems. Leading intellectuals, such as O.D. Skelton, led a push to convince students and colleagues alike of the need for applied knowledge derived from scientific methods.[1]

For historians, the greatest social utility of the discipline was in developing patriotism. In the years after the war, English-speaking Canadians also became more interested in the history of their country. Indeed, the 1920s saw a cultural awakening in anglophone Canada as the war and the new world order it produced invigorated Canadian patriotic pride. Canadians participated in the Paris peace conference and joined the League of Nations. Canada no longer automatically followed the mother country in world affairs, as the 1926 Imperial Conference confirmed. Indeed, though Britain's reputation as a world power survived the war, it was greatly diminished. And Canadians congratulated themselves for having reversed the colonial relationship and having saved the mother country.[2] Nevertheless, it is too simplistic to see the war as a straightforward watershed in Canada's developing autonomy and identity. The decade that followed it was a period of profound contradictions. For instance, in the face of such optimism about the future, mainstream cultural nationalism during the 1920s was framed by a consciousness of history. In 1919, the Imperial Order Daughters of the Empire commissioned patriotic paintings about the war and distributed them in Canadian schools. The Historical Landmarks Association, after gaining an unprecedented number of members in 1919, reorganized itself in 1922 as a body of professional historians, the Canadian Historical Association. Although not directly linked to each other, both the Canadian Historical Association and the *Canadian Historical Review* (founded in 1920) wrestled with the same concerns surrounding Canadian history in the interwar years. Both debated the true nature of history (literary or scientific), and both responded to a widely felt need to correct popular misconceptions about Canada's past and a desire to forge a national consensus that transcended language and regional barriers.[3] Throughout the decade, federal and provincial governments promoted historical understanding through their newly created historic sites boards. And, by the end of the 1920s, the radio branch of the Canadian National Railway pressed dramatists to write historical radio plays to promote a national consciousness. All this expanded attention began to put the established common sense consensus regarding Jacques Cartier in flux. Part of this shift sprang directly from the fact that new participants were involved in the consensus. Certainly, Cartier remained a hero primarily for French Canadians. But, as the previous chapter demonstrated, anglophones were accepting him as well. They were unlikely to embrace the image of a hero developed for ultramontane nationalism and instead began to conceptualize Cartier in a more secular succession of historical events. Meanwhile, in Quebec, the First World War and its crises inspired in many French Canadians a feeling that heritage should be more exclusive.

The Third Voyage
Among the first of the new national institutions to promote Jacques Cartier was the Historic Sites and Monuments Board of Canada (HSMBC), established by the Conservative government of Robert Borden in 1919. But this federal agency was hampered by bureaucratic isolation within the Dominion Parks Branch, as well as a lack of vision for its mandate. Lacking clear funding commitments and a lucid statement of purpose, the board's first years are best characterized by inaction and abortive efforts to define itself. But, following a reorganization in 1923, the HSMBC began to imagine itself as the arbiter of all things historical across the country.[4] Through its structure, regionalism shaped the board's vision of Canadian history. It consisted of Parks Branch Commissioner J.B. "Bunny" Harkin and a secretary from Parks, as well as historians from Ontario, Quebec, the Maritimes, and Western Canada. Every year, at its annual meeting, members proposed locations from their regions for recognition as official Canadian historic sites. Typically, though with a few exceptions, each member was responsible for selecting sites from his own area.[5] Thus, the type of history recognized by the board often reflected as much the interests of the regional representatives as it did any concerted effort to define Canada's past.[6]

During the 1920s, the board revealed a striking inconsistency in distinguishing sites of national historic importance. Partially, this was due to its inability to define exactly what the term "national historic importance" meant, an issue that it debated at its annual meetings throughout the decade. And partially, it was because the range of proposed sites mirrored the individual energies of each member. Thus, by the end of the 1920s, the HSMBC had reviewed some 900 sites, recognized 256 as being of national importance, and marked 151, mostly with its standard plaque and cairn.[7] Standardization was inherent in such statist initiatives, but behind outward displays of it and, one might imagine, of objectivity, the internal workings of the board showed remarkable susceptibility to personal whim. In the selection process, each regional representative suggested people and events worthy of commemoration, researched the case to support his own recommendations, and drafted the wording of the proposed plaques. The other board members functioned largely as editors. As initiative thus lay in the hands of individual members, the likelihood of any proposal being accepted owed as much to the will of the particular member as anything else. Cartier unfortunately lacked a strong champion during the board's initial years. Although the celebrated historian Benjamin Sulte was Quebec's first board member, he died in 1923, leaving a legacy of unfulfilled proposals. Moreover, Sulte was replaced by Victor Morin, Aegidius Fauteux, Philippe Demers, and Maréchal Nantel in rapid succession. Each brought fresh ideas, but more importantly, the board repeatedly reserved decisions about Quebec sites pending the appointment of the next Quebec member. Thus, not surprisingly, it initially showed little interest in Jacques Cartier. Admittedly, this lack of attention also reflected an earlier decision to recognize notable individuals at their places of birth.[8] Nevertheless, ignoring the exploits of the "discoverer" of the country was a curious policy. When the board first took an interest in Cartier, it was for his second and third voyages.

In May 1922, Benjamin Sulte proposed the commemoration of Cartier's fort near Quebec City.[9] Perhaps oddly, he did not select the fort from Cartier's first Canadian winter, that of 1535-36. Instead, he chose the fort, some ten miles upriver, that was occupied by Cartier during the disastrous winter of 1541 and by Roberval during the equally difficult winter of 1543. This decision may be partially explained by Sulte's desire to defer to the existing cross and the Cartier-Brébeuf monument at the presumed site of the 1535-36 fort. The HSMBC was still a fledgling institution in 1922, with limited resources and dependent on local goodwill. Appropriating an existing French Canadian site and marking it with a federal monument might have been seen by some as interloping. But more precisely, given the board's limited resources and constant financial pressures, it would also have been seen as redundant by the other members and by government oversight.

The board accepted Sulte's suggestion and set about its usual procedure of locating a site for the plaque that was historically appropriate, available for use, and in a prominent enough spot to be visible to the public. Further complicating the issue was the fact that Cartier built (and Roberval rebuilt) not one, but two forts. A variety of local experts, including Pierre-Georges Roy of the Archives du Québec, aided in the search for an appropriate site. With a single "exact" location impossible to ascertain, the board was free to consider the most accessible one.[10] Harkin had once claimed that he hoped to teach tourists about Canadian history via the plaques program, so placing the marker on the main tourist road seemed an obvious step to take. A suitable site was secured where the Côte de Cap-Rouge passed a railway bridge near the mouth of the Cap-Rouge River. After some further negotiation, the spot originally chosen was swapped for one on higher ground that was slightly more prominent and visible from the road.[11] Indeed, by the end of the decade, the local caretaker was proudly reporting that as many as sixty cars stopped at the cairn on summer weekends, and more could be expected with further highway improvements in the area.[12]

The board had greater difficulties with the actual wording of the plaque. And the finished result, which remained in place for nearly seventy years, smacks of committee compromise and little more than a passing familiarity with the source materials:

Charlesbourg-Royal

Here Jacques Cartier, in 1541-1542, in his third voyage, and Roberval, in 1542-1543, wintered with their followers some 200 in all, in two forts, upper and lower, built by Cartier and repaired and extended by Roberval, who named the place "France-Roy."

This, the first attempt to colonize Canada, proved a disastrous failure and was abandoned.

In 1543, Cartier was sent by the King to bring Roberval back to France.

Here were grown the first wheat and European vegetables in Canada.

The plaque's reference to the fourth voyage can be partly attributed to unfortunate timing. Sulte, who accepted its existence, had proposed one version of the text but died before it could be carried out. Although, in the early 1920s, the voyage was increasingly the object of skepticism, it was still sometimes accepted as fact. Furthermore, Victor Morin, who replaced Sulte on the board, resigned in 1924, leaving responsibility for any already approved Quebec sites to the board chairman, Brigadier General E.A. Cruikshank.[13] Although Cruikshank was a respected authority on the War of 1812, his historical interests did not extend much beyond military affairs. His knowledge of Quebec's history was poor, and he neither spoke nor read French. The board then relied heavily on the expertise of Quebec archivist Roy and a new edition of Biggar, unaware of the changes in historical understanding this meant. But individual members also felt free to make their own suggestions. The result was the haphazard and disjointed text on the plaque.

More importantly, the text made the third voyage a purely secular affair, and in this, it marks the beginning of a clear trend in official commemorations that divided Cartier from the religious nationalism of the nineteenth century. Certainly, a purely Catholic reading of the third voyage is impossible, given that even its first phase under Cartier's leadership was commanded by a Huguenot. But the HSMBC chose specifically to focus on colonization and cultivation. Although the colonization effort was "a disastrous failure," it set Cartier at the head of a line of colonization. Divorced from his religious connotations by an agency composed of anglophone Protestants, Cartier took on new meaning. His efforts were noble but unsuccessful. Champlain, the first of Canada's "governors," was then reinstated by implication as the true founder of Canada.

The Second Voyage

A more contentious case was the commemoration of Cartier's arrival in Montreal during his second voyage. In February 1920, Benjamin Sulte proposed to the HSMBC that a plaque honour Cartier's Hochelaga visit of fall 1535. The board had no objection to observing an early peaceful encounter between Europe and America, and it quickly approved the plaque during its annual meeting of that spring.[14] Yet, the exact site of Hochelaga had long been a contested issue in Montreal. Anglophones tended to place it somewhere near the McGill University campus, whereas some francophones located it on the other side of Mount Royal, in the modern town of Outremont.[15] The nineteenth-century archaeologist John William Dawson opened the debate in 1860, after he unearthed the remains of what he believed to be Hochelaga – an Aboriginal site on the south flank of Mount Royal.[16] Dawson's site captured the imagination. In 1892, in time for the celebration of Montreal's 250th anniversary, the Antiquarian and Numismatic Society of Montreal marked the site by placing a plaque on the home of Dr. William Hingston at the southwest corner of Metcalfe and Sherbrooke Streets.[17] However, the HSMBC decided that McGill University's campus on the north side of Sherbrooke Street was the best location for the marker. Securing McGill's permission to place a plaque on university grounds, it moved toward an unveiling scheduled for early 1922.[18] But at the last second, these plans nearly collapsed due to the panic caused by a single letter from Aegidius Fauteux, the highly respected Montreal librarian, who wrote Harkin to caution him against staking the board's reputation on the Dawson site.[19] Aristide Beaugrand-Champagne, a Montreal architect and member of the francophone Société historique de Montréal, had discovered "conclusive proof" to counter the Dawson claim and intended to publish his findings establishing the true site of Hochelaga. Beaugrand-Champagne drew on an established tradition that Cartier's voyage had taken him around the northern shore of the Island of Montreal, following the Rivière des Prairies rather than the commonly accepted St. Lawrence route. Relying heavily on Cartier's mention of three rapids, Beaugrand-Champagne argued that he had landed at the Sault-au-Récollet on the north shore of the island rather than at other commonly accepted points, the Lachine Rapids or the St. Mary's current.[20] Using this "northern route thesis," Beaugrand-Champagne read Cartier's *Relations* in a way that placed Hochelaga on the north side of Mount Royal, specifically near the intersection of Maplewood and Pagnuelo Streets in the city of Outremont. In striving for historical accuracy, the HSMBC had unwittingly stepped into a local and exceptionally minor dispute. But the man who initiated the panic found the way out. Fauteux recommended retaining the McGill campus site for the plaque via the ruse of deliberate ambiguity. As no definitive proof could be found for the location of Hochelaga, he suggested simply noting that it had been "near this site." The HSMBC quickly adopted his idea and unveiled the plaque on 22 May 1925.[21]

Continuing disagreement between the predominantly francophone-supported northern route and the largely anglophone-backed southern alternative underscores the social territoriality of historical memory. However, the dispute involved more than mere archaeology, for it enlisted Cartier and Hochelaga in a struggle to claim space in Montreal. In placing Hochelaga in Outremont, Beaugrand-Champagne wrote Cartier's journey so that his route traversed francophone neighbourhoods rather than the primarily anglophone areas associated with Dawson's hypothesis. Although Outremont began as a predominantly anglophone town, it quickly developed into a middle-class francophone community, which was the francophone equivalent of wealthy, anglophone Westmount. But, following the turn of the century, many Jewish Montrealers aspired to live in Outremont. Jacques Cartier, who named Mount Royal, and the narrative of French discovery, reinforced francophone claims to historic occupation of the northeastern flank of Mount Royal.[22] A year after the McGill plaque was unveiled, the Sault-au-Récollet section of the Société Saint-Jean-Baptiste de Montréal (SSJBM) unveiled two plaques to celebrate the 175th anniversary of the Sault-au-Récollet Church. The plaques commemorated the first mass held at Montreal, in 1615, and the martyrdom of the Récollet priest Nicolas Viel. In 1625, Hurons escorting Father Viel back to Quebec City killed him and his Huron companion Ahuntsic, tossing their bodies into the rapids that recall this memory in their name. In a strategy similar to that employed with the Cartier-Brébeuf monument, one plaque also supported the northern route thesis: "Here at the foot of the last rapid of the Rivière des Prairies on 2 October 1535, Jacques Cartier landed en route for Hochelaga."[23] This thesis, then, argued for the recombination of Cartier and Catholicism.

The thesis suffered a blow during the 1934 celebrations marking the quatercentennial of Cartier's first voyage. Although that voyage never reached Montreal, the city's new bridge across the St. Lawrence was rechristened as the Jacques Cartier Bridge that year. The pont du Havre, or Harbour Bridge, as it was initially called, was a project of the Montreal Harbour Commission; it spanned the river at Île Ste-Hélène where the St. Mary's current sped the river's course. Dreams of this second bridge across the St. Lawrence had been in the works since John Young headed the harbour commission in the 1870s. But not until 1924 did the commission finally secure support from the federal government through an act of Parliament.[24] Construction of the bridge began in 1925 and was completed in 1930 at a cost of $23 million. During construction, it was known as the South Shore Bridge but was officially named the Harbour Bridge when inaugurated in the spring of 1930. And, as the 1934 celebrations approached, Georges Pelletier of *Le Devoir* began a campaign to rename it, this time after the great explorer, even though a more appropriate commemorative date might have been the following year.[25] Pelletier's wish was granted through an Order-in-Council in the spring of 1934, but the official inauguration of the new name waited until the arrival of the Cartier celebration dignitaries in Montreal at the end of the summer.

On a Saturday afternoon, 1 September 1934, a crowd of several thousand gathered at the centre of the bridge to witness a formal ceremony unveiling a bust of Cartier and rededicating the bridge. The proceedings opened with the Canadian Grenadier Guards playing "O Canada," followed by a welcome speech given by the harbour commission president. He thanked the French government for having generously donated the sculpture as a physical legacy of its goodwill toward Canada, and he promised that the commission would cherish and care for the gift. Next, as the band played the "Marseillaise," the daughters of three of the French delegates in attendance crossed the roadway to release a silken French Tricolore and reveal the sculpture beneath. At that moment, a local troop of Boy Scouts released flocks of pigeons, dyed red, white, and blue for the occasion, into the air. The frightened and abused birds added an almost comical element to the proceedings, as they flew every which way through the crowd, seeking shelter from the strong winds whipping over the centre of the river. And the ceremony closed with the minister of marine, Alfred Duranleau, formally dedicating the bridge in the name of the Government of Canada, proclaiming that "from now on [it] will officially be known as the Jacques Cartier Bridge, and dedicated to the memory of the Discoverer of Canada." He wondered whether Cartier had grasped the future greatness of the "magnificent country" he discovered. Montreal was a Christian home and a centre of French thought in America, yes, but also "one of the most famous trade counters of the British Empire," one that welcomed the ships of all nations.[26] Once again Ottawa had reoriented Cartier's significance. His legacy could be celebrated by French and English, Catholic and Protestant alike. But even if this legacy could be shared, at least one newspaper perceived that the bridge fixed the memory of Cartier's route to Hochelaga. Commenting in advance of the ceremonies, the *Montreal Gazette* pointed out that "the very spot on which the cornerstone [of the bridge] is sitting" was that where Cartier landed.[27]

Beaugrand-Champagne continued to argue his theory into the 1940s, and he was not without supporters.[28] Proponents of the northern route thesis have included Victor Morin, Lionel Groulx, Gérard Malchelasse, and, more recently, Lucien Campeau. Opposition has come from anglophone scholars, such as William Douw Lighthall, Samuel E. Morison, and Bruce Trigger, or from federalist francophones such as Gustave Lanctôt and Marcel Trudel.[29] This southern landing thesis seems more plausible but does not resolve the question of the exact site of Hochelaga. Had Cartier taken the route described by Beaugrand-Champagne, following the Rivière des Prairies and scaling Mount Royal from the flat plain overlooking the eastern end of the island, he would surely have noticed the St. Lawrence. On the other hand, looking north from Mount Royal, one can easily miss the Rivière des Prairies. There is no indication anywhere that Cartier knew or guessed that Hochelaga was on an island. Yet, there are reasons to support Cartier's landing at the Lachine Rapids or the St. Mary's current. Regardless of where Cartier landed, his descriptions are vague enough to place Hochelaga on the north face of Mount Royal. The issue is not likely to be resolved; neither archaeological nor documentary evidence can produce a clear solution. Nevertheless, the naming of the Jacques Cartier Bridge, although not officially intended to resolve the issue, created a powerful marker in the popular mind that Cartier landed at the St. Mary's current.

Downriver, in the old capital, the provincial Commission des monuments historiques de la province de Québec (CMHQ) helped to preserve Cartier's legacy in Quebec City. Yet, if the federal HSMBC worked to secularize memories of Cartier, the CMHQ continued to connect them to the Catholic faith. It was created in 1922 as a result of growing anxiety among middle-class intellectuals concerning the destruction of the province's heritage. Its aim was neither wholly secular nor wholly religious. Its immediate catalyst was the 1921 sale of Louis-Joseph Papineau's mansion in Montebello and the open letter written by the granddaughter of François-Xavier Garneau to Premier Louis-Alexandre Taschereau condemning it. Pressure also came from an old guard of Quebec's heritage preservation movement, Superior Court justice Antoine-Aimé Bruneau. He likewise demanded legal protection for the province's historical treasures.[30] The resulting Bill 170, "An Act Respecting the Preservation of Monuments and Objects of Art Having an Historic or Artistic Interest," made Quebec the first Canadian province to take an active role in its public heritage: it created the CMHQ, which had the power to designate and mark historic sites throughout the province. CMHQ members included Montrealers Adélard Turgeon, Victor Morin, William Douw Lighthall, and E.-Z. Massicotte, as well as Quebec City's Pierre-Georges Roy. These men set right to work: their first order of business was to draw up an inventory of provincial historic sites, which was ready within a year and published as *Monuments commémoratifs*.[31] They then initiated a plaques program and the planning of ceremonies to honour historic anniversaries. In 1923, the CMHQ also undertook to lobby the provincial public works department to continue the Taché and Bourassa plan for a national pantheon on the facade of the Legislative Assembly.[32]

The province began work on this project during the mid-1920s, designing monuments to Cartier, Iberville, and Jolliet, but numerous problems complicated affairs. The unveiling at the Legislative Assembly was first scheduled for 17 September 1925, but work on the Jolliet statue was held up, and the ceremonies were delayed until the following summer. Also, no one was sure regarding where the figure of Cartier should stand. The design for his statue, entrusted to sculptor Georges Bareau, was an exact replica of the monument unveiled in Saint-Malo in 1905. A committee was struck to find an appropriate spot but could not reach consensus. Part of the problem was that Bareau's statue would not easily fit in the narrow niches of Taché's assembly building. Already in the 1920s, the original plan to place Cartier at the top of the central tower of the parliament building had either been forgotten or was simply recognized as inappropriate for a bicultural province. In the end, the CMHQ opted to donate the Cartier statue to the city of Quebec, which in turn decided to place it at Place Jacques-Cartier in the Faubourg Saint-Roch.[33]

The old Faubourg Saint-Roch, called the Quartier Saint-Roch by the 1920s, had a long association with the memory of Jacques Cartier. But, in contrast to the old walled city or the Grande Allée leading from its St. Louis Gate, this neighbourhood had not been frequented by tourists. One of Quebec City's oldest suburbs, Saint-Roch had developed at the end of the French regime but soon became a working-class district. Hemmed in by the cliffs of Cap Diamant, the St. Charles River, and the Jesuit estates, it was home to most of the city's wage earners and common labourers by midcentury. In the 1920s, it had not lost its working-class flavour – or its memories of Jacques Cartier. Near this industrial area, at least according to the accepted traditions, Cartier had wintered during his second voyage. The district spills into the Pointe-aux-Lièvres, the site of the short-lived 1835 cross, and is across the

St. Charles from the Cartier-Brébeuf monument. In 1848, the Marché Jacques-Cartier opened in the neighbourhood, which was also the end point of the procession that formed after Pierre-J.-O. Chauveau read his poem "Donnacona" during the 1889 Cartier-Brébeuf unveiling. Toward the end of the nineteenth century, as Quebec City grew, the district was divided into the Saint-Roch ward in the north and the Jacques-Cartier ward in the south. The district was a natural place to put the monument.

Inaugurated on 17 October 1926, the Saint-Roch monument represents an effort to maintain the combination of nationality and faith. By placing the monument in this working-class neighbourhood, the CMHQ was affirming the historical connection between the popular classes and a certain brand of nationalism. However, the unveiling was distinguished from those of the federal government by its deliberate combination of civil and religious authorities. At two o'clock in the afternoon, Monsignor Omer Cloutier, representing the archbishop of Quebec, met Lieutenant Governor Narcisse Pérodeau, the mayor, and the interim premier at the square known as Place Jacques-Cartier. Police officers formed an honour guard around the shrouded statue, although they were hardly needed to keep back the orderly crowd, which included the pupils of the city's schools. The children were a key component in these ceremonies, as speaker after speaker addressed his remarks to them or mentioned their presence. In them, the nation saw its future represented. Particularly noteworthy was Pierre-Georges Roy's speech. As representative of the CMHQ, he presented the statue to the city but took the time to "correct" an error in the historical record concerning the first mass held in Quebec. It greatly predated the commonly accepted year of 1617. Cartier had brought two priests with him, Roy proclaimed, and was too good a Catholic to have spent an entire winter without attending mass. Therefore, the first mass must have occurred during the winter of 1535.[34]

Meanwhile, local residents at the Île-aux-Coudres in Charlevoix County, some sixty miles east of Quebec City, were planning to commemorate a sixteenth-century mass that was supported by stronger evidence than was Roy's conjecture. Following a scheme initiated by the local parish priest, and pushed by Quebec City lawyer Georges Bellerive, the HSMBC involved itself in this, paying homage to the Catholic memory of Cartier. At a three-hour ceremony on a rainy Sunday, a large crowd listened to speakers dedicating a stone cross and plaque commemorating the first mass celebrated in Canada. This was a somewhat reluctant federal participation in the linking of Cartier with Catholicism. In connection with this project, Bellerive had begun prodding Aegidius Fauteux, the Quebec member of the HSMBC, as early as 1924. However, a few years and the appointment of a favourable Quebec representative were required before the HSMBC acted on the proposal. Even then, it exhibited some reluctance to erect a specifically confessional national monument. Some board members proposed that the plaque refer to James Wolfe's passage by the island on his 1759 approach to Quebec City.[35] After local protests, Bellerive himself was permitted to draft a text for the plaque, and, as the HSMBC had earlier acquiesced to a cross at Port Dover to commemorate Dollier de Casson and Jolliet's discovery of Lake Erie, he was also able to convince the board to accept this form of monument. Even when the HSMBC discovered that Cartier had not erected a cross at this site, a fact that might have killed the proposal, the cross was retained.[36]

Some of the most important people in Quebec journeyed to the Île-aux-Coudres, or at least sent their proxies, for the 23 September 1928 unveiling. In attendance was His Eminence the archbishop of Quebec; C.J. Magnan represented Premier Taschereau; Solicitor General Lucien Cannon stood in for Ernest Lapointe, one of Quebec's most powerful politicians; and Pamphile Demers represented the HSMBC. Federal representation, although present, was distinctly French and Catholic. Moreover, the arrival of the archbishop on the *Lady Grey* ensured that, for the first time since the Montreal Eucharistic Congress nearly two decades earlier, the colours of the Holy See flew from the masts of a Canadian government ship. Watched over by papal Zouaves who had braved the heavy rain that let up only as the ceremonies began, His Eminence took his place of honour in the first row. Bellerive himself opened the dedication with a promise to publish an account of the day's events and gracefully thanked the HSMBC. Demers then rose to explain the historical message of the plaque. Its text bore only a slight resemblance to Bellerive's earlier draft: "On the 6th September, 1535, Jacques Cartier anchored his three ships near this place, explored the island, and named it Île-aux-Coudres. Next day, he departed after hearing the mass. This is the first recorded Christian service on Canadian soil."

With this text, the HSMBC clearly attempted to dodge the thorny issue of connecting itself too closely to Catholic nationalism in Quebec. The plaque broadened the meaning of the commemoration to the initiation of Christian, not exclusively Catholic, worship in Canada. This was something that, presumably, all Canadians could embrace.[37] However, this broader message was upstaged by the overt Catholicism of the ceremony. In his speech, the archbishop noted that taking possession of Canada for God was the higher significance of Cartier's Gaspé cross and his mass at Île-aux-Coudres a year later. Solicitor General Lucien Cannon went further, claiming that "we are Catholic and French as Cartier had wanted, as he had hoped ... It is in staying Catholic and French that we will be true Canadians."[38] Clearly, more than one nationalism was alive at the ceremony and willing to make use of Cartier's memory. This clash, however blunted, between Catholic Quebec nationalism and a non-denominational Canadian counterpart was more pronounced for federal involvement. The effort to expand the meaning of Cartier to fit a pan-Canadian national identity exposed the weakness of using one nationalism's symbols to achieve the ends of another.

The First Voyage
As early as 1921, an American museum curator, John M. Clarke, urged the
erection of a national monument to commemorate the landing in which
Cartier took possession of Canada in the name of the French king. Clarke's
interest in Cartier stemmed from summers spent in Gaspé. There, in 1908,
he had discovered a wooden medallion that, because it featured the face of
a sea captain and the initials "J.C.," he took to be a depiction of Jacques
Cartier.[39] Clarke's pleas initially went unanswered. The HSMBC contemplated
installing a plaque honouring Cartier's first landing at Gaspé, which was to
be inaugurated in 1925 or 1926, but never followed through.[40] But in 1930,
more powerful voices urged building a monument to celebrate the upcoming
quatercentennial of the discovery of Canada. Rodolphe Lemieux, the long-
serving Speaker of the House of Commons and MP for Gaspé, took up the
cause in 1929. At the same time, the bishop of Gaspé, Monsignor F.-X. Ross,
organized a committee in his diocese to raise a monument and build a commemorative cathedral in time for the quatercentennial.[41] The committee
was chaired by Quebec's well-known conservative historian Thomas Chapais.[42] Ross held to a traditional view of the French Canadian nation as a
rural, agrarian, and Catholic people clinging by divine vocation to a time-
honoured lifestyle. During his tenure, the diocese embarked on a series of
nationalist, corporatist, and cooperative strategies typical of this brand of
nationalism, such as encouraging the caisses populaires. Given the history
of Cartier's place in this nationalism, it is perhaps not surprising that the
diocesan seal included a likeness of Jacques Cartier.[43]

That same year, the abbé Lionel Groulx took a public stance on the issue
in the pages of *Le Devoir*. Groulx proclaimed the necessity that this monument not be simply a local initiative, but "this monument must be the
genuine work of a national subscription, for we need a grand act of faith
and national gratitude." Groulx's position was twofold. First, Cartier represented the opening of Canadian history, the original official contact between
Canada and Europe and the moment at which Canada became a French
country. This national affirmation was crucial because it would help assure
French Canada's traditional rights: "Our country is invaded by all the races
of the world, who do not always have the time to learn our history, who
have too much inclination to misunderstand or underestimate our past, our
privileges, and our rights. Again among the newly arrived, and in spite of
painful experience, we must not fail to make plain our constitutional and
political rights."[44]

Although Groulx played to the political and constitutional significance
of Cartier, he did not ignore the traditionally held religious import of the
arrival of "un thaumaturge fameux." Nor was he content with a proposal
for just one Cartier cross. He imagined the province as a vast sea of them,
symbolically united in cruciform commemoration of its French and Catholic

roots. At a congress of school inspectors for the provincial Department of Public Instruction, he urged every school to put up a commemorative cross. Estimating costs at thirty dollars per cross, the department promptly distributed plans as well as explanations of the symbols involved.[45] The ambition was to erect a cross for every village in Quebec, although one scholar suggests that they were raised in towns that did not already have a wayside cross. The wayside, or roadside, cross was a traditional symbol of Catholic piety in the Quebec countryside. Privately raised, these wooden crosses dotted the province, often accompanied by symbols representing Christ's Passion. Local residents no doubt preferred the spontaneity of their own wayside crosses, but Groulx was not the only enthusiast for this idea. Maurice Brodeur, a heraldist who designed a "national" flag in honour of the Cartier celebrations, organized the Société nationale Jacques-Cartier to take up the cause. Brodeur later borrowed elements from his Cartier flag, as well as from the Carrignan-Sacré-Coeur flag, when he developed the modern flag of Quebec.[46] Indeed, when the Quebec flag was unveiled to the public in 1948, Paul Beaulieu, Duplessis' minister of industry and commerce, commented that it recalled Cartier's act of planting a cross at Gaspé.[47]

Rodolphe Lemieux, appointed to the Senate in 1930, followed Ross and Groulx in insisting that the celebration should be religious because, borrowing from earlier beliefs, he saw Cartier as the first herald of the teachings of Christianity in Canada. Moreover, Cartier's own narrative gave Lemieux "ample evidence of his profound spirituality and his earnest desire to convert the pagan Indians."[48] Obviously, such an emphasis could not unite all Canadians. Nevertheless, interest was not confined to Quebec. In Ontario, for example, Victor Barrette, the children's page editor of the French-language newspaper *Le Droit* (under the pseudonym l'Oncle Jean), launched his own campaign to raise Cartier crosses at schools across Canada's francophone regions.

While this was going on, the federal government, through the offices of the HSMBC, was still contemplating installing a monument somewhere as a commemoration of the discovery of Canada. It had even decided to raise a cross at Gaspé, deviating considerably from its standard cairn and plaque. However, this apparent conformity of plans does not imply a broad consensus on the significance of Cartier in Canadian history. The board chose a cross mostly because it had already helped raise one to honour Cartier's visit to Île-aux-Coudres. That cross was Bellerive's initiative. Cruciform commemoration of Cartier, in mimicry of Cartier's own acts, emerged from the francophone community of Quebec. For the board, the Île-aux-Coudres site was of lesser historical significance than that at Gaspé, and therefore the more important locus of Canada's discovery needed to surpass it.

Once again the board's desire to situate its monuments near the "exact" spot of the event to be commemorated posed problems. This was often the case, but it was particularly so with the Cartier voyages. Not only did Cartier's accounts contain few clues regarding specific locations, but the increased interest in his voyages had given rise to a considerable debate on the subject by the 1930s. This dispute involved some of the most important writers on Canada's early history. The board found itself faced with at least five potential sites, all in or near the entrance to Gaspé harbour: Arnold's Bluff, O'Hara's Point, York Beach, Sandy Beach, and the Gaspé Peninsula (or Pénouille), as well as a last-minute suggestion of Jacques Cartier Point. It was later determined that Jacques Cartier Point was a local name for Arnold's Bluff.[49] That location had the support of Benjamin Sulte. Father Pacifique (Henri Buisson d'Valigny), a Gaspésian priest and local historian, argued for York Beach, whereas Henry Percival Biggar and Marius Barbeau favoured the peninsula. Barbeau (relying on the belief that the Stadaconans were Iroquoian) pointed out that the Iroquois camped only on sand, which existed at O'Hara's Point and the peninsula. However, the approach to O'Hara's Point was through treacherous rocks, which would certainly have dissuaded an experienced mariner such as Cartier.[50] The sole realistic site, then, was the peninsula. W.F. Ganong rejected Barbeau's argument: due to modern improvements to accommodate larger vessels, the peninsula did lie within the boundaries of Gaspé harbour, but his reading of old maps had suggested that such was not the case during the sixteenth century. Ganong had conducted the most detailed surveys of Cartier's landing site and came to accept O'Hara's Point as the most likely spot because it was a high beach of the kind that Native peoples favoured for their seaside encampments. Surely, he concluded, Cartier would have landed where the people were. Lying across from O'Hara's Point, McConnell's Point (Arnold's Bluff) was an abrupt cliff, which would have been densely wooded and therefore unattractive to Cartier.[51] For its part in the investigation, the HSMBC dispatched its latest Quebec representative, Judge Edouard Surveyer, to Gaspé to inspect the options and report back. Surveyer grumbled about the task, his most serious complaint being that the train to Gaspé lacked a buffet car, but nevertheless pressed on to the tiny seaside village. After interviewing local authorities, he determined that Cartier had landed at O'Hara's Point, conveniently next to the parish church. This claim rested on F.J. Richmond's presentation to the 1922 annual meeting of the Canadian Historical Association. Richmond's claim to expertise stemmed mostly from being among the oldest inhabitants of the village, and he founded his research on John M. Clarke's interviews with a local sea captain. In other words, his argument was almost pure speculation, even if Ganong reached the same conclusions.[52] However, the site was also well served by a good road and owned by Bishop Ross, who was quite favourably disposed to leasing a plot for a federal monument. It was a natural, and possibly historically accurate, fit.

Meanwhile, another dispute welled up within the board's ranks to threaten the fragile consensus. This focused on the historical meaning of Cartier's cross, and it provides greater insight into the thinking of non-Quebecers on the question of Jacques Cartier. At its annual meeting in 1933, the board had opted for a simple inscription: "In commemoration of the Four hundredth Anniversary of the landing of Jacques Cartier at the entrance to this harbour on 24th July, 1534." However, unhappy with this sterile interpretation of the discovery of Canada, Surveyer asked Thomas Chapais to draft another version. Chapais added the key phrase "and of his taking possession of Canada." The original wording had been straightforward enough. No one disputed Cartier's arrival at Gaspé in 1534, and the cross fit both the historical events and the precedent of commemoration set by the board at Île-aux-Coudres. But Chapais had drawn from an established consensus among francophones that Cartier had taken possession of Canada for France at Gaspé. Not all anglophones shared this view.

Almost immediately, two board members complained. D.C. Harvey and J.C. Webster protested that Cartier had made no such claim but had explained away his cross as a navigational beacon. The inclusion of the phrase "Vive le roi" on Cartier's cross, they insisted, could not be seen as an indication of taking possession.[53] Harvey and Webster were not simply nitpicking: this was a substantial dispute that questioned the fundamental meaning of Cartier's place in Canadian history. And some scholarly disagreement had developed over the meaning of Cartier's Gaspé cross. Although francophone writers usually accepted the cross as a claim of possession, some anglophone authors were less certain. Justin Winsor dated Cartier's claim of possession from a 3 May 1536 cross-raising at his St. Croix fort, making it one of the last acts he performed before leaving Canada during his second voyage. Arthur Doughty made the same assertions. J.P. Baxter saw through Cartier's explanation to Donnacona, but stated that both the Gaspé and St. Croix crosses constituted a claim of possession.[54]

The difficulty in ascertaining Cartier's intentions at Gaspé is a direct result of the ambiguity in the *Relations*. The Gaspé cross was not the first that Cartier raised on his voyages, but it was the one that the accounts describe in greatest detail. Unlike an earlier cross erected in June at St. Sevran harbour on the north shore of the Gulf of St. Lawrence, the Gaspé cross was raised during a formal ceremony. Moreover, though the former was a simple cross, the latter was decorated with the arms of France and engraved with the words "Vive le Roy de France." This would seem to suggest that Cartier attached some importance to it. The account mentions two purposes for the cross. First, it served a religious function. However, as Cartier and his men prepared to depart, Donnacona harangued them about the cross standing on the shore. At this point, Cartier dismissed it as a navigational beacon, its second purpose, and the account makes no declarations about possession of territory.[55]

Patricia Seed has examined European claims of possession in the New World, and her work sheds some light on Cartier's actions. She comments on the intricacy of sixteenth-century French claims of possession, which drew on a complex understanding of French civic and religious ceremonies. New World rituals of possession were usually carefully planned, subtle occurrences bound by certain understandings and rules, even if the indigenous population was kept in the dark regarding them. Simply planting a cross was not enough. And the French did not behave as though the existence of a cross was sufficient to mark a claim. The planting and blessing of the cross was part of a larger ceremony in which it was also necessary to communicate the meaning to Native peoples and gain their "consent." The French were somewhat unique among European nations in this regard. The English, by contrast, simply presumed that occupying the land was enough to assure their claims. Given Donnacona's reaction to the Gaspé cross, Cartier must have known that he had failed to gain consent, and so his explanation might in fact have been truthful, to an extent. He then negotiated that consent by presenting Donnacona with a series of gifts, construing Donnacona's acceptance of them as acquiescence. Certainly, there was an arrogance in such an interpretation. Likewise, in 1503, Binot Poulmier de Gonneville perceived "consent" in the hand gestures of Brazilian Indians.[56] And certainly, Donnacona read gift giving according to his own cultural understandings of mutual exchange and alliance. Nevertheless, that Cartier felt the need to gain consent suggests that he believed the cross alone had not established possession, but that he had secured it before he left for France with Donnacona's sons. Back in 1934, E.A. Cruikshank dismissed the whole question as ludicrous because even the "untutored Indian" Donnacona recognized Cartier's intent. However, he also felt that the affair embarrassed the board and could not be resolved without initiating a new dispute.[57] Cruikshank's premonition proved accurate.

Working alongside the federal board was a political committee headed by Senators C.P. Beaubien and Raoul Dandurand. This committee met irregularly and, at least as far as the HSMBC could ascertain, did very little. However, from a larger perspective, this National Committee (sometimes styled the Quebec Committee by its detractors) served as a liaison between the Canadian planners and the French Comité France-Amérique, a quasi-governmental goodwill committee that promoted French cultural ties with Canada. In the fall of 1933, Dandurand travelled to France where he met a group of French dignitaries who planned to visit Canada the following summer. Convinced that this occasion could easily become an important international event, he returned to Canada and immediately urged Ottawa to build a monument worthy of international attention and the transatlantic bond.[58]

Indeed, promoting bonds between France and Canada became an important theme in the celebrations that followed, with the first Cartier commemorations of 1934 being held in France during the summer. These opened
with a concert of French Canadian folk songs performed at the Sorbonne in
May, slightly in advance of a delegation of Canadians (including Dandurand),
who arrived a few days later.[59] In honour of their arrival, French and colonial
radio services broadcast a lecture by Philippe Roy, the Canadian envoy in
Paris, on Canada's history and recent development. The next day, after high
mass at Notre-Dame de Paris, Roy hosted a Dominion Day celebration for
eight hundred guests at the Canadian legation. The French historian and
diplomat (and founder of the Comité France-Amérique) Gabriel Hanotaux
set the tone for this event and those to come with his speech. After repeating
the claim that Cartier had inspired Rabelais, Hanotaux drew connections
between Cartier's discoveries and the later colonial expansion of France, and
even of Britain. French Canadians, then, were a product of the union of the
two great European races – French and British – in Confederation and a
continuation of the spirit of French civilization in North America.[60] Later
that evening, the French government put on an open-air concert at the Tuil-
leries Gardens, where the Canadian troupe l'Alouette interpreted Canadian
folk songs. On 2 July, a bust of Cartier, a gift from the Comité France-
Amérique to the city of Paris, was unveiled at Place du Canada in the Eighth
Arrondissement. More luncheons and concerts followed, after which the
Canadian delegation departed for a visit to Saint-Malo to lay wreaths at the
foot of the 1905 Cartier monument before returning to Canada.[61]

Meanwhile, in Canada, the HSMBC had planned for a fifteen-foot cross,
but Dandurand wanted to double its height. He pressed the issue throughout
the winter, meeting with federal ministers, civil servants, newspaper repor-
ters, and especially lobbying Judge Surveyer, the Quebec member of the
HSMBC. Surveyer's correspondence with Harkin became increasingly tense
in the new year. On 4 January 1934, he complained that a thirty-foot cross
would be too large for the selected site. Dandurand had criticized the site as
well, but Surveyer begged Harkin to support his claim that the plans were
already made, the land had been deeded, and nothing could be changed.[62]
A furious round of missives flew between the various members of the board,
and eventually Surveyer won his point. The smaller cross was already under
construction, the site had been chosen, and there just was not enough money
to start over again. Dandurand, however, was undaunted. The *Montreal
Gazette* reported that he had won an additional $5,000 from Ottawa. Although
the *Gazette* article was premature, Harkin later learned that the minister of
the interior, agreeing that the cross was too small, had approved spending
additional money on a larger one.[63]

With only a few months to go before the planned ceremonies, the board
had to abandon the cross it had already constructed and start over with a

larger one. In some ways, this saved it from embarrassment, for it had some-how produced a Celtic cross, which, Prime Minister R.B. Bennett pointed out to Harkin in a phone call, was historically inaccurate. Acting on the advice of the National Committee, Bennett suggested a thirty-foot cross cut from a single block of stone.[64] If Bennett's direct involvement in the minute details of this project seems surprising, it was part of a larger pattern in his government. Bennett was notorious for acting alone on major issues, such as his New Deal broadcasts in January 1935. Secretary of State Charles Cahan later cited the Cartier celebrations as a specific example of Bennett's obses-sion with control.[65] Although, with the prime minister's backing, funding was no longer an issue, Bennett's massive stone cross posed its own problems. Time was obviously required for its creation, and the board was running out of time. There was also the question of what to do with the original fifteen-foot cross. But D.C. Harvey had some more biting concerns: "In regard to Québec's passion for identical measurements of Cartier's cross, I am wonder-ing if historical exactitude would not suggest a pole instead of a granite shaft, particularly in view of the difficulty of having such huge arms of granite suspended as a perpetual warning to tourists not to walk beneath them."[66]

Nonetheless, the prime minister wanted a thirty-foot, single-piece granite cross, and that was that. But the forty-six-ton object cost $6,935, nearly $2,000 over budget. And it could not be transported from Quebec City to Gaspé by train, because the local railway bridges could never handle its weight. It had to be floated by barge, further slowing the project. Still, it was standing in place by 15 August, nine days before the big event.[67]

However, the headaches were not over. In the spring of 1934, Peter John Veniot (Pierre-Jean Vigneau), a New Brunswick Member of Parliament, pointed out in the House of Commons that Cartier's first landfall was at the entrance to Bathurst Harbour in the Baie des Chaleurs.[68] Veniot was frustrated that Bathurst would receive none of the $100,000 he claimed the federal government had allotted to the festival.[69] Another controversy involved the commemorative stamps issued by the post office in 1934. First, the postmaster was called upon to defend the decision to commemorate Cartier rather than the anniversary of the founding of New Brunswick. The explanation was that Cartier's landing was a national anniversary and that the post office had followed its policy of not celebrating individual provinces.[70] Clearly, Ottawa's interpretation was that Cartier was the founder of Canada. Perhaps more worrying was the accusation that the stamps contained historical inaccur-acies, which was levelled by abbé Victor Tremblay, an amateur Cartier en-thusiast. He had been upset about a written description of a stamp's depiction of Cartier, which portrayed him as excited and almost surprised to see land. Repeating Hiram Stephens' comparison to Columbus, Tremblay pointed out that Cartier, unlike Columbus, expected to find land exactly where he found it.[71] Gustave Lanctôt, a professional historian from the Dominion Archives, was called upon to defuse the situation, and once Tremblay saw the stamp itself, he confessed that it was not as bad as he had feared.[72] Yet these annoyances continued to plague the celebrations.

About the time that Dandurand started to pester Surveyer and Harkin concerning the size of the Gaspé cross, another board member, D.C. Harvey, came under increasing pressure from his part of the country to take up the cause of commemorating Cartier's brief landing on western Prince Edward Island in early July 1534. The idea especially appealed to another Maritimer, J.C. Webster, who saw no good reason why "all the honours should go to Québec." Indeed, he felt that Cartier's real "discovery of Canada" had actually occurred at PEI as it was there that he first landed on what would become Canadian soil.[73] H.R. Stewart, the province's deputy secretary, concurred. He felt that, because Cartier had made the "true discovery" of Canada at PEI, holding a ceremony when the French delegation sailed past the island was crucial.[74] Happily, the board seemed to have found a place for its extra cross. Although Harvey believed that PEI had "no claim" for a cross, Harkin promptly offered the original fifteen-footer to its premier. The offer was flatly rejected.[75] The main reason for this was that, as Harvey pointed out, Cartier had not raised one himself when he landed briefly on the island. Therefore, it was historically inaccurate. But, more importantly, the Island Committee (as Webster, Harvey, and the local authorities came to be known) felt that it was staking a claim of priority over Quebec. A smaller cross would imply inferiority. Their assertion of precedence was evident in their enthusiasm for observing that Cartier had visited the Northumberland Strait before heading up to Gaspé. Being first was important to the Island Committee because it lent the right of precedence and a sense of legitimacy to its claim to the Cartier celebrations.[76] It seems to appear in the decision to use, not a modern translation of Cartier, but the Richard Hakluyt 1598 translation in the text of the explanatory plaque erected by the HSMBC in Charlottetown. In some ill-defined way, Hakluyt lent historical authenticity to the claim. After all, Faribault had simply translated the Hakluyt version back to French when he published his edition in 1843. Use of the Hakluyt translation suggested that French ignorance of Cartier had been overcome by English scholarship. Webster complained that members of the National Committee – especially Senators Dandurand and Beaubien – routinely slighted the Island Committee and the historical importance of Prince Edward Island.

Another complicating factor at the 1934 celebrations was the emphasis placed on attracting tourists, a major concern during the 1930s. Indeed, some predicted that the Gaspé festivities could surpass even the 1908 Quebec City tercentenary as a tourist draw. In 1929, tourism added some $300 million to Canada's gross national product, but that figure had slumped to a mere $117 million at the depths of the Great Depression in 1933. Although Michael Dawson has suggested that tourism outperformed other Canadian industries during the depression, this may have been due to the state's increased interest in that decade.[77] For instance, in 1934, the Senate launched a special committee to inquire into what could be done to promote visits to Canada. Chaired by Senator W.H. Dennis of Nova Scotia, the committee recommended a massive and aggressive promotional campaign to draw attention to Canada's numerous attractions.[78] Although the committee met in May 1934, when plans for the Cartier quatercentenary were already advanced, the prospects of using such events to "pep up" Canada's image abroad figured prominently in its vision. The testimony of W.H. Van Allen, the assistant to the director of publicity in the federal Department of Trade and Commerce, produced an exchange between Ontario's Senator Horatio Hocken and Senator Creelman MacArthur of PEI. The latter suggested that though the Chicago World's Fair would probably keep many Americans in the US, the Cartier celebrations could be expected to showcase Gaspé and thus prompt many from Great Britain and France to take advantage of the depression's low steamship rates. Picking up the possibility of using Cartier as a lure, Hocken suggested striking a deal with the Radio Commission for a live broadcast for the thousands outside Quebec who might be interested in him. To this, MacArthur hastened to add that the "French of Louisiana" might also pay attention.[79] The following week, Hocken pursued his radio idea with Theodore Morgan of the Canadian Association of Tourist Bureaus. "Would you focus on this summer's Cartier celebrations?" he asked when Morgan suggested that the government launch an advertising campaign, only to be disappointed with Morgan's dismissive reply: federal advertising should not concentrate on such "passing events."[80] Nonetheless, tourist advertising was a concern during the planning and unveiling of the Cartier monuments of 1934. H.R. Stewart had insisted that the PEI monument be at Charlottetown, miles from any probable historical landing, because it had to be close to tourist traffic. Another argument in favour of the Hakluyt translation was that "the quaintness of the wording will catch the interest of visitors."[81] The finished plaque included the following brief quotation from Hakluyt: "All the said land is low and plaine, and the fairest that may possibly be seene, full of goodly medowes and trees." And indeed, the unveiling ceremonies were enormously popular with the travelling public. Gaspé was expected to be mobbed, as newspapers reported heavy ship, rail, and road traffic, and it was virtually impossible to find a room at any Charlottetown inn by August 1934.[82]

The tourist potential of Cartier was quite significant, but his were not the only festivities designed to lure the travelling public off the beaten track in 1934. Gaspé competed with tourist festivals both major and minor. The Century of Progress exhibition commemorating the centennial of the incorporation of Chicago opened in 1933 but, due to popular demand, was reopened from May to October 1934. In Canada, the birth of the Dionne quintuplets catapulted Corbeil, Ontario, into the international spotlight. In addition, Toronto feted the centennial of its own incorporation with a year of pageants, parades, concerts, and picnics. But Toronto also demonstrated the popular appeal of Cartier, whose landing at Gaspé featured as the first act of a four-act pageant at the Canadian National Exhibition, which was attended by many of the delegates who also witnessed the Gaspé celebrations.[83] Certainly, this honoured the important guests as much as it did the memory of Jacques Cartier. Still, the inclusion of Cartier at the pageant spoke to the renewed popularity of the explorer, even among those who could not attend the official ceremonies. Elsewhere, other spontaneous efforts were made to commemorate Cartier's discoveries. Boy Scouts in Harrington Harbour, Quebec, raised their own Cartier memorial. In North Bay, Ontario, a small monument was erected by the Cercle canadien-français and the Fédération des femmes canadiennes-françaises, and Cartier figured prominently in the city's Old Home Week the following year.[84] Local newspapers across Canada commented on the plans. For instance, the *Ottawa Journal* suggested having the British air fleet retrace Cartier's route from the air as part of the ceremonies, although, due to the limits of 1930s airplane technology, this would require the Royal Navy to transport the planes across the Atlantic to start their journey at Newfoundland.[85] The *Brockville Recorder and Times* erroneously informed its readers that the province of Quebec planned to celebrate the quatercentenary of the first attempt to colonize Canada. Agreeing with the *Brantford Expositor*, the *Recorder and Times* asserted that Cartier should not be dismissed as a French Canadian figure but embraced as the father of "our" country.[86] But once again, the realities of the economic recession quickly scuttled these ambitious plans. Although it did not open until 1935, the New York Public Library also marked "the discovery of the St. Lawrence" with an exhibition of its collections.[87] Cartier's appeal, though clearly still connected to French Canadian nationalism, was also broader in scope.

This popularity carried over into an explosion of song and literature focusing on Cartier. Mary Travers, one of Quebec's most popular folk singers, wrote "La Gaspésienne pure laine" to honour not only Cartier himself but Gaspé's honouring of Cartier:

> Oui tous les pays du monde
> Était tous réprésentés
> Pour fêter nos joies profondes
> l'arrivée de Jacques Cartier.

Reiterating the sentiments expressed at Île-aux-Coudres, as well as those of others in 1934, Travers sang of her pride in her French language and culture:

C'est ici que sur nos côtes
Jacques Cartier planta la croix
France ta langue est le nôtre
On la parle comme autrefois

Si je la chante à ma façon
J'suis Gaspésienne et pis j'ai ça d'bon.[88]

Also known as La Bolduc, Travers sang for an audience of everyday French Canadians. Her record sales demonstrate the popularity of her work, but nothing indicates that this particular song gained any special notoriety. Most probably, she retired it once it was no longer topical. Between 1932 and 1935, La Bolduc focused on her touring review show and made no recordings. "La Gaspésienne pure laine" was recorded on the Starr Records label a year after the Cartier quatercentenary.[89] Nevertheless, La Bolduc was not alone in capitalizing on interest in the 1934 celebrations. In addition to the numerous scholarly and journalistic articles and souvenir brochures, no fewer than fifteen books about Cartier appeared in 1934 alone. But publishers anticipated the events and began to release works in advance of them. In 1931, Charles de La Roncière, a well-known authority on the French navy, published *Jacques Cartier et la découverte de la Nouvelle France* for the French Colonial Exhibition at Vincennes.[90] Riddled with nineteenth-century errors, La Roncière's account might have benefited from reference to N.-E. Dionne's 1889 study, which was reprinted in 1933 and again in 1934. In 1934, Marius Barbeau published *La merveilleuse aventure de Jacques Cartier,* devoting nearly half its space to his theories about Cartier and Rabelais. Camille Pouliot released *La grande aventure de Jacques Cartier.* Abbé Pouliot reprinted the *Relations* of the first two voyages, bound together with his "Glanures gaspésiennes," a few poems, and accounts of John Clarke's medallion, the major sites of Gaspé, and the coming of the Catholic Church to the Gaspé region. C.-E. Roy and Lucien Brault depicted Cartier as a lay propagandist of Catholicism.[91] Adélard Desrosiers, the principal of the École normale Jacques-Cartier, followed Cartier's voyages in his own words in *Notre Jacques Cartier.* Desrosiers' version of history came almost entirely from his own imagination, but it did indicate a claim of possession suggestive of the older French Canadian nationalism. Cartier's three voyages and two years of colonization, Desrosiers argued, secured French rights in North America that not even the powerful Spanish Empire dared challenge. France's history in North America, then, descended via the inheritance from Jacques Cartier and reinforced him as the discoverer and founder of "our" (meaning French Canadian) country.[92]

Most of the Cartier works timed for 1934 were in French. However, anglophone authors also released commemorative works. A collection of poems by Sherman Swift, with prose interpretations by T.G. Marquis, appeared under the title of *The Voyages of Jacques Cartier in Prose and Verse*. Theirs was a typical popular Cartier for anglophone Canadians. He was Catholic but not too Catholic; he was devout but independent and secular. And they dwelt on the second voyage's attack of scurvy and Cartier's material successes.[93] At the 1934 meeting of the Royal Society of Canada, English and French authors read papers dealing with specific details of Cartier's voyages. And Blanche McLeod Lewis followed Cartier's itinerary in the pages of the *Canadian Geographical Journal* for potential English Canadian travellers in the spring of 1934.[94] Still, of the twenty-nine 1934 publications mentioned in the *Canadian Historical Review*'s regular lists of recent works relating to Canada, twenty-four were written in French. Probably the most enduring of these efforts was Lionel Groulx's *La découverte du Canada: Jacques Cartier*. Although Groulx denied timing the publication of this work to coincide with the 1934 celebrations, both the coincidence of dates and his early involvement in pushing for a commemorative festival suggest otherwise.[95] Situating Cartier's exploits in the historical context of European expansion and discovery in the New World – indeed, the discussion of Cartier represented about one-third of the full text – Groulx offered the most sophisticated account of the Malouin explorer to date.

Gaspé, 1934

On 24 August, the first of a series of "big days" arrived. The packet boat *Champlain* landed at Charlottetown where a distinguished French delegation was greeted by Senator Beaubien and ushered to Province House for the unveiling of the cairn bearing the board's plaques recounting Cartier's arrival at PEI. The unveiling showcased the rhetoric of racial fusion that Cartier represented in official Canadian programs. Much as the governor general had for the 1908 Quebec City tercentenary, Ottawa continued to promote an idea of race fusion that was incompatible with French Canadian ideas of identity. The federal finance minister E.N. Rhodes and Premier J.P. MacMillan emphasized the lessons of Canada's past: that two peoples had come together to work in peace to build a new nation. Of course, Canadian politicians were not unique in ignoring the roles of Native peoples in this crucial moment in Canadian history. But, speaking for the French delegation, Henry Bordeaux of the Académie française hinted that France recognized a broader diplomatic meaning behind the summer's commemorations: "We find ourselves ... on Canadian soil but it is not in fact a foreign soil ... We have found descendents of many former families of Europe, among whom many are French." These old families spoke French, "the language of liberty," a concept that Bordeaux developed by remarking that the deeper ties of blood between France and Canada were remembered in Canadian war graves on the battlefields of the western front.[96] Following Bordeaux's speech, the lieutenant governor of Prince Edward Island unveiled the cairn, and the band played

"God Save the King" and the "Marseillaise." The pattern established in the island ceremony repeated itself the next day in Gaspé. For the HSMBC, Cartier represented the European discovery of Canada. For many French Canadians, he symbolized the founding of their people. One newspaper proclaimed that "l'hommage à Cartier fut aussi un hommage au Canada français."[97] For some Canadians, both anglophone and francophone, the veneration of Cartier signified the fusion of Canada's peoples. But for the French dignitaries, and possibly for some astute Canadian politicians, Cartier denoted the Anglo-French alliance. The French delegation had requested that the Charlottetown cairn be draped in the Union Jack and the Tricolore, much to the dismay of the historically minded HSMBC.[98] The Cartier celebrations, then, were part of a line of tributes in Canada and Europe, including the Vimy Ridge memorial, Montreal's statue of Jean Vauquelin, and a Nova Scotian commemoration of the Duc d'Anville, that diplomats employed to keep these two major powers on friendly terms.[99]

Charlottetown was but a prelude to the main festival at Gaspé on 25 August. The *Champlain* arrived in the harbour amid a wondrous salute of seventy fishing boats decked out in flags bearing sixteenth-century Breton and Norman arms. These little vessels had come from far and wide, at their own expense, to acknowledge the dignitaries, and no doubt their crews helped swell the five thousand that gathered that sunny Saturday afternoon on a hill overlooking the harbour. The town was suitably decorated with triumphal arches and flowers, creating a celebratory landscape that assailed the senses. The evening held the prospect of fireworks over the bay, building illuminations, concerts, and feasts. But the focus of the day was the stone cross high above the waterfront. The unveiling ceremony was a thing of legend before it had even begun. As a fitting tribute, the newspapers reported, the thirty-foot cross had been cut from stone sent to Canada from Saint-Malo, Cartier's birthplace. The rumour was untrue, but this bit of popular myth making was an appropriate opening to the quest for symbolism that appeared in the dignitaries' speeches.[100] Quebec's lieutenant governor, E.-L. Patenaude, instigated the discourse, speaking of how the French and English peoples had come together in Canada through a process that evolved from discovery and battle to commerce and art. Speaking directly to English, French, and American visitors, he reminded them that, like their own people, Canadians had sacrificed their young men and resources on the battlefields of Europe. Canada's peaceful development had been interrupted by the Old World, and so it was fitting that the representatives of that world come together to pay homage to the man who had founded this New World of peace. Next, Prime Minister Bennett took the podium and (in English, as *La Presse* noted) repeated the familiar story in which Canada's two founding peoples learned to honour their combined past. The Sulpician priest Pierre Boissard echoed the rhetoric of racial merger: "Cartier's sacrifice was then

Figure 6   The Cartier cross at Gaspé in 2006. It is now located at a modern
cathedral built in the late 1960s. *Photo by the author*

fruitful, thanks to two great peoples who founded and grew a powerful race
with which we will always remain united, the Canadian nation, which remains among the most solid boulevards of Christian civilization."[101]

Meanwhile, the leader of the French delegation, Pierre-Etienne Flandin,
reminded everyone that Cartier symbolized the common past and especially
common sacrifices. The official souvenir book of the French delegation

echoes this effort at instilling a common purpose and sense of common destiny. It remarked that heaven itself confirmed as much with a rainbow linking France and Canada: "The Canadian miracle is thus a French miracle. The day when we inaugurated the Jacques Cartier Bridge at Montreal, at the end of the day, a rainbow, its first arch appearing to rise from the very bank of the St. Lawrence, crossed space, seemed to be lost there, and no one knew where rested the second pillar of this immense vault launched across the sky and the sea. There is no doubt now: the second pillar was planted in France."[102]

As at Charlottetown, Canadian official memories stressed the fusion of Canada's two peoples. France used the same occasion to link Canada to itself and tried to transform the Cartier cross into a surrogate war memorial. The Comité France-Amérique had originally planned that French veterans of the First World War would assemble at Gaspé for the ceremonies, but few of them had the financial means to attend, and the idea was abandoned. The French national veterans' association could not afford to send even one official delegate, and the government apparently declined to supply funding.[103] Still, the message was compelling, especially as the Third Republic nervously eyed events unfolding in the Third Reich.

Official memories of the rites remained linked to the war. Two years later, at a ceremony in Paris following the unveiling of the Vimy Ridge memorial, Maréchal Henri-Philippe Pétain made a curious request: he asked that some grains of wheat grown near the Vimy battlefield be planted at the Gaspé cross.[104] The Vimy wheat, either explicitly or implicitly, symbolizes the body of Christ; planting it at the Gaspé cross connected the exploits of Jacques Cartier with the prophesied arrival of the true faith, following themes of Christian salvation common to both Canadian war memories and earlier accounts of Cartier's voyages. Although Pétain was later disgraced for his leadership of the Vichy government during the Second World War, he was still a French military hero in 1936. During the first war, he was hailed as the saviour of Verdun and eventually became the popular commander-in-chief of the French forces, with a reputation for caring about the welfare of his men. Staunchly conservative, he saw his long-term role as rescuing France from near destruction by left-wing ideologies, a goal he hoped to accomplish by restoring respect for authority and traditional religion. Indeed, even his collaboration with Hitler was designed not only to save French lives but to set up France as a defensive wall against the spread of Bolshevism.[105] It is little surprise that, in 1936, he sought to use biblical imagery and an old hero of Canadian conservatism to encourage Franco-Canadian friendships. The Canadian Legion, through the HSMBC and the Gaspé site caretaker, obliged Pétain's request by sowing the wheat in a little plot behind the cross. Each year, they replanted it, along with a plot of poppies, turning the Cartier cross into a cenotaph. This was a curious step, as the cross stood within a hundred yards of the village war memorial.[106] But the Cartier cross implied a different kind of sacrifice than did the war memorial. Pétain's gift conveyed gratitude for saving France, not sacrifice for king and country, and suggested that the bonds forged during that war might be tested again.

However, in 1934, a more traditional interpretation also wound its way into the Gaspé festivities. Cardinal J.-M.-R. Villeneuve, the archbishop of Quebec, followed the prime minister to the podium. At the time, he was active in the same nationalist circles as Lionel Groulx, and his address returned to a semblance of the nineteenth-century religious Cartier: "But is there, in the splendour of human history, a greater tableau and a more striking figure than this Jacques Cartier 'whose immortal gesture haunts our memory.' The centuries have passed, but his work remains ... You are not surprised, gentlemen, that this fourth centenary is celebrated at Gaspé under the aegis of the Church, as well as the State, that beside a memorial cross a votive temple of granite is rising."[107]

Villeneuve's "temple of granite" was, of course, Bishop F.-X. Ross's planned memorial cathedral, now ambitiously revived four years after its first failure. Villeneuve had come to Gaspé with a papal delegation to bless its cornerstone and hold a pontifical mass on its site. This was a message that the French delegation preferred to ignore. The *Champlain* was scheduled to depart for the St. Lawrence River on Saturday night amid a triumphant send-off of fireworks and ship horns, but public pressure forced a last-minute change. Clearly, many ordinary people continued to associate Cartier with Catholicism.

On Sunday morning, beneath an outdoor altar and a canopy of maple branches and garlands, Villeneuve celebrated mass. Camille Roy, the rector of the Séminaire de Québec, gave the sermon. He opened with a passage from the Good Friday liturgy: "Here, by this wood, a great joy spreads itself through the world."[108] His sermon was an effort to remind French Canadians of the spiritual element of their dual origins. Cartier had chosen Christ's cross as the sign of his "conquest" of the New World, and this symbol united French Canadians, much as Groulx had ambitiously planned: "And the crosses that, on the voyage of 1535, Jacques Cartier will raise on other shores that he discovers in sailing up our great river bear witness again to his design to unite always, in his mind, the legitimate ambitions of his king and the spiritual conquest of souls."[109]

Following Roy's sermon, the papal delegate Monsignor Cassulo blessed the cornerstone of the memorial basilica. Again, the cathedral proved too ambitious a project, and it was not built.[110] With the close of the ceremony, the crowd dispersed, leaving the village of Gaspé, this centre of a nation's origins, an isolated and quiet outpost. Not long after the dignitaries departed and life had returned to its anonymous normality, the local children discovered that the Cartier cross made an excellent subject for target practice and took to throwing stones at it as they walked to and from school.[111]

From Gaspé, the *Champlain* sailed for Quebec City. A flotilla of three French warships, two Canadian destroyers, and two passenger liners converged there for 27 August. That evening, the established themes replayed themselves at a banquet. The prime minister once again referred to the friendship between Canada's two founding peoples and noted his own personal friendship with the Liberal premier of Quebec, Louis-Alexandre Taschereau. After shaking hands with his provincial counterpart, he spoke of Canada's debt to Quebec's preservation of ancient French civilization. Indeed, Bennett almost resembled an anti-modernist in his nostalgic praise of the simplicity of life among Quebec's rural habitants. Even in the depths of the economic depression, Bennett opined, "the people of Québec have maintained a measure of happiness denied to more ambitious people." Taking his cue, Taschereau argued that Quebec could not have preserved its values – its language, its laws, its customs, and its faith – had it not been for the benevolent conquest of the British. Again, domestic harmony was the message of the Cartier celebrations. So, too, was military recruitment, as Admiral Sir Roger Keyes suggested that Cartier's example should serve as encouragement to Canadian boys to join the Royal Canadian Navy. And, of course, Pierre-Etienne Flandin continued to speak of the natural bond between France and Canada, although even he admitted that he was running out of fresh ways to praise the Canadians.[112]

The schedule for the next day allowed for numerous smaller functions. The Quebec City Board of Trade held a luncheon for the visiting members of the French Boards of Trade and Chambers of Commerce. The passenger liner *Champlain* hosted a reception in the afternoon, as did the lieutenant governor at his official residence, Spencer Wood. The evening was devoted to a ball aboard the French warship *Vauquelin,* a concert on the Dufferin Terrace beneath the Chateau Frontenac, and fireworks launched from the *Champlain* in the harbour below. The only "historical" events to take place were the laying of wreaths at the foot of the Champlain monument by the mayor and the captain of the *Champlain,* and another ceremony during which the Duc de Lévis-Mirepoix placed a wreath at the Montcalm monument on the Grande Allée. Curiously, no official observance was scheduled for the 1889 Cartier-Brébeuf monument or the Saint-Roch monument unveiled only eight years earlier. Certainly, use of the Cartier-Brébeuf monument would have raised the concerns with religious sentiment that were avoided at Gaspé. But the Saint-Roch monument offered no such qualms and was, moreover, a replica of the Cartier memorial in Saint-Malo. Apparently, Quebec City had become Champlain's town by the 1930s.

From Quebec City, the dignitaries moved on to Montreal, Ottawa, and Toronto, before completing their goodwill tour in the United States with stops at Niagara, Rochester, and New York. No other occasion rivalled the seriousness of the Gaspé cross unveiling. But 1934 marks a clear break in the old consensus around the meaning of Jacques Cartier. People were no longer debating the minor points and picking at the edges. In 1934, the disagreements drove straight to the heart of the meaning of Jacques Cartier. Public pressures to celebrate mass at Gaspé notwithstanding, the old agreement that Cartier represented religious faith, the initiation of French Canadian history, and the first Canadian hero was lost amid disputes regarding his claims of possession and the lessons of racial fusion or international amity. Moreover, though Ottawa attempted to elevate Cartier into a national bicultural symbol, his association in Quebec was once again becoming localized in Gaspé and in Montreal. Although the old accord began to break down at the moment that anglophones began to focus on this French Canadian national hero, it did not fall apart due to resulting resentment. Instead, anglophone interest opened up new ways of thinking about Cartier's place in history, and it set Cartier at the head of varying lines of historical narrative. The account of the birth and survival of a devout French Catholic nation no longer stood alone, for multiple avenues of history now descended from Cartier. But nor did the old common sense interpretation disappear. It continued to endure, just as its decline had taken several decades.

7
Decline and Dispersal

If 1934 had been Gaspé's year to celebrate Cartier, Montreal's turn came in 1935. That year marked the quatercentennial of the first European visit to what would become Montreal, the metropolis of Canada. Quebec City did honour Cartier's second voyage, but most of the focus was on Montreal, and its celebrations were much more subdued than those of the previous year. In September 1935, as part of the Provincial Exposition, the Société nationale Jacques-Cartier organized a repeat of Faribault's 1835 ceremony, although no one commented on the parallel. It started at 4:15 p.m. on 5 September when Mayor J.-E. Grégoire unveiled a cross near the Colisée and very near the spot of Faribault's cross. Representing Cardinal Villeneuve, Monsignor B.-P. Garneau blessed the cross, and Maurice Brodeur laid a floral anchor at its base. This was clearly a continuation of the campaign of Brodeur and others to rain Cartier crosses throughout the Quebec countryside. After this short and formulaic ritual, the dignitaries spoke briefly regarding the importance of Cartier. As the fair itself was dedicated to Quebec's agricultural vocation, connecting it to the mariner of Saint-Malo often seemed a stretch. A recurring theme was that Cartier's courage and initiative could provide an example for the youth of French Canada. The mayor pointed out that Cartier, who had sailed into the unknown, charted a path that the lost youth of the depression might follow: "as an example to our youth who no longer know where to direct their own steps."[1] In a province promoting the colonization of new agricultural areas as one solution to unemployment, the message would not go unnoticed. Then, at 5:00 p.m., the exposition closed for the year.

Cartier at Hochelaga
Although Cartier had visited Hochelaga during October, Montreal's 1935 quatercentennial events began in early spring. In May, the Montreal Symphony Orchestra held a special concert at Notre-Dame Church in the heart

of Old Montreal under the guest conductorship of New York's Rosario Bour-
don.[2] However, the real festivities opened with the Saint-Jean-Baptiste national holiday in June. These began on the eve of the twenty-fourth, with
a huge bonfire at Montreal's Lafontaine Park, the customary site for this
traditional fire. The next morning likewise began as usual with a mass held
by abbé Albert Pinault of Verdun, who delivered a sermon aimed squarely
at the evils of socialism, the specific threat of the Co-operative Common-
wealth Federation, and the values of a new generation. In the midst of the
depression, Pinault worried that too many young people would turn from
the institute of the family, ignore their civic and religious duties, and forget
that all authority stemmed from God. Following mass, the city's francophones lined the streets to enjoy another annual tradition: the Saint-Jean-
Baptiste parade.

From 1927 onward, the parade was organized by a central committee run
by Emile Vaillancourt and J.-B. Lagacé on behalf of the SSJBM. The committee selected a theme for the parade, and its floats were fitted into that
theme. Vaillancourt, a writer and amateur historian, planned the historical
message of the year as well as each float. Lagacé, an accomplished painter,
developed their specific designs. The themes were not always historical, but
they tended to be. For 1935, the organizing committee chose the theme of
"The St. Lawrence and the Great Lakes," and each float depicted some aspect
of French Canadian history in this Laurentian watershed. Cartier appeared
on a quarter of the parade's twenty floats. Vaillancourt identified him most
clearly with Saint-Malo and Hochelaga, and the floats explicitly represented
him leaving his home and arriving on Mount Royal. Elsewhere, his presence
was suggested by models of his ships crossing the Atlantic or sailing the St.
Lawrence River.[3]

On the anniversary of Cartier's arrival at Hochelaga, another ceremony
was held at the McGill University campus. Ignoring the still current controversy regarding the location of Hochelaga, Cartier's landing place, and
his route to the village, the Civic Improvement League, which organized
the Montreal celebrations, staged an event at the HSMBC plaque of 1923.
Founded in 1909 as part of an effort to clean up corruption in municipal
government, the Civic Improvement League developed into a citizens'
planning and beautification committee whose members were among the
most influential men in Montreal.[4] They included Victor Morin and William
Douw Lighthall, two of the most important figures in the construction of
Montreal public history.[5] At the ceremony, Mayor Camillien Houde placed
a floral bouquet at the base of the boulder supporting the plaque, after which
speeches were read by Houde, Lighthall, Morin, Judge Surveyer of the
HSMBC, and Milton Hersey, president of the Civic Improvement League.
The speeches were short and similar in tone. Each orator honoured the
courage of Cartier, discoverer of Canada, who scaled Mount Royal, named

it, and surveyed the surrounding countryside. Indeed, in the memory of Cartier as presented at these celebrations, Mount Royal assumed a place of importance nearly equal to that of Gaspé. Mayor Houde, however, also took time to praise the league and encourage it to continue its work in helping the public better understand the history of this country.[6]

Mount Royal, and its connection to the name of the modern city, was more than an incidental theme of the festivities. It has long held a central place in the self-image of Montrealers. Today, Mount Royal Park is often heralded as the heart of the city, and the gruelling climb up the mountain is rewarded by a spectacular view of the modern metropolis. In popular imagination, this view reinforced the southern route thesis and cemented Cartier's place in the city's history. Through the nineteenth century, Mount Royal served as an emblematic natural feature of the city in various artists' depictions of the Montreal skyline.[7] More than that, it figured in many, sometimes competing, local expressions of nationalism. Anglophone Canadians of the Victorian age saw in the mountain an example of a "wilderness" landscape and, according to Gillian Poulter, incorporated it into an emerging colonial identity. In this context, snowshoeing across the slopes of Mount Royal was a means of establishing a distinctive Canadian form of Britishness.[8] French Canadians viewed the mountain in historical, rather than spatial, contexts through references to Cartier and Paul Chomedey, sieur de Maisonneuve, the founder of Montreal, who erected a cross on Mount Royal during the colony's first winter. In the twentieth century, they also began to colonize this largely anglophone space, moving into the town of Outremont in numbers and establishing French Catholic institutions on the mountain's slopes, such as the Université de Montréal and St. Joseph's Oratory.[9]

The choice of the mountain for a public park, opened in 1876, reflected contemporary recognition of its cultural significance. The park has always been popular, and for years the mountain was the final resting site for the city's inhabitants, as it holds the Catholic, Protestant, and Jewish cemeteries. Through the nineteenth century, numerous enthusiasts floated proposals to adorn the peak of Mount Royal with an emblem. In 1867, before the park had been designated, a Parisian artist named Louis Rochet suggested that a monument to Jacques Cartier be erected at the summit, where the historical Cartier had reconnoitred the surrounding Montreal Plain. Seven years later, Rochet again offered to cast a colossal bronze statue of Cartier for the summit of Mount Royal, only to have city council reject it again.[10] In 1888, city council entertained another proposal, this time to place a two-hundred-foot bronze statue of the Virgin Mary on the mountain. Sculptor Louis-Philippe Hébert, then a promising young artist, produced a maquette, but this ambitious project was stillborn. A more bizarre scheme involved running a cable car between the mountain and Île Sainte-Hélène. For obvious reasons, this project never went beyond the drawing board.[11] By 1935, however, the mountain had been topped with a massive cross symbolizing the connection between the city's francophones and their faith. Inaugurated in 1924 by the influential SSJBM, it quickly became the emblem of the city.[12] But it did not stand alone atop Mount Royal. The public lookout, or belvedere, along with a nearby chalet, had already become a favourite site in the park for tourists and Montrealers. The chalet was opened in 1932 and instantly panned as a "white elephant."[13] In its original conception, it was to be a place for special occasions, and its great hall would host balls and banquets, but it remained mostly empty.[14] Almost immediately, schemes came forward to turn the empty building into a museum. Léon Trépanier opened the discussion with a suggestion to create a museum of Quebec art in 1933. Two years later, a more complete proposal to build a botanical and geological museum was submitted to the city by McGill University's Museum Committee.[15] This second idea would have included some small displays to Quebec history.

In truth, the chalet already taught a history lesson to those who were willing to read it. Above the hearths of its great hall were mounted the arms of England, France, Champlain, Maisonneuve, and Cartier. And when the chalet opened, its walls displayed seventeen commissioned paintings depicting the history of Montreal. Five of these portrayed Cartier's exploits, whereas the others carried the Montreal story forward through Champlain, Maisonneuve, and Dollard des Ormeaux. Two of the Cartier paintings were maps: one traced the lines of his voyages through the St. Lawrence River and the gulf; the other reproduced the Ramusio plan of Hochelaga. The remaining three showed Cartier's arrival at Hochelaga, his meeting with Hochelaga's chief, and his visit to the summit of Mount Royal. This last example is probably the worst of the three yet also the most iconographic. The painter, Alfred Faniel, posed Cartier on a rock precipice, with his Native companions blending into the forest behind him, as he surveyed the view. None of these paintings are of particular artistic merit, as one critic suggested before the chalet had even opened.[16] However, they helped underpin the notion that here was a place where history unfolded, where average citizens could stand in the footsteps of great men. In combination, the ceremony at McGill, the messages in the chalet's paintings, and the plaque on the lookout reinforced in public memory the southern route thesis. Regardless of its merits, or those of the northern thesis, most Montrealers, and certainly most tourists, were exposed to this unspoken interpretation of Cartier's sojourn in Hochelaga.

The SSJBM also held October ceremonies to honour Cartier's visit. It sponsored a contest for the best short essay on Cartier's second voyage and published Thérèse Tanguay's winning entry in the October issue of *L'Oiseau bleu.* Tanguay drew attention to the importance of the naming of the mountain, and by extension, of the city: "Dazzled by the splendid panorama that unfolded harmoniously at his feet, beyond the enchanting river to the heights that bounded the horizon, he found but one word to express his admiration; he named this mountain of Hochelaga 'Mount Royal,' and it has forever conserved this gracious name."[17] Indeed, Cartier's visit to Mount Royal emerged as a key theme in the popular memory of him and was featured on the official program of the Saint-Jean-Baptiste celebrations in June 1935. Cartier's significance was gradually being reduced to toponymy and his association with Montreal's central geographical feature.

The SSJBM also organized a day of remembrance later in October, the highlight of which was a speech by Lionel Groulx at the Monument national. The day began with a mass at Notre-Dame-de-Bonsecour chapel in Old Montreal. In his sermon, Olivier Maurault, rector of the Université de Montréal, drew attention to the religious elements of Cartier's visit to Hochelaga, referring to his deep piety and his tenderness in dealing with the Hochelagans. Here was the old Catholic Cartier prophesying the coming of the faith to North America. His visit was a portent of the missionary work to follow. The historical lesson Maurault inferred from Cartier was that French Canadians must remain true to their faith and accept God's generosity as Cartier did.[18] After mass, a delegation marched to city hall to unveil a new plaque that commemorated Mount Royal – and the naming of Montreal – as much as it celebrated Cartier: "In honour of Jacques Cartier. The famous French navigator reached Hochelaga in October 1535 and gave the mountain the name of Mount Royal which it still bears today."[19]

The repeated emphasis on the naming of Mount Royal is suggestive. Perhaps Montrealers honoured Cartier not for his historical significance but as an aspect of celebrating their mountain. However, at least some held to the idea of the heroic Cartier and the lessons he taught. Later that night, a crowd of dignitaries took their places in the Monument national to hear the priest-historian Groulx explain the historical importance, and another version of the historical lesson, of Jacques Cartier's arrival at Hochelaga. Patriotism, and the importance of raising French Canadian children in a spirit of patriotism, was the message of Groulx's history. And, like Maurault earlier in the day, he laid at the feet of youth the hopes of building a Catholic nation that would fulfill the promise initiated by Cartier.[20]

Yet, in contrast to those of 1934, these varied Montreal celebrations were muted. Without federal and foreign involvement, the funding simply was not available to stage more elaborate festivities in the middle of the Great Depression. No private philanthropist emerged to play the role of a Vanderbilt and assure a grand event. But the 1935 celebrations were subdued due to more than financial stress. Cartier simply did not command the levels of interest that federal event planners had been able to generate the year before. Although still honoured by historians and dignitaries, he had clearly fallen from his pedestal. Less than a decade later, he had disappeared from the narrative of Montreal as offered by the same Civic Improvement League. Admittedly, for the third centennial of the founding of Ville-Marie, held in 1942 during the Second World War, homage to Cartier could be expected to take second place to that accorded Maisonneuve. However, despite having visited the area in 1541, Cartier did not figure in the celebrations, even as a precursor to Maisonneuve. Indeed, at the anniversary of Cartier's first visit to Hochelaga, the organizing committee held a ceremony to rededicate another HSMBC plaque, this one on the old custom house commemorating Maisonneuve's establishment of the "cradle of Montréal."[21] Another contrast with Cartier's inclusion in the 1908 pageant on the Plains of Abraham is obvious.

Indeed, the twentieth century saw a diminishment in the importance of Cartier in French Canadian identity and nationalism. Cartiermania reached its apogee by 1890, and the long decline of Cartier's stature, especially relative to Champlain's, can be traced. Perhaps the fate of the Cartier-Brébeuf monument most clearly illustrates this process. From its erection in 1889, it gradually ceased to be of value to the local community, even in the birthplace of Cartiermania. The Cercle catholique had donated the land to the Catholic Church, which had entrusted it to Saint-Roch Parish. However, time ravaged the monument, leaving it in a deplorable state as the working-class parish could not afford its upkeep.[22]

Part of the reason for this decline was the change in Quebec society and in French Canadian nationalism. Abbé Pinault had some reason for his concern with the youth of Quebec. Although the church hierarchy remained largely conservative, the 1930s saw increasing ideological diversity in Catholicism. Powerful lay organizations, and in particular youth organizations, emerged to offer a "democratic" critique of the hierarchy and insist that Catholicism adapt to the changing cultural values of a modern society and that the church accept increased lay leadership. Through the 1930s, the clergy responded by organizing a series of youth groups based not on the parish or geographical location but on corporatist notions of social function. The Jeunesse ouvrière catholique, the Jeunesse étudiante catholique, and the Jeunesse agricole catholique, for instance, gathered young people into associations that promoted ideas of social hierarchy and class harmony. Such notions were not new. Through the nineteenth century, Catholic nationalists had been making similar arguments, as seen in the pronouncements of the École sociale populaire. However, as Michael Gauvreau has recently argued, these organizations also reflected a belief that youth constituted a new social category that offered hope for a spiritual renaissance in national life. Faced with the economic and social crisis of the Great Depression, young people were more inclined to embrace new ideas than were their counterparts of earlier in the century.

Moreover, urging young people to take control of their lives, and, by extension, to assume leadership roles in Quebec society, strengthened support for a broad intellectual current known as "personalism."[23] Personalism might be characterized as a loose set of ideals founded on notions that discarded purely material imperatives and placed value in the person. It rejected social and economic determinism, emphasizing personal engagement and realism instead. Personalism extended back into the nineteenth century but became popularized during the crisis of the 1930s. It was particularly strong at Boston University under the influence of Borden Parker Browne but entered Quebec as a neo-scholastic tradition through contacts with France and Belgium. Under Emmanuel Mounier's teachings, personalism was politically flexible but spiritual at root. Not to be confused with individualism, personalism construed the person as linked in spiritual, cultural, and social bonds with others. Therefore, like Marxism and fascism, it offered a critique of the "bourgeois civilization" that had produced the crisis of the 1930s.[24] Within French personalism, a rigorous debate existed between the followers of Emmanuel Mounier, Jacques Maritain, and others, but the youth of Quebec did not forge specific allegiances: instead, they identified broad principles with their own values and a conviction that they formed the vanguard of the coming spiritual revolution.[25] However, if the youth of Action catholique constituted a vanguard that held the key to a "real" Catholicism, a rupture with previous religious tradition was inevitable.

Not everyone has agreed with this interpretation of 1930s Quebec Catholicism as championed by Michael Gauvreau. A recent roundtable in the pages of the *Revue d'histoire de l'Amérique française* has taken up the debate over Catholic reform in which Gauvreau sees personalism as one of the roots of the 1960s Quiet Revolution.[26] Gauvreau's thesis hinges on the idea of generational conflict in which the fundamental role of Action catholique was to promote modern cultural values. In part, this could help explain why youth turned away from the Catholicism represented by Jacques Cartier. Although the Catholic youth group Jeune-Canada was active in the 1934 celebrations, youth organizations more typically began from a negative premise that the values of the previous generation offered no lessons for the crises and pressures of modern life.[27] This was a growing idea of nationalism, rooted in a new understanding of Catholicism, that was fully modernist in that it saw no real value in reference to the past. In a climate of near hostility to preceding generations, young nationalists also began to turn away from their heroes.

Perhaps, then, French Canadian youth discarded the symbol of Jacques Cartier because he had become closely associated with an older clerical nationalism. Some nationalists in the 1930s, such as those who joined the

Ordre de Jacques-Cartier, certainly embraced this old vision and its invocation of Cartier's image. Also known as La Patente, the order was a secret
society established in Ottawa in 1926 by a parish priest, F.-X. Barrette. Hier-
archically structured and conservative, it spread through French Canada
during the 1930s, peaking at an estimated ten thousand members. It championed a number of religious and nationalist causes; its members infiltrated
dozens of other organizations; and they promoted one another's advance-
ment through various domains of public life. Externally, La Patente sponsored
public opinion campaigns linked to faith, morality, education, the French
language, and anti-communism.[28] Its actual influence is debatable, and it
eventually disbanded in 1965. During the Second World War, La Patente
was accused of fascism and its members of plotting against Canada, something that may also help explain Cartier's absence from the 1942 celebrations
in Montreal.[29] But in the 1930s, it certainly held sway for some young nationalists. The nationalist leader André Laurendeau may have been a member.[30] But it never had mass appeal, and its use of Cartier implied secrecy,
not celebration.

Certainly, some members of Catholic youth groups flirted with fascism
and its cult of the leader. Perhaps this fascination with leadership and the
earlier celebration of historical heroes both sprang from similar sources, and
such a shift in attentions may also help explain the decline of recourse to
figures like Cartier. However, as Louise Bienvenue cautions, such flirtations
are nuanced. Catholics could easily reject the overt atheism of the Nazis,
but elements of Mussolini's corporatism were appealing to young nationalists. And the strong leader seemed the very antithesis of the weak and cor-
rupted political leaders they saw in 1930s Canada. Yet, even Mussolini's
leadership, and in particular his treatment of the Holy See, sparked condem-
nation. Prudently, the young nationalists of groups such as the Jeunesse
étudiante catholique and the Jeunesse agricole catholique concluded that
true world leadership resided solely with the pope.[31]

Even had they been interested in elevating historical heroes, the youth of
the 1930s and 1940s might not have embraced Cartier. Hero celebration had
been greatly transformed in early twentieth-century Quebec. Led by Lionel
Groulx, youth groups had earlier turned their attentions to a youth hero,
Adam Dollard des Ormeaux. In 1660, he led a small band of young settlers
and Native allies against an Iroquois war party in battle at the Long Sault of
the Ottawa River. In 1910, a number of young Montrealers initiated a ritual
on the anniversary of the battle. After mass at Notre-Dame Church, they
placed wreaths at the Dollard depiction on the Maisonneuve monument at
Place d'Armes, thus initiating an annual event. When Groulx moved to
Montreal, he quickly recognized in Dollard's story the very essence of his
religiously inspired nationalism. Although Dollard and his followers were
overcome and killed in battle, their sacrifice, performed by the youth in the

name of the patrie, exemplified the kind of nationalism that Groulx wanted to lead Quebec. In 1911, allegorical floats depicting Champlain and Dollard toured a variety of Saint-Jean-Baptiste Day events to help solicit donations to a monument fund.[32] During the First World War, recruiters invoked Dollard's image to inspire French Canadians to enlist. But this effort failed to recognize that the message of Dollard was one of home defence. Although one anglophone remarked that French Canadians did not know of anglophone appreciation for the hero's feats, the source of that appreciation was a more important divide.[33] By 1918, French Canadians had dubbed 24 May la fête de Dollard. And, in the coming years, two Dollard monuments were raised, one at Carillon on the Quebec side of the Ottawa River and the other in Montreal's Lafontaine Park.[34]

However, by the 1930s, Dollard's name was less celebrated, or at least celebrated differently. Throughout the 1920s, young French Canadians led pilgrimages to Carillon, but interest fizzled with time. In 1933, Jeune-Canada renewed the pilgrimage but could not repeat the feat in subsequent years. Historians also began to dispute Groulx's mythic and romantic story of Dollard's defence of the imperilled Ville-Marie colony. Indeed, the decline of the Dollard myth reveals the ways in which professional and amateur historians continued to interact during the 1930s. McGill University historian E.R. Adair initiated an offensive with a lecture to the Women's Historical Society of Montreal, in which he asserted that Dollard was nothing more than an ambitious thief who, completely ignorant of any plot against Ville-Marie, led an ill-conceived attack against Iroquois fur traders. He was not, as the myth contended, the saviour of Ville-Marie and may have done more harm than good.[35] Amateur historians W.H. Atherton and Emile Vaillancourt responded through the newspapers in defence of the traditional version.[36] Adair and Vaillancourt swapped missives in the Montreal press before Lionel Groulx, by then holding the chair of Canadian history at the Université de Montréal, published his own two-part reply in *Le Devoir.*[37] Adair's original lecture appeared, alongside a more balanced companion piece by Gustave Lanctôt of the Dominion Archives, in the professional historical journal the *Canadian Historical Review.* Even there, it continued to attract the attention of amateur historians such as Aegidius Fauteux.[38]

The authenticity of Groulx's version began to come under question, but more importantly, the ideology Dollard supported no longer reflected the needs of Quebec in the crisis of the 1930s.[39] Feeling betrayed, Groulx took the dispute personally and wondered whether the controversy would have occurred had so prominent a figure as himself not been involved. But Adair's assault was relatively minor compared to the government's use of Dollard for wartime recruiting.[40] As historians Colin Coates and Cecelia Morgan argue, Groulx saw the story of Dollard "as part of the unique natural heritage of French Canadians, and [it] belonged only to them."[41] Yet, in the 1930s, this sort of hero worship no longer resonated with the rising generation. The modern historian Patrice Groulx has argued that, in the case of Dollard des Ormeaux, veneration of the hero began to diminish only after 1945. However, this suggestion hinges on the mid-1940s publication of tracts critical of the Dollard legend.[42] A closer look hints at a generational divide. Supporters of the Dollard myth included such men as the author Léo-Paul Desrosiers, who was born before the turn of the twentieth century. At the same time, critics of the myth included the young publisher Lucien Parizeau (born 1910) and Marcel-Pierre Hamel (born 1913), the reformist nationalist and journalist for such publications as *Action catholique*. These young men were more representative of the generation that came of age in the Great Depression and would have begun to formulate their views on traditional nationalism while in their twenties. Thus, despite some brief attention early in the great crisis of modernity that the depression represented, Quebec's youth turned away from the nationalist solutions of earlier generations, discarded the nationalist historical heroes, and demanded new solutions to social crises. As a result, Dollard suffered a decline in the estimation of the youth of the 1930s alongside Jacques Cartier.

Amateur and Professional

If the youth of Quebec, or the people of Quebec's major cities, lost interest in Cartier, the loss was not universal. He remained important to both anglophones and francophones as a historical figure, but he had diminished as a heroic one. Of course, this assertion is a generalization, not a universal truth. At least one man kept alive the vision of an old Cartier: Gustave Lanctôt (see Figure 7). Born in 1883 at Saint-Constant, south of Montreal, Lanctôt was educated at the Collège de Montréal, and he pursued legal training at the Université de Montréal. Although called to the bar in 1907, he quickly abandoned the law for a career in journalism, working for the Montreal dailies *Le Canada* and *La Patrie*. Again, this career was short-lived: awarded a Rhodes Scholarship in 1909, Lanctôt headed off to Oxford to study history and political science, and to play hockey. His studies also took him to Paris and the Sorbonne. Upon his return to Canada in 1912, he found a position in the Dominion Archives, an ideal place from which he could continue his historical studies. Soon afterward, war broke out in Europe. In 1915, he enrolled in the Canadian Expeditionary Force and rose to the rank of major. While in the army, Lanctôt continued to work for his civilian boss, the dominion archivist Arthur Doughty, and with Doughty was assigned to collect Canadian war trophies, as well as amass records of Canada's war effort. Demobilized at the end of the war, Lanctôt completed his doctorate at the Université de Paris with a dissertation on the administration of New France. And, upon his second return to Canada, he again took up a position

Figure 7 Gustave Lanctôt (far right) standing with dominion archivist Arthur Doughty (centre) in France in 1916. *Library and Archives Canada, C-051858*

in the Dominion Archives, becoming director of its French Section and, in 1937, succeeding Doughty as the second dominion archivist.

Despite his education in Montreal, the seat of Quebec nationalism, Lanctôt never strayed into the various camps of French Canadian nationalists. His long years in federal service fit with his own views of Canada and of French Canada's place in the dominion. Fluently bilingual, Lanctôt was comfortable defending his opinions in either language and with both anglophone and francophone scholars. Pursuing scholarship with the professional detachment befitting a doctor of philosophy, he advocated a scientific approach to history and had little time for the nationalist use of the past. Indeed, toward the end of his career, he published an article in *Action universitaire* that denounced the "racist school of thought" in the xenophobic writings of many Quebec historians, including Lionel Groulx. For this reason, Groulx passed over Lanctôt when assembling the Institut d'histoire de l'Amérique française in the 1940s, even though the latter was the dominion archivist with a doctorate from the Sorbonne.[43] Still, Lanctôt was as prolific a writer of historical accounts as Groulx himself. He published at least ten books on topics ranging from the French regime to modern Canada. And he wrote countless articles, pamphlets, and speeches over the course of his long career, both before and after his official retirement in 1947.[44]

Despite these trappings of the professional historian, Lanctôt retained many of the traits of the amateur enthusiast of previous generations. In ways that paralleled Faribault's much earlier interest, Lanctôt was also a Cartier enthusiast. In his writings, he carried on the old glorification of Cartier despite growing discomfort with such goals among professional historians. His was an enthusiast's obsession with the great man and an almost amateur tendency to coordinate all evidence into a clean narrative that connected to famous events and figures. For instance, Lanctôt insisted that Cartier learned of North America by accompanying Verrazano in the *Dauphin* in 1524 and again in 1528.[45] According to Lanctôt, Cartier's comparison of North American maize to Brazilian millet corn, as well as his knowledge of Portuguese, suggested that he had been to Brazil. Although this may well be accurate, there is no need to link any earlier American experience to Verrazano. Lanctôt's claim rests on Cartier's absence from the Malouin birth registers and marriage certificates during the time in which Verrazano was at sea and on Père Biard's confused seventeenth-century references to Cartier's voyages. Responding to Lanctôt's hypothesis, Jesuit historian Lucien Campeau noted that Biard clearly distinguished Verrazano's voyage from Cartier's, even if he sometimes confused their dates.[46] Lanctôt and Campeau battled each other in the pages of the *Revue d'histoire de l'Amérique française* through 1953 to 1954, but the weight of scholarly opinion turned against Lanctôt.[47] A contemporary French author seems to have summed up historical opinion when he characterized the idea of Cartier accompanying Verrazano as seductive rather than convincing.[48]

Other arguments can be raised against Lanctôt. Cartier, a sea captain, was frequently absent from the Malouin registers during the seafaring months. If he was at sea during roughly the same period as Verrazano, it does not follow that the two were at sea together. Secondly, as Marcel Trudel points out, Cartier used none of Verrazano's toponymy, suggesting that he was unfamiliar with it. He made no mention of Verrazano's Nouvelle Gallia or, more spectacularly, of the famous Norumbega. In describing the Richelieu River, Cartier divined that its source was in Florida – that is, to the south. Had he been with Verrazano, he would most certainly have chosen Verrazano's Arcadie, or Virginia, and perhaps even noted that he had personally seen these lands. Indeed, Cartier made no reference whatsoever to either Verrazano's voyage or his own alleged earlier explorations. Trudel has further emphasized that Cartier's name appears nowhere in Verrazano's accounts. But perhaps most fundamentally, Trudel noted that Verrazano equipped his ship in Normandy as Verrazzano doubted that jealous Norman merchants and sailors would have tolerated a Breton from Saint-Malo among the crew.[49]

Nevertheless, not having sailed with Verrazano does not preclude the possibility that Cartier had been to Brazil on some other expedition. The well-established Malouin trade in Brazilian dyewoods, and Cartier's apparent familiarity with Portuguese, suggests that he had an awareness of Brazil and had probably encountered Portuguese shipping prior to 1534. In introducing him to the king in 1532, Jean Le Veneur claimed that Cartier had seen Brazil.[50] Moreover, Bretons were welcome on Dieppois fishing ships and were regularly employed as pilots for the Grand Banks fishery.[51]

Lanctôt and his predecessor Faribault had much in common. Although they lived a century apart, their careers as historians shared certain traits. Both men straddled the amateur-professional divide. Both might be classified as "professionalizing" historians for their own times, Faribault for his work to assemble collections of documents and Lanctôt for his work as an archivist, as well as his university training. However, both men also revealed the amateur's tendency to see the evidence as pointing to the well-known and celebrated aspects of history. As Stephen Bann suggests, the willingness to force probability beyond credibility was also the mark of the early antiquarian.[52] Faribault and Lanctôt tended to find what they were looking for: both showed a willingness to let their desire to unearth the relics of Cartier lead them to conclusions. Much as Faribault had allowed himself to see the *Petite Hermine* in a rotted hulk, Lanctôt was willing to see Cartier himself in some old bones.

After his retirement, Lanctôt led a mission to France to discover Cartier's tomb and, if possible, to transfer his remains to Canada. Corresponding with the French government's chief architect for historical monuments, he learned that local tradition placed Cartier's grave inside the Saint-Malo cathedral, in the St. Julien wing at the foot of the altar of the Virgin.[53] However, this account was imprecise in its descriptions and based on little more than legend and family memories. Moreover, Saint-Malo had been thoroughly destroyed during the war, and much of it remained in ruins when Lanctôt visited it in February 1949. The cathedral itself had been bombed, and following the bombardment, several remains of intra-muros tombs were recovered from the rubble. The bone fragments, being found here and there, were simply transferred as one to the town cemetery.[54] But more than war and reconstruction obscured the memory of Cartier's tomb: the long political turmoil of French history also played a role. In the 1790s, the cathedral was converted to a temple of the Goddess of Reason and used for the storage of fodder.[55] Ten years of revolution eliminated the ornaments of the cathedral, as well as its records, leaving behind only memory and tradition to guide the identification of its tombs. Even a 1790 plan of the cathedral was unhelpful, as it showed no altar in the St. Julien wing. As many of Lanctôt's informants insisted, memory and oral tradition would have to suffice.

Unfortunately, there was more than one set of memories, and more than one oral tradition, to guide the search for Cartier's tomb. Even before leaving Canada, Lanctôt learned of an alternative site, from a *London Times* letter to the editor written some time in 1934. Its author, A.R. Tremearne, an Anglican vicar in Lincolnshire, England, claimed to have located Cartier's tomb in a rural Breton school house. In 1926, having missed their train, he and a friend had decided to walk the ten miles to their destination. About halfway there, they passed a house, one of three being used as a village school, with a cross above the door. For some reason, the matron of the school explained to the friends that Cartier's tomb was in a vault beneath the cottage. Over the course of a few months, Tremearne and Lanctôt exchanged letters (Lanctôt sent butter and sausages as Britain was still under wartime rationing), and the story firmed up. Arriving in France, Lanctôt tracked down a chapel (Saint-Michel des Sablons), then serving as a school, where Sister Germaine confirmed a tradition, itself passed down from the former rector, that Cartier's tomb lay beneath the chapel's altar.[56]

Meanwhile, investigations were continuing at the Saint-Malo cathedral (see Figure 8). During the spring of 1949, workers discovered an intact skeleton buried beneath some of the cathedral pillars, lying in a bed of lime.[57] The remains were examined by a local doctor, who performed his investigation in the presence of abbé Julien Descottes, Raymond Conron, the mayor, and the police chief. Dr. Nicolleau's examination proved inconclusive but did note that Cartier died during an epidemic in Brittany and that, at the time, those who died of plague were inhumed in lime. N.-E. Dionne had

Figure 8   Jacques Cartier's tomb in the Saint-Malo cathedral as it appeared during the summer of 2009. *Photo by the author*

popularized the belief that Cartier died of some plague or another, speculating that an outbreak during the summer provided sufficient evidence to make the claim. However, Dionne admitted that his suggestion was pure guesswork.[58] Nevertheless, it entered into deliberations regarding the remains uncovered at the cathedral. Continuing with this sort of reasoning, medical experts determined that the skull matched the distinctive profile of portraits completed in the tradition of Théophile Hamel's 1845 lithographs. Thus, a largely fictional likeness served to authenticate a real skull. Subsequent inspection concluded that the skull lacked some teeth, which Nicolleau took as consistent with exposure to scurvy. Although François-Xavier de

Charlevoix asserted that Cartier had contracted the disease, there is no explicit record of this in the *Brief recit*.[59] Certain characteristics of the skull suggested rheumatism, which Lanctôt felt explained Cartier's failure to appear at baptisms later in life.[60] Canon Descottes provided further compelling evidence. His own maternal grandmother, who had died in 1922, came from an old Saint-Malo family, and Cartier himself had been the godfather of one of her ancestors, Jean Jallobert. Descottes remembered that every time she entered the cathedral, she would identify the spot where Cartier was interred. The skeleton had been found exactly there.[61] Lanctôt took all this as confirmation and remarked that "unquestionably, the present mission has achieved a complete success."[62] Although he accorded no credit to Lanctôt's efforts, Lionel Groulx reaffirmed his conclusions in the 1966 edition of his *La découverte du Canada*. Raymond Cornon provided Groulx with a copy of a 1949 Interior Ministry report on the skull, as well as a more recent summary by the Historical and Archaeological Society of Saint-Malo.[63] Groulx reprinted these in the revised edition of his book.

One of the original objectives for the mission to find Cartier's tomb was to transfer the remains to Canada. As Lanctôt put it during an interview with a Toronto newspaper, as Columbus had found a resting place in Havana, the discoverer of Canada should find his own final resting place in Canada.[64] However, throughout the entire endeavour, both the minister of external affairs and the ambassador to France repeatedly avoided committing to any repatriation scheme. The final medical report, published in 1952, reinforced this reluctance.[65] Although excavations uncovered "an ensemble of probabilities and conjectures" that made Lanctôt's conclusion seem "reasonable," none of this could constitute legal or medical proof. Moreover, the entire ensemble of probabilities was confined only to one recovered skull, not the full remains. Nothing ever came of Lanctôt's suggestion that Canada and France share the remains, with half being laid to rest in each country.[66] Indeed, the apparent discovery of Cartier's remains provoked a few fleeting commentaries but no outpouring of enthusiasm, particularly as compared with the *Petite Hermine* episode of just over a century earlier: the public yawned. Today, the skeleton, presumed to be Cartier's, rests in St. Vincent Cathedral in Saint-Malo.

The Quiet Revolution and Professional History

Ronald Rudin has argued that, in Quebec, the first steps toward a professionalization of history were taken during the first quarter of the twentieth century, capped by the 1925 Sémaine d'histoire du Canada held in Montreal.[67] However, far more important strides occurred after the Second World War. Even as soldiers were returning from Europe and the Pacific, Quebec's francophone universities moved to expand and improve the quality of the history they taught. In Quebec City, abbé Arthur Maheux was planning the creation of an Institut d'histoire for Laval University. Maheux's approach to the study of history was decidedly amateur, but he maintained regular communications with University of Toronto faculty and hoped to use contacts with anglophone Canadians and Americans to improve the professionalism of the discipline in the province, much as his colleague Georges-Henri Lévesque was doing in the Faculty of Social Sciences.[68] Meanwhile, in Montreal, Lionel Groulx was organizing both the expansion of the history offerings at the Université de Montréal and an independent historical institute. Typically for this nationalist historian, he chose to announce the formation of the Institut d'histoire de l'Amérique française (IHAF) on the fête nationale with a speech at a banquet.[69] Setting nationalism aside for the moment, Groulx claimed that his IHAF would not sacrifice the "truth" for ideological convenience: instead, it would pursue "scientific" history and promote the professionalization of the discipline in Quebec. Indeed, Groulx described the goals of this new institution as professional training, storage of archival materials, and publication of works that met "professional" standards.[70]

Nevertheless, ideology continued to influence historical studies. Laval's new History Department was founded on the premise of teaching history from a "Catholic" perspective, and Groulx's nationalism crept into the workings of the IHAF. Rudin characterizes the IHAF as a "hybrid" institution in its inception. It presented a balance between Groulx's nationalist *parti pris* and his interest in promoting professional or scientific historical methodologies. Membership was likewise determined as much by ideological stance as by professional credentials. For example, perhaps due to personal or political reasons, Groulx excluded Gustave Lanctôt. And, among the first executives of the IHAF, aside from Groulx as president, were his former students Guy Frégault and Maurice Séguin as vice-president and secretary treasurer. The IHAF board similarly reflected Groulx's own balancing act, being a mix of lay experts and clerical historians.[71]

Another case where professional and amateur differed by degrees was with the creation of the *Revue d'histoire de l'Amérique française* (RHAF). The RHAF addressed the third of Groulx's objectives for the IHAF – the publication of professional scholarly historical studies. It was intended to supplant the *Bulletin des recherches historiques* (BRH), founded by Quebec archivist Pierre-Georges Roy in 1895. The BRH was an antiquarian's or enthusiast's publication, and its brief articles did not follow the professional standards for documenting evidence that university historians require. Nor were its contributions subjected to the critical screening characteristic of professional historical journals such as the *American Historical Review,* the *English Historical Review,* or the *Canadian Historical Review.* If Quebec's francophone historians were to be taken seriously, as Groulx intended by this professionalization project, they needed a journal of equal critical stature.[72] To this end, the initial issues allotted considerable space to the discussion of methodology, and submissions were rejected for failing to meet standards of originality and method. Still, as Rudin points out, the RHAF remained closed to scholars whose vision of Quebec history did not accord with those of the nationalists, at least in the early years.[73]

The combined efforts of Laval and Montreal Universities, as well as the enhanced publishing opportunities offered by the new RHAF, allowed the historical profession to expand in the province. By the 1960s, Quebec historiography had coalesced into two dominant approaches, one based at the Université de Montréal and the other at Laval University. The debates between partisans of these approaches have become legendary among Canadian historians, and in many ways they furthered long-seated animosities between the communities, the two universities, some of their key personnel, and, in particular, the priests Groulx and Maheux. At root, the differences were founded on competing political visions of Quebec's place in (or out of) Canada. The Montreal School, led by Guy Frégault, Maurice Séguin, and later Michel Brunet, advocated what has been called a "neo-nationalist" interpretation of the Conquest of 1760 that supported political nationalism. At Laval, Fernand Ouellet emerged as the champion of an alternative interpretation. He and Jean Hamelin were strongly influenced by the Annales School of France, whose method for historical explanation emphasized economics and social forces rather than politics. In the main, Jacques Cartier lay outside these debates, as the professional historians turned their attentions to other issues.

Marcel Trudel's development as a professional historian took an unusual route. He was born in 1917 near Trois-Rivières, but, because his mother died during the early 1920s, his life was repeatedly uprooted. As was common at the time, his father felt he could not raise children alone, and young Marcel was sent away, living first with an aunt and uncle, later in an orphanage, and eventually at a boarding school. As a child, he was a loner, spending solitary time with his books, and he demonstrated the ambition of a small-town Quebecer of his generation. His early dreams were of becoming a Franciscan, but these changed after he was expelled from the seminary in Trois-Rivières. At Laval University, Trudel became a leader of a new generation of historians, even though his doctorate was in literature rather than history. He was hired to teach Canadian history at Laval in 1945, but before he could commence, he was sent to Harvard University where his title of visiting professor disguised the real reason for his presence there – pursuing a reading program to improve his knowledge. He was not permitted to obtain another doctorate, and after two years of auditing courses, he returned to Quebec to join Laval's Institut d'histoire in 1947. There, he championed a new kind of historical study purged of hagiography and ideology, one supported by scientific methods and documentary evidence.[74] He regularly criticized Quebec texts as mired in nationalism and historical grievances. Yet, although his own memoirs suggest that he was criticized for his anti-clerical rebelliousness, he was probably hired because his doctoral thesis largely agreed with the clerical interpretation that Voltaire's influence on Canada was destructive. Yet Trudel, attracted by the IHAF's commitment to professionalism, grew close to his Montreal colleagues, especially Guy Fré-gault.[75] Although, during the early 1960s, his outspoken advocation of civil marriage raised eyebrows and ultimately forced his departure for Ontario universities, he remained influential in the study of New France. He wrote only one piece on Jacques Cartier, but his close attention to detail in his monumental *Histoire de la Nouvelle-France* made his work the definitive word on the Old Regime history of Canada. The first volume of this master study, *Les vaines tentatives*, makes a useful guide to professional historians' assessment of Jacques Cartier at the start of the Quiet Revolution.

Trudel's interpretation of Cartier is strikingly at variance with that of earlier historians. For Trudel, Cartier was no longer a devout proselytizing Catholic sailor but an adventurer primarily interested in material wealth and a passage to Asia. Certainly, Trudel was not the first to make such claims. In a paper delivered to the Canadian Historical Association in 1934, Biggar had also insisted on Cartier's material objectives.[76] But Trudel was more systematic in his depiction of a purely secular Cartier. Indeed, even as he accepted the existence of Dom Guillaume Le Breton and Dom Anthoine as priests on the roll for the second voyage, he questioned their presence on the trip itself. Rehashing the traditional arguments, Trudel simply found the evidence to be inconclusive and even suggested that the priests may have succumbed to scurvy. Yet, despite their possible presence, Trudel insisted that Cartier's voyage was not missionary in the slightest. Citing the commission for the second voyage, he explained it as a simple continuation of the first, also secular, expedition.[77] Moreover, for Trudel, the evidence in support of missionary activity was fraudulent in origin. The commissions supporting Cartier's (and Roberval's) colonization efforts of 1541-43 were equally secular. Cartier's initial commission, issued in March 1538, made no allowance for missionary activity. Later, however, a pious preamble was inserted for reasons of *realpolitik* and repeated nearly verbatim in Roberval's commission. Again, Trudel insisted, the French were interested only in riches.[78]

Trudel's explicitly secular interpretation of history set a tone for Cartier historiography, but it too was a reflection of his times and a theme widely accepted. Whereas the Cartier historians of the 1850-1950 period had unanimously perceived a religious motif in Cartier's voyages, those of the post-war era increasingly attributed a purely secular intent to Cartier. Anglophone scholars, American and Canadian, followed Trudel in hypothesizing a wholly economic incentive. The contrasts between these two approaches are striking. In 1934, in the flurry of publications that coincided with the Cartier celebrations, it was still possible to presume that Cartier's voyages constituted a religious mission, despite Biggar's claims to the contrary. Camille Pouliot, to cite only one example, clung to Cartier's proselytizing purpose in his *La grande aventure de Jacques Cartier.*[79] After the Second World War, such a blithe acceptance was replaced by an equally Manichean assumption that religion had nothing at all to do with it. Among the first works to voice this thought was *Jacques Cartier et la pensée colonisatrice,* published in 1946 by the French historian Eugène Guernier. Guernier continued the tradition of Cartier hagiography, praising the Malouin for being centuries ahead of his time in formulating a notion of a French colonial empire, rather than replicating Spanish conquests and the search for gold. Nevertheless, his motives were as secular as those driving the Spanish conquests.[80] Even Groulx, who reviewed the book in the RHAF, praised Guernier for secularizing Cartier and presenting him as a "simple chercheur d'or et de passage vers l'orient," not an evangelist seeking to convert people whose existence he did not know of in 1534.[81]

The old common sense surrounding Cartier no longer fit with the emerging Québécois nationalism characteristic of the Quiet Revolution. This looked to the future and eschewed the older nationalism of the Duplessis years as backward and counterproductive. Aggressive and secular, it welcomed modernity rather than seeking defences against it. Michael Gauvreau has explained how elements of the new Catholic nationalism of the 1930s evolved into this secular nationalism in the 1960s. However, it retained a distrust of the ideas of previous nationalists. Shifts in portrayals of Cartier also support the idea that the Quiet Revolution had roots in an earlier period and, as Ronald Rudin suggests, can be found in the historical institutions established by the Catholic priests Groulx and Maheux. A consensus about common sense ideas in national history eroded, beginning in the years that straddled the Second World War. The outpouring of publications in 1934 demonstrated a last moment of French Canadian harmony on the meaning of Jacques Cartier in history. But that same outpouring also revealed cracks in the agreement. Post-war studies, building on the pursuits of pre-war amateur historians, continued to tear down the remnants of the old common sense knowledge. Lanctôt's enthusiasm notwithstanding, Cartier no longer stood at the head of Quebec's family tree, and his heroism was no longer celebrated.

As the study of history became more professional in the post-war years, it also moved away from the narrative tradition and the focus on great men. Fernand Ouellet termed this the "modernization" of historiography, but in actuality, the discipline was fragmenting as increasing numbers of young scholars sought out original topics for doctoral theses and publications.[82] This fragmentation, lamented by Michael Bliss and J.L. Granatstein as a recent destruction of historical memory in English Canada, began with their own generation.[83] It was accompanied by a growing interest in new historical topics.

Professional scholars continued to look at Jacques Cartier, but they did so in new ways. Certainly, the old debate over the northern and southern route to Hochelaga persisted. Gérard Malchelosse took it up in the pages of *Cahiers des Dix*, a scholarly journal maintaining the amateur tradition of the man of letters. Writing for the RHAF ten years later, Claude Perrault favoured the northern route.[84] Related to this interest in Hochelaga was the study of Native peoples. This likewise began in the amateur tradition in the person of William Douw Lighthall. Born in Hamilton, Ontario, into a United Empire Loyalist family, Lighthall lived most of his life in Montreal.[85] He was an imperialist, a poet, and a scholar as well as a faithful servant of public life. He served as mayor of Westmount from 1900 to 1903, and he founded the Union of Canadian Municipalities in 1901. He was also fascinated by history and was a member of the Antiquarian and Numismatic Society of Montreal, the HSMBC, and the CMHQ. And the Iroquois reserve near Montreal kept his mind on the place of the "Indian" in Canadian history. In 1898, Lighthall wrote a brochure on a prehistoric burial ground in Westmount and later gained fame as an expert on Ramusio's sixteenth-century plan of Hochelaga. In 1909, in recognition of his service to the federal Indian Department as a special counsel, or possibly as a token of gratitude for his historical romances about the Iroquois, he was named an honorary "Iroquois Chief" with the symbolic name Ticonderoga.[86] Lighthall was enormously proud of his Iroquoian identity, however fictional: he often styled himself Tekenderoken, or Tek, and considered himself a "brother in blood" to his Native friends.[87]

Following Lighthall, Aristide Beaugrand-Champagne turned to the study of the Hochelagans and Stadaconans during the 1940s. However, widespread francophone interest in Aboriginal peoples developed only with the Quiet Revolution.[88] With the post-war professionalization of history, and its branching out to forge links with kindred disciplines, the study of the St. Lawrence Aboriginal societies became a cottage industry. In it, Jacques Cartier was the source of choice. By the end of the 1960s, anthropologists and ethnologists, such as Bruce Trigger, employed Cartier as a resource through which to investigate the St. Lawrence Indians. Cartier had ceased to be an object of study and had become a source, albeit suspect, of information.

Cartier monuments and plaques continued to be unveiled but never with the fanfare of 1934, or even 1935. In 1957, on the anniversary of Cartier's death, local citizens placed a plaque on the main lighthouse in Matane, some two hundred miles downriver from Quebec City. A south shore community, Matane has no real connection to Cartier. Nevertheless, on 8 September 1957, the local historical society placed the plaque on the town's old lighthouse. Its text commemorated Cartier's death and named him the discoverer of Canada:

1557 1957
In memory of the 4th centenary of the death of Jacques Cartier
1491-1557
Illustrious navigator of Saint-Malo, France
Discoverer of Canada.[89]

The lighthouse itself had been turned over to the historical society and had been used as a tourist information bureau for much of the decade.[90] This plaque was clearly intended to capture tourist attention and stimulate interest in the local area.

In 1966, a prominent family of artists from Saint-Jean-Port-Joli produced a series of steles at Gaspé. Even here, the message was that Cartier, and his contact with Native peoples, was part of global, not national, heritage. At Expo 67, Canada's centennial festival, the Canadian government built a replica of the *Grande Hermine* to float in the waters of the St. Lawrence at Montreal, despite the fact that the original ship never made it that far. Sitting in the Lac des Dauphins on the man-made island built up by adding landfill to the once tiny Île Ronde, La Ronde Amusement Park was a feature of Expo 67. Like the Disneyland prototype for post-war amusement parks, La Ronde was divided into theme areas, such as the Klondike (or Wild West) Fort Edmonton. A Toronto reporter lamented that it put the storied midway of the Canadian National Exhibition to shame.[91] The *Grande Hermine* was given a berth in the man-made lake near the replica "eighteenth century Québec village," which served as a shopping centre for handicraft souvenirs.[92] After Expo, the ship was relocated to Cartier-Brébeuf Park in Quebec City, although people in Gaspé thought it rightly belonged to their town. Some fifty supporters of Gaspé picketed the vessel's initial launch in the year before Expo.[93] Perhaps they thought it poetic justice that the *Grande Hermine* sank on its relaunch into a pond at Cartier-Brébeuf Park. Recovered and moored, it was regularly visited by school groups but was never popular as a Quebec City tourist attraction. In 2001, Heritage Canada decided it could no longer keep it, and the ship was destroyed.[94] At about the same time, Parks Canada constructed a mock Indian village at the park that recalls the memory of Stadacona. The commemoration of First Nations supplanted that of European explorers in a reversal of a hundred years of tradition. Other minor Cartier remembrances did continue but without any real consensus. In 1969, the old plaque in Charlottetown was relocated to the new Jacques Cartier Provincial Park at the western end of PEI. Under the sponsorship of the Canadian millionaire and philanthropist David M. Stewart, it was set into a plinth for a new Cartier statue. And in 1971, a plaque was added to the plinth of the Saint-Roch Cartier monument to explain that the monument was a replica of one in Saint-Malo. None of these represented a consensus; they simply provided information. Cartier had been reduced to a curiosity of early Canada. The facts and firsts of his voyages were still routinely cited, but they were stripped of moral, religious, and historical meaning.

8
Failure and Forgetting

The 450th anniversary of Cartier's first voyage arrived in 1984. Although it was marked by a huge festival organized jointly by the federal and provincial governments, it actually demonstrated the extent to which Jacques Cartier had fallen from the lofty position he once enjoyed. On the surface, Québec 84 mirrored the 1934 celebrations: both involved tours of foreign dignitaries and public speeches in Gaspé and Quebec City; both fostered hopes of local economies awash with tourist dollars. Much like that of 1934, the anniversary sparked both popular and scholarly interest. Planning was in full swing by the spring of 1983, and the key events involved a flotilla of seventy-five tall ships from Gaspé up the St. Lawrence River to Quebec City in the summer of 1984. The same two cities that had anchored the festivities half a century earlier were once again the focus of official Cartier memories. Yet, despite the millions of dollars dedicated to the 1984 event, it was a near complete bust.

Québec 84
In the context of the early 1980s, federal-provincial cooperation in this festival might seem awkward. Yet, the federal governments of Pierre Trudeau's and John Turner's Liberals jointly planned and financed Québec 84 with René Lévesque's Parti Québécois provincial government. These governments had fought viciously against one another in the 1980 referendum campaign and again in the subsequent negotiations over patriation of the constitution. John Turner had been out of office at the time; Québec 84 was not his project. It was a public relations exercise that he inherited when he became party leader, and therefore prime minister, in June 1984. Following the defeat of the referendum, and the patriation of the constitution, Lévesque and many Quebecers continued to nurse deep wounds regarding Canadian federalism. In this context, everything was politicized. Attending a Saint-Malo ceremony to mark the start of the 450th anniversary, Lévesque took some pride in the preponderance of blue Quebec flags, which outnumbered the red and white

Canadian flags, implying that Quebec had won this battle of the flags. The wounds reopened easily. The same year was also a bicentennial of the coming of the Loyalists, and minor controversies swirled about the Loyalist celebrations. Francophone groups in Ontario, for instance, pointed out that the Loyalists were not the first Europeans in the province. Queen Elizabeth II was invited to attend this event but pointedly was not invited to Québec 84. Some newspapers suggested that she should also visit Quebec for the Cartier festivities, but the spokesman for the secretary of state insisted that this would not occur.[1] Instead, when the queen's visit was announced, her itinerary included stops in New Brunswick, a flight over Quebec, and stops in Ontario and Manitoba. Organizers of the Quebec celebration had not extended an invitation to her, at least publicly, and Ottawa decided it was best to avoid the issue, although both the president of France and the pope visited Quebec that summer.[2]

The itineraries of visiting world leaders were not the only controversial issues facing Québec 84. As was the case in 1934, interprovincial competition crept into the mix. Many Canadians saw Québec 84 as an attempt by the federal government to buy the loyalty of Quebecers. The tall ships were also to voyage to Toronto, where local journalists mused about the amount of money splashing around in Quebec versus the paltry sums being spent on the Toronto portion of the event. Promotional materials ignored Ottawa's involvement when they began to appear in newspapers in May. Federal officials were accused of apathy and aloofness, which one Toronto journalist attributed to the Liberal leadership campaign and the dying days of the Trudeau-appointed Prime Minister's Office.[3] New Brunswickers, upstaged in the Loyalist celebrations and ignored in the Cartier ones, as in 1934, pointed out that both the Loyalists and Cartier had arrived in New Brunswick first.

The Cartier festivities began in Saint-Malo in April with the official dedication and public opening of Jacques Cartier's manor at Limoilou. This house had been known since Dionne discovered it in the 1880s but had remained in private hands. In 1974, Jean Palardy, historical advisor to the Macdonald-Stewart Foundation, learned that the owner was preparing to modernize the building, significantly affecting its heritage value. He convinced David M. Stewart to intervene. The Macdonald-Stewart Foundation was established in 1973 when Stewart sold Macdonald Tobacco, which he had inherited from his father, and devoted his time and wealth to charitable endeavours. The foundation was involved in numerous hospital charities in Quebec, McGill University's agricultural college, and in historical reconstructions and preservations at Montreal's Chateau Ramezay, the Île Sainte-Hélène fortifications, and at Chateau Dufresne.[4] The Limoilou manor was a natural overseas extension of this work. Mixing his historical periods, Stewart organized a Society of 100 Associates to raise the millions needed to buy and restore the property. The foundation sent out circulars to Canadian corporations, based on a list of Olympic Games donors supplied by Ottawa.[5] It bought the property in May 1978 and began restoration work.

Ottawa also issued stamps and coins to coincide with the anniversary. Ironically, given the non-invitation of the queen, her image featured on the obverse of a special one-dollar coin, which depicted Cartier landing at Gaspé. The mint had already planned a $100 gold Cartier coin for 1984 but rushed out this dollar coin in the spring. The main reason stated for the rush was that the gold coin was scheduled for September release, long after the main tourist events had ended. The dollar coin was designed to counter this misstep and to offer an affordable souvenir that capitalized on the anticipated attentions of Québec 84.[6] Similarly, the post office's special stamps were marked by blunders. In a series of twelve stamps commemorating the provinces, which, in some unspecified way, were intended to honour Jacques Cartier, the captions were incorrect.[7]

The Québec 84 festival itself was a disaster, even if a mini Cartiermania materialized. Certainly, conferences were held, films produced, and important scholarly works published. Indeed, as one *Globe and Mail* reporter noted, if the "disgraceful rip off" constituted one extreme of the Jacques Cartier industry, a flurry of scholarly work on the Malouin explorer embodied the other.[8] Perhaps the most lasting legacy was the creation of the Centre Jacques Cartier, a social science research centre based at the Université Lumière Lyon 2. Although the Centre Jacques Cartier does include a version of Hamel's portrait in some of its branding, it is not greatly concerned with the explorer himself. Its mandate is to foster scholarly exchange between Canadian and French researchers in a vast array of subject fields.[9] Nevertheless, much as had occurred fifty years earlier, the early 1980s produced a spike of literary and academic output to coincide with the commemorative events. Among the first was Michel Bideaux's article "Éditer Cartier," published in the pages of the *Revue d'histoire littéraire du Québec et du Canada français*.[10] Bideaux, now professor emeritus at the Université Montpellier, used this article to launch a new edition of Cartier's *Relations* for 1984.[11] Bideaux's is probably the most thorough edition of Cartier's *Relations* yet published. In deriving a "definitive" text, he drew on a variety of earlier editions, in particular Ramusio and Hakluyt, but also the 1545 *Brief recit,* the Moreau manuscript, and the 1598 Rouen manuscript. Indeed, Bideaux's bibliography lists eighteen editions, many of which might be described as reprints. The result is a heavily annotated text in sixteenth-century French that conveys an aura of authoritative authenticity. This is a thorough literary history of the accounts of Cartier's voyages, with a focus on the creation, provenance, and preservation of the manuscripts. Except for explanations of some of the controversial passages in the texts, Bideaux's work offers little comment on the characters, or the persons of Cartier and Roberval. The focus, then, is on the text rather than the achievements.

Another key scholarly publication was the monumental *Le monde de Jacques Cartier*, edited by the distinguished French historian Fernand Braudel, among others.[12] In the year before his death, this former editor of the journal *Annales E.S.C.* directed the publication of a collection of articles in a superbly illustrated and textured study, not only of Cartier but of his sixteenth-century world, on both sides of the Atlantic. Drawing together an international group of scholars, this volume represents the height of academic writing on Cartier in the 1980s. It featured essays by major scholars such as John Dickinson, Cornelius Jaenen, and Michel Mallet au Jourdin to contextualize the history supposedly commemorated by Québec 84. In three sections, the authors explored the sixteenth century, the contexts of discovery and exchange, and the voyages of Jacques Cartier. Like that of Bideaux, this work engaged in no mythic construction of a great adventurer. The "biography" of Cartier comprised only six pages of text, which focused largely on the few known "facts" of his life. The romance of a founding hero was all but lost to the historical context of Renaissance economics, ethnography, environmental history, and cold dispassionate analyses of the sixteenth-century European imagination. Cartier in the 1980s had become less a discoverer of Canada than a source through which one could better understand the cultural biases of sixteenth-century Europe.

Not all the Cartiermania was so detached. Indeed, the independent filmmaker and comedian Marc Blais dressed himself as Cartier, became the unofficial face of Québec 84, and made himself a minor celebrity in the process.[13] But interest was only fleeting this time, and political controversy was the name of the game. Two main non-profit corporations, the Corporation Québec 1534-1984 and the Corporation Gaspé 84, organized the biggest events at Quebec City and Gaspé respectively. Even before the festivities began, there were warning signs in Gaspé. A strike by municipal workers and an inadequate number of tourist beds prompted fears of a total collapse.[14] One of the tall ships capsized and sank in a storm in the Atlantic, with a loss of nearly two-thirds of the crew.[15] Québec 84 attempted to turn Cartier into a marketing gimmick for tourism but without success. By mid-July, despite large numbers of tourists in Quebec City and support from more established tourist festivals, the Corporation Québec 1534-1984 was in dire financial straits and, according to some journalists, incompetently run. Despite having already spent $20 million on Québec 84, Ottawa had to bail out the organizing committee with an additional $3.5 million to keep the festival running until its official closing date in August.[16] In Gaspé, things were worse. When the tall ships left port, they took the tourists with them. Facing a $400,000 deficit, Corporation Gaspé 84 shut down at the end of July, cutting a full month of events out of its program.[17]

In actuality, Québec 84 was not about Jacques Cartier at all, or even about history itself for that matter. It was meant to be a celebration of modern

Quebec. Even if the tall ships did present an implicit reference to the explorers of the age of sail, they overshadowed any memories of Cartier. Quebec City's daily newspaper, *Le Soleil,* showered the spectacle of the tall ships with coverage, but with the exception of a comic version of Cartier's *Relations* drawn by a school-age boy, it ignored the exploits of the explorer whose anniversary was the excuse for the celebrations. Even Gilles Picard's comic was not about Cartier: it was about the youth of Quebec. One of its panels showed Cartier and his sailors sitting around their cross at Gaspé singing "Gens du pays," Quebec's unofficial national anthem.[18] When a world champion sailor arrived in town, he was hailed, not as a modern Jacques Cartier, but as the "Wayne Gretzky de la mer."[19] Moreover, 1984 was a busy year for Canadians. Three prime ministers held office in the same calendar year, Canadian athletes exceeded expectations at the boycott-plagued Los Angeles Olympics, Steve Fonyo ran across the country, completing Terry Fox's Marathon of Hope, and both the queen and the pope paid visits. Modern Quebec, and modern Canada, turned away from history for their heroes and preferred the excitement of celebrity in their own age.

Peripheral Interest
Even as the cult of celebrity and "star gazing" pushed aside older concerns with historical heroes, some people continued to find figures from the past compelling. Fourteen years after the collapse of Québec 84, Pierre Larouche launched another Cartier scheme. An urban planner and engineer trained at McGill and Yale, Larouche proposed a Cartier statue for the top of Mount Royal. He organized the Compagnons de Jacques Cartier to raise funds and plan the installation, as well as a more ambitious project to construct a millennium tower on the mountain. Here was a strange effort to link Cartier to the millennium celebrations every community was planning by the end of the 1990s. Yet, despite the support of eighty-three of the one hundred people Larouche had polled a few years earlier, the Cartier statue and tower never materialized.[20]

Scholarly interest around Cartier also persisted, even if Cartier himself was no longer a central topic of study. In 1992, at about the time when the memory of Christopher Columbus was taking a beating, Larouche published his own investigation into Cartier's 1535 arrival at Hochelaga. Indeed, he dedicated it to Cartier himself, the "Christophe Colomb de l'Amérique du nord." In fact, his book was written to coincide with the celebration of another historic date: the 350th anniversary of the founding of Montreal. Although the 450th anniversary of Cartier's "discovery" of Hochelaga had passed without notice in 1985, Larouche connected Cartier's sixteenth-century visit with the arrival of Paul Chomedey de Maisonneuve over a century later.[21] This linked Cartier to the founding of Montreal just as the tercentenary on the Plains of Abraham had established his prologue to

Canada's founding by Champlain. In his own way, Larouche continued the tradition established by Faribault, Dionne, and Lanctôt.

Other scholars balked at Larouche's lead and further reduced Cartier's centrality, even in works that focused on his exploits. Ramsay Cook's 1993 edition of Cartier's *Relations* is a case in point. One of Canada's most influential twentieth-century historians, Cook produced a version of Cartier's *Relations* in which the central figure took a supporting role. In the introduction, Cook attempted to shift the focus from the European explorers to the Stadaconan people whom Cartier met. Its title, "Donnacona Discovers Europe," punctuates this shift in historiographical perspective, one that had been building since the 1950s. Sliding quickly over issues of authorship and the authority of the texts, Cook focused on the problems of sources and on using Cartier for ethnography. In the end, his version remains a straightforward and standard narrative of the voyages, little changed from Biggar. The relative repositioning of Jacques Cartier and Donnacona was not entirely successful. However, Cook did make a serious effort to read these European-recorded events from the Stadaconan perspective, an admirable objective that nevertheless furthered the explorer's fall from hero to historical source.[22]

Leading scholars such as Ramsay Cook took the initiative in shifting the use of historical figures like Cartier, but as professional historians, they remained limited by sources and the evidence on which they could rely in support of their arguments. Popular accounts, on the other hand, were less limited, and thus they reveal twenty-first-century Canada's tastes to a greater degree. For instance, Historica's "Heritage Minutes" present an unproblematized interpretation of Canada's past that reflects nation-building mythology more than scholarship. The Heritage Minutes, or Historica Minutes, are minute-long short films illustrating particular episodes in Canada's history. They first appeared in 1991 amid widespread public debate concerning Canadians' knowledge of national history and have subsequently aired regularly on Canadian television and in movie theatres. Accompanied by predesigned lesson plans, they are also distributed for use by school teachers in classrooms across Canada. The Jacques Cartier minute, produced in 1991, re-enacts a fantasy incident in which Cartier walks overland to Stadacona in 1534, and reinforces the popular belief that the word "Canada" is a mistranslation of *kanata*, the Stadaconan word for village, as the Iroquois' name for their country. The minute displays an almost deliberate misreading of history and historiography. Although Cartier was led to Stadacona by Domagaya and Taignoagny, the minute opens with Cartier and his sailors walking over the crest of a hill, accompanied by a priest who claims knowledge of the local language. Soon, they meet an old Aboriginal man, presumably Donnacona, who, in gesturing to his village, gives the priest the false impression that his country's name is Kanata. Even when corrected by a common sailor, whose insubordination is even less probable than his surprisingly better command of the local language, the mistake is left unchecked. Cartier is absolved of it – after all, he relied on the leadership of his priest in this matter – but in so absolving him, the Heritage Minute also reduces his role in history. Far from being the heroic leader of nineteenth-century historiography or of Hamel's portrait, Cartier is simply present as a confused observer at an event memorialized in twentieth-century popular mythology.[23] Even in his own story, he had become a minor character.

A similar nation-building exercise produced *Canada: A People's History* during the first years of the new millennium. The French and English sides of the Canadian Broadcasting Corporation worked together to produce this seventeen-part documentary on Canada's history.[24] In the broadcasts, Cartier's significance was even further reduced. Three short segments present an incomplete vision of his voyages. The first, "The Land God Gave to Cain," depicts a "frustrated" Cartier searching for a trade passage through North America but finding only "confusing shorelines, fog, and dead ends." The segment ends with Cartier claiming possession of this land and the kidnapping of Domagaya and Taignoagny. The second segment takes Cartier to Hochelaga and multiplies the errors. It presents as fact a meeting between André Thevet and Domagaya and Taignoagny, claims that Cartier knew Hochelaga was on an island, and depicts him as a purely secular and unsympathetic figure consciously manipulating the Hochelagans' belief in his divinity. The greatest misconceptions, however, revolve around the iconic mythology of the scurvy incident. According to the documentary, Cartier did not intend to winter in North America, but his ships were unexpectedly caught in the ice. Moreover, it adds that Cartier did not conceal the scurvy of his crew and that Domagaya and Taignoagny brought the cure into his fort. These may appear to be quibbles, but they significantly recast the historical record that is supported by evidence. Moreover, they suit popular ideas regarding early European-Aboriginal contact in which cynical but hapless Europeans survive in the New World only though the benevolence of simple-living, kind-hearted Native peoples. It is an attractive myth. The final segment reveals that Donnacona "languished" in Europe and, like the second segment, elevates Thevet as an authority on the voyages. For the purposes of this documentary, the third voyage did not exist.[25]

Although the companion book corrected many of the errors of the film version, the whole reduces Cartier to snapshots of popular myths and misconceptions.[26] The presentist interpretation of history illustrated by the film serves another purpose, that of fostering national unity through an understanding of the history that unites the country. It is a popularization of history that, in the nature of the genre, sweeps aside the conventions of scholarship in favour of a compelling narrative. However, what stands out in this tiny segment of a thirty-two-hour documentary is how unimportant Jacques Cartier's role in Canadian history has become, especially when contrasted with the enormous significance placed on him by nineteenth-century French Canadians and later by their English-speaking compatriots. Jacques Cartier was once the figure that bound nationalists together, or at least represented the promise of such a unity to some. By the early twenty-first century, he had once again dropped not into obscurity but to the periphery.

Conclusion

For nearly a century, Jacques Cartier had served as a point of (limited) contact between English and French Canadian nationalism. He similarly offered a contact point between amateur and professional traditions of history in the mid-twentieth century. But, as professional history pursued a trajectory away from the celebration of the heroic past, the amateur tradition continued to embrace it. Nevertheless, though Cartier remained a figure for commemoration in the amateur tradition, his "memory" was no longer internal. For modern Québécois, Cartier no longer spoke to their identity in the same manner. He no longer represented values lying at the heart of their national identity. For anglophone Canadians, Cartier remained what he had always been: the first European to visit what would become modern Canada.

By the end of the twentieth century, no real consensus existed about Cartier beyond the basic anglophone idea that he headed the narrative of national historical development and that his objectives were secular and material. A new nationalism, reflecting a post-war modernity, had reduced Cartier from his Victorian status. From obscurity, Cartier was elevated through the works of a few French Canadian intellectuals in the mid-nineteenth century to an exalted position. But his rise resulted from more than the efforts of a few dedicated enthusiasts. The nineteenth-century image of Cartier was a product of, and a reaction to, modernity. A pious and intrepid explorer was inspirational but also verifiable in the scientific evidence uncovered via objective archival research. Over the years, while documented particulars of Cartier's life were debated, the inspirational or emotional meaning of his exploits remained largely untouched. However, in the transition from the era of Faribault and Dionne to that of Lanctôt and Trudel, memories of Jacques Cartier changed in fundamental ways. Anglophone interest, comparisons with Cabot and Champlain, and competing nationalisms in the twentieth century raised questions about the common sense wisdom of Cartier's piety and his connections to Canadian nationality. Moreover, emerging from the great crises of the depression and the Second World War, Canadian society – even in Quebec – no longer sought solace in the old pieties. The continued professionalization (or modernization) of historical research in Canada also helped knock holes in some common sense knowledge. Cartier could no longer represent the traditional meaning, nor did people need him to.

According to the works of Gramscian scholars and others, common sense knowledge is never ideologically neutral. Nor, however, is it a simple tool of domination. Common sense "facts" affected the world view of working-class people, the bourgeoisie, and elites, even if they tended to benefit some more than others. Nor is common sense static. It changes, slowly and gradually, to reflect changes in the material and cultural conditions of everyday life. As Canada developed through the nineteenth and twentieth centuries, common sense evolved to mirror new aspects of modernity. The "modern" of 1893 was not modern in 1934, and that of 1934 was out of date by 1984. The history of Cartiermania, its rise and decline, reflected changes in Canadian common sense and in both the comforts and anxieties of modernity.

By the dawn of Quebec's Quiet Revolution, a new common sense had swept aside the old religious Jacques Cartier. Even the clerical nationalist Lionel Groulx insisted on a secular Cartier in the 1940s. Certainly, hints of the old ideals surfaced from time to time, and Cartier continued to be celebrated in fleeting and idiosyncratic ways. But he no longer spoke to any national identity. Indeed, part of the new common sense was a peculiar localization of Cartier memories in Gaspé and on Mount Royal, which clearly offset any "national" memory. Adopted by English Canadians, he was never internalized as one of their own. And a modernizing Quebec no longer looked to its ultramontane past for inspiration. In an increasingly secular, commercial, and consumerist post-war society, no one identified with a Renaissance explorer.

Cartier was not alone in suffering this decline. Heroes have experienced similar fates across the world. The nature of public memory appears to have undergone a profound change during the second half of the twentieth century. With some notable exceptions, heroes were no longer long-dead explorers and national founding fathers. Instead, in a world in which "democracy" was a new common sense, people turned to contemporary icons of commercial consumerism. Sports, film, and the entertainment industry provided a steady stream of new modern-day heroes. Historical heroes no longer mattered as much. Today, when people think of the heroes of history, they think more of veterans, the common soldier, than they do of leaders.

Some historians have argued that this shift from the leaders of the past toward what they describe as the trivial and empty idols of Hollywood and hockey can be traced to the historical profession itself. In a series of polemical works, Canadian historians such as J.L. Granatstein and Michael Bliss have criticized social history for the "sundering" of the Canadian mind.[27] The turn to private life, to everyday life, and away from "great men" has affected the way in which history is taught and how the past is understood. Opponents of this movement might argue that it has left Canada's professional historians too quick to reflect contemporary cultural values that embrace multiculturalism and a concomitant rejection of the older canon. Or they may state that this presentism and "political correctness" in turn has alienated much of the public and switched off its interest in professional historians. However, similar complaints have been voiced throughout the twentieth century. The example of Jacques Cartier suggests that there is a longer, and perhaps natural, process at work, one that is connected to long-term alterations in the historical discipline. As methods and accepted forms of evidence have changed since the days of Faribault and Dionne, so has the "meaning" of history. The new understanding of the past reflects new forms of common sense knowledge. Nothing in this book is a call to rebuild a lost national identity through the celebration of Sir John A. Macdonald, for example. But perhaps professional historians need to develop new ways to think about their own discipline. They need to recognize their place in the construction of common sense knowledge, as well as the limits on their role in it. But, more centrally, they need to acknowledge more fully how much their interpretations of the past, and more precisely their methods, reflect the common sense of their own times. They must investigate more directly the politics of history writing.

Jacques Cartier has demonstrated one way of thinking about these questions. His twentieth-century decline was no less related to developments in the discipline than was his nineteenth-century rise. Cartier has remained idiosyncratic and is no longer connected to public memory as he once was. Stripped of his religious and nationalist significance, the hero is remembered but not internalized. He rose from obscurity, became the founder of a nation, of a country, and the inspiration to thousands, but was then abandoned once again. He was celebrated in a certain way during the nineteenth century. His meaning changed in the twentieth century. One wonders what 2034 will bring him.

Notes

Introduction

1 Archaeologists discovered the site of Charlesbourg-Royal in modern Cap-Rouge, Quebec, during the summer of 2006. See *Le Soleil* (Quebec City), 19 August 2006; *National Post* (Toronto), 22 August 2006; *The Globe and Mail* (Toronto), 29 August 2006.

2 *La Minerve* (Montreal), 15 June 1893. See, especially, the town council's procès-verbaux, 6 July 1892, 13 July 1892, 25 May 1893, P 23, Fonds de la municipalité de Saint-Henri, Archives de la Ville de Montréal, Montreal.

3 David Karel, ed., *Dictionnaire des artistes de langue française en Amérique du nord* (Quebec City: Presses de l'Université Laval, 1992), 820-21.

4 The French text reads: "À Jacques Cartier né à Saint-Malo le 31 décembre 1491 envoyé par François 1er à la découverte du Canada le 20 avril 1534. Jetant l'ancre le 16 juillet de la même année, dans l'entrée du Saint-Laurent il prit possession de tout le pays au nom du roi son maître, et l'appela Nouvelle-France. 1893."

5 J.N. Wilford, *The Mysterious History of Columbus* (New York: Knopf, 1991), 248-59; Claudia Bushman, *America Discovers Columbus* (Hanover: University Press of New England, 1992). See also Thomas Schlereth, "Columbia, Columbus, and Columbianism," *Journal of American History* 79, 3 (December 1992): 937-68.

6 Peter Pope, *The Many Landfalls of John Cabot* (Toronto: University of Toronto Press, 1997).

7 Graeme Morton, *William Wallace: Man and Myth* (Stroud: Sutton, 2001). Contrast with the more celebratory David R. Ross, *On the Trail of William Wallace* (Edinburgh: Luath Press, 1999).

8 Anthony D. Smith, *The Ethnic Origins of Nations* (London: Basil Blackwell, 1986), 192-202.

9 Benedict Anderson, *Imagined Communities: Reflections on the Origins and Spread of Nationalism* (London: Verso, 1993), 204.

10 Washington Irving, *A History of the Life and Voyages of Christopher Columbus*, 4 vols. (London: John Murray, 1828).

11 David Cannadine, "Imperial Canada: Old History, New Problems," in *Imperial Canada, 1867-1914*, ed. Colin Coates (Edinburgh: University of Edinburgh, Centre of Canadian Studies, 1997), 4.

12 See, especially, Gérard Bouchard, *Les deux chanoines: contradiction et ambivalence dans la pensée de Lionel Groulx* (Montreal: Boréal, 2003). But see also Esther Delisle, *The Traitor and the Jew: Anti-Semitism and Extreme Right-Wing Nationalism in French Canada from 1929 to 1939* (Montreal: Davies, 1993); Susan Mann Trofimenkoff, ed., *Abbé Groulx: Variations on a Nationalist Theme* (Vancouver: Copp Clark, 1973), and her *Action française: French Canadian Nationalism in the Twenties* (Toronto: University of Toronto Press, 1975); Georges-Émile Giguère, *Lionel Groulx: biographie* (Montreal: Bellarmin, 1978); Pierre Hébert, *Lionel Groulx et l'appel de la race* (Saint-Laurent: Fides, 1996). See also Ross Gordon, "The Historiographical Debate on the Charges of Anti-Semitism Made against Lionel Groulx" (MA thesis, University of Ottawa, 1996).

Chapter 1: The Sixteenth-Century World and Jacques Cartier

1 Enrique Dussel, *The Invention of America*, trans. M.D. Barker (New York: Continuum, 1995), 28. See also Samuel E. Morison, *Admiral of the Ocean Sea* (Boston: Little, Brown, 1942), 92-108.

2 On de Gonneville and Essoméricq, see Philippe Bonnichon, *Des cannibales aux castors: les découvertes françaises de l'Amérique, 1503-1788* (Paris: France-Empire, 1994), 19-25.

3 Henry Percival Biggar, *The Precursors of Jacques Cartier, 1497-1534: A Collection of Documents Relating to the Early History of the Dominion of Canada* (Ottawa: Government Printing Bureau, 1911), 102-11.

4 See, in particular, Gustave Lanctôt, *Jacques Cartier devant l'histoire* (Montreal: Éditions Lumen, 1947), 16-19. Lanctôt's thesis will be discussed in greater detail below.

5 Verrazano's western sea was probably today's Pimlico Sound. According to Samuel E. Morison, the modern breaks in the Outer Banks off the Carolina coast did not exist in the sixteenth century. See Morison, *The European Discovery of America*, vol. 1, *The Northern Voyages, AD 500-1600* (New York: Oxford University Press, 1971), 293.

6 Henry Percival Biggar identified Cartier at forty-two baptisms, as either a witness or a godfather, between 1510 and 1552. See his *Collection of Documents Relating to Jacques Cartier and the Sieur de Roberval* (Ottawa: Public Archives of Canada, 1930).

7 Marcel Trudel, "Cartier, Jacques," in *Dictionary of Canadian Biography Online* (Toronto: University of Toronto Press, 2005), Library and Archives Canada, http://www.biographi.ca.

8 To avoid confusion, Cartier's dates from the Julian calendar will be used. The Gregorian calendar, adopted in parts of Catholic Europe in 1582, and in Britain in 1752, typically shifts dates ten to twelve days from the Julian calendar. Further discussion of dating can be found in Hospice-A. Verreau, "Jacques Cartier: questions de calendrier civil et ecclésiastique," *Proceedings and Transactions of the Royal Society of Canada* 10 (1890): 113-14.

9 Henry Percival Biggar, *The Voyages of Jacques Cartier: Published from the Originals, with Translations, Notes, and Appendices* (Ottawa: Public Archives of Canada, 1924), 22.

10 Ibid., 34-35.

11 Ibid., 50-51.

12 Claude Chapdelaine, "Sur les traces des premiers Québécois," *Recherches amérindiens au Québec* 15, 1-2 (1985): 3-6. For an overview of the differing theories regarding the identity of these people, see James F. Pendergast, "The Confusing Identities Attributed to Stadacona and Hochelaga," *Journal of Canadian Studies* 32, 4 (Winter 1998): 149-67.

13 This prophetic coupling of capture and Christianity set the trend for a long tradition of proselytization among the Native peoples of northern North America.

14 Morison, *The European Discovery of America*, 1:391.

15 Biggar, *Voyages of Jacques Cartier*, 114.

16 Jean-Claude Robert, *Atlas historique de Montréal* (Montreal: Art global, 1994), 24.

17 André Thevet, *Les singularitez de la France antarctique* (1578; Paris: Maisonneuve et Cie, 1878), 407.

18 Biggar, *Collection of Documents*, 83 (Sir John Wallop to Cromwell, 18 April 1540), and 135-37 (Spanish ambassador in France to the emperor, fall 1540).

19 Biggar, *Collection of Documents*, 128-31 (Commission of 17 October 1540).

20 Biggar, *Collection of Documents*, 178-85 (Commission of 15 January 1541).

21 Biggar, *Collection of Documents*, 285 (the emperor to the cardinal of Toledo, 7 May 1541).

22 Biggar, *Collection of Documents*, 463 (Examination of Newfoundland Sailors regarding Cartier, 23 September 1542).

23 Marcel Trudel recounts the sanitized version of the story. In it, the lovers are a married couple and are marooned due to the husband's treason. Trudel, *Histoire de la Nouvelle-France*, vol. 1, *Les vaines tentatives, 1524-1603* (Montreal: Fides, 1963), 155. For a Canadian account, see Thomas Guthrie Marquis, *Marguerite de Roberval: A Romance of the Days of Jacques Cartier* (Toronto: Copp Clark, 1899). More recently, Douglas Glover's novel *Elle* (Fredericton: Goose Lane Editions, 2003), a lusty portrayal of the saga, won the Governor General's Award for Fiction.

24 Jean Alfonse's *Cosmographie* reveals that Roberval attempted to supplant Cartier's toponymy. France-Roy is the accepted new name for Charlesbourg-Royal, but some documents suggest

Fort Henri-Charles and France-neufve as other names. Jean Alfonse, *Les voyages adventureux du capitaine Ian Alfonse, Sainctongeois* (Paris: Ian de Marnef, 1559), is an abridgement of the *Cosmographie* of 1545 held in the Bibliothèque nationale, Paris.

25 Serge Courville, ed., *Atlas historique du Québec: population et territoire* (Sainte-Foy: Presses de l'Université Laval, 1996), 6.

26 Peter Pope covers this point at some length in *The Many Landfalls of John Cabot* (Toronto: University of Toronto Press, 1997), 137-41.

27 Francis Parkman, *The Parkman Reader: From the Works of Francis Parkman*, ed. S.E. Morison (Boston: Little, Brown, 1955), 67.

28 Biggar, *The Precursors*, 195-97.

29 Robert Delort, "Les Basques ont-ils atteint le Canada avant 1497?" *Cahiers d'histoire* 13, 2 (Fall 1993): 23-30.

30 Lanctôt, *Jacques Cartier devant l'histoire*, 16-20, 99-135.

31 In "Jacques Cartier et son oeuvre," *Revue de l'Université d'Ottawa* 5, 1 (January-March 1935): 35, Lanctôt suggested that Cartier captained the ship home.

32 Reuben Thwaites, ed., *The Jesuit Relations and Allied Documents* (Cleveland: Burrows, 1897), 3:36.

33 Lucien Campeau, "Encore à propos de Cartier," *Revue d'histoire de l'Amérique française* 7, 4 (March 1954): 558-70.

34 Trudel, *Histoire de la Nouvelle-France*, 1:58-63.

35 Eric Hobsbawm, Introduction to *The Invention of Tradition*, ed. Eric Hobsbawm and Terrence Ranger (Cambridge: Cambridge University Press, 1983), 1-14.

36 Jeffrey Burton Russell, *Inventing the Flat Earth: Columbus and Modern Historians* (New York: Praeger, 1991).

37 Gramsci discussed "common sense" in *Selections from the Prison Notebooks* (New York: International, 1971), 323-43.

38 Michael Billig, *Banal Nationalism* (London: Sage, 1995).

Chapter 2: Forgetting and Remembering

1 See Louis-Léonard Aumasson, sieur de Courville, *Mémoires sur le Canada depuis 1749 jusqu'à 1760: en trois parties, avec cartes et plans lithographiés* (Quebec City: Middleton and Dawson, 1873). See also George Heriot, *The History of Canada, from Its First Discovery, Comprehending an Account of the Original Establishment of the Colony of Louisiana* (London: Longman and Rees, 1804); William Smith, *A History of Canada from Its First Discovery to the Peace of 1763* (Quebec City: J. Neilson, 1815).

2 Brian Young, "Positive Law, Positive State: Class Realignment and the Transformation of Lower Canada, 1815-1866," in *Colonial Leviathan: State Formation in Mid-Nineteenth-Century Canada*, ed. Allan Greer and Ian Radforth (Toronto: University of Toronto Press, 1992), 52.

3 The 1545 edition is entitled *Brief recit* but many subsequent editions use the modern French *Bref récit*, and some employ *Brief récit*. Except when citing a specific edition, I use *Brief recit* generically.

4 Marcel Trudel, *Histoire de la Nouvelle-France*, vol. 1, *Les vaines tentatives, 1524-1603* (Montreal: Fides, 1963), 72-73.

5 Michel Bideaux, "Introduction," in *Relations: Édition critique par Michel Bideaux*, by Jacques Cartier (Montreal: Presses de l'Université de Montréal, 1986), 61-62, 305. Noël's letter is reproduced in Richard Hakluyt, *The Principal Navigations, Voyages, Traffiques and Discoveries of the English Nation, Made by Sea or Overland to the Remote and Farthest Distant Quarters of the Earth at Any Time within the Compasse of These 1600 Years* (London: Dent, 1926), 13:154.

6 A section of the title of Florio's 1580 translation.

7 Christian Morissonneau, "L'oeuvre de Jacques Cartier," in *Le monde de Jacques Cartier*, ed. Fernand Braudel (Montreal: Libre Expression, 1984), 293.

8 W.F. Ganong, *Crucial Maps in the Early Cartography and Place-Nomenclature of the Atlantic Coast of Canada* (Toronto: University of Toronto Press, 1964), 331-54.

9 Dany Larochelle, "Du ciel au bateau: La *Cosmographie* (1544) du pilote Jean Alfonse et la construction du savoir géographique au XVIe siècle" (MA thesis, Université de Sherbrooke, 2001).

10 Jehan Mallard, *Premier livre de la description de tous les portz de mer de l'univers* (N.p., 1545); Guillaume Postel, *De orbis terræ concordia libri quatuor ... Adjectæ sunt quoque annotationes in margine a pio atque erudito quodam viro, etc.* (Paris: Gromorsus, 1544).

11 Ribault's and Laudonnière's accounts of the Huguenot Florida colonies are included in Suzanne Lussagnet, ed., *Les Français en Amérique pendant la deuxième moitié du XVIe siècle*, vol. 2, *Les Français en Floride* (Paris: Presses universitaires de France, 1958), 4, 38.

12 La Popelinière's *Trois mondes* confuses Verrazano and Cartier, who is never named. Anne-Marie Beaulieu, ed., *Les trois mondes de la Popelinière* (Geneva: Librairie Droz, 1997).

13 Thevet, *Cosmographie universelle*, reprinted in Roger Schlesinger and Arthur Stabler, eds., *André Thevet's North America: A Sixteenth Century View* (Montreal and Kingston: McGill-Queen's University Press, 1986), 48.

14 Frank Lestringant, "Nouvelle-France et fiction cosmographique dans l'oeuvre d'André Thevet," *Etudes littéraires* 10, 1-2 (April-August 1977): 150-51.

15 Samuel E. Morison, *The European Discovery of America*, vol. 1, *The Northern Voyages, AD 500-1600* (New York: Oxford University Press, 1971), 457.

16 On this, and on Thevet in general, see Frank Lestringant, *André Thevet: cosmographe des derniers Valois* (Geneva: Librairie Droz, 1991).

17 Marius Barbeau, "Cartier Inspired Rabelais," *Canadian Geographical Journal* 9, 9 (September 1934): 113-25.

18 Pierre Margry, *Les navigations françaises et la révolution maritime du XIVe au XVIe siècle: d'après les documents inédits tirés de France, d'Angleterre, d'Espagne et d'Italie* (Paris: Librairie Tross, 1867), 338.

19 Morison, *The European Discovery of America*, 1:458.

20 The only known copy of Doremet's manuscript is conserved in the Bibliothèque de l'Arsenal, Paris, cote 8306H. It was reprinted by F. Joüon des Longrais as *Jacques Doremet: sa vie et ses ouvrages* (Rennes: Plihon et Hervé, 1894). See also Abel Lefranc, *Les navigations de Pantagruel: étude sur la géographie Rabelaisienne* (Paris: Leclerc, 1905).

21 Voltaire (François-Marie Arouet), *Candide ou l'optimisme*, édition critique, René Pomeau, ed. (Paris: Librairie Nizet, 1959), 188. The original quotation from *Candide* (Chapter 23) reads as follows: "Vous savez que ces deux nations sont en guerre pour quelques arpents de neige vers le Canada."

22 Barbeau, "Cartier Inspired Rabelais," 124-25. Apparently, Adélard Turgeon made a similar point at a 1905 monument unveiling in Saint-Malo. Louis Tiercelin, *Mémorial des fêtes franco-canadiennes pour l'érection du monument de Jacques Cartier* (Paramé: Éditions de l'Hermine, 1905), 70.

23 Lucien Febvre, *L'apparition du livre* (Paris: A. Michel, 1971), 421-23. See also Geoffroy Atkinson, *Les nouveaux horizons de la Renaissance française* (Paris: E. Droz, 1935), 21.

24 André Lespagnol, *Histoire de Saint-Malo et du pays malouin* (Toulouse: Privat, 1984), 101.

25 See E.G.R. Taylor, ed., *The Original Writings and Correspondence of the Two Richard Hakluyts* (London: Hakluyt Society, 1935), 2:288.

26 Documentation to this effect is appended to Alain Beaulieu and Réal Ouellet's edition of Samuel de Champlain's *Des sauvages* (Montreal: Typo, 1993), 203-13.

27 Reproduced as Marc Lescarbot, *Nova Francia, a Description of Acadia, 1606*, trans. P. Erondelle (London: Routledge, 1928), 157.

28 Baron de Lahontan, *Oeuvres complètes*, ed. Réal Ouellet (Montreal: Presses de l'Université de Montréal, 1990), 529. The original version reads, "Jacques Cartier y alla ensuite, mais après monté plus haut que Québec avec son Vaisseau, il repassa en France fort degouté de ce Païs-là."

29 Numa Broc, *La géographie des philosophes: géographie et voyageurs français au XVIIIe siècle* (1971; Paris: Ophrys, 1974), 153-55.

30 Père François-Xavier de Charlevoix, *Histoire et description générale de la Nouvelle France, avec le journal historique d'un voyage fait par ordre du roi dans l'Amérique septentrionale* (Paris: Pierre-François Giffart, 1744), 1:32.

31 J.F. Bosher, *The Canada Merchants* (Oxford: Clarendon, 1987), 18, 113.

32 Hugh Trevor-Roper, *The Romantic Movement and the Study of History* (London: Athlone Press, 1969); Stephen Bann, *Romanticism and the Rise of History* (New York: Twayne, 1995).

33   Aiden Day, *Romanticism* (London: Routledge, 1996).
34   George Heriot, *Travels through the Canadas: To Which Is Subjoined a Comparative View of the Manners and Customs of Several of the Indian Nations of North and South America* (London: Richard Phillips, 1805), 74.
35   Pierre de Grandpré, *Histoire de la littérature française du Québec* (Montreal: Beauchemin, 1967), 135.
36   Mason Wade, *The French Canadians, 1760-1967* (Toronto: Macmillan, 1968), 298-99. See also Séraphin Marion, *Les lettres canadiennes d'autrefois* (Hull: Éditions l'Éclair, 1944), 4:140-42.
37   Maurice Lemire, "Introduction," in *Le romantisme au Canada*, ed. Maurice Lemire (Saint-Laurent: Nuit blanche, 1993), 9-10.
38   David Hayne claimed that the first Romantic work by a French Canadian author was "Repas champêtre" by "un voyageur," published in *Le Canadien* (Quebec City), 26 July 1820. Hayne, "L'influence des auteurs français sur les récits de 1820 à 1845," in Lemire, *Le romantisme*, 44.
39   Kenneth Landry, "Le commerce du livre à Québec et à Montréal avant l'arrivée de *La Capricieuse*, 1815-1854," in Lemire, *Le romantisme*, 108-9; Yvan Lamonde, "La Librairie Hector Bossange de Montréal (1815-1819) et le commerce international du livre," in *Territoires de la culture québécoise* (Quebec City: Presses de l'Université Laval, 1991), 181-218; *Catalogue des livres qui se trouvent aux magazins de Messrs. G. et B. Horan à Québec et chez M. H. Bossange à Montréal* (Montreal, 1816).
40   Richard Switzer, *Chateaubriand* (New York: Twayne, 1971); Paul Comeau, *Die Hards and Innovators: The French Romantic Struggle: 1800-1830* (New York: Peter Lang, 1988).
41   Frederic Boily claims that Herder influenced Lionel Groulx, in *La Pensée nationaliste de Lionel Groulx* (Sillery: Septentrion, 2003).
42   Wade, *The French Canadians*, 298.
43   Serge Gagnon, "Painchaud, Charles-François," *Dictionary of Canadian Biography Online* (Toronto: University of Toronto Press, 2005), Library and Archives Canada, http://www.biographi.ca; N.-E. Dionne, *Vie de C.-F. Painchaud, curé, fondateur du Collège de Sainte-Anne-de-la-Pocatière* (Quebec City: Léger Brousseau, 1894); Joseph-Guillaume Barthe, *Souvenirs d'un demi-siècle; ou, mémoires pour servir à l'histoire contemporaine* (Montreal: J. Chapleau et fils, 1885); *Rapport de l'archiviste de la province du Québec* (Quebec City: Imprimeur du roi, 1921-22), 393.
44   Ghislaine de Diesbach, *Chateaubriand* (Paris: Perrin, 1995), 523.
45   Peter Novik, *That Noble Dream: The "Objectivity Question" and the American Historical Profession* (Cambridge: Cambridge University Press, 1988), 28-29, 48; Dorothy Ross, *The Origins of American Social Science* (Cambridge: Cambridge University Press, 1991), 19-20; Marlene Shore, "'Remember the Future': The *Canadian Historical Review* and the Discipline of History," *Canadian Historical Review* 76, 3 (September 1995): 411.
46   See M. Brook Taylor, *Promoters, Patriots, and Partisans: Historiography in Nineteenth-Century English Canada* (Toronto: University of Toronto Press, 1989), 88-105.
47   Kenneth Hudson, *Social History of Museums: What Visitors Thought* (London: Macmillan, 1975), 6.
48   Philippa Levine, *The Amateur and the Professional: Antiquarians, Historians, and Archaeologists in Victorian England, 1838-1886* (Cambridge: Cambridge University Press, 1986), 37-42.
49   Susan Crane, "Story, History and the Passionate Collector," in *Producing the Past: Aspects of Antiquarian Culture and Practice, 1700-1850*, ed. Martin Myrone and Lucy Peltz (Aldershot: Ashgate, 1999), 191.
50   Stephen Bann, *The Inventions of History: Essays on the Representation of the Past* (Manchester: Manchester University Press, 1990), 102.
51   Arnoldo Momigliano, "The Rise of Antiquarian Research," in *Classical Foundations of Modern Historiography* (Berkeley: University of California Press, 1990), 54.
52   Crane, "Story, History and the Passionate Collector," 187.
53   Levine, *The Amateur and the Professional*, 41-43.
54   Auguste Gosselin, *Un bon patriote d'autrefois: Le Docteur Labrie* (Quebec City: Laflamme et Proulx, 1907), 5-12.

55 Alan Gordon, *Making Public Pasts: The Contested Terrain of Montreal's Public Memories, 1891-1930* (Montreal and Kingston: McGill-Queen's University Press, 2001), 74.
56 Michael Driskel, *As Befits a Legend: Building a Tomb for Napoleon, 1840-1861* (Kent: Kent State University Press, 1993).
57 N.B. Peny, "The Whig Cult of Fox in Early Nineteenth-Century Sculpture," *Past and Present* 70, 1 (February 1976): 94-105.
58 Iain Pears, "The Gentleman and the Hero: Wellington and Napoleon in the Nineteenth Century," in *Myths of the English*, ed. Roy Porter (Cambridge: Polity Press, 1992), 216-36; see also Linda Colley, "The Apotheosis of George III: Loyalty, Royalty and the British Nation, 1760-1820," *Past and Present* 102, 1 (February 1984): 94-129; Gerald Jordan and Nicholas Rogers, "Admirals as Heroes: Patriotism and Liberty in Hanoverian England," *Journal of British Studies* 28, 3 (July 1989): 201-24.
59 Norman Knowles, *Inventing the Loyalists: The Ontario Loyalist Tradition and the Creation of Usable Pasts* (Toronto: University of Toronto Press, 1997), 32.
60 Each of these monuments may have served different purposes. In Dublin, at least, the Nelson Pillar was erected by official decree of the British governor of Ireland.
61 Joseph Bouchette, *The British Dominions in North America* (London: Longman, Rees, Orme, Brown, Green, and Longman, 1832), 243-44.
62 See P.C. Parr, ed., *Carlyle's Lectures on Heroes, Hero-Worship and the Heroic in History* (Oxford: Clarendon Press, 1910).
63 Claudia Bushman, *America Discovers Columbus* (Hanover: University Press of New England, 1992).
64 Charles W. Jones, *Saint Nicholas of Myra, Bari, and Manhattan: Biography of a Legend* (Chicago: University of Chicago Press, 1978).
65 Gerald Izenberg, *Impossible Individuality: Romanticism, Revolution, and the Origins of Modern Selfhood, 1787-1802* (Princeton: Princeton University Press, 1992).
66 Alan Macfarlane, *Origins of English Individualism: The Family, Property, and Social Transition* (New York: Cambridge University Press, 1979); C.B. Macpherson, *The Political Theory of Possessive Individualism: Hobbes to Locke* (Oxford: Clarendon Press, 1964); Stephen Lukes, *Individualism* (New York: Harper and Row, 1973).
67 Edmund Burke, *Reflections on the Revolution in France* (1790; New Haven: Yale University Press, 2003).
68 See, for instance, Bruce Curtis' discussion of the ultramontane J.-C. Taché's development of the 1871 census, in his *The Politics of Population: State Formation, Statistics, and the Census of Canada, 1840-1875* (Toronto: University of Toronto Press, 2001), 285-86.
69 Cited in François Beaudin, "L'influence de la Mennais sur Mgr Lartigue, premier évêque de Montréal," *Revue d'Histoire de l'Amérique française* 25, 2 (September 1971): 232. The French reads: "serons bien vite Ultramontains."
70 Yvan Lamonde, *Histoire sociale des idées au Québec (1760-1896)* (Saint-Laurent: Fides, 2000), 156-61.
71 See *L'Ami du peuple* (Montreal), 18 June 1836.

Chapter 3: The Invention of a Hero

1 The outline of this story has been told by Jacques Robert in "L'invention d'un héros," in *Le monde de Jacques Cartier*, ed. Fernand Braudel (Montreal: Libre Expression, 1984), 295-305.
2 *Le Canadien* (Quebec City), 28 September 1835. The French text reads: "quelque chose d'élégant mais modeste en même temps."
3 The petition is reproduced in N.-E. Dionne, *Jacques Cartier* (Quebec City: Léger Brousseau, 1889), 290-91.
4 Jean-Marie Lebel, "Fisher, John Charlton," *Dictionary of Canadian Biography Online (DCB Online)* (Toronto: University of Toronto Press, 2005), Library and Archives Canada, http://www.biographi.ca.
5 Yvan Lamonde, "Faribault, Georges-Barthélemi, *DCB Online*. See also H.R. Casgrain, *G.B. Faribault* (Quebec City: Léger Brousseau, 1867), 45-50.

6   Examples of these proposals can be located in Polygraphie 6, Nos. 77, 79 A-H, 81, 82, and 83, Archives du Séminaire de Québec, Centre de référence de l'Amérique française, Quebec City, as well as in the Album Jacques Viger at the Archives de la Ville de Montréal, Montreal.

7   G.B. Faribault to L.-F. Hovius, 10 May 1843, published in *Transactions of the Literary and Historical Society of Quebec* 5, 1 (1862): 84-86.

8   Robert, "L'invention d'un héros," 296.

9   Thomas Schlereth, "Columbia, Columbus, and Columbianism," *Journal of American History* 79, 3 (December 1992): 940-44.

10 Barry Schwartz, "Social Change and Collective Memory: The Democratization of George Washington," *American Sociological Review* 56, 2 (April 1991): 221-36.

11 Alan Gordon, *Making Public Pasts: The Contested Terrain of Montreal's Public Memories, 1891-1930* (Montreal and Kingston: McGill-Queen's University Press, 2001), 145-47.

12 Although his name is usually spelled "Lafontaine" today, Louis-Hippolyte LaFontaine typically signed his name with the capital F. I have adopted this convention when discussing the man but have used the modern spelling in places named for him. See Jacques Monet, "Lafontaine, Louis-Hippolyte," *DCB Online*.

13 Allan Greer, *Peasant, Lord, and Merchant: Rural Society in Three Quebec Parishes, 1740-1840* (Toronto: University of Toronto Press, 1985); Christian Dessureault, "L'égalitarisme paysan dans l'ancienne société rurale de la vallée du Saint-Laurent: éléments pour une ré-interprétation," *Revue d'histoire de l'Amérique française* 40, 3 (Winter 1987): 373-407; Christian Dessureault, "Crise ou modernisation? La société rurale maskoutaine durant le premier tiers du XIXe siècle," *Revue d'histoire de l'Amérique française* 42, 3 (Winter 1989): 359-88.

14 Serge Courville, *Entre ville et campagne: l'essor du village dans les seigneuries du Bas-Canada* (Quebec City: Presses de l'Université Laval, 1990).

15 Brian Young, "Positive Law, Positive State: Class Realignment and the Transformation of Lower Canada, 1815-1866," in *Colonial Leviathan: State Formation in Mid-Nineteenth-Century Canada*, ed. Allan Greer and Ian Radforth (Toronto: University of Toronto Press, 1992), 52.

16 For the connection between the Institut-Canadien and Vattemarre, see *La Minerve* (Montreal), 8 July 1847. See also Claude Galarneau, "Vattemarre, Nicolas-Marie-Alexandre," *DCB Online;* Yvan Lamonde, "Les associations au Bas-Canada: de nouveaux marchés aux idées (1840-1867)," *Histoire sociale – Social History* 8, 16 (November 1975): 361-69; Gilles Gallichan, *Livre et politique au Bas-Canada, 1791-1849* (Sillery: Septentrion, 1991); Fernand Hould, "L'Institut canadien de Québec, 1848-1898, agent de promotion de la vie culturelle à Québec: mythes et réalité" (MA thesis, Université Laval, 1997).

17 Hervé Gagnon, "Divertissement et patriotisme: la genèse des musées d'histoire à Montréal au XIXe siècle," *Revue d'histoire de l'Amérique française* 48, 3 (Winter 1995): 317-49.

18 Rev. Henry Esson cited in Nora Robins, "The Montreal Mechanics' Institute: 1828-1870," *Canadian Library Journal* 38, 6 (December 1981): 374.

19 J. Henripin and Yves Péron, "La transition démographique de la Province de Québec," in *La population du Québec: Études retrospectives*, ed. Hubert Charbonneau (Montreal: Boréal Express, 1973), 23-44.

20 See Roger Magnuson, *A Brief History of Québec Education* (Montreal: Harvest House, 1980), 23-33; Hélène Lafrance, "Le fonctionnement idéologique des collèges classiques," in *Idéologies québécoises*, Cahiers d'études littéraires et culturelles 4, ed. Richard Giguère and Liette Audet (Sherbrooke: Université de Sherbrooke, Département d'études françaises, 1980), 126-28.

21 Allan Greer, "The Pattern of Literacy in Québec, 1745-1899," *Histoire sociale – Social History* 11, 22 (November 1978): 293-335.

22 Bruce Curtis, "'The New Studies in Literacy' and Literacy in Lower Canada: Methodological Considerations" (paper presented at the Canadian Historical Association annual meeting, University of Western Ontario, London, Ontario, 1 June 2005).

23 See Benedict Anderson's lengthy discussions of newspaper readership and the development of standardized national languages through literacy efforts in *Imagined Communities: Reflections on the Origins and Spread of Nationalism* (London: Verso, 1993). See also Walter Bagehot, "Charles Dickens," *National Review* 7 (October 1858): 458-86.

24 Figures and dates extracted from André Beaulieu and Jean Hamelin, *La presse québécoise des origines à nos jours,* 10 vols. (Quebec City: Presses de l'Université Laval, 1973).

25 See Norman Knowles, *Inventing the Loyalists: The Ontario Loyalist Tradition and the Creation of Usable Pasts* (Toronto: University of Toronto Press, 1997); Colin Coates and Cecelia Morgan, *Heroines and History: Representations of Madeleine de Verchères and Laura Secord* (Toronto: University of Toronto Press, 2002).

26 Although dealing specifically with England, Lynn Barber's *The Heyday of Natural History, 1820-1870* (London: Jonathan Cape, 1980) offers an amusing historical account of the natural history fad.

27 David Elliston Allen, *The Naturalist in Britain: A Social History* (London: Allen Lane, 1976), 59-60.

28 For discussions of Canadian natural history, see, especially, Suzanne Zeller, *Land of Promise, Promised Land: The Culture of Victorian Science in Canada,* Canadian Historical Association Booklet 56 (Ottawa: Canadian Historical Association, 1996); Carl Berger, *Science, God, and Nature in Victorian Canada* (Toronto: University of Toronto Press, 1996), 22-23.

29 Anthony Rasporich, "Positivism and Scientism in the Confederation Debates," in *Science, Technology, and Culture in Historical Perspective,* Studies in History 1, ed. Louis Knafla, Martin Staum, and T.H.E. Traws (Calgary: Department of History, University of Calgary, 1976), 206-34.

30 Victorian chauvinism classified the Aboriginal peoples of North America among "natural" phenomena.

31 Carl Berger, *The Writing of Canadian History: Aspects of English-Canadian Historical Writing since 1900,* 2nd ed. (Toronto: University of Toronto Press, 1986), 6-8.

32 Colin Coates, *Metamorphoses of Landscape and Community in Early Quebec* (Montreal and Kingston: McGill-Queen's University Press, 2000); Henry David Thoreau, *A Yankee in Canada: With Anti-Slavery and Reform Papers* (Boston: Ticknor and Fields, 1866), 75.

33 Louis Le Jeune, *Dictionnaire général de biographie, histoire, littérature, agriculture, commerce, industrie et des arts, sciences, moeurs, coutumes, institutions politiques et religieuses du Canada* (Ottawa: Université d'Ottawa, 1931), 1:470-71; W. Stewart Wallace and W.A. McKay, eds., *Macmillan Dictionary of Canadian Biography* (Toronto: Macmillan, 1978), 194; Serge Gagnon, "Lareau, Edmond," *DCB Online.*

34 François Daniel, *Histoire des grandes familles françaises du Canada, ou aperçu sur le Chevalier Benoist et quelques familles contemporaines* (Montreal: Sénécal, 1867), 28. The original French reads: "Le Canada échappe à l'absorption."

35 Ibid., 124.

36 My thanks to Maurice Lemire for suggesting this clarification during a personal conversation, Edinburgh, 5 May 2000.

37 Jacques Michon, "Sénécal, Eusèbe," *DCB Online;* Noël Bélanger, "Tanguay, Cyprien," *DCB Online.* See also Monsignor J.-C.-K. Laflamme, "La Dictionanaire généalogique," *Bulletin des recherches historiques* 8, 8 (August 1902): 238-41.

38 J.-C. Taché to John Langton, 21 November 1868, RG 17 AI 2, Records of the Department of Agriculture, Library and Archives Canada (LAC), Ottawa; Bruce Curtis, *The Politics of Population: State Formation, Statistics, and the Census of Canada, 1840-1875* (Toronto: University of Toronto Press, 2001), 249-51.

39 Cyprien Tanguay, *Dictionnaire généalogique des familles canadiennes depuis la fondation de la colonie jusqu'à nos jours* (Montreal: Sénécal, 1871), 1:vi. The French original reads: "les dates, les noms, les généalogies sont des éléments de l'Histoire."

40 Pierre Margry, *Les navigations françaises et la révolution maritime du XIVe au XVIe siècle: d'après les documents inédits tirés de France, d'Angleterre, d'Espagne, et d'Italie* (Paris: Librairie Tross, 1867), 326.

41 Casgrain, *G.B. Faribault,* 50-54.

42 Reproduced in ibid., 60-62.

43 *Québec Gazette* (Quebec City), 23 April 1827.

44 On Chasseur's financial difficulties, see *Le Canadien* (Quebec City), 4 March 1833. On Chasseur's museum, see Hervé Gagnon, "Pierre Chasseur et l'émergence de la muséologie scientifique au Québec, 1824-1836," *Revue d'histoire canadienne* 48, 3 (June 1994): 205-38.

45   See Père François-Xavier de Charlevoix, *Histoire et description générale de la Nouvelle France, avec le journal historique d'un voyage fait par ordre du roi dans l'Amérique septentrionale* (Paris: Pierre-François Giffart, 1744), 1:18-21. See also Amable Berthelot, "Dissertation sur le canon de bronze," *Transactions of the Literary and Historical Society of Quebec* 2 (1830): 198-215, in which Berthelot rather fancifully argues that the cannon was lost by Verrazano.
46   G.-B. Faribault to L.-F. Hovius, 10 May 1843. Reprinted in *Transactions of the Literary and Historical Society of Quebec* 5, 1 (1862): 84-86.
47   *Le Canadien* (Quebec City), 25 August 1843; *Québec Gazette* (Quebec City), 30 August 1843.
48   N.-E. Dionne, *Le fort Jacques-Cartier et la Petite Hermine* (Montreal, 1891). See also Amable Berthelot, *Discours sur le vaisseau abandoné par Jacques Cartier, lors de son second voyage au Canada* (Quebec City: A. Coté, 1844).
49   Quoted in N.-E. Dionne, *Galerie historique* (Quebec City: Laflamme et Proulx, 1913), 8:31-32. The French reads: "ces fragments . . . deviennent de précieux documents pour l'histoire de notre ville; en effet, Messieurs, ils rappellent les plus belles phases de la vie de notre cher compatriote, et ces phases glorifient Saint-Malo, sa ville natale."
50   L.-F. Hovius to G.-B. Faribault, 12 March 1844. Reprinted in *Transactions of the Literary and Historical Society of Quebec* 5, 1 (1862): 86-91.
51   Gustave Lanctôt, *Jacques Cartier devant l'histoire* (Montreal: Éditions Lumen, 1947), 147; Francis Parkman, *France and England in North America* (Boston: Little, Brown, 1874), 180-81; Gustave Lanctôt, "Portraits of Jacques Cartier," *Canadian Geographical Journal* 10, 3 (March 1935): 151.
52   David Karel, ed., *Dictionnaire des artistes de langue française en Amérique du nord* (Quebec City: Presses de l'Université Laval, 1992), 379-81; Raymond Vézina, "Hamel, Théophile," *DCB Online.*
53   Robert, "L'invention d'un héros," 297.
54   Jean-Lucan Leprohon to Pierre Margry, 12 December 1848, in Louis Cormier, ed., *Lettres à Pierre Margry de 1844 à 1886 (Papineau, Lafontaine, Faillon, Leprohon et autres)* (Quebec City: Presses de l'Université Laval, 1968), 130.
55   *La Minerve* (Montreal), 30 March 1848.
56   Denis Martin, *Portraits des héros de la Nouvelle France: images d'un culte historique* (La Salle: Hurtubise, 1988), 75-89. See also Lanctôt, "Portraits of Jacques Cartier," 149-53.

Chapter 4: Cartiermania

1   *Le Courrier du Canada* (Quebec City), 4 October 1858.
2   Ibid. The original French reads: "Il y a dans le Jacques Cartier de M. Bourassa le cachet d'une inspiration réelle; cette figure si fortement burinée, ces traits si marqués sont bien ceux du hardi pilote de Saint Malo, et dans cet oeil qui perce il y a bien le regard d'un découvreur. Nous sommes, comme canadien français, glorieux de cette oeuvre, ce n'est plus ici une figure quelconque, plus ou moins coupée dans la matière première, c'est une création d'artiste, une pensée et non simplement un fait."
3   A.J.H. Richardson, *Quebec City: Architects, Artisans, and Builders* (Ottawa: National Museum of Man, 1984), 101-2.
4   At the time of writing, this statue was on display at the Musée de la Gaspésie in Gaspé.
5   See Alan Gordon, *Making Public Pasts: The Contested Terrain of Montreal's Public Memories, 1891-1930* (Montreal and Kingston: McGill-Queen's University Press, 2001), 148. See also Donald Boisvert, "Religion and Nationalism in Québec: The Saint-Jean-Baptiste Celebration in Sociological Perspective" (PhD diss., University of Ottawa, 1990); Michèle Guay, "Notes de recherche sur la fête nationale des Canadiens-français," in *Que la fête commence!* ed. Diane Pinard (Montreal: Société des festivals populaires du Québec, 1982), 61-72.
6   *La Minerve* (Montreal), 27 June 1850. The French original reads: "représentative[s] allégorique[s] de la nation canadienne." See also *La Minerve* (Montreal), 25 June 1849; *Montreal Gazette,* 26 June 1849.
7   *La Minerve* (Montreal), 27 June 1854.
8   Éveline Bossé, *Un grand représentant de l'élite canadienne-française: Joseph-Charles Taché* (Quebec City: Garneau, 1971), 108-22. See also Elsbeth Heaman, *The Inglorious Arts of Peace:*

Exhibitions in Canadian Society during the Nineteenth Century (Toronto: University of Toronto Press, 1999), 154-62.

9 *Journal de Québec* (Quebec City), 30 June 1855.

10 *Journal de Québec* (Quebec City), 21 August 1855.

11 Mason Wade, *The French Canadians, 1760-1967* (Toronto: Macmillan, 1968), 300.

12 The account of this story can be followed in the transcript of Belvèze's report, which comprises the majority of MG 24 F 42, Collection Paul-Henri de Belvèze, Library and Archives Canada (LAC). See also Éveline Bossé, *La Capricieuse à Québec en 1855* (Montreal: La Presse, 1984).

13 Translated from the inscription on the daguerreotype by Joan Schwartz in "More Than 'Un Beau Souvenir du Canada,'" *The Archivist* 118 (1999): 7.

14 On the daguerreotype, see Brian Carey, "An Imperial Gift," *History of Photography* 10, 2 (April-June 1986): 147-49; George Bolotenko, *A Future Defined: Canada from 1849 to 1873* (Ottawa: National Archives, 1992), 82-84.

15 *La Minerve* (Montreal), 26 June 1855. It should be noted that these boys did not participate in that year's official parade, which was cancelled because of rain. However, they were presented to the congregation at the morning's celebration of mass.

16 Joan Schwartz, "Agent of Sight, Site of Agency: The Photograph in the Geographical Imagination" (PhD diss., Queen's University, 1998), 475-80.

17 Reginald Hamel, John Hare, and Paul Wyczynski, eds., *Dictionnaire des auteurs de langue française en Amérique du Nord* (Montreal: Fides, 1989), 298-300. Chevalier became a member of the Paris municipal council in 1871. He died in 1879. See also Marc La Terreur, "Chevalier, Henri-Émile," *Dictionary of Canadian Biography Online (DCB Online)* (Toronto: University of Toronto Press, 2005), Library and Archives Canada, http://www.biographi.ca.

18 The original French reads: "Une signe me rappelât notre Jacques Cartier, lui que connaissent, que vénèrent les plus ignorants des Canadiens-français, à qui tous ont élevé un autel dans leur coeur; lui dont j'avais vu le portrait, le nom, en vingt endroits, dans les édifices publics, sur les places, les routes, les navires, soit à Montréal, soit à Québec." Henri-Émile Chevalier, *Jacques Cartier* (1860; Paris: Lebigre-Duquesne, 1868), 2. The quotation is taken from the 1868 edition.

19 Peter Novik, *That Noble Dream: The "Objectivity Question" and the American Historical Profession* (Cambridge: Cambridge University Press, 1988), 21-24.

20 Philip Massolin, *Canadian Intellectuals, the Tory Tradition and the Challenge of Modernity, 1939-1970* (Toronto: University of Toronto Press, 2001), 22-23.

21 A.B. McKillop, *Matters of Mind: The University in Ontario, 1791-1951* (Toronto: University of Toronto Press, 1994), 109-11.

22 Pierre de Grandpré, *Histoire de la littérature française du Québec* (Montreal: Beauchemin, 1967), 294-96.

23 Gabriel Monod, "Avant propos," *Revue historique* 1 (1873): 2. The French reads: "chaque affirmation soit acompagné de preuve." See also Alice Gerard, "À l'origine des combats des Annales," in *Au berceau des Annales*, ed. Charles-Olivier Carbonell and Georges Livet (Toulouse: Presses de l'IEP, 1983), 79-88.

24 Donald Wright, *The Professionalization of History in English Canada* (Toronto: University of Toronto Press, 2005), 172.

25 See, for example, Wendy Mitchinson's examination of gender and professionalization in medicine in *The Nature of Their Bodies: Women and Their Doctors in Victorian Canada* (Toronto: University of Toronto Press, 1991).

26 C. Desmazières de Séchelles, "Documents sur les voyages et sur la vie de Jacques Cartier," *Transactions of the Literary and Historical Society of Quebec* 5, 1 (1862): 81-145. Reprinted as C. Desmazières de Séchelles, *Notes sur la vie et les trois voyages de Jacques Cartier: mémoires de la Société littéraire et historique de Québec* (Quebec City: Société littéraire et historique de Québec, 1862); Jacques Cartier, *Bref récit et succincte narration de la navigation faite en MDXXXV et MDXXXVI par le capitaine Jacques Cartier aux îles de Canada, Hochelaga, Saguenay et autres; précédée d'une brève succincte introduction historique par M. d'Avézac* (Paris: Librairie Tross, 1863); Marie Armand Pascal d'Avézac, *Jacques Cartier au Canada et ses précurseurs à la côte nord-ouest de l'Amérique* (Paris: Librairie Tross, 1864); H. Michelant and Alfred Ramé, eds.,

Discours du voyage fait par le capitaine Jacques Cartier aux Terres-Neufves de Canada (Paris: Librairie Tross, 1865); H. Michelant and Alfred Ramé, eds., *Relation originale du voyage de Jacques Cartier au Canada en 1534: documents inédits sur Jacques Cartier et le Canada* (Paris: Librairie Tross, 1867).

27 Ronald Rudin, *Making History in Twentieth Century Quebec: Historians and Their Society* (Toronto: University of Toronto Press, 1997), 4-14; Marcel Fournier, *L'entrée dans la modernité: science, culture et société au Québec* (Montreal: Éditions Saint-Martin, 1986), 76-77.

28 See, for example, John Dickinson, "Commentaire sur le critique de Ronald Rudin," *Bulletin d'histoire politique* 4, 2 (Winter 1995): 21-24; Paul-André Linteau and Fernand Harvey, "Les étranges lunettes de Ronald Rudin," *Revue d'histoire de l'Amérique française* 51, 3 (Winter 1998): 419-24; Jean-Marie Fecteau, "Between Scientific Enquiry and the Search for a Nation: Quebec Historians as Seen by Ronald Rudin," *Canadian Historical Review* 80, 4 (December 1999): 641-66; Serge Gagnon, *Le passé composé: de Ouellet à Rudin* (Montreal: VLB Éditeur, 1999).

29 Monsignor L.F.R. Laflèche, *Quelques considérations sur les rapports de la société civile avec la religion et la famille* (Montreal: Sénécal, 1866), translated by Ramsay Cook in his *French-Canadian Nationalism: An Anthology* (Toronto: Macmillan, 1969), 95.

30 The French original reads, "Ce n'est qu'avec celle de M. De Champlain que nous devons commencer la longue série généalogique du peuple canadien. Oui, c'est à l'immortel fondateur de la ville de Québec, que revient l'honneur de l'établissement permanent des premières familles en Canada." Cyprien Tanguay, "Des noms et des familles canadiennes," *Revue canadienne* 10 (1873): 129.

31 See Benjamin Sulte, "Pretendues origines des Canadiens français," *Proceedings and Transactions of the Royal Society of Canada* 3 (1885): 13-28. The Baron de Léry's colony is often presented as fact, but few serious scholars accept it as such. The theory of its existence is based on Marc Lescarbot's unsubstantiated claim, which may have confused a Portuguese interest with a French colony. De Léry has also been difficult to locate in documentary evidence.

32 See, as an example, Fernand Ouellet, "Nationalisme canadien-française et laïcisme au XIXe siècle," *Recherches sociographiques* 4, 1 (January-April 1963): 47-70.

33 Calculated from figures given in Paul-André Linteau, *Histoire du Québec contemporain* (Montreal: Boréal Express, 1981), 1:271.

34 *L'Avenir* (Montreal), 14 April 1848.

35 See Yvan Lamonde, *Louis-Antoine Dessaulles, 1818-1895: un seigneur libéral et anticlerical* (Saint-Laurent: Fides, 1994), 60-62.

36 F.-X. Garneau, *Histoire du Canada,* 5th ed. (Paris: Librairie Félix Alcan, 1913), 256. The French reads: "la plus grande liberté qui venait d'être accordée au commerce."

37 J.-B.-A. Ferland, *Cours d'histoire du Canada* (1861; Wakefield: S.R. Publishers, 1969), 20-21.

38 Quoted in *200e anniversaire de la découverte du Mississipi [sic] par Jolliet et le P. Marquette: soirée littéraire et musicale à l'Université Laval le 17 juin 1873* (Quebec City: L.H. Huot, 1873), 28. The French reads: "Disons-le, Messieurs: Les Espagnols ont découvert le Mississippi, comme les Scandanaves l'ont fait de l'Amérique avant Colomb, comme les Basques et les Bretons ont découvert le golfe du St. Laurent avant Jacques Cartier."

39 *La Minerve* (Montreal), 26 June 1874.

40 *Canadian Illustrated News* (Montreal), 22 August 1874; *L'Opinion publique* (Montreal), 27 August 1874.

41 *Souvenir de 24 juin 1874* (Montreal: Sénécal, 1874), 8.

42 Joseph Tassé, "Discours," *Revue canadienne* 10 (1873): 270. The French reads: "Ces études, Mesdames et Messieurs, ont pour but non seulement de faire revivre notre passé sous ses traits les plus saisissants, de servir d'enseignement au peuple, mais elles contribuent encore à tirer de la poussière d'oubli des héros et des faits inconnus, à jeter un nouveau jour sur des points obscurcis et à nous faire rechercher en tout la verité historique."

43 Bruno Hébert, *Monuments et patrie: une réflexion philosophique sur un fait historique: la célébration commémorative au Québec de 1881 à 1929* (Joliette: Éditions Pleins bords, 1980), 254-57. My own claims for 1891 as a turning point apply only to Montreal's monuments. Gordon, *Making Public Pasts,* 34.

44 Luc Noppen and Gaston Deschenes, *Québec's Parliament Buildings: Witness to History* (Quebec City: Gouvernement du Québec, 1986), 137-43.

45 Ibid., 141.

46 Ibid., 152.

47 Cercle catholique de Québec, *Constitution du Cercle catholique de Québec* (Quebec City, 1878). On *Le Courrier du Canada* and its politics, see André Beaulieu and Jean Hamelin, *La presse québécoise des origines à nos jours* (Quebec City: Presses de l'Université Laval, 1973), 1:203-6.

48 *Le Courrier du Canada* (Quebec City), 24 September 1885.

49 Hospice-A. Verreau, "Jacques Cartier: questions de calendrier civil et ecclésiastique," *Proceedings and Transactions of the Royal Society of Canada* 10 (1890): 113-14.

50 Gordon Smith, "Gagnon, Ernest," *DCB Online*.

51 A full treatment of this issue can be found in J.R. Miller, *Equal Rights: The Jesuits' Estates Act Controversy* (Montreal and Kingston: McGill-Queen's University Press, 1979).

52 This figure is a crude estimate based on the 1891 census (Table 2), which notes total wages of $30,699,115 paid to 117,389 men, women, and children at 23,037 Quebec industrial establishments.

53 Figures compiled from Cercle catholique de Québec, *Premier bulletin du comité littéraire et historique du Cercle catholique de Québec: oeuvre du monument Jacques-Cartier* (Quebec City, 1888), 6-14, and Cercle catholique de Québec, *Deuxième bulletin du comité littéraire et historique du Cercle catholique de Québec: oeuvre du monument Jacques-Cartier* (Quebec City, 1890).

54 There is, however, some evidence that, in social environments, people rely on the lead of their "betters" in recalling stories. See Mary Susan Weldon, "Collective Memory: Collaborative and Individual Processes in Remembering," *Journal of Experimental Psychology: Learning, Memory, and Cognition* 23, 5 (September 1997): 1160-75.

55 Félix Martin, *Le P. Jean de Brébeuf* (Paris: G. Tequi, 1877), 26.

56 See *Le Canadien* (Quebec City), 28 May 1845; *Le Canadien* (Quebec City), 28 June 1845.

57 John Hare, Marc Lafrance, and David-Thiery Ruddel, *Histoire de la Ville de Québec, 1608-1871* (Montreal: Boréal, 1987), 225-27.

58 Ronald Rudin, *Founding Fathers: The Celebration of Champlain and Laval in the Streets of Quebec, 1878-1908* (Toronto: University of Toronto Press, 2003), 214-15.

59 The French reads: "Jacques Cartier et ses hardis compagnons les marins de la Grande Hermine, la Petite Hermine et de l'Émerillon passèrent ici l'hiver de 1535-36" and "Le 3 mai 1536 Jacques Cartier fit planter, à l'endroit où il venait de passer l'hiver, une croix de 35 pieds de hauteur portant l'écusson fleurdelisé et l'inscription franciscus primus dei gratia rex regnat."

60 "Le 23 septembre 1625 les pères Jean de Brébeuf, Ennemond Massé et Charles Lalemant prirent solennellement possession du terrain appelé Fort-Jacques-Cartier situé au confluent des Rivières St-Charles et Lairet pour y ériger la première résidence des missionnaires jésuites à Québec."

61 Pierre-J.-O. Chauveau, *Discours prononcé lors de l'inauguration du monument Cartier-Brébeuf le 24 juin 1889* (Montreal: Beauchemin et fils, 1889), 241, 248-9.

62 Canada, Canadian Heritage, *Cartier-Brébeuf National Historic Site: In Search of Jacques Cartier*, Research Bulletin 312 (Ottawa: Parks Canada, 1994).

63 Quoted in Robert Rumilly, *Honoré Mercier et son temps* (Montreal: Fides, 1975), 2:94-95. "Quand nous disparaîtrons, nous dirons à la génération appelée à nous succéder: Nous sommes catholiques et français, et quand vous, nos successeurs disparaîtrez à votre tour, vous devrez dire à la génération qui vous remplacera: Nous mourons catholiques et français! Ce sera notre testament et le leur; dernières volontés suprêmes d'un peuple héroïque, transmises de père en fils, de génération en génération, jusqu'à la consommation des siècles.
    Pour obtenir ce grand résultat et consolider ainsi nos destinées, nous avons un devoir impérieux, urgent, solonnel, à remplir."
    "Cessons nos luttes fratricides; unissons-nous!"

64 On this, see Gérard Bergeron, *Révolutions tranquilles à la fin du XIXe siècle* (Montreal: Fides, 1997), 49-50; Gilles Gallichan, *Honoré Mercier: la politique et la culture* (Sillery: Septentrion,

1994), 52-53. It should be noted that Robert Rumilly counted sixteen speakers at the evening's banquet, including Wilfrid Laurier, who spoke for a different brand of nationalism.
65   *Le monde illustré* (Paris), 27 August 1898.

Chapter 5: Common Sense

1   Louis Tiercelin, *Mémorial des fêtes Franco-Canadiennes pour l'érection du monument de Jacques Cartier* (Paramé: Éditions de l'Hermine, 1905); "Proceedings," *Proceedings and Transactions of the Royal Society of Canada* 2nd series, vol. 12 (1906): xix. A copy of this monument was erected in Quebec City in 1971. Rodolphe Fournier, *Lieux et monuments historiques de Québec et environs* (Quebec City: Éditions Garneau, 1976), 9.
2   Ernest Myrand, *Une fête de Noël sous Jacques Cartier* (Quebec City: Demers et frère, 1888).
3   Reginald Hamel, John Hare, and Paul Wyczynski, eds., *Dictionnaire des auteurs de langue française en Amérique du Nord* (Montreal: Fides, 1989), 1018-19.
4   Ernest Myrand, *1690, Sir William Phips devant Québec: histoire d'un siège* (Quebec City: Demers et frère, 1893); Ernest Myrand, *Frontenac et ses amis: étude historique* (Quebec City: Dussault et Proulx, 1902); Ernest Myrand, *Noëls anciens de la Nouvelle-France: étude historique* (Quebec City: Dussault et Proulx, 1899).
5   Jean-Louis Trudel, "French-Canadian Science Fiction and Fantastique," in *French Science Fiction, Fantasy, Horror and Pulp Fiction: A Guide to Cinema, Television, Radio, Animation, Comic Books and Literature from the Middle Ages to the Present,* ed. Jean-Marc Lofficier and Randy Lofficier (Jefferson: McFarland, 2000), 460-61; Claude Janelle, *Le XIXe siècle fantastique en Amérique française* (Quebec City: Éditions Alire, 1997), 7.
6   Charles-Honoré Laverdière, *Découverte du tombeau de Champlain* (Quebec City: Darveau, 1866). See also Ronald Rudin, *Founding Fathers: The Celebration of Champlain and Laval in the Streets of Quebec, 1878-1908* (Toronto: University of Toronto Press, 2003), 53-58.
7   W. Stewart Wallace, ed., *The Encyclopedia of Canada* (Toronto: University Associates of Canada, 1948), 4:3; Hamel, Hare, and Wyczynski, *Dictionnaire des auteurs,* 823-24.
8   One of the more curious aspects of Myrand's work is his argument that, seen from above, the course of the Lairet River traces the profile of Cartier's face.
9   Myrand's story also seems to have been submitted to the contest, as a speech by Angers was appended to the published version.
10   Gilles Gallichan, "Dionne, Narcisse-Eutrope," *Dictionary of Canadian Biography Online (DCB Online)* (Toronto: University of Toronto Press, 2005), Library and Archives Canada, http://www.biographi.ca.
11   N.-E. Dionne, *Jacques Cartier* (Quebec City: Léger Brousseau, 1889), 13-19.
12   Ibid., 180-81. The French reads: "aller planter sa tente dans chacune des paroisses, et compulser les archives, soit de l'état civil, soit des notaires ou des greffes, et en trier tout le parti dont un homme d'expérience est capable. Sans ce travail, jamais nous ne parviendrons à débrouiller la véritable généalogie d'une famille aussi nombreuse que celle des Cartier."
13   J.-B.-A. Ferland, *Cours d'histoire du Canada* (1861; Wakefield: S.R. Publishers, 1969), 45.
14   Paul de Cazes, "Deux points d'histoire," *Proceedings and Transactions of the Royal Society of Canada* 2 (1884): 1-3.
15   Dionne, *Jacques Cartier* (1889), 26-31.
16   *Toronto Star,* 25 April 1928. One expert who continued to credit the fourth voyage was Pierre-Georges Roy; despite its dwindling support, he claimed that it was "admis par tous aujourd'hui," in P.-G. Roy, "Où hiverna Jacques Cartier en 1541-42?" *Bulletin des recherches historiques* 30, 11 (November 1924): 353.
17   J.P. Baxter, *A Memoir of Jacques Cartier* (New York: Dodd, 1906), 50, see also 51-53.
18   Henry Harrisse, *Notes pour servir à l'histoire, à la bibliographie et à la cartographie de la Nouvelle France et des pays adjacents, 1545-1700* (Paris: Librairie Tross, 1872).
19   Robert La Roque de Roquebrune, "La Rocque de Roberval, Jean-François de," *DCB Online.*
20   Baxter, *A Memoir,* 53.
21   On the destruction of Saint-Malo, see Paul Aubry, *L'agonie de Saint-Malo* (Rennes: Éditions l'ancre de marine, 1994).
22   "Of the third ship, please put 17 months for the said voyage of the said Cartier, and for eight months that it was to return to seek the said Roberval." Henry Percival Biggar, *A*

Collection of Documents Relating to Jacques Cartier and the Sieur de Roberval (Ottawa: Public Archives of Canada, 1930), 480-84 (Statement of Cartier's Account, 21 June 1544).

23 Arthur Doughty and Adam Shortt, *Canada and Its Provinces* (Toronto: Publishers Association of Canada, 1914), 1:42; Stephen Leacock, *The Mariner of St. Malo: A Chronicle of the Voyages of Jacques Cartier* (Toronto: Glasgow, Brook, 1915), 109.

24 Maurice Lemire, *Dictionnaire des oeuvres littéraires du Québec: des origines à 1900* (Montreal: Fides, 1978), 401. The French reads: "porter les lumières de la civilisation et de la foi ... [aux] aborigènes, qu'il a toujours traités avec humanité."

25 Dionne, *Jacques Cartier* (1889), 191.

26 See Cornelius Jaenen, *Friend and Foe: Aspects of French-Amerindian Cultural Contact in the Sixteenth and Seventeenth Centuries* (New York: Columbia University Press, 1976), 96.

27 H.B. Stephens, *Jacques Cartier and His Four Voyages to Canada* (Montreal: W. Drysdale, 1890); Joseph Pope, *Jacques Cartier: His Life and Voyages* (Ottawa: Woodburn, 1890).

28 See T.D. McGee, "Jacques Cartier," and "Jacques Cartier and the Child," in *Canadian Ballads and Occasional Verses* (Montreal: Lovell, 1858), 12-16.

29 Mary Anne McIver, "On Seeing a Portrait of Jacques Cartier," in M.A. McIver, *Poems* (Ottawa: I.B. Taylor, 1869), 170.

30 Rosanna Leprohon, "Jacques Cartier's First Visit to Mount Royal," in *The Poetical Works of Mrs. Leprohon* (Montreal: Lovell, 1881), 66-67.

31 M. Brook Taylor, *Promoters, Patriots, and Partisans: Historiography in Nineteenth-Century English Canada* (Toronto: University of Toronto Press, 1989), 258-59.

32 John George Bourinot, *The Intellectual Development of the Canadian People: An Historical Review* (Toronto: Hunter, Rose, 1881), 127.

33 A.H. Walle, "Habits of Thought and Cultural Tourism," *Annals of Tourism Research* 23, 4 (October 1996): 874-90.

34 Henry James Morgan, *Sketches of Celebrated Canadians and Persons Related to Canada* (Quebec City: Hunter, Rose, 1862), 1.

35 *Montreal Star*, 30 January 1885.

36 *The Globe* (Toronto), 26 June 1889.

37 W.F. Ganong, "Jacques Cartier's First Voyage," *Proceedings and Transactions of the Royal Society of Canada* 5 (1887): 121-36.

38 In a review of Ganong's essay, one francophone author noted this developing interest. T.H., "Compte rendu de 'Jacques Cartier's First Voyage,'" *Canada français* 1 (1888): 305.

39 B.M. Greene, ed., *Who's Who in Canada* (Toronto: International Press, 1925-26), 1084; Joseph Pope, *Public Servant: The Memoirs of Joseph Pope*, Maurice Pope, ed. (Toronto: Oxford University Press, 1960), 71-72.

40 Pope, *Jacques Cartier*, 121.

41 Ibid., 51.

42 Francis Parkman, *France and England in North America* (Boston: Little, Brown, 1874), 202.

43 Charles Cunat, *Saint-Malo illustré par ses marins* (Rennes: Péalat, 1857), cited in Dionne, *Jacques Cartier* (1889), 155.

44 Dionne, *Jacques Cartier* (1889), 149-56; Pope, *Jacques Cartier*, 131.

45 Jacques Cartier, *Relations: Édition critique par Michel Bideaux*, ed. Michel Bideaux (Montreal: Presses de l'Université de Montréal, 1986), 371.

46 Régis Roy, "Jacques Cartier: était-il noble?" *Proceedings and Transactions of the Royal Society of Canada* 3rd series, vol. 13 (1919): 67, see also 61-67. The French reads: "Nous en attendons de plus probants pour nous convaincre que notre héros n'était pas homme de qualité."

47 S.E. Dawson, *The Saint Lawrence Basin and Its Borderlands* (London: Lawrence and Butler, 1905), 210-11.

48 Régis Roy, "Guillaume de Caën," *Bulletin des recherches historiques* 32, 9 (September 1926): 531; Marcel Trudel, "Caën, Guillaume de," *DCB Online*.

49 *La Patrie* (Montreal), 24 August 1944. See also Mariel O'Neill-Karch and Pierre Karch, eds., *Régis Roy (1864-1944): choix de nouvelles et de contes* (Ottawa: Éditions David, 2001), 14-19.

50 Dawson, *The Saint Lawrence Basin*, 185.

51 Paul de Cazes, "Les points obscurs des voyages de Jacques Cartier," *Proceedings and Transactions of the Royal Society of Canada* 8 (1890): 26-28.

52 Pope, *Jacques Cartier*, 63-69. This practice is permissible in canon law.
53 Ibid., 86-87, 133.
54 Terence J. Fay, *A History of Canadian Catholics* (Montreal and Kingston: McGill-Queen's University Press, 2002), 77-81, 95-96.
55 François Lebrun, *Être chrétien en France sous l'Ancien Régime, 1516-1790* (Paris: Seuil, 1996), 16-17; A.N. Galpern, *The Religions of the People in Sixteenth-Century Champagne* (Cambridge, MA: Harvard University Press, 1976).
56 Pope, *Jacques Cartier*, 133.
57 William Kingsford, *History of Canada* (Toronto: Rowsell and Hutchinson, 1887), 1:4.
58 Ferland, *Cours d'histoire du Canada*, 21.
59 Francis Parkman, *The Parkman Reader: From the Works of Francis Parkman*, ed. S.E. Morison (Boston: Little, Brown, 1955), 71.
60 Biggar, *Collection of Documents*, 82 (Baptism of the Savages of Canada, 25 March 1539).
61 Biggar, *Collection of Documents*, 128 (Cartier's Commission for his Third Voyage, 17 October 1540) and 178 (Roberval's Commission, 15 January 1541). Cartier's commission aimed to "induire les autres peuples d'iceux pays à croire en nostre saincte foy," while Roberval's spoke of "l'augmentation de nostre foy crestienne et accroissement de nostre mère saincte église catholique."
62 Marcel Trudel, *Histoire de la Nouvelle-France*, vol. 1, *Les vaines tentatives, 1524-1603* (Montreal: Fides, 1963), 131.
63 F.B. Tracy, *The Tercentenary History of Canada: From Champlain to Laurier* (New York and Toronto: P.F. Collier and Son, 1908), 26.
64 Doughty and Shortt, *Canada and Its Provinces*, 1:38.
65 Peter Pope, *The Many Landfalls of John Cabot* (Toronto: University of Toronto Press, 1997), 109-15.
66 See *Toronto Star*, 20 May 1896.
67 *Toronto Empire*, 7 December 1894.
68 O.A. Howland, *The New Empire: Reflections upon Its Origin and Constitution and Its Relation to the Great Republic* (Toronto: Hart, 1891).
69 R.B. Flemming, "Howland, Sir William Pearce," *DCB Online*.
70 "Proceedings," *Proceedings and Transactions of the Royal Society of Canada* 2nd series, vol. 1 (1895): xxii-xxiv.
71 Canada, *Senate Debates* (18 March 1896), 335-38; *Toronto Star*, 13 February 1896.
72 *Toronto Star*, 25 June 1897. Although some scholars have suggested that the planned historical exhibition went ahead in modified form in 1899, this was actually a separate event born of different motivations and pursued by different historical organizations. See *The Globe* (Toronto), 13 January 1899; *Toronto Star*, 4 January 1899; *Toronto Star*, 30 June 1899.
73 George L. Parker, "Dawson, Samuel Edward," *DCB Online*.
74 S.E. Dawson, "The Voyages of the Cabots," *Proceedings and Transactions of the Royal Society of Canada* 2nd series, vol. 2 (1896): 26-27.
75 Dawson, *The Saint Lawrence Basin*, 114, 211.
76 Pope, *Many Landfalls*, 112.
77 Cited in ibid., 113.
78 Michael Kammen, *Mystic Chords of Memory: The Transformation of Tradition in American Culture* (New York: Vintage Books, 1993), 242; Thomas Schlereth, "Columbia, Columbus, and Columbianism," *Journal of American History* 79, 3 (December 1992): 958-59.
79 Arthur Doughty insisted on this point. See Doughty and Shortt, *Canada and Its Provinces*, 1:20.
80 Justin Winsor, *Cartier to Frontenac: Geographical Discovery in the Interior of North America in Its Historical Relations, 1534-1700* (Boston and New York: Houghton, Mifflin, 1894), dedication.
81 Pope, *Many Landfalls*, 137-39. See also Edmundo O'Gorman, *The Invention of America: An Inquiry into the Historical Nature of the New World and the Meaning of Its History* (Bloomington: Indiana University Press, 1961).
82 Dionne, *Jacques Cartier* (1889), 187.

83 P.-J.-O. Chauveau, "Encore Jacques Cartier," *Canada Français* 1 (1888): 292. The French reads: "ces savants-là, selon moi, sont ... trops savants!"

84 Quoted in *Montreal Gazette*, 24 August 1934.

85 See, for example, *Le Devoir* (Montreal), 6 October 1933; *Le Canada* (Montreal), 6 October 1933.

86 *Toronto Mail and Empire*, 25 August 1934.

87 The original French reads: "a laissé aussi une trace impérissable dans le champ des découvertes." *La Patrie* (Montreal), 26 May 1935.

88 *La Patrie* (Montreal), 25 May 1935.

89 See *Montreal Gazette*, 23 October 1922; Alan Gordon, *Making Public Pasts: The Contested Terrain of Montreal's Public Memories, 1891-1930* (Montreal and Kingston: McGill-Queen's University Press, 2001), 125.

90 *Le Journal de Québec* (Quebec City), 12 November 1866; Rudin, *Founding Fathers*, 53-59.

91 James Stevenson, "Opening Address," *Transactions of the Literary and Historical Society of Quebec, 1879-80* New series, 13 (1880): 9.

92 Rudin, *Founding Fathers*, 60-101.

93 Cyprien Tanguay, *Dictionnaire généalogique des familles canadiennes depuis la fondation de la colonie jusqu'à nos jours* (Montreal: Sénécal, 1871), 1:vi.

94 Alan McNairn, *Behold the Hero: General Wolfe and the Arts in the Eighteenth Century* (Montreal and Kingston: McGill-Queen's University Press, 1997). See also Gerald Jordan and Nicholas Rogers, "Admirals as Heroes: Patriotism and Liberty in Hanoverian England," *Journal of British Studies* 28, 3 (July 1989): 201-24; Linda Colley, "The Apotheosis of George III: Loyalty, Royalty and the British Nation, 1760-1820," *Past and Present* 102, 1 (February 1984): 94-129; Linda Colley, "Whose Nation? Class and National Consciousness in Britain, 1750-1830," *Past and Present* 113, 1 (November 1986): 97-117.

95 Rudin, *Founding Fathers*, 218-19.

96 Anon., *Pageants du tricentenaire de Québec, 1608-1908, mis en scène par M. Frank Lascelles; dialogues et discours par M. Ernest Myrand; musique préparée par M. Joseph Vézina* (Quebec City: Laflamme et Proulx, 1908).

97 H.V. Nelles, *The Art of Nation-Building: Pageantry and Spectacle at Quebec's Tercentenary* (Toronto: University of Toronto Press, 1999), 185.

98 Chauveau, "Encore Jacques Cartier," 303.

99 Jarrett Rudy has recently revealed the close connection between tobacco smoking and early twentieth-century French Canadian nationalism in his *The Freedom to Smoke: Tobacco Consumption and Identity* (Montreal and Kingston: McGill-Queen's University Press, 2005).

Chapter 6: The Many Meanings of Jacques Cartier

1 Philip Massolin, *Canadian Intellectuals, the Tory Tradition and the Challenge of Modernity, 1939-1970* (Toronto: University of Toronto Press, 2001), 24, 68-69. See also Terry Crowley, *Marriage of Minds: Isabel and Oscar Skelton Reinventing Canada* (Toronto: University of Toronto Press, 2003), 117-20.

2 Joseph Levitt, *A Vision beyond Reach* (Ottawa: Deneau, 1982), 77.

3 Marlene Shore, "'Remember the Future': The *Canadian Historical Review* and the Discipline of History," *Canadian Historical Review* 76, 3 (September 1995): 412.

4 C.J. Taylor, *Negotiating the Past: The Making of Canada's National Historic Parks and Sites* (Montreal and Kingston: McGill-Queen's University Press, 1990), 32-40.

5 Membership was entirely male until 1960, when Margaret Ormsby joined to represent British Columbia.

6 On this, see Alan Gordon, *Making Public Pasts: The Contested Terrain of Montreal's Public Memories, 1891-1930* (Montreal and Kingston: McGill-Queen's University Press, 2001), 60-64.

7 A.A. Pinard to J.B. Harkin, 16 January 1930, RG 84, vol. 1172, Records of the Canadian Parks Service, Library and Archives Canada (LAC), Ottawa.

8 F.H.H. Williamson to R.A. Gibson, 12 June 1929, RG 84, vol. 1172, LAC.

9 E.A. Cruikshank to J.B. Harkin, 29 May 1922, RG 84, vol. 1253, LAC.

10 P.-G. Roy to J.B. Harkin, 25 February 1924, RG 84, vol. 1253, LAC.
11 J.B. Harkin to W.W. Cory, 13 October 1920, RG 84, vol. 1172, LAC; J.H. Byrne to T.S. Mills, 6 June and 18 June 1925, RG 84, vol. 1253, LAC.
12 Edgar Gauvin to J.B. Harkin, 23 October 1929, RG 84, vol. 1254, LAC.
13 J.B. Harkin to James Coyne, 29 July 1924, RG 84, vol. 1253, LAC.
14 J.B. Harkin to B. Sulte, 19 November 1920, RG 84, vol. 1241, LAC.
15 A more complete discussion of this dispute can be found in Bruce Trigger, "Hochelaga: History and Ethnohistory," in *Cartier's Hochelaga and the Dawson Site*, by Bruce Trigger and James F. Pendergast (Montreal and Kingston: McGill-Queen's University Press, 1972), 21-32. See also Gordon, *Making Public Pasts*, 131-33.
16 John William Dawson, "Notes on Aboriginal Antiquities Recently Discovered in the Island of Montréal," *Canadian Naturalist and Geologist* 5 (1860): 430-49.
17 Antiquarian and Numismatic Society of Montreal, "Tablettes historiques," 1892, Musée du Chateau Ramezay, Montreal; *Lovell's Montréal Directory for 1891-92* (Montreal: John Lovell and Son, 1891), 269.
18 Benjamin Sulte to J.B. Harkin, 13 December 1920, RG 84, vol. 1241, LAC. In exchange for permission to erect its monument on the McGill campus, the board agreed to alter its standard cairn design. Ramsay Traquair to A.P.S. Glassco, 8 March 1921, RG 84, vol. 1241, LAC.
19 Aegidius Fauteux to J.B. Harkin, 23 December 1921, RG 84, vol. 1241, LAC.
20 Aristide Beaugrand-Champagne, "Le chemin d'Hochelaga," *Proceedings and Transactions of the Royal Society of Canada* 3rd series, vol. 17 (1923): 17-24. This article developed out of a 1917 paper presented to the Montreal Antiquarian and Numismatic Society by Montarville Boucher de la Bruyère.
21 Aegidius Fauteux to J.B. Harkin, 3 June 1922, RG 84, vol. 1241, LAC.
22 Census of Canada (1881), 1:256-57; (1901), 1:366-67; (1921), 1:434-35; (1931), 2:374-75. Robert Rumilly claimed that no real French-Jewish animosity existed in Outremont, yet he described a heated battle concerning publicly supported Jewish schools in the early 1930s and characterized the period as a "mouvement de francisation." Rumilly, *Histoire d'Outremont, 1875-1975* (Montreal: Leméac, 1975), 81-86, 157-60, 241-48.
23 *Le Canada* (Montreal), 8 March 1924; *La Presse* (Montreal), 12 July 1926. The French reads: "Ici au pied du dernier sault de la Rivière des Prairies le 2 octobre 1535 est debarqué Jacques Cartier en route pour Hochelaga."
24 An Act to amend the Montreal Harbour Commissioners' Act, 1894, Act 14-15, George V, chapter 58.
25 See *Le Devoir* (Montreal), 23 June 1934; *Le Devoir* (Montreal), 24 June 1934. The bridge was also known colloquially as the "pont croché" due to the odd jog in its approach. Pierre Turgeon, *Les bâtisseurs du siècle* (Montreal: Lanctôt, 1996), 72-73.
26 *Montreal Gazette*, 3 September 1934.
27 *Montreal Gazette*, 1 September 1934. The francophone press made no such pronouncements regarding the site of Cartier's landing but did repeatedly proclaim Cartier the "Discoverer of Canada." See, for example, *La Patrie* (Montreal), 4 September 1934; *La Presse* (Montreal), 1 September 1934.
28 See Aristide Beaugrand-Champagne, "Le chemin et l'emplacement de la Bourgade d'Hochelaga," *Cahiers des Dix* 12 (1947): 115-60.
29 The literature on the site of Hochelaga is extensive. For the most thorough summary of the dispute, see Trigger, "Hochelaga: History and Ethnohistory," 21-32. See also W.D. Lighthall, "Hochelaga and the Hill of Hochelaga," *Proceedings and Transactions of the Royal Society of Canada* 3rd series, vol. 18 (1924): 91-106; Gustave Lanctôt, "L'itinéraire de Cartier à Hochelaga," *Proceedings and Transactions of the Royal Society of Canada* 3rd series, vol. 24 (1930): 115-41; Samuel E. Morison, *The European Discovery of America*, vol. 1, *The Northern Voyages, AD 500-1600* (New York: Oxford University Press, 1971), 413; Marcel Trudel, *Histoire de la Nouvelle-France*, vol. 1, *Les vaines tentatives, 1524-1603* (Montreal: Fides, 1963), 97-98, 161; Lionel Groulx, *La découverte du Canada: Jacques Cartier*, rev. ed. (Montreal and Paris: Fides, 1966), 123-26; Jacques Cartier, *Relations: Édition critique par Michel Bideaux*, ed. Michel Bideaux (Montreal: Presses de l'Université de Montréal, 1986), 372; Jean-Claude Robert,

Atlas historique de Montréal (Montreal: Art global, 1994), 24-25. For a modern, popular account of the debate, see Mark Abley, "Where Was Hochelaga?" *Canadian Geographic,* November-December 1994, 63-68.

30 See *La Presse* (Montreal), 24 August 1921. Antoine-Aimé Bruneau's heritage involvement dated from 1887 when, as editor of a local paper, he denounced the proposed destruction of a windmill at Sorel. Cited in Paul-Louis Martin, "La conservation du patrimoine culturel: origines et évolution," in *Les Chemins de la mémoire: monuments et sites historiques du Québec* vol. 1, ed. Paul-Louis Martin (Quebec City: Les publications du Québec, 1990), 8-9. See also Béatrice Chassé, "Manoir Louis-Joseph Papineau," in *Les Chemins de la mémoire*, 2:510. On the CMHQ's early activities, see also Gordon, *Making Public Pasts*, 64-71.

31 Pierre-Georges Roy, *Les monuments commémoratifs de la province de Québec* (Quebec City: Commission des monuments historiques de la province de Québec, 1923).

32 Commission des monuments historiques de la provincec de Québec, Minute Books, 14 February 1923, E 52, Bibliothèque et Archives nationales du Québec, Section de Québec, Montreal.

33 Ibid., 22 June 1923, 21 April 1925, 9 June 1925.

34 *La Patrie* (Montreal), 18 October 1926. Pierre-Georges Roy had earlier made this claim in his *Les petites choses de notre histoire* (Lévis, 1919), 5:3-5.

35 Pamphile Demers to J.B. Harkin, 15 June 1927 and Georges Bellerive to A.A. Pinard, 5 November 1927, RG 84, vol. 1277, LAC.

36 Pamphile Demers to A.A. Pinard, 15 March 1928, RG 84, vol. 1227, LAC.

37 Gary Miedema has argued that this federal policy of broadening interfaith Christianity was a product of 1960s liberalism, a means to retain Canada's Christian foundations while promoting multiculturalism and toleration. The Île-aux-Coudres cross, and other commemorative examples, suggest that federal government agencies were pursuing these goals even before the Second World War. See Miedema, *For Canada's Sake: Public Religion, Centennial Celebrations, and the Re-Making of Canada in the 1960s* (Montreal and Kingston: McGill-Queen's University Press, 2005).

38 Comité d'organisation, *Monument Jacques-Cartier, première messe au pays: fête d'inauguration à l'Île-aux-Coudres, Comté de Charlevoix, 23 septembre 1928: notes et discours* (Quebec City: Cie d'imprimerie commerciale, 1929), 18. The French reads: "Nous sommes catholiques et français comme Cartier l'a voulu, comme il l'ésperait ... c'est en restant catholiques et français que nous serons de vrais canadiens."

39 See John M. Clarke to C.C. Ballantyne, 3 May 1921, reprinted in *Bulletin de la Société de Géographie de Québec* 15, 4 (1957): 195-97; see also John M. Clarke, "Un médaillon de Jacques Cartier," *Revue canadienne* 5 (January-June 1910): 6-15. The medallion is part of the permanent collection of the Musée de la Gaspésie, Gaspé.

40 A.A. Pinard, "Memorandum," 28 July 1924, RG 84, vol. 1253, LAC.

41 Lionel Groulx, *Mes mémoires* (Montreal: Fides, 1972), 3:48.

42 F.-X. Ross to J.B. Harkin, 16 March 1933, RG 84, vol. 1250, LAC. Chapais had succeeded his boyhood friend Narcisse-Eutrope Dionne as editor of *Le Courrier du Canada* in 1884.

43 Jules Bélanger, Marc Desjardins, and Jean-Yves Frenette, *Histoire de la Gaspésie* (Montreal: Boréal Express, 1981), 625-67.

44 *Le Devoir* (Montreal), 22 October 1930. Groulx's French: "il faut que ce monument soit l'oeuvre véritable d'une souscription nationale, comme il faut un grand acte de foi et de gratitude national [sic]" and "Notre pays est envahi par toutes les races du monde, lesquelles n'ayant pas toujours le temps d'apprendre notre histoire, n'ont que trop d'inclination à méconnaître ou à sousestimer notre passé, nos privilèges et nos droits. Encore qu'aux nouveaux venus, et en dépit des pénibles expériences, il ne faille pas négliger de faire savoir nos droits constitutionnels et politiques."

45 "L'enseignement primaire," *Education-Instruction* (September 1934) cited in Paul Carpentier, *Les croix de chemin: au-delà du signe* (Ottawa: Musées nationaux du Canada, 1981), 61, see also 62-63.

46 *La Nation* (Montreal), 9 July 1936. On Brodeur and the Société nationale Jacques-Cartier, see Fonds Maurice Brodeur, P209, Archives de l'Université Laval, Montreal, and Fonds Maurice Brodeur, P574, Bibliothèque et Archives nationales du Québec, Montreal. A copy

of the 1934 "Drapeau national 'Jacques Cartier'" is at the Bibliothèque nationale du Québec, Quebec City, cote CP 3498.

47 *The Globe and Mail* (Toronto), 23 January 1948.

48 Rodolphe Lemieux, "Canada's Quadcentenary, 1934," *Canadian Geographical Journal* 1 (November 1930): 564.

49 J.A. Bastien to G.W. Bryan, 1 May 1933; E.-F. Surveyer to J.B. Harkin, 3 April 1934; E.-F. Surveyer to J.B. Harkin, 9 May 1934, RG 84, vol. 1250, LAC; *L'Événement* (Quebec City), 29 March 1934.

50 Marius Barbeau, "La croix de Cartier," *Revue de l'Université d'Ottawa* 11, 4 (October 1941): 440-43.

51 W.F. Ganong, *Crucial Maps in the Early Cartography and Place-Nomenclature of the Atlantic Coast of Canada* (Toronto: University of Toronto Press, 1964), 196.

52 G.W. Bryan to J.B. Harkin, 1 September 1933, RG 84, vol. 1250, LAC; F.J. Richmond, "The Landing Place of Jacques Cartier at Gaspé in 1534," *Canadian Historical Association Annual Report* 1 (1922): 38-46.

53 J.B. Harkin to E.-F. Surveyer, 27 July 1933; J.C. Webster to J.B. Harkin, 1 August 1933, RG 84, vol. 1250, LAC.

54 J.P. Baxter, *A Memoir of Jacques Cartier* (New York: Dodd, 1906), 23; Justin Winsor, *Cartier to Frontenac: Geographical Discovery in the Interior of North America in Its Historical Relations, 1534-1700* (Boston and New York: Houghton, Mifflin, 1894), 35; Arthur Doughty and Adam Shortt, *Canada and Its Provinces* (Toronto: Publishers Association of Canada, 1914), 1:33-38.

55 See Brian Slattery, "French Claims in North America, 1500-59," *Canadian Historical Review* 59, 2 (June 1978): 147-49.

56 Patricia Seed, *Ceremonies of Possession in Europe's Conquest of the New World, 1492-1620* (New York: Cambridge University Press, 1995), 41-67.

57 E.A. Cruikshank to J.B. Harkin, 7 August 1933, RG 84, vol. 1250, LAC.

58 Raoul Dandurand to J.B. Harkin, 29 November 1933 and 16 December 1933, RG 84, vol. 1250, LAC.

59 *Ottawa Citizen*, 29 May 1934.

60 *L'Harvus* (Paramé), 2 July 1934, 1.

61 Philippe Roy to O.D. Skelton, 13 July 1934, RG 25 G 1, vol. 1674, Records of the Department of External Affairs, LAC. See also *La Patrie* (Montreal), 5 July 1934.

62 E.-F. Surveyer to J.B. Harkin, 4 January 1934, RG 84, vol. 1250, LAC.

63 *Montreal Gazette*, 5 February 1934; H.H. Rowatt to J.B. Harkin, 29 March 1934, RG 84, vol. 1250, LAC.

64 J.B. Harkin to H.H. Rowatt, 9 April 1934, RG 84, vol. 1250, LAC.

65 Cahan in a private conversation with William Lyon Mackenzie King, 15 March 1935, Diaries of Prime Minister William Lyon Mackenzie King, MG 26 J 13, LAC. See also Larry Glassford, *Reaction and Reform: The Politics of the Conservative Party under R.B. Bennett, 1927-1938* (Toronto: University of Toronto Press, 1992), 100-2; Donald Forster and Colin Read, "The Politics of Opportunism: The New Deal Broadcasts," *Canadian Historical Review* 60, 3 (September 1979): 324-49.

66 D.C. Harvey to J.B. Harkin, 10 April 1934, RG 84, vol. 1213, LAC.

67 R.A. Gibson to J.B. Harkin, 30 May 1934; T.S. Mills to J.B. Harkin, 24 August 1934, RG 84, vol. 1250, LAC.

68 Vigneau was the first Acadian premier of New Brunswick. The official records of Canada's Parliament use the anglicized name Peter John Veniot.

69 Canada, *House of Commons Debates* (16 March 1934), 1150, and *House of Commons Debates* (11 June 1934), 4076.

70 Ibid. (29 June 1934), 4437-38.

71 *Le Devoir* (Montreal), 16 March 1934.

72 Gustave Lanctôt to Victor Tremblay, 30 April 1934; Gustave Lanctôt to Arthur Sauvé, 30 April 1934; Victor Tremblay to Gustave Lanctôt, 5 May 1934, MG 30 D 95, vol. 9, LAC.

73 J.C. Webster to J.B. Harkin, 4 March 1934 and 8 March 1934, RG 84, vol. 1213, LAC. In the 1930s, Newfoundland had not yet become part of Canada.

74 H.R. Stewart to J.C. Webster, 9 April 1934, RG 84, vol. 1213, LAC.

75 D.C. Harvey to J.B. Harkin, 10 April 1934; J.C. Webster to J.B. Harkin, 10 May 1934, RG 84, vol. 1213, LAC.

76 Raphael Samuel, "Continuous National History," in *Patriotism: The Making and Unmaking of British National Identity*, ed. Raphael Samuel (London and New York: Routledge, 1989), 1:9-17.

77 Michael Dawson, *Selling British Columbia: Tourism and Consumer Culture, 1890-1970* (Vancouver: UBC Press, 2004), 78, 92.

78 Canada, Senate, *Report and Proceedings of the Special Committee on Tourist Traffic* (Ottawa: King's Printer, 1934), ix-xiv.

79 Ibid., 19.

80 Ibid., 57-58.

81 H.R. Stewart to J.C. Webster, 9 April 1934; Fred Landon to J.B. Harkin, 26 April 1934, RG 84, vol. 1213, LAC.

82 See *Halifax Chronicle*, 19 July 1934; *Le Soleil* (Quebec City), 27 August 1934.

83 *Toronto Star*, 4 September 1934.

84 *The Globe* (Toronto), 8 August 1935; see also Françoise Noël, "Old Home Week Celebrations as Tourism Promotion: North Bay, Ontario, 1925 and 1935," *Urban History Review* 37, 1 (Fall 2008): 35-46.

85 *Ottawa Journal*, 5 April 1934.

86 *Brockville Recorder and Times*, 31 October 1930.

87 New York Public Library, *Canada: An Exhibition Commemorating the Four-Hundredth Anniversary of the Discovery of the Saint Lawrence by Jacques Cartier, 1534-1535* (New York: New York Public Library, 1935).

88 Mary Travers, "La Gaspésienne pure laine," reproduced in Philippe Laframboise, ed., *La Bolduc: Soixante-douze chansons populaires* (Montreal: VLB Éditeur, 1992), 34.

89 See David Lonergan, *La Bolduc: La vie de Mary Travers, 1894-1941* (Quebec City: Isaac-Dion Éditeur, 1992), 129; Mme Édouard Bolduc, "La Gaspésienne pure laine" (sound recording), Starr Records 15907.

90 Charles de La Roncière, *Jacques Cartier et la découverte de la Nouvelle France* (Paris: Plon, 1931).

91 N.-E. Dionne, *Jacques Cartier*, 2nd ed. (Quebec City: Robitaille, 1933) and *Jacques Cartier*, 3rd ed. (Quebec City: Robitaille, 1934); Marius Barbeau, *La merveilleuse aventure de Jacques Cartier* (Montreal: Éditions Albert Lévesque, 1934); Camille Pouliot, *La grande aventure de Jacques Cartier* (Quebec City, 1934). See also C.-E. Roy and Lucien Brault, *Gaspé depuis Cartier* (Quebec City: Au moulin des lettres, 1934).

92 Adélard Desrosiers, *Notre Jacques Cartier* (Montreal: Éditions Albert Lévesque, 1934).

93 Sherman Charles Swift and T.G. Marquis, *The Voyages of Jacques Cartier in Prose and Verse* (Toronto: Thomas Allen, 1934).

94 Blanche McLeod Lewis, "Along the North Shore in Cartier's Wake," *Canadian Geographical Journal* 8, 5 (May 1934): 209-21.

95 Lionel Groulx, *La découverte du Canada: Jacques Cartier* (Montreal: Granger frères, 1934); Groulx, *Mes mémoires*, 4:214. See also *Le Canada* (Montreal), 9 November 1933.

96 *Le Soleil* (Quebec City), 25 August 1934. The French reads: "Nous nous trouvons ... sur le sol canadien mais ce n'est pas de fait un sol étranger ... Nous avons trouvé des descendents de nombreuses anciennes familles d'Europe dont plusieurs françaises."

97 *La Presse* (Montreal), 27 August 1934.

98 A.G. Doughty to J.B. Harkin, 13 July 1934, RG 84, vol. 1213, LAC.

99 Gordon, *Making Public Pasts*, 116-17.

100 See, especially, *Ottawa Citizen*, 30 March 1934; "Great Cross of Saint-Malo Quarry Stone Unveiled," *Ottawa Citizen*, 27 August 1934.

101 *La Presse* (Montreal), 27 August 1934. The original French reads: "Le sacrifice de Cartier a donc été fécond par l'apport des deux grands peuples, qui a fondé et fait grandir une race puissante à qui nous resterons toujours unis, la nation canadienne, qui demeure l'un des boulevards les plus solides de la civilisation chrétienne."

102 Comité France-Amérique, *Voyage au Canada: la mission Jacques Cartier* (Paris: Éditions de l'Atlantique, 1935), 24. "Le miracle canadien est ainsi un miracle français. Le jour où nous

inaugurâmes le pont Jacques Cartier à Montréal, à la tombée du jour, un arc-en-ciel, dont la première arche semblait partir de la rive même du Saint-Laurent, franchissait l'espace, semblait s'y perdre et l'on ne savait où reposait le second pilier de l'immense voûte lancée à travers le ciel et la mer. Nul doute maintenant: le second pilier s'appuyait sur la France."

103 Gabriel-Louis Jarray to M. Labonne, 31 July 1934, MG 5 F, vol. 23, Fonds de la Ministère des affaires étrangères (France), LAC.

104 On Vimy wheat, see John Pierce, "Constructing Memory: The Idea of Vimy Ridge" (MA thesis, Wilfrid Laurier University, 1993), 73.

105 Marc Ferro, *Pétain* (Paris: Fayard, 1987). Pierre-Etienne Flandin, leader of the French delegation to Gaspé, also collaborated with the Nazis and was convicted of treason after the war. *The Globe and Mail* (Toronto), 12 January 1944.

106 M.F. Gregg to F.H.H. Williamson, 12 April 1937, RG 84, vol. 1250, LAC. The wheat and poppies were still growing in the 1940s when an American tourist complained to the Parks Branch that, compared to the immaculate war memorial nearby, the cross site was deplorably maintained and covered with weeds and "hay." B.R. Thompson to "The Department," 11 July 1941, RG 84, vol. 1250, LAC.

107 Quoted in *La Presse* (Montreal), 27 August 1934. The French reads: "Mais est-il dans les fastes de l'histoire humaine un tableau plus grand et une figure plus saisissante que ce Jacques Cartier 'dont le geste immortel hante notre mémoire.' Les siècles ont passé mais son oeuvre demeure ... Vous ne vous étonnez point, messieurs, que ce quatrième centenaire soit célébré à Gaspé sous l'égide de l'Église, en même temps que l'État, qu'à côté d'une croix souvenir s'élève un temple votif de granit."

108 Quoted in Ibid. "Voici que par ce bois une grande joie s'est répandue dans le monde."

109 Quoted in Ibid. "Et les croix, qu'au voyage de 1535, Jacques Cartier va élever sur d'autres rivages, qu'il découvre en remontant notre grand fleuve, témoignent encore de son dessein d'unir toujours dans sa pensée, et les ambitions légitimes de son roi, et la conquête spirituelle des âmes."

110 The cathedral was never completed. In the 1960s, another cathedral drive was initiated, resulting in today's Christ the Lord Cathedral, consecrated in 1969.

111 J.B. Harkin to S.R. Sams, 18 May 1936, RG 84, vol. 1250, LAC.

112 *La Presse* (Montreal), 27 August 1934.

Chapter 7: Decline and Dispersal

1 *Le Soleil* (Quebec City), 6 September 1935. The French reads: "en exemple à notre jeunesse qui ne sait plus où diriger ses pas."

2 *La Patrie* (Montreal), 22 May 1935.

3 *Le Devoir* (Montreal), 22 June 1935.

4 See Gabriel Rioux, "Émergence d'une réflexion moderne en planification urbaine: apports de la Ligue du Progrès Civique pour la métropole montréalaise" (MA thesis, Université du Québec à Montréal, 2005).

5 Alan Gordon, *Making Public Pasts: The Contested Terrain of Montreal's Public Memories, 1891-1930* (Montreal and Kingston: McGill-Queen's University Press, 2001), 52-56.

6 *La Patrie* (Montreal), 3 October 1935.

7 François-Marc Gagnon, "Vues de Montréal," in *Montréal au XIXe siècle: des gens, des idées, ses arts, une ville*, ed. Jean-Rémi Brault (Ottawa: Leméac, 1990), 204-8. See also the official opening of the park in *Canadian Illustrated News* (Montreal), 3 June 1876.

8 Gillian Poulter, "Montreal and Its Environs: Imagining a National Landscape, c. 1867-1885," *Journal of Canadian Studies* 38, 3 (Fall 2004): 69-100.

9 Bernard Debarbieux and Claude Marois, "Le Mont Royal: forme naturelle, paysages et territorialités urbaines," *Cahiers de géographie du Québec* 41, 113 (September 1997): 185-87.

10 *L'Opinion publique* (Montreal), 30 July 1874; 5 November 1874. See also Janice E. Seline, "Frederick Law Olmsted's Mount Royal Park, Montreal: Design and Context" (MA thesis, Concordia University, 1983), 25; David Karel, ed., *Dictionnaire des artistes de langue française en Amérique du nord* (Quebec City: Presses de l'Université Laval, 1992), 700-1.

11 Léon Trépanier, *On veut savoir* (Montreal: La Patrie, 1960), 1:58-59.

12 Robert Rumilly, *Histoire de la Société Saint-Jean-Baptiste de Montréal* (Montreal: L'Aurore, 1975), 316. Rumilly makes an explicit comparison between the Mount Royal cross and Cartier's Gaspé cross. See also Gaston Côté, "L'érection de la croix du Mont Royal," *MENS: Revue d'histoire intellectuelle de l'Amérique française 7*, 1 (Fall 2006): 47-72.
13 *Montreal Standard,* 16 July 1932.
14 See, for example, *La Patrie* (Montreal), 1 September 1933.
15 *La Patrie* (Montreal), 17 February 1933; *Montreal Standard,* 19 January 1935.
16 *Montreal Standard,* 16 July 1932.
17 *L'Oiseau bleu* (Montreal), October 1935, 35-36. *L'Oiseau bleu* was the SSJBM's monthly children's magazine. The winning essay ignored the issue of Cartier's route to Hochelaga. In French, Tanguay's quote reads: "Émerveillé du splendide panorama qui se déroulait si harmonieusement à ses pieds, au-delà du fleuve féerique et jusqu'aux hauteurs qui bornent l'horizon, il ne trouva qu'un mot pour exprimer son admiration; il appela 'Mont Royal' cette montagne d'Hochelaga qui a conservé depuis cette gracieuse appelation."
18 *Le Devoir* (Montreal), 29 October 1935.
19 Société Saint-Jean-Baptiste de Montréal, *Jacques Cartier sur le Mont Royal en octobre 1535: programme-souvenir, 24 juin 1935* (Montreal: SSJBM, 1935), unnumbered plate; Société Saint-Jean-Baptiste de Montréal, *Hommage à Jacques Cartier* (Montreal: SSJBM, 1936).
20 *La Patrie* (Montreal), 30 October 1935.
21 J.P. Héroux, *Troisième centenaire de Montréal: compte rendu des fêtes* (Montreal: Commission du IIIe centenaire de Montréal, 1942). See also Harold Berubé, "Commémorer la ville: une analyse comparative des célébrations du centenaire de Toronto et du tricentenaire de Montréal," *Revue d'histoire de l'Amérique française 57*, 2 (Fall 2003): 209-36.
22 Commission des monuments historiques de la province de Québec, Minute Books, 14 January 1925, E 52, Bibliothèque et Archives nationales du Québec, Section de Québec.
23 Michael Gauvreau, *The Catholic Origins of Quebec's Quiet Revolution, 1931-1970* (Montreal and Kingston: McGill-Queen's University Press, 2005), 18-23. See also Louise Bienvenue, *Quand la jeunesse entre en scène: L'Action catholique avant la Révolution tranquille* (Montreal: Boréal, 2003); É.-A. Martin and Jean-Philippe Warren, *Sortir de la Grande Noirceur: l'horizon personnaliste de la Révolution tranquille* (Sillery: Septentrion, 2002).
24 Joseph Amato, *Mounier and Maritain: A French Catholic Understanding of the Modern World* (Tuscaloosa: University of Alabama Press, 1975).
25 Gauvreau, *The Catholic Origins,* 25.
26 See the following three essays in *Revue d'histoire de l'Amérique française 60*, 3 (Winter 2007): Lucia Ferreti, "L'Église catholique des années 1930-1970: avant tout celle des laïcs de l'Action catholique," 373-77; Yvan Lamonde, "Un arc en ciel," 377-81; Denyse Baillargeon, "Une révolution religieuse," 381-85.
27 Mason Wade, *The French Canadians, 1760-1967* (Toronto: Macmillan, 1968), 903. On Jeune-Canada's role, see Jeune-Canada, *Sur les pas de Cartier: Discours prononcés par les Jeune-Canada lors de leur assemblée "Hommage à Jacques Cartier"* (Montreal: Jeune-Canada, 1934).
28 See Roger Cyr, *La Patente; tous les secrets de la maçonnerie canadienne-française: L'Ordre de Jacques-Cartier* (Montreal: Éditions du Jour, 1964); G. Raymond Laliberté, *Une société secrète: l'Ordre de Jacques Cartier* (Montreal: Hurtubise HMH, 1983).
29 See *The Globe and Mail* (Toronto), 23-24 June 1944; *The Globe and Mail* (Toronto), 21 July 1944.
30 *The Globe and Mail* (Toronto), 28 June 1944.
31 Bienvenue, *Quand la jeunesse entre en scène,* 120-21.
32 *La Presse* (Montreal), 23 June 1911.
33 Indeed, the editor of the *Montreal Daily Herald,* J.C. Walsh, urged the creation of the monument committee. *Montreal Daily Herald,* 26 March 1910. See also Patrice Groulx, *Pièges de la mémoire: Dollard des Ormeaux, les Amérindiens, et nous* (Hull: Vents d'Ouest, 1998), 201-2.
34 J.-D. Tourigny, *Fêtes patriotiques et récits populaires des événements qui s'y rapportent* (Montreal: La Salle, 1921), 45-56.
35 *Montreal Gazette,* 21 March 1932.

36   See *Montreal Gazette,* 26 March 1932; *Le Devoir* (Montreal), 29 March 1932.
37   *Le Devoir* (Montreal), 7 May 1932; *Le Devoir* (Montreal), 11 May 1932. The most detailed summary of the Dollard dispute is found in Groulx, *Pièges de la mémoire,* 249-65. The debate can also be followed in André Vachon, "Dollard des Ormeaux," *Dictionary of Canadian Biography Online (DCB Online)* (Toronto: University of Toronto Press, 2005), Library and Archives Canada, http://www.biographi.ca.
38   E.R. Adair, "Dollard des Ormeaux and the Fight at the Long Sault," *Canadian Historical Review* 13, 1 (June 1932): 121-38; Gustave Lanctôt, "Was Dollard the Saviour of New France?" *Canadian Historical Review* 13, 1 (June 1932): 138-46. See also George Brown to Aegidius Fauteux, 13 May 1932, George Brown Collection, University of Toronto Archives, Toronto, cited in Colin Coates and Cecelia Morgan, *Heroines and History: Representations of Madeleine de Verchères and Laura Secord* (Toronto: University of Toronto Press, 2002), 98.
39   Fernande Roy, "Une mise en scène de l'histoire: la fondation de Montréal à travers les siècles," *Revue d'histoire de l'Amérique française* 46, 1 (Summer 1992): 7-36.
40   Lionel Groulx, *Mes mémoires* (Montreal: Fides, 1972), 2:57-58.
41   Coates and Morgan, *Heroines and History,* 98.
42   Groulx, *Pièges de la mémoire,* 300-5.
43   Gustave Lanctôt, "Évolution de notre historiographie," *Action universitaire* 13 (1946-47): 3-6; Ronald Rudin, *Making History in Twentieth Century Quebec: Historians and Their Society* (Toronto: University of Toronto Press, 1997), 76-77.
44   Lanctôt's papers are held at Library and Archives Canada (Fonds Gustave Lanctôt, MG 30 D 95), the Centre de recherche sur la civilisation canadienne française, University of Ottawa (Fonds Gustave Lanctôt, P137), the Université de Moncton (Fonds d'archives no. 99 Gustave Lanctôt), and the Université de Montréal (as part of the Fonds du Centre de Documentation des Lettres Canadiennes-Françaises).
45   Gustave Lanctôt, *Jacques Cartier devant l'histoire* (Montreal: Éditions Lumen, 1947), 16-20, 99-135.
46   Lucien Campeau, "Encore à propos de Cartier," *Revue d'histoire de l'Amérique française* 7, 4 (March 1954): 558-70.
47   See Lucien Campeau, "Autour de la relation du P. Pierre Biard," *Revue d'histoire de l'Amérique française* 6, 4 (March 1953): 517-35; Campeau, "Encore à propos de Cartier"; Gustave Lanctôt, "Cartier au Canada en 1524," *Revue d'histoire de l'Amérique française* 7, 3 (December 1953): 413-25; Gustave Lanctôt, "Cartier en Nouvelle France en 1524," *Revue d'histoire de l'Amérique française* 8, 2 (September 1954): 213-19.
48   Michel Mollat, *Le commerce maritime normand à la fin du moyen âge* (Paris: Plon, 1952), 266.
49   Marcel Trudel, *Histoire de la Nouvelle-France,* vol. 1, *Les vaines tentatives, 1524-1603* (Montreal: Fides, 1963), 58-63.
50   Marcel Trudel, "Cartier, Jacques," *DCB Online.*
51   Samuel E. Morison, *The European Discovery of America,* vol. 1, *The Northern Voyages, AD 500-1600* (New York: Oxford University Press, 1971), 263.
52   Stephen Bann, *The Inventions of History: Essays on the Representation of the Past* (Manchester: Manchester University Press, 1990), 111.
53   Raymond Conron to Gustave Lanctôt, 14 March 1948, MG 30 D 95, vol. 9, Fonds Gustave Lanctôt, LAC.
54   M. de Menthon to Gustave Lanctôt, 20 December 1948, MG 30 D 95, vol. 9, Fonds Gustave Lanctôt, LAC.
55   Father Julien Descottes, a French correspondent of Lanctôt's, supplied a date of 14 August 1790 for the closing of the cathedral. However, this appears to be too early in the French Revolution for the Dechristianization movement.
56   Gustave Lanctôt to A.R. Tremearne, 17 September 1948; A.R. Tremearne to Gustave Lanctôt, 24 September 1948; A.R. Tremearne to Gustave Lanctôt, 15 November 1948; Gustave Lanctôt to Georges Vanier, ambassador to France, 7 February 1949, all held in MG 30 D 95, vol. 9, Fonds Gustave Lanctôt, LAC.
57   Commandant Khanzadian to Gustave Lanctôt, 12 April 1949, MG 30 D 95, vol. 9, Fonds Gustave Lanctôt, LAC.

58 N.-E. Dionne, *Jacques Cartier* (Quebec: Léger Brousseau, 1889), 166-69.
59 Père François-Xavier de Charlevoix, *Histoire et description générale de la Nouvelle France, avec le journal historique d'un voyage fait par ordre du roi dans l'Amérique septentrionale* (Paris: Pierre-François Giffart, 1744), 1:21.
60 "Procès Verbal – Ministère de l'intérieur, 11 avril 1949" and "Note sur le squelette dit de 'Jacques Cartier,'" MG 30 D 95, vol. 9, Fonds Gustave Lanctôt, LAC.
61 Father Descottes to Gustave Lanctôt, 15 April 1949, MG 30 D 95, vol. 9, Fonds Gustave Lanctôt, LAC.
62 "Report on the Special Mission for the Discovery of Jacques Cartier's Burial Place," MG 30 D 95, vol. 9, Fonds Gustave Lanctôt, LAC.
63 Lionel Groulx, *La découverte du Canada: Jacques Cartier*, rev. ed. (Montreal and Paris: Fides, 1966), 175-78.
64 *The Globe and Mail* (Toronto), 7 June 1949.
65 "Étude et identification des restes de Jacques Cartier," *Bulletin de l'Académie de medecine* 136, 7-8 (26 February 1952): 103-9.
66 *The Globe and Mail* (Toronto), 7 June 1949.
67 Rudin, *Making History,* 41-47.
68 On Lévesque, see Robert Parisé, *Georges-Henri Lévesque: père de la renaissance québécoise* (Montreal: Stanké, 1976). See also Groulx, *Pièges de la mémoire,* 294.
69 *Le Devoir* (Montreal), 29 June 1946.
70 *Le Devoir* (Montreal), 26 October 1946.
71 Rudin, *Making History,* 74-77.
72 See Lionel Groulx, "Un institut d'histoire," *Revue d'histoire de l'Amérique française* 2, 3 (December 1948): 475.
73 Rudin, *Making History,* 79. Although Rudin cites Lanctôt as an example, he did publish articles in the RHAF during the early 1950s.
74 Marcel Trudel, *Mémoires d'un autre siècle* (Montreal: Boréal, 1987), 160-66.
75 Rudin, *Making History,* 82-85. Relying on his correspondence, Rudin suggests that Trudel rewrote his own past to augment his anti-clericalism yet, paradoxically, to reduce the animosity between himself and abbé Maheux, the clerical historian and director of the IHAF.
76 Henry Percival Biggar, "Cartier's Objective," *Report of the Annual Meeting of the Canadian Historical Association* 13 (1934): 121-23.
77 Trudel, *Histoire de la Nouvelle-France,* 1:87-90.
78 Ibid., 122-23.
79 Camille Pouliot, *La grande aventure de Jacques Cartier* (Quebec City, 1934).
80 Eugène Guernier, *Jacques Cartier et la pensée colonisatrice* (Paris: Éditions de l'encyclopédie de l'Empire Français, 1946).
81 Lionel Groulx, "Compte rendu de Guernier," *Revue d'histoire de l'Amérique française* 1, 4 (March 1948): 603.
82 Fernand Ouellet, "La modernisation de l'historiographie et l'émergence de l'histoire sociale," *Recherches sociographiques* 26, 1-2 (1985): 11-83.
83 Michael Bliss, "Privatizing the Mind: The Sundering of Canadian History, the Sundering of Canada," *Journal of Canadian Studies* 26, 4 (Winter 1991-92): 5-17; J.L. Granatstein, *Who Killed Canadian History?* (Toronto: HarperCollins, 1998).
84 Gérard Malchelosse, "Jacques Cartier va à Hochelaga," *Cahiers des Dix* 21 (1956): 31-53; Claude Perrault, "La découverte de Montréal par Jacques Cartier," *Revue d'histoire de l'Amérique française* 20, 2 (September 1966): 235-61.
85 On Lighthall and his friend David Ross McCord, see Donald Wright, "W.D. Lighthall and David Ross McCord: Antimodernism and English-Canadian Imperialism, 1880s-1918," *Journal of Canadian Studies* 32, 2 (Summer 1997): 134-53. See also Gordon, *Making Public Pasts,* 51-54.
86 *Montreal Daily Witness,* 9 July 1909.
87 W.D. Lighthall to J.W. Jocks, 8 July 1909, W.D. Lighthall Papers, McGill University Archives, Montreal.

88 Norman Clermont, "Les premiers recherches archéologiques dans la région de Montréal," in Brault, *Montréal au XIXe siècle*, 111. See also Groulx, *Pièges de la mémoire*, 292-93.
89 1557 1957
En souvenir du 4e centenaire du décès de Jacques Cartier
1491-1557
Illustre navigateur de Saint-Malo France
Découvreur du Canada
90 Monsignor Antoine Gagnon, *Histoire de Matane* (Rimouski: Impressions des associés, 1977), 321, 615.
91 *The Globe and Mail* (Toronto), 26 April 1967.
92 "18th Century Swinger," *Montreal Magazine* 4, 9 September 1967, 28-29.
93 *Toronto Star*, 28 October 1966.
94 The ship was built by Davies Shipyards in Lévis. Parks Canada, *La Grande Hermine* (Ottawa: Supply and Services Canada, 1977); Parks Canada, *Cartier-Brébeuf National Historic Park: Management Plan* (Ottawa: Supply and Services Canada, 1993), 19-29. According to a local legend, a wrecked vessel beached at the Lake Ontario entrance to the Welland Canal is the remnant of this *Grande Hermine* or of another replica of it. See *St. Catharines Standard*, 28 January 2003; *Hamilton Spectator*, 13 September 2003.

Chapter 8: Failure and Forgetting

1 *The Globe and Mail* (Toronto), 9 November 1983.
2 *The Globe and Mail* (Toronto), 23 November 1983.
3 *Toronto Star*, 27 May 1984.
4 Jean Palardy, "Manoir de Jacques Cartier," MG 30 D 395, vol. 5, Fonds Jean Palardy, Library and Archives Canada, Ottawa.
5 John W. Fisher to David M. Stewart, 24 June 1975, MU 4284, F1193, John W. Fisher Fonds, Archives of Ontario, Toronto.
6 *Saturday Night Magazine*, 22 May 1984.
7 *Toronto Star*, 30 June 1984.
8 *The Globe and Mail* (Toronto), 4 July 1984.
9 For more information on the Centre Jacques Cartier, visit its website at http://cjc.univ-lyon2.fr/.
10 Michel Bideaux, "Éditer Cartier," *Revue d'histoire littéraire du Québec et du Canada français* 4 (Summer-Fall 1982): 10-21. See also René Dionne, "La Revue d'histoire littéraire du Québec et du Canada français," *Voix et images* 12, 2 (Winter 1987): 287-94.
11 Jacques Cartier, *Relations: Édition critique par Michel Bideaux*, ed. Michel Bideaux (Montreal: Presses de l'Université de Montréal, 1986).
12 Fernand Braudel, Michel Mollat, and Maurice Aymard, eds., *Le monde de Jacques Cartier: l'aventure au XVIe siècle* (Montreal: Libre Expression, 1984).
13 *Le Soleil* (Quebec City), 20 June 1984; *The Globe and Mail* (Toronto), 4 July 1984.
14 *Le Soleil* (Quebec City), 15 June 1984.
15 *Le Soleil* (Quebec City), 4 June 1984.
16 *Le Soleil* (Quebec City), 14 July 1984; *Le Soleil* (Quebec City), 17 July 1984; *Le Soleil* (Quebec City), 20 July 1984; *Toronto Star*, 25 July 1984.
17 *Le Soleil* (Quebec City), 23 July 1984.
18 *Le Soleil* (Quebec City), 1 August 1984.
19 *Le Soleil* (Quebec City), 9 July 1984.
20 *Montreal Gazette*, 27 July 1998. The Compagnons de Jacques Cartier website is still active at http://www.jacquescartier.org.
21 Pierre Larouche, *Montréal 1535: Le redécouverte de Hochelaga* (Outremont: Éditions Villes nouvelles – villes anciennes, 1992).
22 Ramsay Cook, ed., *The Voyages of Jacques Cartier* (Toronto: University of Toronto Press, 1993).
23 *Jacques Cartier* (DVD, Historica Heritage Minute, 1991).
24 The French version was broadcast as *Le Canada: Une histoire populaire*, reflecting different sensibilities around the nature of the country.

25 *Canada: A People's History* (DVD, Canadian Broadcasting Corporation, 2000).
26 Don Gillmor, Pierre Turgeon, and Achile Michaud, *Canada: A People's History* (Toronto: McClelland and Stewart, 2000).
27 J.L. Granatstein, *Who Killed Canadian History?* (Toronto: HarperCollins, 1998); Michael Bliss, "Privatizing the Mind: The Sundering of Canadian History, the Sundering of Canada," *Journal of Canadian Studies* 26, 4 (Winter 1991-92): 5-17.

Bibliography

The argument in this book is historiographical in nature. However, it takes an expanded view of historiography to include poetry, song, celebrations, monuments, and historical plaques as part of the writing of Jacques Cartier's history. This bibliography is laid out to reflect this approach so that entries are grouped according to how they have been used. The primary sources used to support the argument include archival collections, coverage of events in the periodical press, versions of Cartier's *Relations*, and collections of documents related to his life and exploits, as well as publications and historical studies by amateur and professional historians that reveal what historians thought about Cartier at different points in time. Works grouped as secondary sources are those that provide the context and help with the interpretation of the primary source materials.

Primary Sources

Archival Sources

Archives de la Ville de Montréal, Montreal
Album Jacques Viger
Fonds de la Commission du troisième centenaire de Montréal, VM 12
Fonds de la municipalité de Saint-Henri, P 23
Fonds du Service des travaux publics, VM 4

Bibliothèque et Archives nationales du Québec, Section de Québec
Commission des monuments historiques de la province de Québec, Minute Books, E 52

Library and Archives Canada (LAC), Ottawa
Diaries of Prime Minister William Lyon Mackenzie King, MG 26 J 13
Fonds de la Ministère des affaires étrangères (France), MG 5
Fonds Gustave Lanctôt, MG 30 D 95
Fonds Jean Palardy, MG 30 D 395
Fonds Paul-Henri de Belvèze, MG 24 F 42
Records of the Canadian Parks Service, RG 84
Records of the Department of Agriculture, RG 17 AI 2
Records of the Department of External Affairs, RG 25

McGill University Archives, Montreal
W.D. Lighthall Papers

Archives of Ontario, Toronto
John W. Fisher Fonds, F1193

Primary Printed Materials

Anon. *Jacques Cartier, 1491-1557: exposition organisée pour le quatrième centenaire de sa mort.* Saint-Malo: Musée de Saint-Malo, 1957.

Anon. *Pageants du tricentenaire de Québec, 1608-1908, mis en scène par M. Frank Lascelles; dialogues et discours par M. Ernest Myrand; musique préparée par M. Joseph Vézina.* Quebec City: Laflamme et Proulx, 1908.

Anon. *Souvenir des fêtes de Tadoussac pour célébrer le quatrième centenaire de la découverte du Saguenay par Jacques Cartier.* N.p., 1935.

Anon. *Souvenir du quatrième centenaire de la découverte de l'Île d'Orléans et du dévoilement d'une croix Jacques-Cartier à Saint-Jean, dimanche, le 15 septembre 1935.* Quebec City: Société nationale Jacques-Cartier, 1935.

Canada. House of Commons. *Debates of the House of Commons.* Ottawa: Queen's Printer, 1890-1970.

Canada. Senate. *Report and Proceedings of the Special Committee on Tourist Traffic.* Ottawa: King's Printer, 1934.

Catalogue des livres qui se trouvent aux magazins de Messrs. G. et B. Horan à Québec et chez M. H. Bossange à Montréal. Montreal, 1816.

Cercle catholique de Québec. *Deuxième bulletin du comité littéraire et historique du Cercle catholique de Québec: oeuvre du monument Jacques-Cartier.* Quebec City, 1890.

–. *Premier bulletin du comité littéraire et historique du Cercle catholique de Québec: oeuvre du monument Jacques-Cartier.* Quebec City, 1888.

Chauveau, Pierre-J.-O. *Discours prononcé lors de l'inauguration du monument Cartier-Brébeuf le 24 juin 1889.* Montreal: Beauchemin et fils, 1889.

Comité d'organisation. *Monument Jacques-Cartier, première messe au pays: fête d'inauguration à l'Île-aux-Coudres, Comté de Charlevoix, 23 septembre 1928: notes et discours.* Quebec City: Cie d'imprimerie commerciale, 1929.

Comité France-Amérique. *Voyage au Canada: la mission Jacques Cartier.* Paris: Éditions de l'Atlantique, 1935.

Dugas, Jocelyne. *Le quatrième voyage de Jacques Cartier: programme souvenir officiel: Québec 1534-1984 / Jacques Cartier, the Fourth Voyage: Official Souvenir Programme: Québec 1534-1984.* Quebec City: Edimédia, 1984.

Héroux, J.P. *Troisième centenaire de Montréal: compte rendu des fêtes.* Montreal: Commission du IIIe centenaire de Montréal, 1942.

Jeune-Canada. *Sur les pas de Cartier: Discours prononcés par les Jeune-Canada lors de leur assemblée "Hommage à Jacques Cartier."* Montreal: Jeune-Canada, 1934.

Literary and Historical Society of Quebec. *Transactions of the Literary and Historical Society of Quebec: Session of 1862.* Quebec City: Literary and Historical Society of Quebec, 1862.

–. *Transactions of the Literary and Historical Society of Quebec: Session of 1879-80.* Quebec City: Literary and Historical Society of Quebec, 1880.

New York Public Library. *Canada: An Exhibition Commemorating the Four-Hundredth Anniversary of the Discovery of the Saint Lawrence by Jacques Cartier, 1534-1535.* New York: New York Public Library, 1935.

Parks Canada. *Cartier-Brébeuf National Historic Park: Management Plan.* Ottawa: Supply and Services Canada, 1993.

–. *La Grande Hermine.* Ottawa: Supply and Services Canada, 1977.

Quebec. Assemblée législative. *Débats de l'Assemblée législative du Québec.* Quebec City: Assemblée nationale, 1890-1935.

Société Saint-Jean-Baptiste de Montréal. *Hommage à Jacques Cartier.* Montreal: Société Saint-Jean-Baptiste de Montréal, 1936.

–. *Jacques Cartier sur le Mont Royal en octobre 1535: programme-souvenir, 24 juin 1935.* Montreal: Société Saint-Jean-Baptiste de Montréal, 1935.

Tiercelin, Louis. *Mémorial des fêtes Franco-Canadiennes pour l'érection du monument de Jacques Cartier.* Paramé: Éditions de l'Hermine, 1905.

Tourigny, J.-D. *Fêtes patriotiques et récits populaires des événements qui s'y rapportent.* Montreal: La Salle, 1921.

Newspapers
L'Ami du peuple (Montreal), selected dates.
L'Avenir (Montreal), selected dates.
Brockville Recorder and Times, 1930.
Le Canada (Montreal), 1922-35.
Canadian Illustrated News (Montreal), 1869-83.
Le Canadien (Quebec City), selected dates.
Le Courrier du Canada (Quebec City), selected dates.
Le Devoir (Montreal), 1930-46.
L'Événement (Quebec City), selected dates.
The Globe (Toronto), 1889-1936.
The Globe and Mail (Toronto), 1936-2006.
Halifax Chronicle, selected dates.
L'Harvus (Paramé), selected dates.
Le Journal de Québec (Quebec City), selected dates.
La Minerve (Montreal), 1847-93.
Le monde illustré (Paris), selected dates.
Montreal Gazette, 1849-1998.
Montreal Standard, selected dates.
Montreal Star, selected dates.
National Post (Toronto), 2006.
L'Oiseau bleu (Montreal), selected dates.
L'Opinion publique (Montreal), 1870-83.
Ottawa Citizen, selected dates.
Ottawa Journal, 1934.
La Patrie (Montreal), 1926-44.
La Presse (Montreal), 1911-35.
Québec Gazette / Gazette de Québec (Quebec City), selected dates.
Le Soleil (Quebec City), 1934-2006.
Toronto Daily Star, 1896-1984.
Toronto Mail and Empire, selected dates.

Accounts of Voyages (Relations) and Collections of Documents
Alfonse, Jean. *Les voyages adventureux du capitaine Ian Alfonse, Sainctongeois.* Paris: Ian de Marnef, 1559.
Aumasson, Louis-Léonard, sieur de Courville. *Mémoires sur le Canada depuis 1749 jusqu'à 1760: en trois parties, avec cartes et plans lithographiés.* Quebec City: Middleton and Dawson, 1873.
Beaulieu, Anne-Marie, ed. *Les trois mondes de la Popelinière.* Geneva: Librairie Droz, 1997.
Biggar, Henry Percival. *A Collection of Documents Relating to Jacques Cartier and the Sieur de Roberval.* Ottawa: Public Archives of Canada, 1930.
–. *The Precursors of Jacques Cartier, 1497-1534: A Collection of Documents Relating to the Early History of the Dominion of Canada.* Ottawa: Government Printing Bureau, 1911.
–. *Voyages of Jacques Cartier: Published from the Originals, with Translations, Notes, and Appendices.* Ottawa: Public Archives of Canada, 1924.
Cartier, Jacques. *Bref récit et succincte narration de la navigation faite en MDXXXV et MDXXXVI par le capitaine Jacques Cartier aux îles de Canada, Hochelaga, Saguenay et autres; précédée d'une brève succincte introduction historique par M. d'Avézac.* Paris: Librairie Tross, 1863.
– [?]. *Brief recit, et succincte narration, de la nauigation faicte es ysles de Canada, Hochelage et Saguenay et autres, auec particulieres meurs, langaige, et cerimonies des habitans d'icelles: fort delectable à veoir.* Paris: Ponce Roffet, 1545.
–. *Relations: Édition critique par Michel Bideaux,* ed. Michel Bideaux. Montreal: Presses de l'Université de Montréal, 1986.
–. *A Short and Brief Narration of the Navigation Made by the Commandment of the King of France, to the Islands of Canada, Hochelaga, Saguenay, and Divers Others, Which Now Are Called New France.* London, 1809.

–. *Voyage de Jacques Cartier au Canada en 1534, nouvelle édition publiée d'après l'édition de 1598 et d'après Ramusio, par M.H. Michelant, avec deux cartes: documents inédits sur le Canada communiqués par M. Alfred Ramé.* Paris: Librairie Tross, 1865.

Charlevoix, Père François-Xavier de. *Histoire et description générale de la Nouvelle France, avec le journal historique d'un voyage fait par ordre du roi dans l'Amérique septentrionale.* 3 vols. Paris: Pierre-François Giffart, 1744.

Faribault, G.-B., ed. *Voyages de découverte au Canada entre les années 1534 et 1542, par Jacques Quartier, le sieur de Roberval, Jean Alphonse de Xaintonage, et c.; suivis de la description de Québec et de ses environs en 1608, et de divers extraits relativement au lieu de l'hivernement de Jacques Quartier en 1535-36.* Quebec City: William Cowan et fils, 1843.

Hakluyt, Richard. *The Principal Navigations, Voyages, Traffiques and Discoveries of the English Nation, Made by Sea or Overland to the Remote and Farthest Distant Quarters of the Earth at Any Time within the Compasse of These 1600 Years.* 8 vols. London: Dent, 1926.

Joüon des Longrais, Frédéric. *Jacques Cartier: documents nouveaux.* Paris: Alphonse Picard, 1888.

Julien, Charles-André. *Les Français en Amérique pendant la première moitié du XVIe siècle, textes des voyages de Verrazano, Cartier et Roberval.* Paris: Presses universitaires de France, 1946.

Lahontan, Baron de. *Oeuvres complètes.* Edited by Réal Ouellet. Montreal: Presses de l'Université de Montréal, 1990.

Lussagnet, Suzanne, ed. *Les Français en Amérique pendant la deuxième moitié du XVIe siècle.* Vol. 2, *Les Français en Floride.* Paris: Presses universitaires de France, 1958.

Mallard, Jehan. *Premier livre de la description de tous les portz de mer de l'univers.* N.p., 1545.

Maran, René. "Biographie de Jacques Cartier." In *Voyages de découverte au Canada entre les années 1534 et 1542,* Jacques Cartier, 133-206. Paris: Anthropos, 1968 [1843].

Michelant, H., and Alfred Ramé, eds. *Discours du voyage fait par le capitaine Jacques Cartier aux Terres-Neufves de Canada.* Paris: Librairie Tross, 1865.

–. *Relation originale du voyage de Jacques Cartier au Canada en 1534: documents inédits sur Jacques Cartier et le Canada.* Paris: Librairie Tross, 1867.

Postel, Guillaume. *De orbis terræ concordia libri quatuor ... Adjectæ sunt quoque annotationes in margine a pio atque erudito quodam viro, etc.* Paris: Gromorsus, 1544.

Taylor, E.G.R., ed. *The Original Writings and Correspondence of the Two Richard Hakluyts.* Vol. 2. London: Hakluyt Society, 1935.

Thevet, André. 1578. *Les singularitez de la France antarctique.* Paris: Maisonneuve et Cie, 1878.

Thwaites, Reuben, ed. *The Jesuit Relations and Allied Documents.* Vol. 3. Cleveland: Burrows, 1897.

Publications Relating to Jacques Cartier

Achard, Eugène. *Le chemin de Jacques Cartier vers la bourgade d'Hochelaga.* Montreal: Éditions Eugène Achard, 1969.

–. *L'homme blanc de Gaspé.* Montreal: Librairie générale canadienne, 1937.

–. *Le royaume du Saguenay.* Montreal: Librairie générale canadienne, 1942.

–. *Sur le grand fleuve de Canada.* Montreal: Librairie générale canadienne, 1940.

–. *Le vice-roi du Canada.* Montreal: Librairie générale canadienne, 1942.

Alexandre, Marie. *L'espion de Jacques Cartier.* Montreal: Librairie générale canadienne, 1946.

Anon. "Ce que fut Jacques Cartier." *La Revue populaire* 11, 7 (July 1918): 9-14.

Anon. *Quatre gloires canadiennes: Jacques Cartier, Samuel de Champlain, RR. PP. de Brébeuf et Lalemant.* Montreal: Cadieux et Derome, 1887.

Archambault, J.L. *Jacques Cartier ou Canada vengé: drame historique en cinq actes.* Montreal: Sénécal, 1879.

Averill, Esther Holden. *Cartier Sails the St. Lawrence.* New York: Harper and Row, 1956.

Barbeau, Marius. "Cartier Inspired Rabelais." *Canadian Geographical Journal* 9, 3 (September 1934): 113-25.

–. "La croix de Cartier." *Revue de l'Université d'Ottawa* 11, 4 (October 1941): 440-43.

–. *La merveilleuse aventure de Jacques Cartier.* Montreal: Éditions Albert Lévesque, 1934.

Barette, Victor. *Veille de Noël St-Malo en 1535.* Trois-Rivières, 1934.

Baxter, J.P. *A Memoir of Jacques Cartier.* New York: Dodd, 1906.

Beaugrand-Champagne, Aristide. "Le chemin d'Hochelaga." *Proceedings and Transactions of the Royal Society of Canada* 3rd series, vol. 17 (1923): 17-24.

–. "Le chemin et l'emplacement de la Bourgade d'Hochelaga." *Cahiers des Dix* 12 (1947): 115-60.

–. "Introduction aux voyages de Jacques Cartier: Des origines à Jean Cabot." *Canadian Historical Association Annual Report* 13 (1934): 97-104.

–. "Introduction aux voyages de Jacques Cartier: Jean Cabot." *Canadian Historical Association Annual Report* 14 (1935): 88-109.

–. "Les origines de Montréal." *Cahiers des Dix* 13 (1948): 39-62.

Berrong, Richard. "The Nature and Function of the Savage in Jacques Cartier's *Récits de voyage.*" *Romance Notes* 22, 2 (Winter 1981): 213-17.

Berthelot, Amable. *Discours sur le vaisseau abandoné par Jacques Cartier, lors de son second voyage au Canada.* Quebec City: A. Coté, 1844.

–. "Dissertation sur le canon de bronze." *Transactions of the Literary and Historical Society of Quebec* 2 (1830): 198-215

Berthiaume, André. "Bref récit." In *Dictionnaire des oeuvres littéraires du Québec.* Vol. 1, *Des origines à 1900,* ed. M. Lemire, 64-67. Montreal: Fides, 1978.

–. *La découverte ambiguë: Essai sur les récits de voyage de Jacques Cartier et leur fortune littéraire.* Montreal: Pierre Tisseyre, 1976.

–. "La fortune d'un couple mythique: Jacques Cartier et l'amérindien." *Études littéraires* 8, 1 (April 1975): 81-102.

–. "Le soleil, la croix, l'épée." *Études littéraires* 7, 1 (April 1974): 183-90.

Besson, Maurice. "Jacques Cartier et la découverte du Canada." *Le Monde colonial illustré,* July 1934, 107-8.

Beunat, Mario. *Jacques Cartier: l'aventurier exemplaire.* Paris: Acropole, 1984.

–. *Jacques Cartier: l'aventurier exemplaire.* Longueuil: Institut Nazareth et Louis-Braille, 1984. In Braille.

Bideaux, Michel. "Éditer Cartier." *Revue d'histoire littéraire du Québec et du Canada français* 4 (Summer-Fall 1982): 10-21.

–. "Qui est l'auteur de la Relation de 1534?" *Études canadiennes* 10, 17 (December 1984): 83-90.

Biggar, Henry Percival. "Cartier's Objective." *Report of the Annual Meeting of the Canadian Historical Association* 13 (1934): 121-23.

–. "Jacques Cartier's Portrait." *Canadian Historical Review* 6, 2 (June 1925): 155-57.

Boissonnault, Réal, Kenneth Kidd, John Rick, and Marcel Moussette. *Étude sur la vie et l'oeuvre de Jacques Cartier (1491-1557)* Ottawa: Parks Canada, 1977.

Bordeaux, Henry. "La mission française au Canada." *L'Illustration,* 15 September 1934, 66-68.

–. *Nouvelle et Vieille France: une mission au Canada.* Paris: Plon, 1934.

Bosseboeuf, C.F. *Quatrième centenaire de la découverte du Canada, par Jacques Cartier.* Tours: Maison Mame, 1934.

Bouniol, Bathild. *Les marins français.* Paris: Bray, 1867.

Bourinot, J.G. "Cape Breton and Its Memorials of the French Regime." *Proceedings and Transactions of the Royal Society of Canada* 11 (1891): 173-343.

Braudel, Fernand, Michel Mollat, and Maurice Aymard, eds. *Le monde de Jacques Cartier.* Montreal: Libre Expression, 1984.

Brault, Lucien. "Bibliographie." *Bulletin des recherches historiques* 41, 12 (December 1935): 724-35.

Brito, G. "Les manuscrits de Jacques Cartier." *Arts et métiers graphiques* 44 (1934): 49-53.

Brodeur, Maurice. "La croix de la découverte du Canada ou croix Jacques Cartier." *Le Documentaire encyclopédie populaire Québec* 5 (December 1942): 147-49.

–. "Le drapeau Jacques-Cartier." *La Revue populaire* 27, 7 (July 1934): 10, 52-53.

Bruchési, Jean. "Pour fêter Jacques Cartier." *La Revue moderne* 15, 11 (September 1934): 3.

Burland, C.A. "A Map of Canada in 1546." *Geographical Magazine* 24, 2 (February 1951): 103-10.

Buron, Edmond. "Le quatrième centenaire du Canada." *Canada français* 18 (1930): 164-73.

Burpee, Lawrence J. *The Discovery of Canada*. Ottawa: Graphic, 1929.
–. "Trailing Jacques Cartier." *Canadian National Magazine,* November 1938, 10-11, 31.
Campeau, Lucien. "Encore à propos de Cartier." *Revue d'histoire de l'Amérique française* 7, 4 (March 1954): 558-70.
–. "Sur le pas de Cartier et de Champlain." *Cahiers de l'académie canadienne-française* 8 (1964): 29-38.
Canada. Canadian Heritage. *Cartier-Brébeuf National Historic Site: In Search of Jacques Cartier.* Research Bulletin 312. Ottawa: Parks Canada, 1994.
Caron, Louis. *Le vrai voyage de Jacques Cartier*. Montreal: Art global, 1984.
Carter, Wilfred. "Canada's Most Sacred Acre." *Revue d'histoire de la Gaspésie* 1, 2 (May-June 1963): 71-77.
Cathelineau, Emmanuel de. "D'une epitaphe sur Roberval." *Nova Francia* 6 (1931): 302-12.
–. "Jacques Cartier, Roberval, et quelques-uns de leurs compagnons." *Revue des questions historiques* 62, 5 (October-November 1934): 15-25.
–. "Quel jour Cartier rentra-t-il de son troisième voyage?" *Nova Francia* 5 (1930): 97-99.
Cazes, Paul de. "Deux points d'histoire." *Proceedings and Transactions of the Royal Society of Canada* 3 (1884): 1-6.
–. "Les points obscurs des voyages de Jacques Cartier." *Proceedings and Transactions of the Royal Society of Canada* 9 (1890): 25-34.
Chabannes, Jacques. *Jacques Cartier*. Paris: La Table ronde, 1960.
Chapelle, Baron de la. "Jean Le Veneur et le Canada." *Nova Francia* 6 (1931): 341-43.
Chapman, William. *Aux Bretons: à l'occasion du dévoilement de la statue de Jacques Cartier à Saint Malo, le 30 juin 1905*. Ottawa, 1905.
Charton, Edouard. *Jacques Cartier, voyageur français*. Paris: Magasin pittoresque, 1857.
Chauveau, P.-J.-O. "Encore Jacques Cartier." *Canada Français* 1 (1888): 292-303.
Chevalier, Henri-Émile. 1860. *Jacques Cartier*. Paris: Lebigre-Duquesne, 1868.
Clarke, John. "Un monument à Jacques Cartier." *Bulletin de la société de géographie de Québec* 15, 4 (1921): 197-95.
–. *A Recently Discovered Portrait Medallion of Jacques Cartier*. Glens Falls, NY: Glens Falls, 1909.
Clément, Béatrice. *Jacques Cartier, 1491-1557*. Quebec City: Jeunesse, 1962.
Comité France-Amérique. "La mission nationale française au IVème centenaire de la découverte du Canada." *France-Amérique* 25, 276 (December 1934): 169-96.
Coté, Louis. *Jacques Cartier*. Ottawa, 1934.
Coverdah, W.H. *Tadoussac Then and Now*. Montreal: Charles Francis Press, 1942.
Cunat, Charles. *Saint-Malo illustré par ses marins*. Rennes: Péalat, 1857.
Da Costa, B.F. "Jacques Cartier and His Successors." In *Narrative and Critical History of America,* vol. 4, ed. Justin Winsor, 47-80. Boston and New York: Houghton, Mifflin, 1884.
Daveluy, Marie Claire. "Lecture faite ... qu'y a-t-il d'inédit dans l'article de M. Robert La Roque de Roquebrune." *Revue d'histoire de l'Amérique française* 7, 3 (December 1953): 435-39.
d'Avézac, Marie Armand Pascal. *Jacques Cartier au Canada et ses précurseurs à la côte nord-ouest de l'Amérique*. Paris: Librairie Tross, 1864.
De Celles, A.D. *Cartier et son temps*. Montreal: Beauchemin, 1907.
Delanglez, Jean. "A Mirage: The Sea of the West." Part 1. *Revue d'histoire de l'Amérique française* 1, 3 (December 1947): 346-81.
–. "A Mirage: The Sea of the West." Part 2. *Revue d'histoire de l'Amérique française* 1, 4 (March 1948): 541-68.
Desmazières de Séchelles, C. *Notes sur la vie et les trois voyages de Jacques Cartier: mémoires de la Société littéraire et historique de Québec*. Quebec City: Société littéraire et historique de Québec, 1862.
Desrosiers, Adélard. *Notre Jacques Cartier*. Montreal: Éditions Albert Lévesque, 1934.
Desrosiers, Leo-Paul. *Commencements*. Montreal: Éditions de l'Action canadienne-française, 1939.
Dionne, N.-E. *Le fort Jacques-Cartier et la Petite Hermine*. Montreal, 1891.
–. *Jacques Cartier*. Quebec City: Léger Brousseau, 1889.
–. *Jacques Cartier*. 2nd ed. Quebec City: Robitaille, 1933.

–. *Jacques Cartier.* 3rd ed. Quebec City: Robitaille, 1934.

–. *La Nouvelle France de Cartier à Champlain.* Quebec City: Darveau, 1891.

Doughty, Arthur. *Report of the Public Archives for the Year 1934.* Ottawa: J.O. Patenaude, 1935.

Doughty, Arthur, and Adam Shortt. *Canada and its Provinces.* Vol. 1. Toronto: Publishers Association of Canada, 1914.

Douro, José. *Les aventures de Jacques Cartier.* Paris: Éditions Jules Tallandier, 1933.

Dumais, Joseph. *Jacques Cartier et Samuel de Champlain: Héros d'autrefois.* Quebec City: Imprimerie de l'Action sociale, 1913.

–. *Le Capitaine malouin Jacques Cartier, découvreur officiel du Canada.* Quebec City: La Fierté française, 1934.

–. *Le souvenir patriotique: Jacques Cartier et Samuel de Champlain.* Quebec City: Imprimerie de l'Action sociale, 1913.

Dumont, Jean, ed. *La découverte du Canada.* 3 vols. Montreal: Amis de l'histoire, 1969. Vol. 1 deals with Cartier.

Dupuy, Paul. *Les illustrations canadiennes: Jacques Cartier, Samuel de Champlain, le bienheureux Jean de Brébeuf, Marie-Madeleine de La Peltrie.* Montreal: Granger frères, 1929.

Ehm, Toufik. *Jacques Cartier raconte.* Montreal: Héritage, 1984.

Evans, Walter Norton. *Cartier and Hochelaga: Maisonneuve and Ville-Marie: Two Historic Poems of Montreal.* Montreal: W. Drysdale, 1895.

Ferguson, Robert Douglas. 1959. *Man from St. Malo: The Story of Jacques Cartier.* Toronto: Macmillan, 1966.

Franc-Nohain (Maurice Legrand). *Comment les Français redécouvrirent le Canada lors des fêtes de la commémoration de l'arrivée de Jacques Cartier à Gaspé, avant-propos de Damase Potvin.* Quebec City: Éditions du Cri de Québec, 1935.

Gagnon, François-Marc. *Jacques Cartier et la découverte du Nouveau Monde.* Quebec City: Musée du Québec, 1984.

–. "Note sur la designation de l'indien chez Jacques Cartier." *Recherches amerindiennes au Québec* 10, 1-2 (1980): 24-36.

Galtier, Gaston. "Jacques Cartier." *Revue de l'alliance française* 57 (April 1934): 54-60.

Ganong, W.F. "The Cartography of the Gulf of St. Lawrence." *Proceedings and Transactions of the Royal Society of Canada* 8 (1889): 17-58.

–. "Jacques Cartier's First Voyage." *Proceedings and Transactions of the Royal Society of Canada* 6 (1887): 121-36.

–. "Voyages of Cartier and Contemporaries." *Proceedings and Transactions of the Royal Society of Canada* 8 (1889): 17-58.

–. "The Voyages of Jacques Cartier." *Proceedings and Transactions of the Royal Society of Canada* 3rd series, vol. 28 (1934): 149-294.

Gérin, Léon. "Les gentilhommes français et la colonisation du Canada." *Proceedings and Transactions of the Royal Society of Canada* 2nd series, vol. 2 (1896): 65-94.

–. "Jacques Cartier, notre découvreur." *Proceedings and Transactions of the Royal Society of Canada* 3rd series, vol. 28 (1934): xlv-lxvi.

–. "Jacques Cartier, sa langue et sa religion." *Canadian Historical Association Annual Report* 13 (1934): 68-70.

–. "Review Essay." *Canadian Historical Review* 16, 3 (September 1935): 323-25.

Greene, Meg. *Jacques Cartier Navigating the St. Lawrence River.* New York: Rosen, 2004.

Groulx, Lionel. *La découverte du Canada: Jacques Cartier.* Montreal: Granger frères, 1934.

–. *La découverte du Canada: Jacques Cartier.* Rev. ed. Montreal and Paris: Fides, 1966.

Guégan, Bertrand. 1929. *Trois voyages au Canada: Jacques Cartier, 1534 et 1536, Samuel de Champlain, 1608 et 1611, et Gabriel Sagard, 1624.* Paris: Éditions du Carrefour, 1934.

–. *Trois voyages au Canada: voyages faits en la Nouvelle France en 1534 et 1536.* Paris: Éditions du Carrefour, 1929.

Guernier, Eugène. *Jacques Cartier et la pensée colonisatrice.* Paris: Éditions de l'encyclopédie de l'Empire Français, 1946.

Guitard, Michelle. *Jacques Cartier in Canada / Jacques Cartier au Canada.* Ottawa: National Library of Canada, 1984.

Harvut, Hippolyte. *Les grands hommes de Saint Malo.* Saint-Malo: Imprimerie Benderitler, 1882.

–. *Jacques Cartier: recherches sur sa personne et sur sa famille.* Nantes: Forest et Grimaud, 1884.
Heurlipes, Frédéric. *Jacques Cartier: ou la découverte du Canada: drame historique en quatre actes, un prologue et un sixième tableau (ad libitum) mêlé de chant.* Paris: H. Gautier, 1892.
Hoffmann, Bernard. *From Cabot to Cartier.* Toronto: University of Toronto Press, 1961.
Howley, M.F. "Cartier's Course: A Last Word." *Proceedings and Transactions of the Royal Society of Canada* 12 (1894): 151-82.
"H.V.C." "Jacques Cartier and the Little Indian Girl." *Literary Garland and British North American Magazine,* October 1848, 461-68.
Jacob, Yves. *Jacques Cartier: de Saint-Malo au Saint-Laurent.* Paris: Éditions Maritimes, 1984.
Jones, Gwyn. "The First Europeans in America." *The Beaver* 44, 3 (Winter 1964): 4-17.
Josseaume, Michel. "Autour de Jacques Cartier, sa famille." *Mémoires de la Société généalogique canadienne-française* 21, 1 (March 1970): 26-46.
Joüon des Longrais, Frédéric. *Le drapeau de Cartier.* Rennes: Prost, 1903.
Julien, Charles-André. *Les voyages de découverte et les premiers établissements (XVe-XVIe siècle).* Paris: Presses universitaires de France, 1948.
King, Joseph. "The Glorious Kingdom of the Saguenay." *Canadian Historical Review* 31, 4 (December 1950): 390-400.
La Roncière, Charles de. *Jacques Cartier et la découverte de la Nouvelle France.* Paris: Plon, 1931.
–. "The New France of Jacques Cartier." *Legion d'honneur* 5, 2 (October 1934), 97-101.
–. *Notre première tentative de colonisation au Canada.* Paris: Bibliothèque de l'école des chartes, 1912.
Lacoursière, Jacques. *Jacques Cartier, l'or du Canada.* Sainte-Foy: Publications Charles-Huot, 1984.
Lahaise, Robert. *Jacques Cartier: voyage en Nouvelle France.* Quebec City: Hurtubise HMH, 1977.
Lailler, Dan. *Le bateau de Jacques Cartier.* Paris: Berger-Levrault, 1984.
Lanctôt, Gustave. "L'aterrissage de Jacques Cartier dans l'île de Montréal." *Canadian Historical Association Annual Report* 21 (1942): 42-43.
–. "Cartier au Canada en 1524." *Revue d'histoire de l'Amérique française* 7, 3 (December 1953): 413-25.
–. "Cartier en Nouvelle France en 1524." *Revue d'histoire de l'Amérique française* 8, 2 (September 1954): 213-19.
–. *Cartier visite la rivière Nicolet en 1535.* Montreal: Ducharme, 1945.
–. "L'itinéraire de Cartier à Hochelaga." *Proceedings and Transactions of the Royal Society of Canada* 3rd series, vol. 24 (1930): 115-41.
–. *Jacques Cartier devant l'histoire.* Montreal: Éditions Lumen, 1947.
–. "Jacques Cartier et son oeuvre." *Revue de l'Université d'Ottawa* 5, 1 (January-March 1935): 33-48.
–. "Jacques Cartier et son oeuvre." *Revue de l'Université d'Ottawa* 5, 2 (April-June 1935): 213-30.
–. "Montréal avant Maisonneuve." *Revue de l'Université Laval* 11, 7 (March 1957): 576-83.
–. "Portraits of Jacques Cartier." *Canadian Geographical Journal* 10, 3 (March 1935): 149-53.
–. "Quelques notes sur Cartier." *Canadian Historical Association Annual Report* 13 (1934): 40-47.
–. *Realisations françaises de Cartier à Montcalm.* Montreal: Éditions Chantecler, 1951.
Laverdière, Charles-Honoré. *Histoire du Canada à l'usage des maisons d'éducation.* Quebec City: A. Coté, 1869.
Laviolette, Guy. *Jacques Cartier (1491-1557), découvreur du Canada.* Montreal: Librairie générale canadienne, 1943.
Le Blant, Robert. "Deux procurations inédites de Jacques Cartier." *Revue d'histoire de l'Amérique française* 15, 3 (December 1961): 443-49.
–. "Les écrits attribués à Jacques Cartier." *Revue d'histoire de l'Amérique française* 15, 1 (June 1961): 90-103.
–. "Notes sur les découvreurs français de l'Amérique du Nord au XVIe siècle: Roberval, Dyel et Lhéry" *Revue d'histoire de l'Amérique française* 11, 4 (March 1958): 563-74.

Le Moine, Roger. "Un compagnon oublié de Roberval." *Revue de l'Université d'Ottawa* 41, 4 (September-December 1971): 556-62.

Leacock, Stephen. *The Mariner of St. Malo: A Chronicle of the Voyages of Jacques Cartier.* Toronto: Glasgow, Brook, 1915.

Lee, David. "Les Français en Gaspésie." *Revue d'histoire de la Gaspésie* 11, 2 (April-June 1973): 79-85.

–. "Les Français en Gaspésie." *Revue d'histoire de la Gaspésie* 11, 3 (July-September 1973): 168-73.

–. "Les Français en Gaspésie." *Revue d'histoire de la Gaspésie* 11, 4 (October-December 1973): 229-35.

Lemieux, Rodolphe. "Canada's Quadcentenary, 1934." *Canadian Geographical Journal* 1 (November 1930): 557-73.

–. "Quatrième centenaire du Canada, 1934." *Canadian Historical Association Annual Report* 9 (1930): 5-10 .

Lespagnol, André. *Jacques Cartier.* Rennes: Ouest-France, 1984.

Lewis, Blanche McLeod. "Along the North Shore in Cartier's Wake." *Canadian Geographical Journal* 8, 5 (May 1934): 209-21.

Lewis, Harrison. "Notes on Some Details of the Explorations of Jacques Cartier." *Proceedings and Transactions of the Royal Society of Canada* 3rd series, vol. 28 (1934): 117-48 .

Leymarie, A.-Léo. *Jacques Cartier, découvreur, explorateur, colonisateur du Canada.* St. Jerome: Avenir du Nord, 1913.

–. *Le premier ouvrage français sur le Canada.* Paris: Jouve, 1925.

Lighthall, W.D. "The False Plan of Hochelaga." *Proceedings and Transactions of the Royal Society of Canada* 3rd series, vol. 26 (1932): 181-92 .

–. "Hochelaga and the Hill of Hochelaga." *Proceedings and Transactions of the Royal Society of Canada* 3rd series, vol. 18 (1924): 91-106 .

–. "New Hochelagan Finds in 1933." *Proceedings and Transactions of the Royal Society of Canada* 3rd series, vol. 28 (1934): 103-8.

Loiselle-Blais, Micheline. *Trois compagnons sur les traces de Jacques Cartier.* Montreal: Héritage, 1984.

Malchelosse, Gérard. "Jacques Cartier va à Hochelaga." *Cahiers des Dix* 21 (1956): 31-53.

Marichal, Robert. "Les compagnons de Roberval." *Humanisme et renaissance* 1 (1934): 51-122.

–. "Postel, Cartier, Rabelais, et les 'paroles gelées.'" *Études Rabelaisiennes* 1 (1956): 181-82.

Marquis, Thomas Guthrie. *Marguerite de Roberval: A Romance of the Days of Jacques Cartier.* Toronto: Copp Clark, 1899.

Martin, Gaston. *Jacques Cartier et la découverte de l'Amérique du Nord.* Paris: Gallimard, 1938.

Massicotte, E.-Z. "Le faux plan de la bourgade d'Hochelaga." *Bulletin des recherches historiques* 41, 8 (August 1935): 478-80.

Maxine (Marie-Caroline-Alexandra Bouchette). *Jacques Cartier 1534.* Montreal: Éditions Albert Lévesque, 1933.

–. *Jacques Cartier 1534: récits canadiens empruntés à l'histoire.* Montreal: Éditions Beauchemin, 1957.

McNeil, Everett. *The Shores of Adventure: Exploring the New World with Jacques Cartier.* New York: Dutton, 1929.

Melançon, Robert. "Terre de Cain, âge d'or, prodiges du Saguenay: Représentations du Nouveau Monde dans les voyages de Jacques Cartier." *Studies in Canadian Literature* 4, 2 (1979): 22-34.

Mériem [pseud.]. *Jacques Cartier.* Tours: Maison Mame, 1899.

Morin, Victor. "Quatre centenaires." *Proceedings and Transactions of the Royal Society of Canada* 3rd series, vol. 28 (1934): 61-96.

Moussonneau, Christian. *Le langage géographique de Cartier et de Champlain.* Quebec City: Presses de l'Université Laval, 1978.

Myrand, Ernest. *Une fête de Noël sous Jacques Cartier.* Quebec City: Demers et frère, 1888.

Néret, Jean-Alexis. *Le capitaine Jacques Cartier.* Paris: Éditions Sulliver, 1949.

Pacifique, Père (Henri Buisson d'Valigny). "Jacques Cartier à Carleton." *Bulletin de la société de géographie de Québec* 17 (1923): 6-12.
–. "Jacques Cartier à l'Île du Prince Édouard." *Bulletin de la société de géographie de Québec* 17 (1923): 3-12.
–. "Jacques Cartier à Port-Daniel." *Bulletin de la société de géographie de Québec* 16 (1922): 137-42.
Peisson, Edouard. *Jacques Cartier, navigateur.* Toulouse: Marcel Didier, 1944.
–. *Jacques Cartier, navigateur.* 2nd ed. Paris: Éditions France Club, 1956.
Perrault, Claude. *La découverte de Montréal par Jacques Cartier.* Montreal: Loisirs St-Edouard, 1984.
–. "La découverte de Montréal par Jacques Cartier." *Revue d'histoire de l'Amérique française* 20, 2 (September 1966): 236-61.
Pope, Joseph. *Jacques Cartier: His Life and Voyages.* Ottawa: Woodburn, 1890.
Pouliot, Camille. *La grande aventure de Jacques Cartier.* Quebec City, 1934.
Quinel, Charles, and A. de Montagon. *Jacques Cartier, le découvreur du Canada.* Paris: Nathan, 1936.
Ramé, Alfred. *Note sur le manoir de Jacques Cartier.* Paris: Librairie Tross, 1867.
Richmond, F.J. "The Landing Place of Jacques Cartier at Gaspé in 1534." *Canadian Historical Association Annual Report* 1 (1922): 38-46.
Riotor, Léon. *Jacques Cartier et le voyage au Canada.* Paris: Pierre Roger, 1937.
Robinson, P.J. "Huron Equivalents of Cartier's Second Vocabulary." *Proceedings and Transactions of the Royal Society of Canada* 3rd series, vol 42 (1948): 127-46.
–. "The Origin of the Name Hochelaga." *Canadian Historical Review* 23, 3 (September 1942): 295-96.
–. "Some of Cartier's Place-Names 1535-1536." *Canadian Historical Review* 26, 4 (December 1945): 401-5.
Roquebrune, Robert La Roque de. "L'acte de baptême du fils de Jamet Quartier." *Revue d'histoire de l'Amérique française* 7, 4 (March 1954): 571-72.
–. "Documents inédits: l'acte de baptême de Jacques Cartier." *Revue d'histoire de l'Amérique française* 7, 2 (September 1953): 293-95.
–. "La découverte du Canada." *Revue de France,* 15 July 1934, 268-84.
–. "Un rival de Jacques Cartier: Roberval." *Revue des questions historiques* 62, 5 (September 1934): 9-14.
–. "Roberval et sa colonie canadienne au XVIe siècle." *Revue d'histoire des colonies* 43, 151 (1956): 125-37.
–. "Roberval, sa généalogie, son père et le procès du Maréchal de Gié, le portrait de Chantilly." *Revue d'histoire de l'Amérique française* 9, 2 (September 1955): 157-75.
Rouse, W.H.D., ed. *Voyages and Plantations of the French in Canada.* London: Blackie and Son, 1908.
Rousseau, Jacques. "L'Annedda et l'arbre de vie." *Revue d'histoire de l'Amérique française* 8, 2 (September 1954): 171-212.
–. "La botanique canadienne à l'époque de Jacques Cartier." *Contributions du laboratoire de botanique de l'Université de Montréal* 28 (1937): 1-77.
–. "Les gens qu'on dit sauvages." *Cahiers des Dix* 23 (1958): 53-90.
Roy, C.-E. "Cartier à Gaspé." *Canada français* (1934): 502-15.
Roy, C.-E., and Lucien Brault. *Gaspé depuis Cartier.* Quebec City: Au moulin des lettres, 1934.
–. *Historical Gaspé.* Quebec City: Au moulin des lettres, 1934.
Roy, P.-G. "Où hiverna Jacques Cartier en 1541-42?" *Bulletin des recherches historiques* 30, 11 (November 1924): 253-55.
–. "Le site du fort Jacques Cartier sur les bords de la rivière Lairet." *Bulletin des recherches historiques* 29, 9 (September 1923): 257-59.
Roy, Régis. "Les compagnons de Jacques Cartier." *Bulletin des recherches historiques* 25, 5 (May 1919): 155-57 .
–. "Jacques Cartier: était-il noble?" *Proceedings and Transactions of the Royal Society of Canada* 3rd series, vol. 13 (1919): 61-67.

Saint-Mieux, Georges. *Les écrits et le parler de Jacques Cartier.* Saint-Malo: Annales de la Société historique et archéologique de Saint Malo, 1905.

Saint-Pierre, Arthur. *Jacques Cartier.* Montreal: Éditions de la Bibliothèque canadienne, 1922.

Scott, H.A. "Au berceau de notre histoire." *Proceedings and Transactions of the Royal Society of Canada* 3rd series, vol. 16 (1922): 39-74.

–. "Les aumoniers de Jacques Cartier." *Bulletin des recherches historiques* 30, 6 (June 1924): 168-74.

Stephens, H.B. *Jacques Cartier and His Four Voyages to Canada.* Montreal: W. Drysdale, 1890.

Sulte, Benjamin. "Le golfe du St Laurent." *Proceedings and Transactions of the Royal Society of Canada* 5 (1886): 7-18.

–. "Pretendues origines des Canadiens français." *Proceedings and Transactions of the Royal Society of Canada* 4 (1885): 13-28 .

Sutherland, John Campbell. *Jacques Cartier.* Toronto: Ryerson Press, 1926.

Swift, Sherman Charles, and T.G. Marquis. *The Voyages of Jacques Cartier in Prose and Verse.* Toronto: Thomas Allen, 1934.

Tiercelin, Louis. "Ce qu'on sait de Jacques Cartier: à propos des fêtes de l'érection de sa statue, à Saint-Malo, le 23 juillet 1905." *L'Hermine: revue littéraire et artistique de Bretagne,* 20 July 1905, 97-113.

Tilly, Raoul de. *Premier voyage de Jacques Cartier au Canada: édition canadienne du discours du voyage fait par le capitaine Jacques Cartier.* Levis: Imprimerie du Travailleur de Lévis, 1890.

Toye, W. *Cartier Discovers the St. Lawrence.* Toronto: Oxford University Press, 1971.

Tremblay, Victor. *Le temps de Jacques Cartier.* Chicoutimi: Société historique du Saguenay, 1934.

Trigger, Bruce. "Cartier's Hochelaga and the Dawson Site." In *Iroquois Culture,* ed. E. Tooker, 63-66. Albany: University of the State of New York, 1967.

–. "Who Were the Laurentian Iroquois?" *Canadian Review of Sociology and Anthropology* 3, 4 (November 1966): 201-13.

Trigger, Bruce, and James F. Pendergast. *Cartier's Hochelaga and the Dawson Site.* Montreal and Kingston: McGill-Queen's University Press, 1972.

Trudel, Marcel. *Jacques Cartier: textes choisis et presentés par Marcel Trudel.* Montreal: Fides, 1968.

Vattier, Georges. *Jacques Cartier et la découverte du Canada.* Paris: Hachette, 1937.

Verreau, Hospice-A. "Jacques Cartier: questions de calendrier civil et ecclésiastique." *Proceedings and Transactions of the Royal Society of Canada* 8 (1890): 113-52 .

–. "Jacques Cartier: questions de droit public, de législation et d'usages maritimes." *Proceedings and Transactions of the Royal Society of Canada* 9 (1891): 77-83.

–. "Jacques Cartier: questions de lois et coutumes maritimes." *Proceedings and Transactions of the Royal Society of Canada* 2nd series, vol. 3 (1897): 119-33.

Ville, Léon. *Un pacifique conquérant: Jacques Cartier.* Paris: Tolra, 1934.

Winsor, Justin. *The Anticipations of Cartier's Voyages.* Cambridge: John Wilson and Son, 1893.

–. *Cartier to Frontenac.* Boston and New York: Houghton, Mifflin, 1900.

–. *Cartier to Frontenac: Geographical Discovery in the Interior of North America in Its Historical Relations, 1534-1700.* Boston and New York: Houghton, Mifflin, 1894.

–. *The Results in Europe of Cartier's Explorations.* Cambridge: John Wilson and Son, 1892.

Wintemberg, W.J. "The Probable Location of Cartier's Stadacona." *Proceedings and Transactions of the Royal Society of Canada* 3rd series, vol. 30 (1936): 19-21.

Wood, William. "Jacques Cartier's Island." *University Magazine,* 1913, 47-63.

Secondary Sources

Allen, David Elliston. *The Naturalist in Britain: A Social History.* London: Allen Lane, 1976.

Anderson, Benedict. *Imagined Communities: Reflections on the Origins and Spread of Nationalism.* London: Verso, 1993.

Atkinson, Geoffroy. *Les nouveaux horizons de la Renaissance française.* Paris: E. Droz, 1935.

Bann, Stephen. *The Inventions of History: Essays on the Representation of the Past.* Manchester: Manchester University Press, 1990.

–. *Romanticism and the Rise of History*. New York: Twayne, 1995.

Barber, Lynn. *The Heyday of Natural History, 1820-1870*. London: Jonathan Cape, 1980.

Barthe, Joseph-Guillaume. *Souvenirs d'un demi-siècle; ou, mémoires pour servir à l'histoire contemporaine*. Montreal: J. Chapleau et fils, 1885.

Beaulieu, André, and Jean Hamelin. *La presse québécoise des origines à nos jours*. 10 vols. Quebec City: Presses de l'Université Laval, 1973-90.

Bélanger, Jules, Marc Desjardins, and Jean-Yves Frenette. *Histoire de la Gaspésie*. Montreal: Boréal Express, 1981.

Berger, Carl. *Science, God, and Nature in Victorian Canada*. Toronto: University of Toronto Press, 1996.

–. *The Writing of Canadian History: Aspects of English-Canadian Historical Writing since 1900*. 2nd ed. Toronto: University of Toronto Press, 1986.

Berubé, Harold. "Commémorer la ville: une analyse comparative des célébrations du centenaire de Toronto et du tricentenaire de Montréal." *Revue d'histoire de l'Amérique française* 57, 2 (Fall 2003): 209-36.

Bienvenue, Louise. *Quand la jeunesse entre en scène: L'Action catholique avant la Révolution tranquille*. Montreal: Boréal, 2003.

Billig, Michael. *Banal Nationalism*. London: Sage, 1995.

Boisvert, Donald. "Religion and Nationalism in Québec: The Saint-Jean-Baptiste Celebration in Sociological Perspective." PhD diss., University of Ottawa, 1990.

Bolotenko, George. *A Future Defined: Canada from 1849 to 1873*. Ottawa: National Archives, 1992.

Bonnichon, Philippe. *Des cannibales aux castors: les découvertes françaises de l'Amérique, 1503-1788*. Paris: France-Empire, 1994.

Bosher, J.F. *The Canada Merchants*. Oxford: Clarendon, 1987.

Bossé, Éveline. *La Capricieuse à Québec en 1855*. Montreal: La Presse, 1984.

–. *Un grand représentant de l'élite canadienne-française: Joseph-Charles Taché*. Quebec City: Garneau, 1971.

Brault, Jean-Rémi, ed. *Montréal au XIXe siècle: des gens, des idées, ses arts, une ville*. Ottawa: Leméac, 1990.

Broc, Numa. 1971. *La géographie des philosophes: géographie et voyageurs français au XVIIIe siècle*. Paris: Ophrys, 1974.

Bushman, Claudia. *America Discovers Columbus*. Hanover: University Press of New England, 1992.

Cannadine, David. "Imperial Canada: Old History, New Problems." In *Imperial Canada, 1867-1914*, ed. Colin Coates, 1-19. Edinburgh: University of Edinburgh, Centre of Canadian Studies, 1997.

Carey, Brian. "An Imperial Gift." *History of Photography* 10, 2 (April-June 1986): 147-49.

Carpentier, Paul. *Les croix de chemin: au-delà du signe*. Ottawa: Musées nationaux du Canada, 1981.

Chapdelaine, Claude. "Sur les traces des premiers Québécois." *Recherches amérindiens au Québec* 15, 1-2 (1985): 3-6.

Coates, Colin. *Metamorphoses of Landscape and Community in Early Québec*. Montreal and Kingston: McGill-Queen's University Press, 2000.

Coates, Colin, and Cecelia Morgan. *Heroines and History: Representations of Madeleine de Verchères and Laura Secord*. Toronto: University of Toronto Press, 2002.

Colley, Linda. "The Apotheosis of George III: Loyalty, Royalty and the British Nation, 1760-1820." *Past and Present* 102, 1 (February 1984): 94-129.

Cook, Ramsay, ed. *French-Canadian Nationalism: An Anthology*. Toronto: Macmillan, 1969.

Côté, Gaston. "L'érection de la croix du Mont Royal." *MENS: Revue d'histoire intellectuelle de l'Amérique française* 7, 1 (Fall 2006): 47-72.

Courville, Serge, ed. *Atlas historique du Québec: population et territoire*. Sainte-Foy: Presses de l'Université Laval, 1996.

Curtis, Bruce. *The Politics of Population: State Formation, Statistics, and the Census of Canada, 1840-1875*. Toronto: University of Toronto Press, 2001.

Cyr, Roger. *La Patente; tous les secrets de la maçonnerie canadienne-française: L'Ordre de Jacques-Cartier.* Montreal: Éditions du Jour, 1964.

Daniel, François. *Histoire des grandes familles françaises du Canada, ou aperçu sur le Chevalier Benoist et quelques familles contemporaines.* Montreal: Sénécal, 1867.

Dawson, John William. "Notes on Aboriginal Antiquities Recently Discovered in the Island of Montréal." *Canadian Naturalist and Geologist* 5 (1860): 430-49.

Dawson, S.E. *The Saint Lawrence Basin and Its Borderlands.* London: Lawrence and Butler, 1905.

Day, Aiden. *Romanticism.* London: Routledge, 1996.

Debarbieux, Bernard, and Claude Marois. "Le Mont Royal: forme naturelle, paysages et territorialités urbaines." *Cahiers de géographie du Québec* 41, 113 (September 1997): 185-87.

Delort, Robert. "Les Basques ont-ils atteint le Canada avant 1497?" *Cahiers d'histoire* 13, 2 (Fall 1993): 23-30.

Dickinson, John. "Commentaire sur le critique de Ronald Rudin." *Bulletin d'histoire politique* 4, 2 (Winter 1995): 21-24.

Dionne, N.-E. *Vie de C.-F. Painchaud, curé, fondateur du Collège de Sainte-Anne-de-la-Pocatière.* Quebec City: Léger Brousseau, 1894.

Dussel, Enrique. *The Invention of America.* Trans. M.D. Barker. New York: Continuum, 1995.

Fay, Terence J. *A History of Canadian Catholics.* Montreal and Kingston: McGill-Queen's University Press, 2002.

Febvre, Lucien. *L'apparition du livre.* Paris: A. Michel, 1971.

Fecteau, Jean-Marie. "Between Scientific Enquiry and the Search for a Nation: Quebec Historians as Seen by Ronald Rudin." *Canadian Historical Review* 80, 4 (December 1999): 641-66.

Ferland, J.-B.-A. 1861. *Cours d'histoire du Canada.* Wakefield: S.R. Publishers, 1969.

Fournier, Rodolphe. *Lieux et monuments historiques de Québec et environs.* Quebec City: Garneau, 1976.

Gagnon, Monsignor Antoine. *Histoire de Matane.* Rimouski: Impressions des associés, 1977.

Gagnon, François-Marc. *Ces hommes dits sauvages: l'histoire fascinante d'un préjugé qui remonte aux premiers découvreurs du Canada.* Montreal: Libre Expression, 1984.

Gagnon, Hervé. "Divertissement et patriotisme: la genèse des musées d'histoire à Montréal au XIXe siècle." *Revue d'histoire de l'Amérique française* 48, 3 (Winter 1995): 317-49.

Gagnon, Serge. *Le passé composé: de Ouellet à Rudin.* Montreal: VLB Éditeur, 1999.

–. *Quebec and Its Historians, 1840-1920.* Montreal: Harvest House, 1982.

–. *Quebec and Its Historians: The Twentieth Century.* Montreal: Harvest House, 1985.

Gallichan, Gilles. *Livre et politique au Bas-Canada, 1791-1849.* Sillery: Septentrion, 1991.

Galpern, A.N. *The Religions of the People in Sixteenth-Century Champagne.* Cambridge, MA: Harvard University Press, 1976.

Garneau, F.-X. *Histoire du Canada.* 5th ed. Paris: Librairie Félix Alcan, 1913.

Gauvreau, Michael. *The Catholic Origins of Quebec's Quiet Revolution, 1931-1970.* Montreal and Kingston: McGill-Queen's University Press, 2005.

Gordon, Alan. *Making Public Pasts: The Contested Terrain of Montreal's Public Memories, 1891-1930.* Montreal and Kingston: McGill-Queen's University Press, 2001.

Grandpré, Pierre de. *Histoire de la littérature française du Québec.* Montreal: Beauchemin, 1967.

Greer, Allan. "The Pattern of Literacy in Québec, 1745-1899." *Histoire sociale – Social History* 11, 22 (November 1978): 293-335.

Groulx, Lionel. "Un institut d'histoire." *Revue d'histoire de l'Amérique française* 2, 3 (December 1948): 472-79.

–. *Mes mémoires.* 4 vols. Montreal: Fides, 1972.

Groulx, Patrice. *Pièges de la mémoire: Dollard des Ormeaux, les Amérindiens, et nous.* Hull: Vents d'Ouest, 1998.

Hamel, Reginald, John Hare, and Paul Wyczynski, eds. *Dictionnaire des auteurs de langue française en Amérique du Nord.* Montreal: Fides, 1989.

Hare, John, Marc Lafrance, and David-Thiery Ruddel. *Histoire de la Ville de Québec, 1608-1871.* Montreal: Boréal, 1987.

Harrisse, Henry. *Notes pour servir à l'histoire, à la bibliographie et à la cartographie de la Nouvelle France et des pays adjacents, 1545-1700.* Paris: Librairie Tross, 1872.

Heaman, Elsbeth. *The Inglorious Arts of Peace: Exhibitions in Canadian Society during the Nineteenth Century.* Toronto: University of Toronto Press, 1999.

Hébert, Bruno. *Monuments et patrie: une réflexion philosophique sur un fait historique: la célébration commémorative au Québec de 1881 à 1929.* Joliette: Éditions Pleins bords, 1980.

Heriot, George. *The History of Canada, from Its First Discovery, Comprehending an Account of the Original Establishment of the Colony of Louisiana.* London: Longman and Rees, 1804.

–. *Travels through the Canadas: To Which Is Subjoined a Comparative View of the Manners and Customs of Several of the Indian Nations of North and South America.* London: Richard Phillips, 1805.

Hobsbawm, Eric. Introduction to *The Invention of Tradition,* ed. Eric Hobsbawm and Terrence Ranger, 1-14. Cambridge: Cambridge University Press, 1983.

Hould, Fernand. "L'Institut canadien de Québec, 1848-1898, agent de promotion de la vie culturelle à Québec: mythes et réalité." MA thesis, Université Laval, 1997.

Hudson, Kenneth. *Social History of Museums: What Visitors Thought.* London: Macmillan, 1975.

Irving, Washington. *A History of the Life and Voyages of Christopher Columbus.* 4 vols. London: John Murray, 1828.

Izenberg, Gerald. *Impossible Individuality: Romanticism, Revolution, and the Origins of Modern Selfhood, 1787-1802.* Princeton: Princeton University Press, 1992.

Jones, Charles W. *Saint Nicholas of Myra, Bari, and Manhattan: Biography of a Legend.* Chicago: University of Chicago Press, 1978.

Jordan, Gerald, and Nicholas Rogers. "Admirals as Heroes: Patriotism and Liberty in Hanoverian England." *Journal of British Studies* 28, 3 (July 1989): 201-24.

Kammen, Michael. *Mystic Chords of Memory: The Transformation of Tradition in American Culture.* New York: Vintage Books, 1993.

Karel, David, ed. *Dictionnaire des artistes de langue française en Amérique du nord.* Quebec City: Presses de l'Université Laval, 1992.

Kelly, E.A. "Bones of Contention: Gustave Lanctôt's Pursuit of Jacques Cartier's Remains." *Archivaria* 20 (Summer 1985): 105-15.

Kingsford, William. *History of Canada.* Vol. 1. Toronto: Rowsell and Hutchinson, 1887.

Knafla, Louis, Martin Staum, and T.H.E. Traws, eds. *Science, Technology, and Culture in Historical Perspective.* Studies in History 1. Calgary: Department of History, University of Calgary, 1976.

Laliberté, G. Raymond. *Une société secrète: l'Ordre de Jacques Cartier.* Montreal: Hurtubise HMH, 1983.

Lamonde, Yvan. "Les associations au Bas-Canada: de nouveaux marchés aux idées (1840-1867)." *Histoire sociale – Social History* 8, 16 (November 1995): 361-69.

–. *Histoire sociale des idées au Québec (1760-1896).* Saint-Laurent: Fides, 2000.

–. *Louis-Antoine Dessaulles, 1818-1895: un seigneur libéral et anticlérical.* Saint-Laurent: Fides, 1994.

–. *Territoires de la culture québécoise.* Quebec City: Presses de l'Université Laval, 1991.

Lamonde, Yvan, and Didier Pothon, eds. *La Capricieuse (1855): poupe et proue: Les Relations France-Québec (1760-1914).* Quebec City: Presses de l'Université Laval, 2006.

Larochelle, Dany. "Du ciel au bateau: La *Cosmographie* (1544) du pilote Jean Alfonse et la construction du savoir géographique au XVIe siècle." MA thesis, Université de Sherbrooke, 2001.

Le Jeune, Louis. *Dictionnaire général de biographie, histoire, littérature, agriculture, commerce, industrie et des arts, sciences, moeurs, coutumes, institutions politiques et religieuses du Canada.* Vol. 1. Ottawa: Université d'Ottawa, 1931.

Lebrun, François. *Être chrétien en France sous l'Ancien Régime, 1516-1790.* Paris: Seuil, 1996.

Lemire, Maurice. *Dictionnaire des oeuvres littéraires du Québec: des origines à 1900.* Montreal: Fides, 1978.

–, ed. *Le romantisme au Canada.* Saint-Laurent: Nuit blanche, 1993.

Lespagnol, André. *Histoire de Saint-Malo et du pays malouin.* Toulouse: Privat, 1984.

Lestringant, Frank. *André Thevet: cosmographe des derniers Valois*. Geneva: Librairie Droz, 1991.

–. "Nouvelle-France et fiction cosmographique dans l'oeuvre d'André Thevet." *Études littéraires* 10, 1-2 (April-August 1977): 145-73.

Levine, Philippa. *The Amateur and the Professional: Antiquarians, Historians, and Archaeologists in Victorian England, 1838-1886*. Cambridge: Cambridge University Press, 1986.

Linteau, Paul-André. *Histoire du Québec contemporain*. 2 vols. Montreal: Boréal Express, 1981.

Linteau, Paul-André, and Fernand Harvey. "Les étranges lunettes de Ronald Rudin." *Revue d'histoire de l'Amérique française* 51, 3 (Winter 1998): 419-24.

Lukes, Stephen. *Individualism*. New York: Harper and Row, 1973.

Macfarlane, Alan. *Origins of English Individualism: The Family, Property, and Social Transition*. New York: Cambridge University Press, 1979.

Macpherson, C.B. *The Political Theory of Possessive Individualism: Hobbes to Locke*. Oxford: Clarendon Press, 1964.

Margry, Pierre. *Les navigations françaises et la révolution maritime du XIVe au XVIe siècle: d'après les documents inédits tirés de France, d'Angleterre, d'Espagne et d'Italie*. Paris: Librairie Tross, 1867.

Marion, Séraphin. *Les lettres canadiennes d'autrefois*. Vol. 4. Hull: Éditions l'Éclair, 1944.

Martin, Denis. *Portraits des héros de la Nouvelle France: images d'un culte historique*. La Salle: Hurtubise, 1988.

McKillop, A.B. *Matters of Mind: The University in Ontario, 1791-1951*. Toronto: University of Toronto Press, 1994.

Morgan, Henry James. *Sketches of Celebrated Canadians and Persons Related to Canada*. Quebec City: Hunter, Rose, 1862.

Morison, Samuel E. *Admiral of the Ocean Sea*. Boston: Little, Brown, 1942.

–. *The European Discovery of America*. Vol. 1, *The Northern Voyages, AD 500-1600*. New York: Oxford University Press, 1971.

Morton, Graeme. *William Wallace: Man and Myth*. Stroud: Sutton, 2001.

Miller, J.R. *Equal Rights: The Jesuits' Estates Act Controversy*. Montreal and Kingston: McGill-Queen's University Press, 1979.

Momigliano, Arnoldo. "The Rise of Antiquarian Research." Chapter 3 in *Classical Foundations of Modern Historiography*. Berkeley: University of California Press, 1990, 54-79.

Myrone, Martin, and Lucy Peltz, eds. *Producing the Past: Aspects of Antiquarian Culture and Practice, 1700-1850*. Aldershot: Ashgate, 1999.

Nelles, H.V. *The Art of Nation-Building: Pageantry and Spectacle at Quebec's Tercentenary*. Toronto: University of Toronto Press, 1999.

Noppen, Luc, and Gaston Deschenes. *Québec's Parliament Buildings: Witness to History*. Quebec City: Gouvernement du Québec, 1986.

Novik, Peter. *That Noble Dream: The "Objectivity Question" and the American Historical Profession*. Cambridge: Cambridge University Press, 1988.

Parkman, Francis. *France and England in North America*. Boston: Little, Brown, 1874.

–. *The Parkman Reader: From the Works of Francis Parkman*. Edited by S.E. Morison. Boston: Little, Brown, 1955.

Pendergast, James F. "The Confusing Identities Attributed to Stadacona and Hochelaga." *Journal of Canadian Studies* 32, 4 (Winter 1998): 149-67.

Peny, N.B. "The Whig Cult of Fox in Early Nineteenth-Century Sculpture." *Past and Present* 70, 1 (February 1976): 94-105.

Pope, Peter. *The Many Landfalls of John Cabot*. Toronto: University of Toronto Press, 1997.

Porter, Roy, ed. *Myths of the English*. Cambridge: Polity Press, 1992.

Rioux, Gabriel. "Émergence d'une réflexion moderne en planification urbaine: apports de la Ligue du Progrès Civique pour la métropole montréalaise." MA thesis, Université du Québec à Montréal, 2005.

Robert, Jean-Claude. *Atlas historique de Montréal*. Montreal: Art global, 1994.

Robins, Nora. "The Montreal Mechanics' Institute: 1828-1870." *Canadian Library Journal* 38, 6 (December 1981): 372-79.

Ross, David R. *On the Trail of William Wallace*. Edinburgh: Luath Press, 1999.

Ross, Dorothy. *The Origins of American Social Science*. Cambridge: Cambridge University Press, 1991.

Roy, Fernande. "Une mise en scène de l'histoire: la fondation de Montréal à travers les siècles." *Revue d'histoire de l'Amérique française* 46, 1 (Summer 1992): 7-36.

Roy, Pierre-Georges. *Les monuments commémoratifs de la province de Québec*. Quebec City: Commission des monuments historiques de la province de Québec, 1923.

Rudin, Ronald. *Founding Fathers: The Celebration of Champlain and Laval in the Streets of Quebec, 1878-1908*. Toronto: University of Toronto Press, 2003.

–. *Making History in Twentieth Century Quebec: Historians and Their Society*. Toronto: University of Toronto Press, 1997.

Rumilly, Robert. *Histoire de la Société Saint-Jean-Baptiste de Montréal*. Montreal: L'Aurore, 1975.

Russell, Jeffrey Burton. *Inventing the Flat Earth: Columbus and Modern Historians*. New York: Praeger, 1991.

Schlereth, Thomas. "Columbia, Columbus, and Columbianism." *Journal of American History* 79, 3 (December 1992): 937-68.

Seed, Patricia. *Ceremonies of Possession in Europe's Conquest of the New World, 1492-1620*. New York: Cambridge University Press, 1995.

Seline, Janice E. "Frederick Law Olmsted's Mount Royal Park, Montreal: Design and Context." MA thesis, Concordia University, 1983.

Shore, Marlene. "'Remember the Future': The *Canadian Historical Review* and the Discipline of History." *Canadian Historical Review* 76, 3 (September 1995): 410-63.

Slattery, Brian. "French Claims in North America, 1500-59." *Canadian Historical Review* 59, 2 (June 1978): 139-69.

Smith, Anthony D. *The Ethnic Origins of Nations*. London: Basil Blackwell, 1986.

Smith, William. *A History of Canada from Its First Discovery to the Peace of 1763*. Quebec City: J. Neilson, 1815.

Taylor, C.J. *Negotiating the Past: The Making of Canada's National Historic Parks and Sites*. Montreal and Kingston: McGill-Queen's University Press, 1990.

Taylor, M. Brook. *Promoters, Patriots, and Partisans: Historiography in Nineteenth-Century English Canada*. Toronto: University of Toronto Press, 1989.

Tracy, F.B. *The Tercentenary History of Canada: From Champlain to Laurier*. New York and Toronto: P.F. Collier and Son, 1908.

Trépanier, Léon. *On veut savoir*. Vol. 1. Montreal: La Patrie, 1960.

Trevor-Roper, Hugh. *The Romantic Movement and the Study of History*. London: Athlone Press, 1969.

Trudel, Marcel. *Histoire de la Nouvelle-France*. Vol. 1, *Les vaines tentatives, 1524-1603*. Montreal: Fides, 1963.

–. *Mémoires d'un autre siècle*. Montreal: Boréal, 1987.

Wade, Mason. *The French Canadians, 1760-1967*. Toronto: Macmillan, 1968.

Wallace, W. Stewart, and W.A. McKay, eds. *Macmillan Dictionary of Canadian Biography*. Toronto: Macmillan, 1978.

Walle, A.H. "Habits of Thought and Cultural Tourism." *Annals of Tourism Research* 23, 4 (October 1996): 874-90.

Wilford, J.N. *The Mysterious History of Columbus*. New York: Knopf, 1991.

Wright, Donald. *The Professionalization of History in English Canada*. Toronto: University of Toronto Press, 2005.

–. "W.D. Lighthall and David Ross McCord: Antimodernism and English-Canadian Imperialism, 1880s-1918." *Journal of Canadian Studies* 32, 2 (Summer 1997): 134-53.

Young, Brian. "Positive Law, Positive State: Class Realignment and the Transformation of Lower Canada, 1815-1866." In *Colonial Leviathan: State Formation in Mid-Nineteenth-Century Canada*, ed. Allan Greer and Ian Radforth, 50-63. Toronto: University of Toronto Press, 1992.

Zeller, Suzanne. *Land of Promise, Promised Land: The Culture of Victorian Science in Canada*. Canadian Historical Association Booklet 56. Ottawa: Canadian Historical Association, 1996.

Index

Printed and bound in Canada by Friesens
Set in Stone by Artegraphica Design Co. Ltd.
Copy editor: Deborah Kerr
Proofreader: Jenna Newman